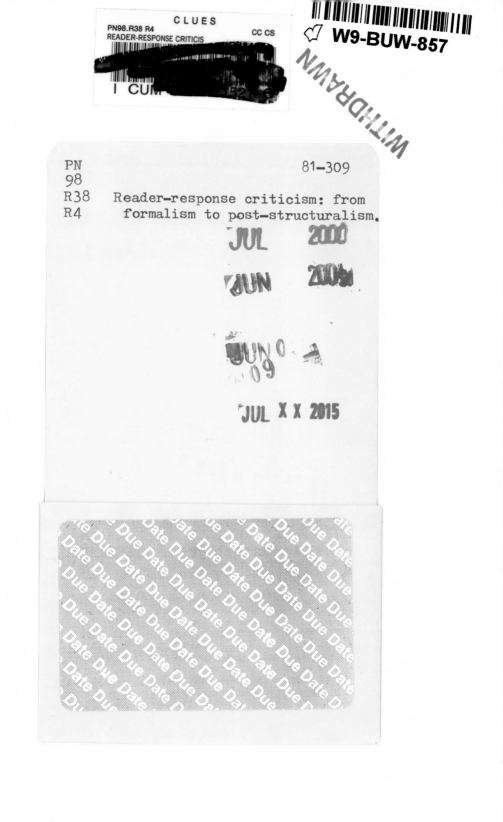

Reader-Response Criticism

FROM FORMALISM TO POST-STRUCTURALISM

Edited by Jane P. Tompkins

The Johns Hopkins University Press

Baltimore and London

Copyright © 1980 by The Johns Hopkins University Press
All rights reserved
Printed in the United States of America

The Johns Hopkins University Press, Baltimore, Maryland 21218
The Johns Hopkins Press Ltd., London

Library of Congress Cataloging in Publication Data

Main entry under title:

Reader-response criticism.

   Bibliography: pp. 233-70
   Includes index.
   1. Reader-response criticism—Addresses, essays,
lectures.   I. Tompkins, Jane P.
PN98.R38R4   801'.95   80-7996
ISBN 0-8018-2400-1
ISBN 0-8018-2401-X (pbk.)

CONTENTS

ACKNOWLEDGMENTS

I wish to acknowledge, first of all, Robert Crosman's contribution to the planning of this anthology in its initial stages.

I would like to thank Steve Mailloux and Joe Harari for their helpful criticisms of the Introduction. I am grateful to Jonathan Goldberg, Joe Harari, George McFadden, Susan Suleiman, Dan O'Hara, Jerry McGann, Walter Michaels, Frances Ferguson, and Richard Macksey, all of whom read the concluding essay and gave me their comments, suggestions, corrections, encouragement, and bibliographic aid. To Jay Cooke, Bill Cain, and, especially, Paul Hiles, I am indebted for the scope and accuracy of the bibliography; to Ellen Mankoff, Marilyn Sides, Terry Ross, and Sonia Maasik, for help in preparing the manuscript. I want to thank Mary Lou Kenney, the copy editor of this book, and Charlie West, the book's designer, for their friendliness and cooperation. I am deeply obliged to Jack Goellner, director of the Hopkins Press, for his support of the project, and to Francis Murnaghan, Jr., for his graciously given, expert advice.

Finally, I would like to express my most heartfelt thanks to Sharon Cameron whose professional expertise and personal generosity saw me through the most difficult part of the concluding chapter and to Stanley Fish, who, in addition to helping at every turn, made this enterprise possible in the first place.

AN INTRODUCTION
TO READER-RESPONSE CRITICISM

Jane P. Tompkins

Reader-response criticism is not a conceptually unified critical position, but a term that has come to be associated with the work of critics
who use the words *reader, the reading process,* and *response* to mark out an
area for investigation. In the context of Anglo-American criticism, the
reader-response movement arises in direct opposition to the New Critical dictum issued by Wimsatt and Beardsley in "The Affective Fallacy"
(1949): "The Affective Fallacy is a confusion between the poem and its
results. . . . It begins by trying to derive the standard of criticism from
the psychological effects of a poem and ends in impressionism and relativism" (p. 21). Reader-response critics would argue that a poem cannot
be understood apart from its results. Its "effects," psychological and
otherwise, are essential to any accurate description of its meaning, since
that meaning has no effective existence outside of its realization in the
mind of a reader.

The essays collected here refocus criticism on the reader. They examine authors' attitudes toward their readers, the kinds of readers various texts seem to imply, the role actual readers play in the determination
of literary meaning, the relation of reading conventions to textual interpretation, and the status of the reader's self. While they focus on the
reader and the reading process, the essays represent a variety of theoretical orientations: New Criticism, structuralism, phenomenology,
psychoanalysis, and deconstruction shape their definitions of the reader,
of interpretation, and of the text. Yet when read in roughly chronologi-
cal order, and with certain issues in view, the essays organize the critical
movements they reflect into a coherent progression and point toward a
new understanding of discourse.

The central issue in this progression is the status of the literary text.
As Edward Wasiolek has observed in his introduction to Serge Doub-
rovsky's *The New Criticism in France:*

> There were many movements during the years 1930–1960, but they di-
> verged like spokes from a hub, and what brought them together was a
> common and unquestioned assumption that critical discourse was a com-
> mentary about, and measured by, an objective text. . . . Supporters and an-
> tagonists of New Criticism never questioned that criticism was an act of
> approximating in language a work that had objective status, and that its
> intelligibility and worth were measured by that objectivity. (P. 6)

The objectivity of the text is the concept that these essays, whether they
intended it or not, eventually destroy. What that destruction yields, ultimately, is not a criticism based on the concept of the reader, but a way of
conceiving texts and readers that reorganizes the distinctions between
them. Reading and writing join hands, change places, and finally become distinguishable only as two names for the same activity.

As emphasis on the reader tends first to erode and then to destroy
the objective text, there is an increasing effort on the part of reader-
oriented critics to redefine the aims and methods of literary study. The
change in theoretical assumptions forces a change in the kinds of moral
claims critics can make for what they do. What began as a small shift of
emphasis from the narrator implied by a literary work to the reader it
implies ends by becoming an exchange of world views. The introduction
that follows will describe this evolution; it will outline the critical positions of each of the essays included here, focusing on their treatment of
textual objectivity and on the kind of moral justification each author
makes for his approach. The concluding essay offers a new perspective
on critical history from the vantage point of reader-response criticism
and redefines the movement in the light of its historical antecedents.

Reader-response criticism could be said to have started with I. A.
Richards's discussions of emotional response in the 1920s or with the
work of D. W. Harding and Louise Rosenblatt in the 1930s; I have
chosen to begin this anthology with Walker Gibson's essay on the mock
reader, written in 1950, because it shows how reader-response criticism
began to evolve within the confines of a formalist position.[1] Gibson's essay
makes no theoretical moves not already provided for by New Critical
doctrine. His view of literature, like that of many reader-critics who
come after him, is text-centered. It assumes the value and uniqueness of
the literary work of art; it assumes that literary meaning is contained in
the words on the page; and it assumes that special training in the critical
process is necessary if the student of literature is to grasp the full extent
of what the work has to offer. The concept of the reader, in Gibson's
essay, is introduced only as a way of unlocking further treasures in the
text: the "mock reader," as its name suggests, is not a "real" reader in any

[1]See editor's note on p. xxvi.

sense at all; yet in retrospect, it constitutes the first step in a series that gradually breaks through the boundaries that separate the text from its producers and consumers and reconstitutes it as a web whose threads have no beginning and no end.

Gibson introduced the notion of a mock reader, as opposed to a real reader, by analogy with the well-established distinction between the *persona* and the author of flesh and blood. In a formalist context, the *persona* had served to create distance between a literary text and its origin in history by inserting between the author and his product another "author" whose existence was entirely a function of the text. Gibson's mock reader is purely textual also but directs attention away from the text and toward the effects it produces. The mock reader is a role that the real reader is invited to play for the duration of the novel. "We assume, for the sake of experience, that set of attitudes and qualities which the language asks us to assume." The key phrase here is "for the sake of experience." The mock reader implied by the text gives the reader's experience its shape and valorizes that experience as an object of critical attention.

Gibson's notion of a speaker addressing a mock reader enables him to overhear a dialogue passing between the two that, when paraphrased, reveals the strategies the author uses to position his readers with respect to a whole range of values and assumptions he wishes them to accept or reject. The concept of the mock reader allows the critic to dramatize the social attitudes implicit in a text by reconstructing the kinds of understandings and complicities narrators and mock readers arrive at over the heads of the characters and quite apart from the manifest content of the prose. Gibson also argues for the usefulness of the concept on pedagogical and moral grounds. Students who are conscious of the various identities they assume as readers will be better able to make value judgments about literature: "A bad book is a book in whose mock reader we discover a person we refuse to become." Conversely, by allowing the student to accept or reject the role a novelist offers him, the concept of the mock reader makes him more aware of his own value system and better able to deal with problems of self-definition.

While Gibson's mock reader is a property of the text and not a real reader at all, his belief that real readers try on the roles thus offered them recognizes that their activities are relevant to an understanding of literature and gives the experience of reading evidential value in literary criticism. Thus, while it shares many New Critical assumptions, Gibson's essay anticipates the direction that reader-response criticism will subsequently take: it moves the focus of attention away from the text and toward the reader, it uses the idea of the reader as a means of producing a new kind of textual analysis, and it suggests that literary criticism be seen as part of larger, more fundamental processes such as the forming of an identity.

Gerald Prince's essay on the narratee has different, though equally

ambitious, aims. His position resembles Gibson's in its fundamental
premises. He begins by affirming a parallelism between the narrator and
the narratee that is roughly analogous to the relation between Gibson's
speakers and mock readers. But instead of investigating the authorial
values that the application of this concept reveals, Prince uses it to
generate a system of classification. He posits first a series of distinctions
among the kinds of readers to whom a text can be addressed: the real
reader (the person who holds the book in hand), the virtual reader (the
kind of reader the author thinks he is writing for, whom he endows with
certain qualities, capacities, and tastes), and the ideal reader (one who
understands the text perfectly and approves its every nuance). All of
these are to be distinguished, although it is not always clear how, from
the narratee—a person to whom a narration is directed either explicitly,
like the Caliph in *The Thousand and One Nights,* or implicitly, like the
unnamed narratee of *The Sun Also Rises.* The point to recognize here is
that once the idea of the reader has come into view it provides the critic
with the opportunity to invent a new set of analytical tools. Prince
devotes most of his essay to describing the instruments of exegesis he
derives from the concept of the narratee. His classificatory system posits
a "zero-degree narratee" who possesses certain minimum characteristics
such as knowing the language but exists in a kind of cultural vacuum,
apart from any value system that would allow him to make judgments.
The zero-degree narratee serves as a reference point for the description
of actual narratees, whose characters come into focus as deviations from
this hypothetical norm. Prince offers a series of suggestions for identifying the traits of a narratee, sketches in several ways of classifying narratees, and enumerates the functions a narratee may perform; for
example, the narratee may forge a link between the author and the
reader, help to characterize the narrator, clarify a theme. The aim of the
essay, finally, is to lay the groundwork for a typology of narrative in
which fictions are classified not only according to the traditional distinctions among various kinds of narrators but also according to the types of
narratees to whom the story is addressed.

Prince does not imply, as Gibson does, that his method of analysis
will make its users better human beings. Influenced by structuralist critics such as Tzvetan Todorov and Gerard Genette, he regards the concept of the narratee as a newly discovered element of narrative, which,
when thoroughly investigated, will be a significant addition to the science
of literary structures. But while the terminology he proposes is innovative and offers critics the chance to produce new descriptions of old
works, Prince's assumptions about the status of the text and its relation to
real readers differ in no way from those of the New Critics. Reading
for him, as for Gibson, consists of discovering what is already there on
the page. His narratees, like Wayne Booth's narrators, belong to the text.
Thus, the focus on mock readers and narratees is ultimately a way of

re-focusing on the text; it does not endow the reader with any powers he did not already have, but leaves him in the same position he had occupied in formalist criticism—that of a flawed but reverential seeker after the truths, in this case the structures, preserved in literary art.

Michael Riffaterre shares with Gibson and Prince the assumption that literary meaning resides in the language of the text, but he attacks the idea that meaning exists independently of the reader's relation to it. His critique of the Lévi-Strauss–Jakobson analysis of "Les Chats" bases itself on the notion that literary meaning is a function of the reader's response to a text and cannot be described accurately if that response is left out of account. Riffaterre criticizes the structuralists' reading of the poem because it relies on phonological and grammatical patterns that are imperceptible to the reader and consequently cannot be "active" components of the poetry. He proposes instead to arrive at an understanding of the poetically significant linguistic features of the sonnet by focusing only on those features that have consistently arrested the attention of readers of various persuasions. The subjective element in these responses is screened out by ignoring the specific content of the readers' responses and focusing only on the *fact* of response to a given locution. "The subjective interpretation of . . . response . . . depends on elements exterior to the act of communication but the response itself testifies objectively to the actuality of a contact." In his analysis of Baudelaire's sonnet, Riffaterre takes into account the reactions of a "superreader," a theoretical construct that includes French poets and critics, translators of the poem, students, "and other souls whom fate has thrown my way." By tallying the effects of the poem's language on this array of respondents Riffaterre believes he can isolate those linguistic features that are poetically significant. His description of these features of the text is notable for its emphasis on the emotional and intellectual activities of the reader moving through the sonnet line by line. His key terms, predictability and unpredictability, are derived from a temporal model of the reading process that views the text as arousing certain expectations which it then either satisfies or frustrates. The frustration of expectation, i.e., the unpredictability of a given locution, is synonymous, for him, with poetic significance.

Riffaterre's attention to the way poetic meaning is reflected in the reader's moment-by-moment reactions to its unfolding represents a new way of performing close stylistic analysis. The analysis remains, however, firmly committed to the assumption of textual objectivity. In its effort to avoid placing any value on the reader's interpretation of his response, it asserts that meaning is a property of the language itself and not of any activities the reader performs. The reader's response is evidence of the presence of poetic meaning at a given point in the text but is not constitutive of it.

Riffaterre's goal in calling the reader into play is the specification of poetically significant linguistic features. According to Georges Poulet, to read is precisely not to be aware of the structural and stylistic properties of the work but to be immersed in the author's mode of experiencing the world. Attention to the reader's experience and the faithful description of it are central tasks for phenomenological critics like Poulet, but the activities they report look nothing like those described by Riffaterre. Poulet does not assume that the meaning of literary works is in any way dependent upon the reader but that their "fate" or mode of existence does. They "wait for someone to come and deliver them from their materiality, their immobility." Up until the moment he has released the book from its speechlessness by opening it, the reader remains all-powerful in relation to the text, but once he has begun to read he becomes the prisoner of the author's consciousness. For the space of time that his mind is occupied by the mind of another the reader's awareness of the text is dissolved. Poulet's emphasis is all on the intimate personal quality of the relation between author and reader and not on the text and its formal features. He regards the text as a magical object that allows the interiority of one human being to play host to the interiority of another and ends his essay by warning against a complete reliance on the objective features of the literary work as an adequate index to the subjectivity of its author. "There is in the work a mental activity profoundly engaged in objective forms; and there is, at another level, forsaking all forms, a subject which reveals itself to itself (and to me) in its transcendence over all which is reflected in it. . . . It seems then that criticism, in order to accompany the mind in this effort of detachment from itself, needs to annihilate, or at least momentarily to forget, the objective elements of the work, and to elevate itself to the apprehension of a subjectivity without objectivity." Poulet's focus on the consciousness of the reader is aimed not so much at using it as a reflector of the specific properties of a literary text as it is at describing the kind of mental attitude, the stance vis-à-vis the text, that will produce the most complete apprehension of the text's subjectivity. His criticism holds out the promise of a moment in which the critic transcends materiality and particularity and stands in presence of the work's "ineffability." The way to achieve this almost mystical moment of insight is by a determined submission of one's own subjectivity to the consciousness that generates the work. "The consciousness inherent in the work is active and potent; it occupies the foreground; it is clearly related to its *own* world, to objects which are *its* objects. In opposition, I myself, although conscious of whatever it may be conscious of, I play a much more humble role, content to record passively all that is going on in me."

When Poulet examines the internal processes through which literature realizes itself in the individual reader, he is struck by the essentially passive nature of the reader's role. The reader gains his experience by forgetting, foregoing himself; dying, so to speak, in order that the text may live. What Wolfgang Iser sees when he examines the same process is exactly the opposite phenomenon: a reader actively participating in the production of textual meaning. For both Iser and Poulet, the literary work is actualized only through a convergence of reader and text, but whereas for Poulet this means allowing one's consciousness to be invaded by the consciousness of another, to Iser it means that the reader must act as co-creator of the work by supplying that portion of it which is not written but only implied. The "concretization" of a text in any particular instance requires that the reader's imagination come into play. Each reader fills in the unwritten portions of the text, its "gaps" or areas of "indeterminacy," in his own way. But this is not to say that the text thus arrived at is a mere subjective fabrication of the reader's. The range of interpretations that arise as a result of the reader's creative activity is seen rather as proof of the text's "inexhaustibility." "By reading," says Iser, "we uncover the unformulated part" of a literary work and what we uncover "represents its [the text's] 'intention.'" The text's intentions may be manifold, they may even be infinite, but they are always present embryonically in the work itself, implied by it, circumscribed by it, and finally traceable to it.

In fully accepting the individual reader's interpretative activity, Iser moves beyond the position adopted by Riffaterre. But he does not grant the reader autonomy or even a partial independence from textual constraints. The reader's activity is only a fulfillment of what is already implicit in the structure of the work—though exactly how that structure limits his activity is never made clear.

Iser's phenomenology of the reading process, with its movement from anticipation to retrospection, its making and unmaking of gestalts, like Prince's taxonomy of readers and narratees, provides critics with a new repertoire of interpretive devices and thus brings to light a new set of facts for observation and description. Iser claims, as Gibson did, that his method will be beneficial for its practitioners. "The need to decipher gives us the chance to formulate our own deciphering capacity. . . . The production of the meaning of literary texts . . . does not merely entail the discovery of the unformulated . . . it also entails the possibility that we may formulate ourselves and so discover what had previously seemed to elude our consciousness." Iser's position extends the field of critical activity to include not only a new subject matter—the phenomenology of the reading process—but also a new moral emphasis. Like Gibson, he views the application of his insights as therapeutic, leading to fuller knowledge of the self and even to self-creation.

By this point it is possible to see that focusing on the reader engenders a species of moral drama in the domain of criticism. To adopt a particular conception of the reader is to engage in a particular kind of virtuous action—the refining of one's moral sensors (Gibson), adding to the sum of human knowledge (Prince), coming ever closer to the truth through attention to linguistic detail (Riffaterre), achieving self-transcendence through self-effacement (Poulet), or building a better self through interpretive enterprise (Iser). What is important about these claims is that although they never deny that the ultimate object of attention is the literary text, they endow the process of reading the text, of receiving it and responding to it, with value. The next event in the drama of the reader's emergence into critical prominence is that instead of being seen as instrumental to the understanding of the text, the reader's activity is declared to be *identical with* the text and therefore becomes itself the source of all literary value. If literature *is* what happens when we read, its value depends on the value of the reading process.

Stanley Fish, the first critic to propose this theory of reading, claims benefits for the reading process similar to those claimed by Iser in that he characterizes reading as an activity that "processes its own user." The therapeutic effects he describes do not involve discovering new areas of the self but concern, rather, a sharpened awareness of the mental processes that language engages us in. His method resembles Iser's, broadly, in that it turns the mind to an investigation of its own activities; the focus, however, is narrowed and foreshortened, concentrating on the reader's moment-to-moment reactions to the language, or, in Fish's words, on "the developing responses of the reader in relation to the words as they succeed one another in time." Whereas Iser chronicles broad-gauge shifts in the reader's attitude toward the text—his construction and reconstruction of a character or his emerging apprehension of a theme— Fish rivets attention on the sequence of decisions, revisions, anticipations, reversals, and recoveries that the reader performs as he negotiates the text sentence by sentence and phrase by phrase. "Essentially what the method does," Fish explains, " is *slow down* the reading experience so that 'events' one does not notice in normal time, but which do occur, are brought before our analytical attention. It is as if a slow-motion camera with an automatic stop action effect were recording our linguistic experiences and presenting them to us for viewing." The essay offers several precise and detailed demonstrations of this critical technique, which, like those previously discussed, owes its existence to the idea that the activity of reading is essential to our understanding of what literature is. What distinguishes Fish's work from that of his predecessors, however, is its much more fully articulated conception of what it means, theoretically, to hold such a position. The notion that readers actively participate in the creation of meaning entails, for him, a re-definition of meaning and of literature itself. Meaning, according to Fish, is not something one extracts from a poem, like a nut from its shell, but an experience one has in the course of reading. Literature, as a consequence, is not regarded as a fixed object of attention but as a sequence of events that unfold within the reader's mind. Correspondingly, the goal of literary criticism becomes the faithful description of the activity of reading, an activity that is minute, complicated, strenuous, and never the same from one reading to the next. This re-definition of what literature is, i.e., not an object but an experience, obliterates the traditional separation between reader and text and makes the responses of the reader rather than the contents of the work the focus of critical attention. Fish's reader, unlike Iser's, is not in the business of filling in gaps left by the text or extrapolating from its hints; and unlike Riffaterre's reader he is not merely an indicator of poetic significance in the text. Instead, he is the source of all possible significations because "the place where sense is made or not made is the reader's mind rather than the printed page or the space between the covers of a book."

The position Fish argues in this essay does not deny that words have meanings, nor does it assert that the reader's response is untrammeled and free from textual constraints. The kinds of experience that literature affords are regulated by the linguistic and literary competence of the individual reader. "If the speakers of a language share a system of rules that each of them has somehow internalized, understanding will, in some sense, be uniform. . . . And insofar as these rules are constraints on production . . . they will also be constraints on the range, and even the direction, of response." The reader reacts to the words on the page in one way rather than another because he operates according to the same set of rules that the author used to generate them. The reader's experience, then, is the creation of the author; he enacts the author's will. The important point is that literature *is* the activity that the reader performs and not a stable artifact: "it refuses to stay still."

Fish's essay, "Literature in the Reader," makes the crucial move in reader-oriented criticism by removing the literary text from the center of critical attention and replacing it with the reader's cognitive activity. The decisive shift in focus opens a new field of inquiry. If meaning is no longer a property of the text but a product of the reader's activity the question to answer is not "what do poems mean?" or even "what do poems do?" but "how do readers make meaning?" Jonathan Culler's *Structuralist Poetics* provides an answer to this question based on the central insights of French structuralism from Saussure to Derrida.

Culler's basic assumption is that the shape a text assumes for its readers is determined not by the text itself but by the complex of sign systems readers conventionally apply to literature. "To read a text as literature is not to make one's mind a *tabula rasa* and approach it without preconceptions; . . . the semiological approach suggests, rather, that the poem be thought of as an utterance that has meaning only with respect to a system of conventions which the reader has assimilated. If other conventions were operative its range of potential meanings would be

different." Like Fish, Culler bases his understanding of how we make
sense of literary texts on a linguistic model. "To speak of the structure of
a sentence is necessarily to imply an internalized grammar that gives it
that structure." Analogously, to speak of the structure of a literary work
implies an internalized "grammar" of literature, or what Culler terms
"literary competence": that set of conventions that directs the reader to
pick out certain features of the work corresponding to public notions of
what constitutes an "acceptable" or "appropriate" interpretation. Literary meaning, then, is not the result of a reader responding to an author's
cues, as Iser would have it, but is an institutional matter, a function of
conventions that are publicly agreed upon. These conventions currently
include the "rule of significance" (i.e., the assumption that a poem expresses "a significant attitude to some problem concerning man and/or
his relation to the universe"), metaphorical coherence, and thematic unity. Culler's concern, however, is not to examine the way these conventions are applied by particular readers to particular works, but rather "to
make explicit the underlying system which makes literary effects possible. . . . The question is not what actual readers happen to do [this was
Fish's question] but what an ideal reader must know implicitly in order to
read and interpret works in ways which we consider acceptable."

Culler's focus on the internalized system of rules that make literature intelligible to us locates the organizing principle of textual interpretation not in the reader but in the institutions that teach readers to read.
Thus, his position pushes both the text *and* the reader into the background, although it does not do away with them altogether, and trains its
sights instead on the theory of literary discourse implicit in any and all
acts of textual interpretation. But despite this apparently anti-
humanistic orientation, Culler concludes his chapter on literary competence by making the same kinds of moral claims for his method that
Gibson, Iser, and Fish made for theirs. He finds an acknowledgment of
the reader's dependence on reading conventions more honest than the
struggle to identify objective features of the text, points to the gain in
self-awareness consequent upon a recognition of the conventional nature of literary activity, and suggests that by making received modes of
understanding explicit readers will become aware of how innovatory
literature "challenges the limits we set to the self as a device of order and
allows us, painfully and joyfully, to accede to an expansion of self."
When Culler speaks of "innovatory literature," which catalyzes the process of self-expansion, the text as an object of knowledge and the self
that responds to it seem to creep back into his theory. His position,
finally, seems to hover between a structuralist rejection of self as an
organizing principle and a liberal humanism that defines moral and
intellectual growth in terms of self-awareness and self-development.

While Culler recognizes the moral claims of individual consciousness almost as an afterthought, and without directly acknowledging the consequences of his doing so, Norman Holland and David Bleich put questions of personal identity and self-awareness at the center of their critical theories. The structuralist drive to de-emphasize individual consciousness in favor of systems of intelligibility that operate through individuals is antithetical to the psychoanalytic model of interpretation these critics adopt and to their moral perspectives as well. The practical goal of their work is to achieve knowledge of the self, of its relation to other selves, to the world, and to human knowledge in general. Much more than for other critics, their moral aims seem to determine the nature of their literary theories.

Norman Holland's central thesis, arrived at over a period of years, is that people deal with literary texts the same way they deal with life-experience. Each person develops a particular style of coping—what Holland calls an identity theme—which imprints itself on every aspect of his behavior, including acts of textual interpretation. The reader will filter a text through his characteristic patterns of defense, project onto it his characteristic fantasies, translate the experience into a socially acceptable form, and thus produce what we would call an interpretation. Whether or not the interpretation is based on something that is really "in" the text is a question Holland refuses to answer directly, but his language constantly suggests that he believes the answer is "yes, partly." At the opening of the essay reprinted here, he speaks of readers "replenishing" a text "by infinitely various *additions* of subjective to objective" (my italics), a phrase that implies that textual meaning is a combination of what readers project onto a text and what the words actually mean. Later, he describes his epistemology, in opposition to Cartesian dualism, as one which conceives experience as "an in-gathering and in-mixing of self and other." He writes of readers "matching" their adaptive patterns to a text, and of the reader who "shapes the materials the literary work offers him." These formulations imply that textual data exist prior to and independent of the reader's interpretive activity and that the reader absorbs them somehow and makes them over in his own image. But how these objective elements of the text take shape for the reader in the first place is not a question Holland seems able to answer, nor is he much concerned to. What he is sure of is that "*interpretation is a function of identity.*" He reasons that since all explanations of the world, including scientific explanations, are interpretations of it, and all interpretation is a human act, the science of human behavior (psychoanalysis) must lie at the base of all human knowledge, for it enables us to apprehend the identity themes that inform all expressions of knowledge about the world. If one were to object to the circularity of this argument by pointing out that psychoanalysis itself is only another interpretation, Holland would reply that that objection confirms his belief in the "creative and relational quality of all our experience."

The aim of Holland's method is, as he puts it (quoting Freud), to foster "the ability to break through the repulsion associated with 'the barriers that rise between each single ego and the others.'" The critic merges his identity with that of the author he is studying by recreating the author's identity theme according to his own characteristic patterns of response. Though Holland locates meaning primarily in the reader rather than in the text, his theory nevertheless retains an idea of the text as "other." If it did not, there would be no barriers to break through or separations to close. In order to overcome the subject-object dichotomy, Holland must maintain the terms that keep that dualism in force. If criticism is to be an activity that effects a "sharing" and "mingling" of the identities of author and reader, the text and the interpreting self must exist independent of one another.

Holland must maintain the autonomy of textual meaning in order to supply literary criticism with its goal—the merging of self and other. It is by denying the autonomy of textual meaning and the persistence of individual identity themes that David Bleich distinguishes his position from Norman Holland's. While Holland eventually brackets the subject-object problem, Bleich centers his theory on it because he views literary response as essentially an epistemological issue. In keeping with this emphasis, he labels the position he has developed "subjective" criticism. According to Bleich, adult individuals universally distinguish among three kinds of entities: objects, symbols, and people. Literary works, in this frame of reference, fall into the category of symbols, which are mental creations. The text is an object only insofar as it has a physical existence; its meaning depends entirely on the process of symbolization that takes place in the mind of the reader. This initial symbolization is what Bleich calls "response." The effort to understand that response, to give it coherence or point, is a process of resymbolization that he calls "interpretation." Neither "response" nor "interpretation" are in any way constrained by the action of the text, as they are for Holland. The question is whether they are constrained by anything outside the interpreting subject. The degree to which Bleich sees the self as shaped by its social context is not altogether clear in the chapter reprinted here. When he says, for example, that "response can acquire meaning only in the context of a predecided community . . . interest in knowledge," it is hard to tell whether the response exists prior to and independent of social definitions or whether it is always the expression of a self formed by communal systems of intelligibility. But elsewhere in *Subjective Criticism*, Bleich commits himself on this point; ultimately, he wishes to preserve the notion of an independent self in the interests of holding on to the possibility of free human initiative. Thus, he distinguishes between an individual's response to literature, which is purely subjective, and the process by which his response becomes a form of knowledge, a process that is determined by the community of interpreters to which the reader belongs.

Bleich defines knowledge as the product of negotiation among members of an interpretive community, as the product of a collective decision about what it is desirable to know, rather than something that is truly independent of human purposes. He concludes from this that "when knowledge is no longer conceived as objective, the purpose of pedagogical institutions from the nursery through the university is to synthesize knowledge rather than to pass it along. . . ." He substitutes for the paradigm of teaching and learning the paradigm of "developing knowledge," replacing the idea of education as an activity in which there are agents and patients (teachers and learners) with the idea of education as a communal pursuit in which all parties are engaged on an equal footing in deciding what counts as true. He wants to take responsibility for the production of knowledge away from traditional sources of authority—texts, teachers, institutions—and place it in the hands of all who are engaged in seeking it. What sets Bleich apart from the other critics represented in this collection is his perception of the effects a theory of reading can have on the way students respond to literature, on classroom procedures, and on the authorization of interpretations.

The phrase "community of interpreters" or "interpretive community" plays a crucial role in the more recent theories of reading advanced by Bleich, Fish, Culler, and Walter Michaels. First developed by Fish in "Interpreting the *Variorum*," it is shorthand for the notion that since all sign systems are social constructs that individuals assimilate more or less automatically (or, more accurately, that pervade and constitute individual consciousness), an individual's perceptions and judgments are a function of the assumptions shared by the groups he belongs to. Bleich, however, in keeping with his desire to safeguard the freedom of individual initiative, uses the term in a different sense. He makes it refer not to shared perceptual strategies that operate through individuals, but to a conscious process of negotiation that takes place within a framework where agreement on what reality is can be given or withheld. Thus, Bleich's position is more conservative than Fish's since, by retaining the notion of an independent self he retains the subject-object model of reality. Fish, however, in "Interpreting the *Variorum*" collapses the distinction entirely, with consequences that at first appear to lay waste the foundations of criticism and pedagogy alike.

Fish begins by recapitulating the position outlined in "Literature in the Reader," preparatory to overturning it. He argues that one cannot decide what a difficult line means by seeing which of two diametrically opposed readings does a better job of marshaling the textual data (often the evidence is equally strong on both sides); rather, one must consult the reader's experience of the line as he encounters it in the temporal sequence of the poem. If the line seems ambiguous, to mean now one thing, now another, then its meaning is neither *a* nor *b* but the fact that the reader must decide for himself what the meaning is. Meaning, in other words, is to be defined in experiential terms. It is what happens to a reader as he negotiates the text and is not something that was already in place before he experienced it.

When Fish made this argument in 1970, and in Part I of "Interpreting the *Variorum*," the reader's experience was described as a response to authorial intentions realized in the formal features of the text. Although the locus of meaning was held to be in the reader's mind and not between the pages of a book, the mental events that constituted literary meaning were assumed to be the effects of specifiable properties of the text, particularly line-endings. In Part II of "Interpreting the *Variorum*," those specifiable properties "disappear"; they are no longer seen as autonomous but as constituted in the act of criticism. There is no preexistent text to which the reader responds, nor is there "reading" in the traditional sense. Texts are written by readers, not read, since, the argument now states, the formal features of the text, the authorial intentions they are normally taken to represent, and the reader's interpretive strategies are mutually interdependent.

When one consults his experience as a reader, the shape it has will be the consequence of a particular set of perceptual categories, categories that do not reflect the world (or the words on the page) but constitute it. To describe the features of a literary work—to say, for example, that it is written in iambic pentameter or has a preponderance of active verbs—is to impose an interpretation on it. Therefore, any features to which one could point as having occasioned this or that response are themselves the product of a particular interpretive framework. The framework creates the data *and* the response and produces the work, so to speak, from the ground up.

Fish's attack on the independence of textual meaning destroys the claims not only of the positivist-formalist position it was mounted against, but those of his own brand of reader-response criticism as well and along with it the theoretical basis of most other reader-oriented work. The question that arises at the end of his essay is: If texts have no specifiable properties, then what is reader-response a response to? Or, as he puts it, What is interpretation an interpretation of? The framing of this question, however, ignores the force of the argument that has just been made by separating the response from its object, the interpretation from what is being interpreted. As Fish himself points out, our perceptual habits are so automatic that we regard as brute facts data that are the result of interpretive conventions. The text does not disappear in the sense that we no longer perceive it; poems still have line-endings and patterns of alliteration; there are still data to interpret; but these data are themselves the products of interpretation and do not have objective status. The position argued for in this essay, although it seems to remove the possibility of literary criticism by making the text disappear, in fact allows criticism to go on as before but with this difference: instead of claiming that one's interpretations of literature are a response to what the author meant, or to what is there on the page, one must acknowledge that they are the result of the interpretive strategies one possesses. The choice, Fish writes, is really

> between an interpretation that is unacknowledged as such and an interpre-
> tation that is at least aware of itself. It is this awareness that I am claiming for
> myself, although in doing so I must give up the claims implicitly made in the
> first part of this paper. There I argue that a bad (because spatial) model had
> suppressed what was really happening, but by my own declared principles
> the notion "really happening" is just one more interpretation.

In explaining why his theory is preferable to the formalist position, Fish makes a familiar appeal to moral values. Like Culler, he believes that giving up the claim to objectivity (which means relinquishing the claim that one knows the truth) is an honest position because it does not pretend to knowledge that is really unavailable. Implicit in this appeal to honesty are an appeal to humility ("I humbly acknowledge the limita-tions of my own discourse") and an appeal to the notion of self-development. By admitting that his own experiential analysis of litera-ture is "just one more interpretation" Fish shows that he is open to change, ready to learn, not the prisoner of an unchanging set of assump-tions.

Fish's moral claims for his theory imply a self that is independent, free, and responsible for its own choices, but the self that his theory posits is one constituted by its own interpretive categories, which are public and shared. In that case, the self as an independent entity van-ishes and, in Culler's words, "its functions are taken up by a variety of interpersonal systems that operate through it." In their theories of read-ing both Fish and Culler subscribe explicitly to this second description of the self, though their appeals to moral value seem to be predicated on the first. Thus, the powerful arguments these critics launch against the objectivity of the text make the nature of the interpreter's self into a problematic issue. As meaning comes to be defined more and more as a function of the reader's consciousness, the powers and limitations of that consciousness become an object of critical debate. This is the subject of the last of the essays reprinted here.

In "The Interpreter's Self" Walter Michaels suggests that American

formalist and French post-structuralist attitudes toward the self have a
common if unacknowledged meeting ground in American pragmatism.
Commenting on a recent debate between Hillis Miller and Meyer Abrams over whether or not texts have determinate meanings, Michaels
observes that the desire to preserve textual objectivity has its roots in a
long-standing American "fear of subjectivity, of the individual interpreter's self." This fear derives from the idea that "if there were no determinate meanings the interpreter's freedom could make of a text anything it wanted." People would "feel free to impose their own subjective
interpretations on any and all texts," a position that makes "a solipsistic
mockery of literary criticism and at worst give[s] sanction to a thoroughgoing and destructive moral scepticism." This fear of an anarchic self,
Michaels argues, is both reflected in and obviated by the American
pragmatists, particularly Josiah Royce and C. S. Peirce. Peirce's attack on
the Cartesian concept of the self asserts that the self is not primary, not
intuited directly, not independent or free, but perceived, like everything
else, by inference. Since, according to Peirce, all our thoughts are signs
(for it can't be proven that thought precedes signs) the only way we can
know the self is *as* a sign. Translating Peirce's theory into deconstructionist terminology, Michaels states that for Peirce "the self, like the
work, is a text" that is "already embedded in a context, the community of
interpretation or system of signs." In this way Michaels shows that since
the self is already an interpretation as well as an interpreter, it is not
radically free, as Abrams supposes, to impose its own meanings on any
and all texts.

   In overturning the neo-Cartesian model of the autonomous reader
confronting an autonomous text, Michaels presents the self as a function
of its interpretive strategies. According to this model, the only mistake
the critic can make is to imagine that he is free to impose his own
subjective fabrications on the text. The fear that without determinate
meaning interpretations can run wild, and interpreters along with them,
is forestalled by Michaels's conception of a self constituted and re-
strained by shared standards of cognition and judgment. In his theory,
the self that actively and freely constructs its own meanings is just as
illusory as the text that contains meanings independent of the reader's
perceptual habits. Thus the position that appears to enfranchise the
reader entirely by releasing him once and for all from the domination of
the text, in fact places the reader under greater constraints than any
prior theory by reconceiving the self as *another* text.

   It is misleading, however, to speak of the reader as free or unfree in
the context of this position. The idea of freedom presupposes that individual selves exist apart from an external reality that either constrains
them or leaves them free from constraint. But the opposition between
self and world on which the notion of freedom (and of determinism)

depends is excluded by the concept of a self that is constituted by interpretive codes that define it and the world simultaneously. Since what we
choose is determined by our beliefs, which we have not chosen, the
notion of free choice dissolves, and along with it a whole range of moral
arguments that can be made on behalf of a critical theory. There is no
point in crediting the interpreter who admits the stipulative nature of his
own assumptions with candor or humility or willingness to grow if the
freedom of chòice that these virtues presuppose is not a possibility. In a
world where free choice is not a meaningful issue, questions of moral
responsibility must assume another shape or drop from sight altogether.

At this juncture, the critics against whom Michaels argued might
well decide that their worst fears about the "moral scepticism" implicit in
his position had been confirmed. But the condition of moral anarchy
that was the object of those fears has not emerged. Instead what Fish and
Michaels variously assert is that, far from there being no values to which
one can appeal, no criteria for judging what is good or true, there is
never a moment when we are not in the grip of some value-system, never
a statement we make that is not value-laden. What they deny is the
possibility of neutral description or of values that are absolute—or, in
other words, of statements that exist apart from a human structure of
interests.

The assertion that all discourse is "interested" amounts to a reinser-
tion of literature into the stream of ordinary discourse from which formalism had removed it. The New Critics had objected to confusing the
poem with its results in order to separate literature from other kinds of
discourse and to give criticism an objective basis for its procedures. The
later reader-response critics deny that criticism has such an objective
basis because they deny the existence of objective texts and indeed the
possibility of objectivity altogether. Relocating meaning first in the
reader's self and then in the interpretive strategies that constitute it, they
assert that meaning is a consequence of being in a particular situation in
the world. The net result of this epistemological revolution is to re-
politicize literature and literary criticism. When discourse is responsible
for reality and not merely a reflection of it, then whose discourse prevails
makes all the difference.

This view of language as the ultimate form of power is not unlike
that of the Greek rhetoricians who believed that speech was a "great
prince" able to transform human experience. Both views of language
restore to literature what literary theorists since the middle of the
eighteenth century, in the interests of literature itself, had been denying
that it possesses—the ability to influence human behavior in a direct and
practical manner. In order for literature to perform its function as a
civilizing agent, it was thought necessary to set it apart from the merely
mechanical and practical spheres of human life. This divorce between

literature and politics, which was finally effected with the advent of formalism, radically changed the definition of what literary response was or could be. The significance that that definition has had in the work of contemporary reader-response critics, and its anomalous relation to the traditional view of literary response, form the subject of the final essay in this volume.

Note

1. The essays in this volume present the major theoretical positions adopted by contemporary critics who have written about the reader's response to literature. In the interests of coherence, I have excluded works which, although important, do not clarify the main line of theoretical development in this field. The annotated bibliography that concludes this volume will fill the gaps that my principles of selection unavoidably create, but I would like to mention here the omissions that seem to me most significant.

Louise Rosenblatt deserves to be recognized as the first among the present generation of critics in this country to describe empirically the way the reader's reactions to a poem are responsible for any subsequent interpretation of it. Her work and later the work of Walter Slatoff raise issues central to the debates that have arisen since.

Alongside each of the pieces included here lie important books and essays that share a similar orientation. Passages from Wayne Booth's *Rhetoric of Fiction* go hand in hand with Walker Gibson's essay on the mock reader. Peter Rabinowitz's "Four Levels of Audience" is a companion piece to the article by Gerald Prince. George Dillon's *Language Processing and the Reading of Literature* and Eugene Kintgen's work in stylistics take in two different directions the question of the reader's response to linguistic phenomena explored here by Michael Riffaterre and Stanley Fish. Murray Schwartz's "Where Is Literature" complements substantially the psychoanalytically oriented work of Norman Holland and David Bleich. Most notably, the rapidly increasing output of critics who practice reception-aesthetics—particularly the essays of Hans Robert Jauss—constitutes an essential development of theoretical work begun by Wolfgang Iser.

Another category of omissions includes critics whose work stands behind that of the writers represented here. The theories of Roman Ingarden undergird those of Wolfgang Iser at almost every point. The enterprise of French post-structuralism, especially the work of Roland Barthes and Jacques Derrida, without whom reader-criticism in its present form would hardly exist, is crucial to the essays by Stanley Fish, Jonathan Culler, and Walter Michaels, although these are important pieces in their own right.

A number of excellent articles have been excluded because they are, for various reasons, eccentric to the purposes of this volume. Of these the most outstanding are D. W. Harding's essay comparing the reading of literature to the overhearing of gossip, Walter Ong's discussion of literary audiences from the writer's point of view, James F. Ross's comprehensive survey of attempts to define the features essential to reading activity, and Stephen Booth's "On the Value of *Hamlet*," which, although it legitimately falls outside the confines of a volume concerned with literary theory, must be mentioned because it illustrates so brilliantly what an accomplished close reader operating from within this perspective can do.

Since any list of omissions, seriously pursued, is endless, I will refer the reader instead to the inclusions, which have been chosen to provide a conceptual framework for organizing the ever-growing quantity of reader-oriented work.

Reader-Response Criticism

1

AUTHORS, SPEAKERS, READERS, AND MOCK READERS

Walker Gibson

I t is now common in the classroom as well as in criticism to distinguish carefully between the *author* of a literary work of art and the fictitious *speaker* within the work of art. Most teachers agree that the attitudes expressed by the "lover" in the love sonnet are not to be crudely confused with whatever attitudes the sonneteer himself may or may not have manifested in real life. Historical techniques are available for a description of the sonneteer, but the literary teacher's final concern must be with the speaker, that voice or disguise through which someone (whom we may as well call "the poet") communicates with us. It is this speaker who is "real" in the sense most useful to the study of literature, for the speaker is made of language alone, and his entire self lies on the page before us in evidence.

Closely associated with this distinction between author and speaker, there is another and less familiar distinction to be made, respecting the *reader*. For if the "real author" is to be regarded as to a great degree distracting and mysterious, lost in history, it seems equally true that the "real reader," lost in today's history, is no less mysterious and sometimes as irrelevant. The fact is that every time we open the pages of another piece of writing, we are embarked on a new adventure in which we become a new person—a person as controlled and definable and as remote from the chaotic self of daily life as the lover in the sonnet. Subject to the degree of our literary sensibility, we are recreated by the language. We assume, for the sake of the experience, that set of attitudes and qualities which the language asks us to assume, and, if we cannot assume them, we throw the book away.

Reprinted from *College English* 11 (February 1950): 265–69 by permission of the author.

I am arguing, then, that there are two readers distinguishable in every literary experience. First, there is the "real" individual upon whose crossed knee rests the open volume, and whose personality is as complex and ultimately inexpressible as any dead poet's. Second, there is the fictitious reader—I shall call him the "mock reader"—whose mask and costume the individual takes on in order to experience the language. The mock reader is an artifact, controlled, simplified, abstracted out of the chaos of day-to-day sensation.

The mock reader can probably be identified most obviously in sub-literary genres crudely committed to persuasion, such as advertising and propaganda. We resist the blandishments of the copywriter just in so far as we refuse to become the mock reader his language invites us to become. Recognition of a violent disparity between ourself as mock reader and ourself as real person acting in a real world is the process by which we keep our money in our pockets. "Does your toupee collect moths?" asks the toupee manufacturer, and we answer, "Certainly not! My hair's my own. You're not talking to *me,* old boy; I'm wise to you." Of course we are not always so wise.

Consider the mock reader in a case only slightly less obvious, the following opening paragraph from a book review of Malcolm Cowley's recent collection, *The Portable Hawthorne*:

> Our thin self-lacerating and discontinuous culture automatically pro-
> duces such uneasy collaborations as this one between Mr. Cowley, the
> hard-working scribe and oddly impressionable cultural sounding board, and
> the publishing industry with its concept of the "Portable." The Hawthorne
> who emerges has had such a bad fall between stools, or clichés, that he
> appears almost as giddy and shattered as we. . . .

The assumptions buried rather shallowly in this passage can very easily be brought to light. A nimble and sympathetic conversation is passing back and forth here—as always—between the speaker and the mock reader, a conversation that goes in part something like this:

> You and I, in brave rebellion against the barbarousness of a business
> culture, can see this book for what of course it is—an "uneasy collaboration"
> and a defamation of that fine Hawthorne whom you and I know and love.
> *We* would not be content, would we, to be mere "scribes"; how stupid other
> people are to think that industry alone is sufficient. You and I are quickly
> able to translate "oddly impressionable" into what of course more literally
> describes the situation, though we were too polite to say so—namely, that
> Cowley is a weak sister. Nothing "odd" about it—you and I know what's
> going on all right.

It is interesting to observe how frankly the speaker throws his arm around the mock reader at the end of the passage I have quoted, as the two comrades experience their common giddiness at the appalling quality of this book. Remember that the *real* reader has in all likelihood not even seen the book yet, and, if he takes his own mock-reader-personality seriously enough, he probably never will.

An opening paragraph from another book review requires us to take on another character:

> I never got around to the early books of the Pasquier series, Georges Duhamel's multigeneration history of a French family, but after reading "Suzanne and Joseph" (Holt), the two-volume novel that closes the series, I can't see any very pressing reason for flying in the face of prevailing opinion about M. Duhamel. He is, as has been claimed by such admirers of his as Kate O'Brien and Sean O'Faolain, quite a good writer. He deals in honored narrative methods and old truths, and he turns out the kind of novel that can be recognized from afar as A Story. . . .

Again, some obvious portion of the between-the-lines dialogue between speaker and mock reader might be paraphrased as follows:

> You and I are persons of leisure and taste, but unostentatious about it; we make no pretense of having Big Ideas, and we "can't see any very pressing reason for flying in the face of prevailing opinion" (you'll excuse my casual, homely phrase) merely because it *is* prevailing. We favor comfort, after all, and we won't lament over the things we never got around to. On the other hand we recognize competence and talent when we see it; we'll certainly listen to whatever Kate O'Brien and Sean O'Faolain have to say; and though we are enlightened enough to realize that A Story (you'll appreciate my capitals) won't in itself do in this complex age, nevertheless the honored methods and old truths are after all the Honored Methods and Old Truths. . . .

Here again it is worth pointing out that many successful readers of this passage—perhaps most of them—never even heard of Kate O'Brien or Sean O'Faolain. It is possible to imagine a reader saying, "I never heard of Kate O'Brien; this review isn't addressed to the likes of me; I'll read something else." But a more plausible response, I believe, would be this: "It's true I never heard of Kate O'Brien, but in my status as mock reader I'm going to pretend that I have; after all, it's obvious how highly I would think of her if I had heard of her."

It will surprise no one to learn that the first passage was taken from a recent issue of the *Partisan Review,* and that the second is from the *New Yorker.* Perhaps it is fair to say that the mock readers addressed by these speakers represent ideal audiences of the two periodicals. In any case it seems plain that the job of an editor is largely the definition of his magazine's mock reader and that an editorial "policy" is a decision or prediction as to the role or roles in which one's customers would like to imagine themselves. Likewise, a man fingering the piles at a magazine stand is concerned with the corollary question, Who do I want to pretend I am today?

(The mock reader of this article numbers among his many impressive accomplishments the feat of having participated at various times as mock reader of both the *New Yorker* and the *Partisan.*)

It is evident that imaginative literature too makes similar demands on its readers. There is great variation from book to book in the ease and particularity with which one can describe the mock reader, but he is always present, and sometimes is so clearly and rigorously defined as to suggest serious limitations on the audience. The mock reader of the opening paragraphs of *The Great Gatsby,* for instance, is a person determined within fairly rigid limits of time and space.

> In my younger and more vulnerable years my father gave me some advice that I've been turning over in my mind ever since.
> "Whenever you feel like criticising any one," he told me, "just remember that all the people in this world haven't had the advantages that you've had."
> He didn't say any more, but we've always been unusually communicative in a reserved way, and I understood that he meant a good deal more than that. In consequence, I'm inclined to reserve all judgments, a habit that has opened up many curious natures to me and also made me the victim of not a few veteran bores. The abnormal mind is quick to detect and attach itself to this quality when it appears in a normal person, and so it came about that in a college I was unjustly accused of being a politician, because I was privy to the secret griefs of wild, unknown men. Most of the confidences were unsought—frequently I have feigned sleep, preoccupation, or a hostile levity when I realized by some unmistakable sign that an intimate revelation was quivering on the horizon. . . .

Here the mock reader must not only take in stride a series of "jokes" formed by some odd juxtapositions—vulnerable years, not a few veteran bores, etc.—but must also be quick to share the attitudes and assumed experiences of the speaker. For instance, the speaker by overt statement and the mock reader by inference have both attended a particular kind of college in a particular way; notice how "in college" appears grammatically as a dependent phrase within a dependent clause, support-ing the casual, offhand tone.

> Of course we remember, you and I, how it was in college, where as normal persons we certainly had no wish to be confused with campus politi-cians, yet were even warier of the wild unknown men, those poets, those radicals and misfits. You and I understand with what deliberate and delicate absurdity I make fun of both the wild unknown men and the formal-literary language to which you and I have been exposed in the course of our expen-sive educations: "an intimate revelation was quivering on the horizon."

It is probable that *Gatsby* today enjoys a greater reputation among real-life wild unknown men than it does among the equivalents of Nick Carraway's class. Somehow many people are able to suspend their antagonisms against Nick's brand of normalcy in order to participate in the tone. Yet it is neither necessary nor desirable to suspend all one's judgments against Nick and his society, for in so far as Nick himself is self-critical, of course we can and must join him. And, finally, Nick is not the speaker at all, I think, but a kind of mock speaker, as our mock reader is a more complex and discerning person than Nick himself. There is another speaker somewhere—almost as if this novel were written in the third person—and it is from this other speaker that the mock reader ultimately takes on some important attitudes. They speak right over Nick Carraway's head.

> You and I recognize the weaknesses in Nick, do we not: his snobbery and his facile assumptions. But we like him pretty well, after all—and it's a question whether his shallowness is really his fault. . . .

The concept of the mock reader need not be "taught" in so many words to be useful to the teacher of literature. The question the teacher might well ask himself is no more than this: Is there among my students a growing awareness that the literary experience is not just a relation between themselves and an author, or even between themselves and a fictitious speaker, but a relation between such a speaker and a projection, a fictitious modification of themselves? The realization on the part of a student that he is many people as he reads many books and responds to their language worlds is the beginning of literary sophistication in the best sense. One crucial objective of the teacher, I take it, is simply the enlargement of his "mock" possibilities. But this is not to imply that one reading experience is as good as another or that there are not value discriminations that are appropriate among various mock readers. In fact, the term may be particularly useful in recognizing just such discriminations and in providing one way of pointing out what we mean by a bad book. A bad book, then, is a book in whose mock reader we discover a person we refuse to become, a mask we refuse to put on, a role we will not play. If this seems to say little more than "A bad book is a bad book," consider an example:

> Alan Foster wanted to go to Zagazig. He wasn't exactly sure why, except that he liked the name, and after having spent four months in Cairo Alan was ready to go places and do things. Twenty-two years old, tall, blond, with powerful shoulders and trim waist, Alan found no difficulty in making friends. He had had a good time in Egypt. Now he wanted to leave Cairo and try out Zagazig.

What is so irritating about this? Many things, but if we isolate the third sentence and describe its mock reader, we can begin to express why this is bad writing. For the mock reader of the third sentence is a person for whom there is a proper and natural relation between powerful shoulders and making friends. No student in a respectable English course, I assume, should be willing to accept such a relation except perhaps as part of an irony. Only by irony could this passage be saved. ("You and I recognize that he makes friends all right, but what friends! This parody of a matinee idol is of course an ass.") No such irony is perceptible, however; the mock reader is expected to make one simple assumption only, and if the real reader has any sophistication at all, the passage collapses. It collapses precisely because the real reader finds in the mock reader a fellow of intolerable simplicity.

It is a question of rejecting the toupee ad, of recognizing that one's hair is one's own. However, the possibility must immediately suggest itself that a skillful control of tone could persuade us in an instant to don a fictitious toupee and to feel in all possible vividness the tug of a textile scalp against our own suddenly naked head. It is, finally, a matter of the details of language, and no mock reader can be divorced for long from the specific words that made him.

And the question remains: By what standard does one judge mock readers, how does one arrive at the decision that this one or that one is intolerable? Often it is as easy as in the case above—a case of oversimple assumptions. But obviously the problem is larger than that, and the tremendous importance, as it seems to me, of distinguishing for students between the mock world of the literary experience and the real world of everyday experience must not obscure the fact that in the end our appeals for decisions of value are toward sanctions of society in a very real world indeed. For the student, the problem of what mock reader—or part of a mock reader—it is proper for him to accept, and what to reject, involves the whole overwhelming problem of learning to read and learning to act. No terminology can remove his hesitations over attempting the enormously difficult job of becoming the mock reader of *Paradise Lost,* or *Antigone,* or Wallace Stevens. The student's hesitation is no more than a part of a larger question that possibly no teacher can presume to answer for him: Who do I want to be?

2

INTRODUCTION
TO THE STUDY OF THE NARRATEE

Gerald Prince

A ll narration, whether it is oral or written, whether it recounts real or
mythical events, whether it tells a story or relates a simple sequence
of actions in time, presupposes not only (at least) one narrator but also
(at least) one narratee, the narratee being someone whom the narrator
addresses. In a fiction-narration—a tale, an epic, a novel—the narrator is
a fictive creation as is his narratee. Jean-Baptiste Clamence, Holden
Caulfield, and the narrator of *Madame Bovary* are novelistic constructs as
are the individuals to whom they speak and for whom they write. From
Henry James and Norman Friedman to Wayne C. Booth and Tzvetan
Todorov, numerous critics have examined the diverse manifestations of
the narrator in fictive prose and verse, his multiple roles and his importance.[1] By contrast, few critics have dealt with the narratee and none to
date has undertaken an in-depth study;[2] this neglect persists despite the
lively interest raised by Benveniste's fine articles on discourse *(le discours)*,
Jakobson's work on linguistic functions, and the evergrowing prestige of
poetics and semiology.

Nowadays, any student minimally versed in the narrative genre differentiates the narrator of a novel from its author and from the novelistic *alter ego* of the author and knows the difference between Marcel and
Proust, Rieux and Camus, Tristram Shandy, Sterne the novelist, and
Sterne the man. Most critics, however, are scarcely concerned with the
notion of the narratee and often confuse it with the more or less adjacent
notions of receptor *(récepteur)*, reader, and arch-reader *(archilecteur)*. The
fact that the word *narratee* is rarely employed, moreover, is significant.

Reprinted from *Poétique* no. 14 (1973): 177–96 by permission of the author.

This lack of critical interest in narratees is not inexplicable. Indeed, their study has been neglected, more than likely, because of a characteristic of the narrative genre itself; if the protagonist or dominant personality of a narration often assumes the role of the narrator and affirms himself as such (Marcel in *A la recherche du temps perdu,* Roquentin in *La Nausée,* Jacques Revel in *L'Emploi du temps*), there is no hero who is above all a narratee—unless one includes narrators who constitute their own narratee,[3] or perhaps a work like *La Modification.* Besides, it should not be forgotten that the narrator, on a superficial if not a profound level, is more responsible than his narratee for the shape and tone of the story as well as for its other characteristics. Finally, many problems of poetic narrative that might have been approached from the angle of the narratee have already been studied from the point of view of the narrator; after all, the individual who relates a story and the person to whom the story is told are more or less interdependent in any narration.

Whatever the case may be, narratees deserve to be studied. Major storytellers and novelists, as well as the less important, bear out this point. The variety of narratees found in fictive narrations is phenomenal. Docile or rebellious, admirable or ridiculous, ignorant of the events related to them or having prior knowledge of them, slightly naive as in *Tom Jones,* vaguely callous as in *The Brothers Karamazov,* narratees rival narrators in their diversity. Moreover, many novelists have in their own way examined the distinctions that should be maintained between the narratee and the receptor or between the narratee and the reader. In a detective novel by Nicholas Blake, for example, and in another by Philip Loraine, the detective succeeds in solving the crime when he realizes that the narratee and the receptor are not the same. In addition, there is no want of narratives that underscore the importance of the narratee, *A Thousand and One Nights* providing an excellent illustration. Scheherazade must exercise her talent as a storyteller or die, for as long as she is able to retain the attention of the caliph with her stories, she will not be executed. It is evident that the heroine's fate and that of the narration depend not only upon her capabilities as a storyteller, but also upon the humor of the narratee. If the caliph should become tired and stop listening, Scheherazade will die and the narrative will end.[4] The same fundamental situation can be found in the encounter of Ulysses with the Sirens,[5] as well as in a more recent work. Like Scheherazade, the hero of *La Chute* has a desperate need for a certain type of narratee. In order to forget his own guilt, Jean-Baptiste Clamence must find someone who will listen to him and whom he will be able to convince of everyone's guilt. He finds this someone at the Mexico City Bar in Amsterdam and it is at that moment that his narrative account begins.

The Zero-Degree Narratee

In the very first pages of *Le Père Goriot,* the narrator exclaims: "That's what you will do, you who hold this book with a white hand, you who settle back in a well-padded armchair saying to yourself: perhaps this is going to be amusing. After reading about old Goriot's secret misfortunes, you'll dine with a good appetite attributing your insensitivity to the author whom you'll accuse of exaggeration and poetic affectation." This "you" with white hands, accused by the narrator of being egotistical and callous, is the narratee. It's obvious that the latter does not resemble most readers of *Le Père Goriot* and that consequently the narratee of a novel cannot be automatically identified with the reader: the reader's hands might be black or red and not white; he might read the novel in bed instead of in an armchair; he might lose his appetite upon learning of the old merchant's unhappiness. The reader of a fiction, be it in prose or in verse, should not be mistaken for the narratee. The one is real, the other fictive. If it should occur that the reader bears an astonishing resemblance to the narratee, this is an exception and not the rule.

Neither should the narratee be confused with the virtual reader. Every author, provided he is writing for someone other than himself, develops his narrative as a function of a certain type of reader whom he bestows with certain qualities, faculties, and inclinations according to his opinion of men in general (or in particular) and according to the obligations he feels should be respected. This virtual reader is different from the real reader: writers frequently have a public they don't deserve. He is also distinct from the narratee. In *La Chute,* Clamence's narratee is not identical to the reader envisioned by Camus: after all, he's a lawyer visiting Amsterdam. It goes without saying that a virtual reader and a narratee can be alike, but once again it would be an exception.

Finally, we should not confuse the narratee with the ideal reader, although a remarkable likeness can exist between the two. For a writer, an ideal reader would be one who would understand perfectly and would approve entirely the least of his words, the most subtle of his intentions. For a critic, an ideal reader would perhaps be one capable of interpreting the infinity of texts that, according to certain critics, can be found in one specific text. On the one hand, the narratees for whom the narrator multiplies his explanations and justifies the particularities of his narrative are numerous and cannot be thought of as constituting the ideal readers dreamed up by a novelist. We need only think of the narratees of *Le Père Goriot* and *Vanity Fair.* On the other hand, these narratees are too inept to be capable of interpreting even a rather restricted group of texts within the text.

If narratees are distinct from real, virtual, or ideal readers,[6] they very often differ from each other as well. Nonetheless, it should be possible to describe each one of them as a function of the same categories and according to the same models. It is necessary to identify at least some of these characteristics as well as some of the ways in which they vary and combine with each other. These characteristics must be situated with reference to a sort of "zero-degree" narratee, a concept which it is now time to define.

In the first place, the zero-degree narratee knows the tongue *(langue)* and the language(s) *(langage[s])* of the narrator. In his case, to know a tongue is to know the meanings *(dénotations)*—the signifieds as such and, if applicable, the referents—of all the signs that constitute it; this does not include knowledge of the connotations (the subjective values that have been attached to them). It also involves a perfect mastery of grammar but not of the (infinite) paragrammatical possibilities. It is the ability to note semantic and/or syntactic ambiguities and to be able to resolve these difficulties from the context. It is the capacity to recognize the grammatical incorrectness or oddness of any sentence or syntagm— by reference to the linguistic system being used.[7]

Beyond this knowledge of language, the zero-degree narratee has certain faculties of reasoning that are often only the corollaries of this knowledge. Given a sentence or a series of sentences, he is able to grasp the presuppositions and the consequences.[8] The zero-degree narratee knows narrative grammar, the rules by which any story is elaborated.[9] He knows, for example, that a minimal complete narrative sequence consists in the passage from a given situation to the inverse situation. He knows that the narrative possesses a temporal dimension and that it necessitates relations of causality. Finally, the zero-degree narratee possesses a sure memory, at least in regard to the events of the narrative about which he has been informed and the consequences that can be drawn from them.

Thus, he does not lack positive characteristics. But he also does not want negative traits. He can thus only follow a narrative in a well-defined and concrete way and is obliged to acquaint himself with the events by reading from the first page to the last, from the initial word to the final word. In addition, he is without any personality or social characteristics. He is neither good nor bad, pessimistic nor optimistic, revolutionary nor bourgeois, and his character, his position in society, never colors his perception of the events described to him. Moreover, he knows absolutely nothing about the events or characters mentioned and he is not acquainted with the conventions prevailing in that world or in any other world. Just as he doesn't understand the connotations of a certain turn of phrase, he doesn't realize what can be evoked by this or that situation, this or that novelistic action. The consequences of this are very important. Without the assistance of the narrator, without his explanations and the information supplied by him, the narratee is able neither to interpret the value of an action nor to grasp its repercussions. He is incapable of determining the morality or immorality of a character, the realism or extravagance of a description, the merits of a rejoinder, the satirical intention of a tirade. And how would he be able to do so? By virtue of what experience, what knowledge, or what system of values?

More particularly, a notion as fundamental as verisimilitude only counts very slightly for him. Indeed, verisimilitude is always defined in relation to another text, whether this text be public opinion, the rules of a literary genre, or "reality." The zero-degree narratee, however, is acquainted with no texts and in the absence of commentary, the adventures of Don Quixote would seem as ordinary to him as those of Passemurailles (an individual capable of walking through walls) or of the protagonists of *Une Belle Journée*.[10] The same would hold true for relations of implicit causality. If I learn in *La Légende de Saint Julien l'Hospitalier* that "Julien believes he has killed his father and faints," I establish a causal relationship between these two propositions founded upon a certain common sense logic, my experience of the world, and my knowledge of certain novelistic conventions. We are, moreover, aware that one of the mechanisms of the narrative process "is the confusion of consecutiveness and consequence, what comes *after* being read in the narrative as *caused by*. . . ."[11] But the narratee with no experience and no common sense does not perceive relations of implicit causality and does not fall victim to this confusion. Finally, the zero-degree narratee does not organize the narrative as a function of the major codes of reading studied by Roland Barthes in *S/Z*. He doesn't know how to unscramble the different voices that shape the narration. After all, as Barthes has said: "The code is a convergence of quotations, a structural mirage . . . the resulting units . . . made up of fragments of this something which always has *already* been read, seen, done, lived: the code is the groove of this *already*. Referring back to what has been written, that is, to the Book (of culture, of life, of life as culture), the code makes the text a prospectus of this Book."[12] For the zero-degree narratee, there is no *already*, there is no Book.

The Signals of the Narratee

Every narratee possesses the characteristics that we have enumerated except when an indication to the contrary is supplied in the narration intended for him: he knows, for example, the language employed by the narrator, he is gifted with an excellent memory, he is unfamiliar with everything concerning the characters who are presented to him. It is not rare that a narrative might deny or contradict these characteristics:

a certain passage might underline the language-related difficulties of the narratee, another passage might disclose that he suffers from amnesia, yet another passage might emphasize his knowledge of the problems being discussed. It is on the basis of these deviations from the characteristics of the zero-degree narratee that the portrait of a specific narratee is gradually constituted.

Certain indications supplied by the text concerning a narratee are sometimes found in a section of the narrative that is not addressed to him. One has only to think of *L'Immoraliste*, the two *Justines*, or *Heart of Darkness* to verify that not only the physical appearance, the personality, and civil status of a narratee can be discussed in this fashion, but also his experience and his past. These indications may precede the portion of the narrative intended for the narratee, or may follow, interrupt, or frame it. Most often, they confirm what the rest of the narration has revealed to us. At the beginning of *L'Immoraliste*, for example, we learn that Michel has not seen his narratees for three years and the story he tells them quickly confirms this fact. Nonetheless, sometimes these indications contradict the narrative and emphasize certain differences between the narratee as conceived by the narrator and as revealed by another voice. The few words spoken by Doctor Spielvogel at the end of *Portnoy's Complaint* reveal that he is not what the narrative has led us to believe.[13]

Nevertheless, the portrait of a narratee emerges above all from the narrative addressed to him. If we consider that any narration is composed of a series of signals directed to the narratee, two major categories of signals can be distinguished. On the one hand there are those signals that contain no reference to the narratee or, more precisely, no reference differentiating him from the zero-degree narratee. On the other hand, there are those signals that, on the contrary, define him as a specific narratee and make him deviate from the established norms. In *Un Coeur simple* a sentence such as "She threw herself on the ground" would fall into the first category; this sentence reveals nothing in particular about the narratee while still permitting him to appreciate the sorrow of Félicité. On the contrary, a sentence such as "His entire person produced in her that confusion into which we are all thrown by the spectacle of extraordinary men" not only records the reactions of the heroine in the presence of M. Bourais, but also informs us that the narratee has experienced the same feelings in the presence of extraordinary individuals. By interpreting all signals of the narration as a function of the narratee, we can obtain a partial reading of the text, but a well-defined and reproducible reading. By regrouping and studying the signals of the second category, we can reconstruct the portrait of the narratee, a portrait more or less distinct, original, and complete depending upon the text considered.

The signals belonging to the second category are not always easy to recognize or to interpret. In fact, if many of them are quite explicit, others are much less so. The indications supplied on the narratee at the beginning of *Le Père Goriot* are very clear and present no problem: "That's what you will do, you who hold this book with a white hand, you who settle back in a well-padded armchair...." But the first two sentences of *The Sun Also Rises* present more difficulty. Jake does not explicitly state that, according to his narratee, to say that a man has been a boxing champion is to express admiration for him. It is enough for him to imply this: "Robert Cohn was once middleweight boxing champion of Princeton. Do not think that I am very much impressed by that as a boxing title, but it meant a lot to Cohn." A greater number of indications concerning this or that narratee are even more indirect. Obviously, any indication, whether explicit or indirect, should be interpreted on the basis of the text itself, using as a guide the language employed, its presuppositions, the logical consequences that it entails, and the already established knowledge of the narratee.

The signals capable of portraying the narratee are quite varied and one can easily distinguish several types that are worth discussing. In the first place, we should mention all passages of a narrative in which the narrator refers directly to the narratee. We retain in this category statements in which the narrator designates the narratee by such words as "reader" or "listener" and by such expressions as "my dear" or "my friend." In the event that the narration may have identified a specific characteristic of the narratee, for example, his profession or nationality, passages mentioning this characteristic should also be considered in this first category. Thus, if the narratee is a lawyer, all information concerning lawyers in general is pertinent. Finally, we should retain all passages in which the addressee is designated by second-person pronouns and verb forms.

Besides those passages referring quite explicitly to the narratee, there are passages that, although not written in the second person, imply a narratee and describe him. When Marcel in *A la recherche du temps perdu* writes: "Besides, most often, we didn't stay at home, we went for a walk," the "we" excludes the narratee. On the contrary, when he declares: "Undoubtedly, in these coincidences which are so perfect, when reality withdraws and applies itself to what we have dreamt about for so long a time, it hides it from us entirely," the "we" includes the narratee.[14] Often an impersonal expression or an indefinite pronoun can only refer to the narratee: "But, the work completed, perhaps one will have shed a few tears *intra muros* and *extra.*"

Then again, there are often numerous passages in a narrative that, though they contain apparently no reference—even an ambiguous one—to a narratee, describe him in greater or lesser detail. Accordingly, certain parts of a narrative may be presented in the form of questions or pseudo-questions. Sometimes these questions originate neither with a character nor with the narrator who merely repeats them. These questions must then be attributed to the narratee and we should note what excites his curiosity, the kinds of problems he would like to resolve. In *Le Père Goriot,* for example, it is the narratee who makes inquiries about the career of M. Poiret: "What had he been? But perhaps he had been employed at the Ministry of Justice. . . ." Sometimes, however, the narrator addresses questions to the narratee himself, some of whose knowledge and defenses are thus revealed in the process. Marcel will address a pseudo-question to his narratee asking him to explain the slightly vulgar, and for that reason surprising, behavior of Swann: "But who has not seen unaffected royal princesses . . . spontaneously adopt the language of old bores? . . ."

Other passages are presented in the form of negations. Certain of these passages are no more the extension of a given character's statement than they are the response to a given narrator's question. It is rather the beliefs of the narratee that these passages contradict, his preoccupations that are attacked, and his questions that are silenced. The narrator of *Les Faux-Monnayeurs* vigorously rejects the theory advanced by the narratee to explain Vincent Molinier's nocturnal departures: "No, it was not to his mistress that Vincent Molinier went each evening." Sometimes a partial negation can be revelatory. In *A la recherche du temps perdu,* the narrator, while believing that the narratee's conjectures about the extraordinary suffering of Swann are wellfounded, at the same time finds them insufficient: "This suffering which he felt resembled nothing he had ever thought possible. Not only because in his hours of deepest doubt he had rarely imagined anything so painful, but because even when he imagined this thing, it remained vague, uncertain. . . ."

There are also passages that include a term with demonstrative significance that instead of referring to an anterior or ulterior element of the narrative, refers to another text, to extra-textual experience *(hors-texte)* known to the narrator and his narratee. "He looked at the tomb and there buried his final tear as a young man . . . one of those tears which though they fall to the earth flow upward to the heavens." From these few lines, the narratee of *Le Père Goriot* recognizes the kind of tears buried by Rastignac. He has certainly already heard about them, without a doubt he has seen them, perhaps he has shed some himself.

Comparisons or analogies found in a narration also furnish us with information more or less valuable. Indeed, the second term of a comparison is always assumed to be known better than the first. On this basis, we can assume that the narratee of *The Gold Pot,* for example, has already heard the bursting of thunder ("The voice faded like the faraway muffled rumbling of thunder"), and we can accordingly begin the partial reconstruction of the type of universe with which he is familiar.

But perhaps the most revelatory signals and at times the most difficult to grasp and describe in a satisfactory way are those we shall call—for lack of a more appropriate term—*over-justifications (surjustifications)*. Any narrator more or less explains the world inhabited by his characters, motivates their acts, and justifies their thoughts. If it occurs that these explanations and motivations are situated at the level of meta-language, meta-commentary, or meta-narration, they are over-justifications. When the narrator of *La Chartreuse de Parme* advises the narratee that at La Scala "it's customary for visits to the boxes to last only twenty minutes or so," he is only thinking about supplying the narratee with information necessary for the understanding of the events. On the other hand, when he asks to be excused for a poorly phrased sentence, when he excuses himself for having to interrupt his narrative, when he confesses himself incapable of describing well a certain feeling, these are over-justifications that he employs. Over-justifications always provide us with interesting details about the narratee's personality, even though they often do so in an indirect way; in overcoming the narratee's defenses, in prevailing over his prejudices, in allaying his apprehensions, they reveal them.

The narratee's signals—those that describe him as well as those that only provide him with information—can pose many problems for the reader who would wish to classify them in order to arrive at a portrait of the narratee or a certain reading of the text. It's not simply a question of their being sometimes difficult to notice, to grasp, or to explain, but in certain narratives, one can find contradictory signals. Sometimes they originate with a narrator who wishes to amuse himself at the expense of the narratee or underscore the arbitrariness of the text; often the world presented is a world in which the principles of contradiction known to us don't exist or are not applicable; finally, the contradictions—the entirely obvious ones—often result from the different points of view that the narrator strives to reproduce faithfully. Nonetheless it occurs that not all contradictory data can be entirely explained in this fashion. In these cases, they should be attributed to the author's ineptness—or temperament. In many pornographic novels, in the worst as well as in the best, the narrator, like the heroes of *La Cantatrice chauve*, will first describe a character as having blond hair, large breasts, and a bulging stomach and then on the following page will speak with as much conviction of her black hair, her flat stomach, and her small breasts. Coherence is certainly not an imperative for the pornographic genre in which a wild variation is the rule rather than the exception. It nonetheless remains that in these cases, it is difficult—if not impossible—to interpret the semantic material presented to the narratee.

Sometimes it is the signals describing the narratee that form a strangely disparate collection. Indeed, every signal relating to a narratee need not continue or confirm a preceding signal or announce a signal to follow. There are narratees who change much as narrators do or who have a rich enough personality to embrace various tendencies and feelings. But the contradictory nature of certain narratees does not always result from a complex personality or a subtle evolution. The first pages of *Le Père Goriot* indicate that a Parisian narratee would be able to appreciate "the particularities of this scene full of local observations and color." But these opening pages contradict what they have just asserted in accusing the narratee of insensitivity and in judging him guilty of mistaking reality for fiction. This contradiction will never be resolved. On the contrary, other contradictions will be added and it will become more and more difficult to know whom the narrator addresses. A case of ineptitude? Perhaps Balzac does not worry about technical details and sometimes commits errors which in a Flaubert or a Henry James would be shocking. But this is a revelatory instance of ineptitude: Balzac, who is obsessed with problems of identity—these problems are certainly very important in *Le Père Goriot*—does not manage to decide who will be his narratee.

Despite the questions posed, the difficulties raised, the errors committed, it is evident that the kinds of signals used, their respective numbers, and their distribution determine to a certain extent the different types of narrative.[15] Narratives in which explanations and motivations abound (*Don Quixote* and *Tristram Shandy*, *Les Illusions perdues* and *Le Temps retrouvé*) are very different from those in which explanations and motivations play a limited role (*The Killers*, *The Maltese Falcon*, *La Jalousie*). The former are often by narrators who find the dimension of discourse (*discours*) more important than that of narrative (*récit*) or who are acutely aware of the gratuitousness—and even the falseness—of any narrative or of a certain type of narrative and consequently try to exorcise it. The latter are produced by narrators who feel perfectly at ease in the narrative (*récit*) or who, for different reasons, wish to be transported from their usual surroundings. Moreover, explanations and motivations can present themselves for what they are or, on the other hand, can dissimulate their nature by disguising themselves more or less completely. A narrator of Balzac or Stendhal does not hesitate to declare the necessity of explaining a thought, an act, or a situation. "We are obliged at this point to interrupt for a moment the story of this bold undertaking in order to supply an indispensable detail which will explain in part the duchess' courage in advising Fabrice upon this quite dangerous flight." But Flaubert's narrators—in particular after *Madame Bovary*—often play upon ambiguity and we no longer know exactly if one sentence explains another or if it merely follows or precedes it: "He assembled an army. It became bigger. He became famous. He was sought after." Explanations can also be presented in the form of universal rules or general laws as in Balzac and Zola or can avoid as much as possible all generality as in the novels of Sartre and Simone de Beauvoir. Explanations can contradict or confirm one another, be repeated or used a single time, appear only at strategic moments or occur anywhere in the narrative. Each time a different type of narration is constructed.

Classification of Narratees

Thanks to the signals describing the narratee, we are able to characterize any narration according to the type of narratee to whom it is addressed. It would be useless, because too long, too complicated, and too imprecise, to distinguish different categories of narratees according to their temperament, their civil status, or their beliefs. On the other hand, it would be comparatively easy to classify narratees according to their narrative situation, to their position in reference to the narrator, the characters, and the narration.

Many narrations appear to be addressed to no one in particular: no character is regarded as playing the role of narratee and no narratee is mentioned by the narrator either directly ("Without a doubt, dear reader, you have never been confined in a glass bottle") or indirectly ("We could hardly do otherwise than pluck one of its flowers and present it to the reader"). Just as a detailed study of a novel such as *L'Education sentimentale* or *Ulysses* reveals the presence of a narrator who tries to be invisible and to intervene as little as possible in the course of the events, so too a thorough examination of a narration that appears to have no narratee—the two works mentioned above as well as *Sanctuary*, *L'Etranger*, and *Un Coeur simple*—permits his discovery. The narrator of *Un Coeur simple*, for example, does not refer a single time to a narratee in an explicit manner. In his narrative, nonetheless, there are numerous passages indicating more or less clearly that he is addressing someone. It is thus that the narrator identifies the individuals whose proper names he mentions: "Robelin, the farmer from Geoffosses . . . Liébard, the farmer from Touques . . . M. Bourais, a former lawyer." It cannot be for himself that he identifies Robelin, Liébard, or M. Bourais; it must be for his narratee. Moreover, the narrator often resorts to comparisons in order to describe a character or situate an event, and each comparison defines more precisely the type of universe known to the narratee. Finally, the narrator sometimes refers to extra-textual experiences ("that confusion into which we are all thrown by the spectacle of extraordinary men"),

which provide proof of the narratee's existence and information about
his nature. Thus, even though the narratee may be invisible in a narration, he nonetheless exists and is never entirely forgotten.

In many other narrations, if the narratee is not represented by a character, he is at least mentioned explicitly by the narrator. The latter refers
to him more or less frequently and his references can be quite direct
(*Eugene Onegin, The Gold Pot, Tom Jones*) or quite indirect (*The Scarlet
Letter, The Old Curiosity Shop, Les Faux-Monnayeurs*). Like the narratee of
Un Coeur simple, these narratees are nameless and their role in the narrative is not always very important. Yet because of the passages that designate them in an explicit manner, it is easy to draw their portrait and to
know what their narrator thinks of them. Sometimes, in *Tom Jones,* the
narrator supplies so much information about his narratee, takes him
aside so often, lavishes his advice upon him so frequently, that the latter
becomes as clearly defined as any character.

Often instead of addressing—explicitly or implicitly—a narratee
who is not a character, the narrator recounts his story to someone who is
(*Heart of Darkness, Portnoy's Complaint, Les Infortunes de la vertu*). This
character can be described in a more or less detailed manner. We know
practically nothing about Doctor Spielvogel in *Portnoy's Complaint,* except
that he is not lacking in perspicacity. On the other hand, in *Les Infortunes
de la vertu,* we are informed about all of Juliette's life.

The narratee-character might play no other role in the narrative
than that of narratee (*Heart of Darkness*). But he might also play other
roles. It is not rare, for example, for him to be at the same time a
narrator. In *L'Immoraliste,* one of the three individuals listening to
Michel writes a long letter to his brother. In this letter, he repeats the
story told to him by his friend, entreats his brother to shake Michel from
his unhappiness, and records his own reactions to the narrative as well as
the circumstances that led to his being present at its telling. Sometimes
the narratee of a story can be at the same time its narrator. He doesn't
intend the narration to be for anyone other than himself. In *La Nausée,*
for example, as in most novels written in the form of a diary, Roquentin
counts on being the only reader of his journal.

Then again, the narratee-character can be more or less affected,
more or less influenced by the narrative addressed to him. In *Heart of
Darkness,* the companions of Marlowe are not transformed by the story
that he recounts to them. In *L'Immoraliste,* the three narratees, if they are
not really different from what they were before Michel's account, are
nonetheless "overcome by a strange feeling of malaise." And in *La
Nausée,* as in many other works in which the narrator constitutes his own
narratee, the latter is gradually and profoundly changed by the events
he recounts for himself.

Finally, the narratee-character can represent for the narration someone more or less essential, more or less irreplaceable as a narratee. In *Heart of Darkness,* it's not necessary for Marlowe to have his comrades on the *Nellie* as narratees. He would be able to recount his story to any other group; perhaps he would be able to refrain from telling it at all. On the other hand, in *L'Immoraliste,* Michel wished to address his friends and for that reason gathered them around him. Their presence in Algeria holds out hope: they will certainly not condemn him, they will perhaps understand him, and they will certainly help him get over his current situation. And in *A Thousand and One Nights,* to have the caliph as narratee is the difference between life and death for Scheherazade. If he refuses to listen to her, she will be killed. He is thus the only narratee whom she can have.

Whether or not he assumes the role of character, whether or not he is irreplaceable, whether he plays several roles or just one, the narratee can be a listener (*L'Immoraliste, Les Infortunes de la vertu, A Thousand and One Nights*) or a reader (*Adam Bede, Le Père Goriot, Les Faux-Monnayeurs*). Obviously, a text may not necessarily say whether the narratee is a reader or a listener. In such cases, it could be said that the narratee is a reader when the narration is written *(Hérodias)* and a listener when the narration is oral *(La Chanson de Roland).*

. . . We could probably think of other distinctions or establish other categories, but in any case, we can see how much more precise and more refined the typology of narrative would be if it were based not only upon narrators but also upon narratees. The same type of narrator can address very different types of narratees. Thus, Louis *(Le Noeud de vipères),* Salavin *(Journal de Salavin),* and Roquentin *(La Nausée)* are three characters who all keep a journal and who are very conscious of writing. But Louis changes narratees several times before deciding to write for himself; Slavin does not regard himself as the sole reader of his journal; and Roquentin writes exclusively for himself. Then again, very different narrators can address narratees of the same type. The narrators of *Un Coeur simple* and *La Condition humaine* as well as Meursault in *L'Etranger* all address a narratee who is not a character, who doesn't know them and who is not familiar with the individuals presented in the text nor with the events recounted.

Nonetheless, it is not only for a typology of the narrative genre and for a history of novelistic techniques that the notion of the narratee is important. Indeed, this notion is more interesting, because it permits us to study better the way in which a narration functions. In all narrations, a dialogue is established between the narrator(s), the narratee(s), and the character(s).[16] This dialogue develops—and consequently the narration also—as a function of the distance separating them from each other. In distinguishing the different categories of narratees, we have already used this concept, but without dwelling upon it too much: it is clear that a narratee who has participated in the events recorded is, in one sense, much closer to the characters than a narratee who has never even heard of them. But the notion of distance should be generalized. Whatever the point of view adopted—moral, intellectual, emotional, physical— narrator(s), narratee(s), and character(s) can be more or less close to each other ranging from the most perfect identification to the most complete opposition.

    ... As there are often several narrators, several narratees, and several characters in a text, the complexity of the rapports and the variety of the distances that are established between them can be quite significant. In any case, these rapports and these distances determine to a great extent the way in which certain values are praised and others are rejected in the course of a narration and the way in which certain events are emphasized and others are nearly passed over in silence. They determine as well the tone and the very nature of the narration. In *Les Cloches de Bâle*, for example, the tone changes completely—and cannot but change—once the narrator decides to proclaim his friendship for the narratee and to speak to him more honestly and more directly than he had previously: abandoning romantic extravagance, he becomes quasi-documentary; leaving behind false detachment, he becomes brotherly. On the other hand, many ironic effects in narration depend upon the differences existing between two images of the narratee or between two (groups of) narratees *(Les Infortunes de la vertu, Werther)*, upon the distance existing between narrator and narratee on the one hand and character on the other *(Un Amour de Swann)*, or yet again upon the distance existing between narrator and narratee *(Tom Jones)*. The complexity of a situation results sometimes from the instability of the distances existing between the narrator, the narratee, and the characters. If Michel's guilt—or innocence—is not clearly established, it is partly because several times he shows himself capable of overcoming the distance separating him from his friends, or, if one prefers, because his friends are unsure of how much distance to put between themselves and him. . . .

The Narratee's Functions

    The type of narratee that we find in a given narrative, the relations that tie him to narrators, characters, and other narratees, the distances that separate him from ideal, virtual, or real readers partially determine the nature of this narrative. But the narratee exercises other functions that are more or less numerous and important and are more or less specific to him. It will be worth the effort to enumerate these functions and to study them in some detail.
    The most obvious role of the narratee, a role that he always plays in a

certain sense, is that of relay between the narrator and the reader(s), or rather between the author and the reader(s). Should certain values have to be defended or certain ambiguities clarified, this can easily be done by means of asides addressed to the narratee. Should the importance of a series of events be emphasized, should one reassure or make uneasy, justify certain actions or underscore their arbitrariness, this can always be done by addressing signals to the narratee. In *Tom Jones,* for example, the narrator explains to the narratee that prudence is necessary for the preservation of virtue, an explanation that allows us to judge better his hero, virtuous but imprudent: "Prudence and circumspection are necessary even to the best men. . . . It is not enough that your designs, nay, that your actions, are intrinsically good, you must take care they shall appear so." Likewise, we know that although Legrandin is a snob, he is not lying when he protests against snobbery because Marcel says quite clearly to his narratee: "And indeed, that doesn't mean that Legrandin was not sincere when he inveighed against snobs." Indeed, the mediation doesn't always operate that directly: thus, narrator-narratee relations are sometimes developed in the ironic mode and the reader cannot always interpret literally the statements of the former to the latter. There exist other conceivable relays than direct and explicit asides addressed to the narratee, other possibilities of mediation between authors and readers. Dialogues, metaphors, symbolic situations, allusions to a particular system of thought or to a certain work of art are some of the ways of manipulating the reader, guiding his judgments, and controlling his reactions. Moreover, those are the methods preferred by many modern novelists, if not the majority of them; perhaps because they accord or seem to accord more freedom to the reader, perhaps because they oblige him to participate more actively in the development of the narrative, or perhaps simply because they satisfy a certain concern for realism. The role of the narratee as mediator is rather reduced in these cases. Everything must still pass via the narratee since everything—metaphors, allusions, dialogues—is still addressed to him; but nothing is modified, nothing is clarified for the reader by this passage. Whatever the advantages may be of this type of mediator it should nonetheless be recognized that from a certain point of view, direct and explicit statements by the narrator to the narratee are the most economical and the most effective sort of mediation. A few sentences suffice to establish the true significance of an unexpected act or the true nature of a character; a few words suffice to facilitate the interpretation of a complex situation. Although we can question indefinitely Stephen's esthetic maturity in *Portrait of the Artist as a Young Man* or the significance of a particular act in *A Farewell to Arms,* we always know exactly—or almost always—according to the text, what to think of Fabrice and la Sanseverina or of the intrigues of Mlle. Michonneau.[17]

Besides the function of mediation, the narratee exercises in any narration a function of characterization. . . . In the case of narrator-characters, the function of characterization is important although it can be reduced to a minimum even here: because he is at a distance from everything and from himself, because his strangeness and solitude depend upon this distance, Meursault would not know how to engage in a true dialogue with his narratee and, thus, cannot be described by this dialogue. Nonetheless, the relations that a narrator-character establishes with his narratee reveal as much—if not more—about his character than any other element in the narrative. In *La Religeuse,* Sister Suzanne, because of her conception of the narratee and her asides addressed to him, emerges as much less naïve and much more calculating and coquettish than she would like to appear.

. . . Moreover, the relations between the narrator and the narratee in a text may underscore one theme, illustrate another, or contradict yet another. Often the theme refers directly to the narrative situation and it is the narration as theme that these relations reveal. In *A Thousand and One Nights,* for instance, the theme of narration as life is emphasized by the attitude of Scheherazade toward the caliph and vice-versa: the heroine will die if her narratee decides not to listen to her any more, just as other characters in the narrative die because he will not listen to them: ultimately, any narrative is impossible without a narratee. But often, themes that do not concern the narrative situation—or perhaps concern it only indirectly—reveal the positions of the narrator and the narratee in relation to each other. In *Le Père Goriot,* the narrator maintains relations of power with his narratee. From the very beginning, the narrator tries to anticipate his narratee's objections, to dominate him, and to convince him. All means are used: the narrator coaxes, entreats, threatens, derides, and in the final analysis we suspect that he succeeds in getting the better of his narratee. In the last part of the novel, when Vautrin has been put in prison and Goriot is advancing more and more quickly toward death, the narrator rarely addresses his narratee. This is because the narrator has won the battle. He is now sure of his effects, of his domination, and he need no longer do anything but recount the story. This sort of war, this desire for power, can be found at the level of the characters. On the level of the events as well as on the level of narration, the same struggle takes place.

If the narratee contributes to the thematic of a narrative, he is also always part of the narrative framework, often of a particularly concrete framework in which the narrator(s) and narratee(s) are all characters *(Heart of Darkness, L'Immoraliste, The Decameron).* The effect is to make the narrative seem more natural. The narratee like the narrator plays an undeniable *verisimilating (vraisemblabilisant)* role. Sometimes this concrete framework provides the model by which a work or narration develops.

In *The Decameron* or in *L'Heptameron,* it is expected that each of the narratees will in turn become a narrator. More than a mere sign of realism or an index of verisimilitude, the narratee represents in these circumstances an indispensable element for the development of the narrative.

. . . Finally it sometimes happens that we must study the narratee in order to discover a narrative's fundamental thrust. In *La Chute,* for example, it is only by studying the reactions of Clamence's narratee that we can know whether the protagonist's arguments are so powerful that they cannot be resisted, or whether, on the contrary, they constitute a skillful but unconvincing appeal. To be sure, the narratee doesn't say a single word throughout the entire novel and we don't even know if Clamence addresses himself or someone else: we only understand, from the narrator's remarks, that his narratee, like himself, is a bourgeois, in his forties, a Parisian, familiar with Dante and the Bible, a lawyer. . . . Nevertheless, this ambiguity emphasizing the essential duplicity of the protagonist's world does not represent a problem for the reader who would wish to discover the way in which Clamence is judged in the novel: whatever the identity of the narratee may be, the only thing that counts is the extent of his agreement with the theses of the hero. The latter's discourse shows evidence of a more and more intense resistance on the part of his interlocutor. Clamence's tone becomes more insistent and his sentences more embarrassed as his narrative progresses and his narratee escapes him. Several times in the last part of the novel he even appears seriously shaken. If at the end of *La Chute* Clamence is not defeated, he certainly has not been triumphant. If his values and his vision of the world and men are not entirely false, neither are they incontestably true. There are perhaps other professions than that of judge-penitent and there are perhaps other acceptable ways to live than Clamence's.

The narratee can, thus, exercise an entire series of functions in a narrative: he constitutes a relay between the narrator and the reader, he helps establish the narrative framework, he serves to characterize the narrator, he emphasizes certain themes, he contributes to the development of the plot, he becomes the spokesman for the moral of the work. Obviously, depending upon whether the narrator is skillful or inept, depending upon whether or not problems of narrative technique interest him, and depending upon whether or not his narrative requires it, the narratee will be more or less important, will play a greater or lesser number of roles, will be used in a way more or less subtle and original. Just as we study the narrator to evaluate the economy, the intentions, and the success of a narrative, so too we should examine the narratee in order to understand further and/or differently its mechanisms and significance.

The narratee is one of the fundamental elements of all narration. The thorough examination of what he represents, the study of a narrative work as constituted by a series of signals addressed to him, can lead to a more sharply delineated reading and a deeper characterization of the work. This study can lead also to a more precise typology of the narrative genre and a greater understanding of its evolution. It can provide a better appreciation of the way a narrative functions and a more accurate assessment of its success from a technical point of view. In the final analysis, the study of the narratee can lead us to a better understanding not only of the narrative genre but of all acts of communication.

Translated by Francis Mariner

Notes

1. See, for example, Henry James, *The Art of Fiction and Other Essays,* ed. Morris Roberts (New York: Oxford University Press, 1948); Norman Friedman, "Point of View in Fiction: The Development of a Critical Concept," *PMLA* 70 (December 1955): 1160-84 Wayne C. Booth, *The Rhetoric of Fiction* (Chicago: University of Chicago Press, 1961) Tzvetan Todorov, "Poétique" in Oswald Ducrot et al., *Qu'est-ce que le structuralisme?* (Paris Seuil, 1968), pp. 97-166; and Gérard Genette, *Figures III* (Paris: Seuil, 1972).

2. See, among others, Walker Gibson, "Authors, Speakers, Readers, and Moc Readers," *College English* 9 (February 1950): 265-69 (chap. 1 in this volume); Rolan Barthes, "Introduction à l'analyse structurale des récits," *Communications* 8 (1966): 18-1⁹ Tzvetan Todorov, "Les Catégories du récit littéraire," *Communications* 8 (1966): 146-4² Gerald Prince, "Notes Towards a Categorization of Fictional 'Narratees,'" *Genre* 4 (Marc 1971): 100-105; and Genette, *Figures III*, pp. 265-67.

3. In a certain sense, every narrator is his own narratee. But most narrators hav other narratees as well.

4. See Tzvetan Todorov, "Les Hommes-récits," *Poétique de la prose* (Paris: Seui 1971), pp. 78-91.

5. See Tzvetan Todorov, "Le Récit primitif," in ibid., pp. 66-77.

6. For convenience's sake, we speak (and will speak often) of readers. It is obviou: that a narratee should not be mistaken for a listener—real, virtual, or ideal.

7. This description of the linguistic capabilities of the zero-degree narratee nonetheless raises many problems. Thus, it is not always easy to determine the meaning(s) *(dé-notation[s])* of a given term and it becomes necessary to fix in time the language *(langue)* known to the narratee, a task that is sometimes difficult when working from the text itself. In addition, the narrator can manipulate a language in a personal way. Confronted by certain idiosyncrasies that are not easy to situate in relation to the text, do we say that the narratee experiences them as exaggerations, as errors, or on the contrary do they seem perfectly normal to him? Because of these difficulties and many others as well, the description of the narratee and his language cannot always be exact. It is, nevertheless, to a large extent reproducible.

8. We use these terms as they are used in modern logic.

9. See in this regard, Gerald Prince, *A Grammar of Stories: An Introduction* (The

Hague: Mouton, 1973). A formal description of the rules followed by all narratives can be found in this work.

10. On verisimilitude, see the excellent issue 11 of *Communications* (1968).

11. Barthes, "Introduction à l'analyse structurale des récits," p. 10. It should be noted that while this confusion has been very much exploited, it is not at all necessary for the development of a narrative.

12. Roland Barthes, *S/Z* (Paris: Seuil, 1970), pp. 27–28.

13. We should undoubtedly distinguish the "virtual" narratee from the "real" narratee in a more systematic manner. But this distinction would perhaps not be very helpful.

14. Note that even an "I" can designate a "you."

15. See, in this regard, Gérard Genette, "Vraisemblance et motivation," in his *Figures II* (Paris: Seuil, 1969).

16. We follow here in modifying the perspective, Booth, *The Rhetoric of Fiction,* pp. 155 ff.

17. See, in this regard, the book by Wayne C. Booth already mentioned.

3

DESCRIBING POETIC STRUCTURES: TWO APPROACHES TO BAUDELAIRE'S "LES CHATS"

Michael Riffaterre

Poetry is language, but it produces effects that language in everyday speech does not consistently produce; a reasonable assumption is that the linguistic analysis of a poem should turn up specific features, and that there is a causal relationship between the presence of these features in the text and our empirical feeling that we have before us a poem. The act of communication—the sending of a message from speaker to addressee—is conditioned by the need it fills: the verbal structure of the message depends upon which factor of communication is focused on. In everyday language, used for practical purposes, the focus is usually upon the situational context, the mental or physical reality referred to; sometimes the focus is upon the code used in transmitting the message, that is, upon language itself, if there seems to be some block in the addressee's understanding, and so forth. In the case of verbal art, the focus is upon the message as an end in itself, not just as a means, upon its form as a permanent, unchangeable monument, forever independent of external conditions. The naked eye attributes this enduring, attention-getting quality to a higher unity and more intricate texture: the poem follows more rules (e.g. meter, lexical restrictions, etc.) and displays more conspicuous interrelationships between its constitutive elements than do casual utterances.

For these features Roman Jakobson has proposed a general formula. Selection and combination are the two basic ordering principles of speech. Selection is based upon equivalence (metaphoric relationship), either similarity or dissimilarity; the speaker designates his topic (subject) by choosing one among various available synonyms and then says what he has to say about it (predicate) by another selection from another set of interchangeable words (paradigm). The combining of these words, that is, their contiguity, produces a sentence. Jakobson defines a poetic structure as one characterized by the projection of the principle of equivalence from the axis of selection to the axis of combination.[1] For instance, words are combined into rhythmic, alliterative, and rhymic sequences because of their equivalence in sound, and this inevitably establishes semantic equations between these words; their respective meanings are consequently perceived as related by similarity (hence a metaphor or simile) or dissimilarity (hence an antithesis).

Which is to say that the recurrence of equivalent forms, *parallelism*, is the basic relationship underlying poetry. Of course, since language is a system made up of several levels superimposed one on top of the other (phonetic, phonological, syntactical, semantic, etc.), parallelism manifests itself on any level: so then, a poem is a verbal sequence wherein the same relations between constituents are repeated at various levels and the same story is told in several ways at the same time and at several times in the same way. This can be usefully restated in structural terms once we have called to mind basic definitions: a structure is a system made up of several elements, none of which can undergo a change without effecting changes in all the other elements; thus the system is what mathematicians call an invariant; transformations within it produce a group of models of the same type (that is, mechanically interconvertible shapes), or variants. The invariant, of course, is an abstraction arrived at by defining what remains intact in the face of these conversions; therefore we are able to observe a structure only in the shape of one or another variant. We are now ready to agree with Claude Lévi-Strauss that a poem is a structure containing within itself its variants ordered on the vertical axis of the different linguistic levels. It is thus possible to describe the poem in isolation, so that we need not explain its singularity by dragging in hard-to-define concepts like non-grammaticalness or departure from the norm. Comparison of variants, prerequisite to analysis, is accomplished by simply scanning the text at its various linguistic levels one after the other.

Such is the approach tried out by Jakobson and Lévi-Strauss on "Les Chats," a sonnet of Baudelaire's, and with extraordinary thoroughness.[2] They modestly declare that they are interested only in describing what the poem is made of. Nevertheless they do draw conclusions as to the meaning of the poem and try to relate it to the esthetics and even the psyche of the poet, purlieu of literary scholars. This raises a question: how are we to pass from description to judgment—that is, from a study of the text to a study of its effect upon the reader? The sonnet is a good occasion for such discussion, for critics generally downgrade the poem (*Fleurs du Mal*, LXVI), a product of Baudelaire's early period (1847), and find it less Baudelairean than most of the others. But the poet did not feel that way about it: he thought it good enough to publish in the feuilleton of a friend, in hopes of drumming up some interest; then he selected it for a preview of his abortive *Limbes* (1851); finally, he thought it worth keeping in the editions of the *Fleurs* that he was able to prepare himself. If structuralism can help determine who is right here, we shall have tested its practical workability in matters of literary criticism.

Far more important, however, is the question as to whether unmodified structural linguistics is relevant at all to the analysis of poetry. The author's method is based on the assumption that any structural system they are able to define in the poem is necessarily a poetic structure. Can we not suppose, on the contrary, that the poem may contain certain structures that play no part in its function and effect as a literary work of art, and that there may be no way for structural linguistics to distinguish between these unmarked structures and those that are literarily active? Conversely, there may well be strictly poetic structures that cannot be recognized as such by an analysis not geared to the specificity of poetic language.

"Les Chats"
[1]Les amoureux fervents et les savants austères
[2]Aiment également, dans leur mûre saison,
[3]Les chats puissants et doux, orgueil de la maison,
[4]Qui comme eux sont frileux et comme eux sédentaires.

[5]Amis de la science et de la volupté,
[6]Ils cherchent le silence et l'horreur des ténèbres;
[7]L'Erèbe les eût pris pour ses coursiers funèbres,
[8]S'ils pouvaient au servage incliner leur fierté.

[9]Ils prennent en songeant les nobles attitudes
[10]Des grands sphinx allongés au fond des solitudes,
[11]Qui semblent s'endormir dans un rêve sans fin;

[12]Leurs reins féconds sont pleins d'étincelles magiques,
[13]Et des parcelles d'or, ainsi qu'un sable fin,
[14]Etoilent vaguement leurs prunelles mystiques.[3]

Jakobson and Lévi-Strauss submit the text to scannings of its meter, sound texture, grammar, and meaning; they are thus able to collect several sets of the equivalent signs that actualize the sonnet's structure. Let me describe briefly the systems thus obtained, with a sampling of the variants comparatively studied in order to establish these systems. My aim here is only to show how the authors' analysis is carried through. The most significant of their arguments omitted here will be taken up in my discussion of the validity of their approach.

Jakobson and Lévi-Strauss recognize the following complementary or intersecting structures:

1. a *tripartite division* into: *quatrain I*, which represents the cats as passive creatures, observed by outsiders, lovers, and scholars; *quatrain II*, where the cats are active but, again, seen as such from the outside, by the powers of darkness; the latter, also seen from outside, are active: they have designs on the cats and are frustrated by the independence of the little beasts; *sestet*, which gives us an inside view of the cat life-style: their attitude may be passive, but they assume that attitude actively. Thus is the active-passive opposition reconciled, or perhaps nullified, and the circle of the sonnet closes.

This tripartite structure is defined by two equivalent models: one grammatical, formed by three complex "sentences" delimited by periods, and further defined by an arithmetic progression in the number of their independent clauses and personal verbal forms (as distinct from forms in the infinitive or participle); one metric (the rhyme systems unify the tercets into a sestet while separating it from the quatrains). These two models are further bound together by the relationship between rhyme and categories: every feminine rhyme coincides with a plural ending, every masculine one with a singular.

2. a *bipartite division* that opposes the octet and the sestet. In the *octet* the cats are seen from an outside observer's point of view and are imprisoned within time and space ([2]*saison* and [3]*maison*, which rhyme and meaning make equivalent). In the *sestet* both viewpoint and space-time limits drop away: the desert bursts the house wide open; the eternity of [11]*dans un rêve sans fin* annuls [2]*dans leur mûre saison:* in this case the equivalence is an antinomy and is formally established by the parallelism of the *dans* constructions, the only two in the poem. This overall opposition combines with two secondary ones: *quatrain I tercet I* ([3]*maison:* [10]*solitudes ::* [2]*saison:* [11]*sans fin*) and *quatrain II tercet II* (cats in darkness vs. cats radiating light).

To take only one of these secondary oppositions: in *quatrain II tercet II*, on the one hand, [12]*Leurs reins féconds sont pleins* is synonymous with [5]*Amis . . . de la volupté* (p. 16), and one of the subjects in the quatrain and three subjects in the tercet all alike designate inanimate things; on the other hand, the antinomy of darkness and light is backed up by corresponding sets of equatable items: [7]*Erèbe* and [6]*ténèbres* echo each other in meaning and in sound, as do [12]*étinCELLES*, [13]*parCELLES d'or* and [14]*prunELLES*.

3. a *chiasma-like division* linking quatrain I and tercet II, where the cats function as objects ([3]*chats*, [12,14]*Leurs*) and, on the other hand, quatrain II and tercet I, where they are subjects. The *quatrain I-tercet II* coupling, to which I shall limit this summary, contains the following formal equivalences: both stanzas have more adjectives than the internal

strophes; the first and last verbs are both modified by rhyming adverbs
(*²Aiment également;* *¹⁴Etoilent vaguement*); these are the only two stanzas
made up of sentences with two subjects for one verb and one object, each
subject and object being modified by one adjective, etc. A semantic relationship underlies these formal features: in *quatrain I* a metonymic relationship between the animals and their worshippers (i.e. cats and people
live in the same house) generates a metaphoric similarity (*⁴comme eux*
twice repeated); the same thing in *tercet II,* where a synecdochic (*pars pro
toto*) description of the cats, using different parts of their body, permits
their metaphoric identification with the cosmos, or so say the two
analysts.

These three systems fit one inside the other and together make of
the sonnet a "closed" structure, but they coexist with a *fourth system* that
makes the poem an open-ended structure which develops dynamically
from the first line to the last: two equal *sestets* (1. 1–6 and 9–14), separated by a *distich.* Of the four structures, this last is the one most at
variance with the stanza and rhyme architecture that defines the sonnet
as a genre: the aberrant distich presents features that do not occur
anywhere else, against a background of features that occur only elsewhere in the poem, some of them related to those of the distich by
antonymy (every single subject-verb group is plural except for *⁷L'Erèbe
les eût pris;* against the rule followed throughout the rest of the poem,
⁷funèbres-⁸fierté alliterate, etc.). Now Jakobson and Lévi-Strauss regard
this distich as a transition: the pseudo-sestet describes objectively a factual situation of the real world; two opposite human categories, sensual
and intellectual, are reconciled through their identification with the
animal endowed with the diametric traits of both types of men; these
traits in turn explain the cats' love for silence and darkness—a predilec-
tion that exposes them to temptation. Erebus threatens to confine them
to their animal nature by taming them; we are relieved to see him fail.
This episode, translated in terms of parallelism, should be seen not just
as another antonymy but as "l'unique équivalence rejetée" (p. 14).

Nevertheless, this rejection has its positive effect: an equivalence
with the sphinx can substitute for it. The sphinx, with a human head on
an animal body, transposes into myth the identification between real cats
and people. Also, the monsters' motionless daydreaming and the cats'
sedentariness (likewise characteristic of the human types they symbolize)
are synonymous; and the way the cats ape the sphinxes is a new equivalence stated simultaneously at the grammatical level, in the narrative (it is
⁹en songeant that they look like the *¹⁰sphinx allongés*), at the morphological
level (*allongés* and *songeant* are the only participles in the text) and at the
sound level the two verbs are related by paronomasia. The second *sestet*
is devoted to the deepening mystery of this *miracle des chats* (p. 15).
Tercet I still sustains the ambiguity: it is difficult to decide whether cats

and sphinxes are linked merely to magnify the image of the cats stylistically, or whether we have here the description of actual similarity, the
racial bond between the household sphinx and the desert cat. In tercet
II, however, substitution of parts of his body for the whole cat dissolves
the beast into particles of matter, and the final identification associates
these particles with desert sands and transmutes them into stars: the
fusion of cats and cosmos has been accomplished. This apotheosis to
infinity does not exclude a circular structure from the text. The authors
believe there is a parallelism between tercet II and line 1, the myth being
seen as a variant on a universal scale of the "constricting" union, inward-
turning, when the lover folds his love into his arms, and of the expansive
union, outward-turning, when the scholar takes the universe in his embrace; similarly, cats either interiorize the universe, or else they spread
themselves out beyond the bounds of time and space (p. 20).

From all the foregoing, we can at least draw the conclusion that these
mutually combinatory and complementary structures interplay in a way
unique. The poem is like a microcosm, with its own system of references
and analogies. We have an absolutely convincing demonstration of the
extraordinary concatenation of correspondences that holds together the
parts of speech.

The Irrelevance of Grammar

But there is no telling which of these systems of correspondences contribute to the poetry of the text. And there is much to be said about the
systems that do not.

The divisions proposed explain a good deal of the tension between
symmetrical and asymmetrical rhymes and the grammar arrangements
upon which the composition of the sonnet rests. The first division is
beyond criticism; the second is well substantiated, since it hinges on an
articulation (the octet-sestet boundary) which corresponds to a change so
sharp that it prompted postulation of the fourth division. Divisions three
and four, especially the last, make use of constituents that cannot possibly be perceived by the reader; these constituents must therefore remain
alien to the poetic structure, which is supposed to emphasize the form of
the message, to make it more "visible," more compelling.

Equivalences established on the basis of purely syntactic similarities
would seem particularly dubious—for instance, the parallelism pointed
to between the relative clauses of lines 4 and 11: this last allegedly draws
the "contour of an imaginary quatrain, a make-believe homologue of the
first quatrain" (p. 13). At most, this might be conceivable if the clauses
appeared against an empty or uniform context; not in an actual sonnet,
whose continual variation of verbal shapes makes a marked contrast

necessary in order to impose perception. Even there, the parallelism
from one line to another can be superseded by a stronger relation within
one of the two lines involved. This happens in the case of the equation
urged by Jakobson and Lévi-Strauss between [4]*Qui comme eux sont frileux*
and [12]*Leurs reins féconds sont pleins,* on account of their syntactic parallelism and their internal rhymes. In context the difference outweighs the
similarities: an internal rhyme like [5]*Science-*[6]*silence* is obvious, and so is
eux-frileux, because identical stresses "confirm" them; but a natural reading of line 12 will have to take into account the tight unity of *Leurs reins
féconds,* which demands a pause after *féconds,* the normal caesura disap-
pearing almost because *pleins* cannot be severed from *d'étincelles; pleins* is
enclitic, which practically cancels out the rhyme. Suppose we read without regard for meaning or grammar: the rhyme resuscitates, but any
responsion to the rhyme in line 4 still appears purely theoretical, for
comme eux sont frileux is homologous only to *comme eux sédentaires* and is
not free to connect elsewhere. For the significant rhyme system, the one
that organizes the rhythm and "illustrates" the meaning, is the
homophony under equal stress of *comme eux* repeated twice. The *frileux*
rhyme is a secondary modulation: it "makes believe" that the line ends at
the caesura,[4] thus getting the rhythm off to a fresh start and making the
"unexpected" repetition all the more striking; the fact that it rhymes
with *comme eux* lays emphasis upon *sédentaires* by contrast—a second
comme eux led the reader's subconscious sense of balance to expect a
second rhyme, and the expectation is beautifully frustrated. We did find
a parallelism anyway, but the remoter one has lost the contest, and this
suffices to make homologue-collecting an unreliable tool. Extensive
similarities at one level are no proof of correspondence: a parallelism is
seen between quatrain I and tercet II, based upon the equivalence of two
subjects ([1]*Les amoureux fervents, les savants austères/*[13]*des parcelles d'or, un
sable fin),* one verb with rhyming adverb ([2]*Aiment également/*[14]*Etoilent vaguement),* one adjective-noun object ([3]*Les chats puissants et doux/*[14]*leurs
prunelles mystiques)* in identical sequence (p. 9). But, in any verse structure, I
do not see how two variants can be equivalent if the positions of their components are not homologous: meter lends significance to the space occupied by the sentence. The relation of object to verb in line 14 is not the
same as in quatrain I, since the quatrain keeps them apart with par-
entheses and enjambement, whereas the tercet unites them. Hence inevitably a difference in emphasis and a shift in respective positions
within the line. Furthermore, the equation of the subjects is all askew:
the components are alike, and we could link *amoureux fervents* vertically
with *parcelles d'or* or diagonally with *sable fin;* but the systems they enter
are not comparable, for *sable fin* does not stand in the same relation to
parcelles d'or as *savants* does to *amoureux.* These last two are opposite
equals, and their contiguity expresses their polarity; but the contiguity

of *parcelles* and *sable* simply repeats twice the same meaning, *ainsi que* indicating a metaphorical relation. *Ainsi que* and *et* may have the same virtual function in language and be classifed alike: but not here, where they are neither synonymous nor antonymous. The parallelism suggested by grammar remains virtual because it has no homologue in the meter or in the semantic system.

No segmentation can be pertinent that yields, indifferently, units that *are* part of the poetic structure, and neutral ones that are not. The weak point of the method is indeed the categories used. There is a revealing instance where Jakobson and Lévi-Strauss take literally the technical meaning of *feminine* as used in metrics and grammar and endow the formal feminine categories with esthetic and even ethical values. They are trying to prove a sexual ambiguity in the poem, the motif of the androgyne, and they find some evidence in the "paradoxical choice of feminine substantives as masculine rhymes" (p. 21). True, the gender of French nouns does orient the associations they trigger: this kind of effect is conceivable with words that signify concrete objects or even abstract concepts, as long as they can be humanized or personified—for example, [5]*volupté,* which is more female than *plaisir* would be. It hardly holds, however, in the case of purely technical terminology, where *masculine* means merely "ending on a fully pronounced syllable" and *feminine* merely "ending on an unstressed syllable" (especially where one need not even be aware of these conventions in order to perceive an alternance). By stretching this to the limit, we may discover cases where the feminine rhyme does evoke some such associations because it coincides with the specific feminine gender ending; it is altogether unlikely with masculine rhymes, which do not offer any similar concurrence. Only technicians would think of it (they have thought of it); metalinguistic rationalization of this sort betrays how easily the wariest of analysts slips into a belief in the intrinsic explanatory worth of purely descriptive terms.

The two critics obviously assume that the definition of categories used to collect data is also valid to explain their function in the poetic structure—that linguistic oppositions for example, automatically entail stylistic differences. The role of liquid phonemes in the sonnet's sound texture, for example, is declared to be significant: quatrain II is certainly characterized by noticeable variations, since this is a stanza where the phonetic dominance shifts from nasal vowels (only 3) to liquid consonants (24); extreme variations cannot fail of their effect. There is, however, a linguistic opposition between /l/ and /r/, particularly marked in French, and this is frequently exploited in poetry in a manner consistent with the phonetic nature of the opposing features. A slight regression of /r/ before /l/ in the tercets is interpreted as "eloquently accompanying the passage from the empirical feline to his mythic transfigurations" (p. 12).

But no one is likely to believe that there is any significance in a difference as imperceptible as that between fourteen /l/ and eleven /r/, especially when tercet II, with /l/ enjoying a majority of two, begins with an /r/ cluster (*Leurs reins*) which will surely catch the eye and ear sooner than an inequality attenuated by distribution along the lines. If we look only for sharp changes, then the drop in the number of liquids from quatrain II to tercet I affects both contenders equally, /l/ ending on top by one point; the one smashing victory of /l/ over /r/—three to nothing—occurs in line 5 *before* the transfiguration; in quatrain II, which is also the only place where brutal variations can be found, the liquids go hand in hand for the whole stanza, rejoicing at the peak of their power. Since liquids as a group do appear significant, the authors assume that every essential linguistic feature of the group must also be significant. The fact is, however, that it does not work out that way: the liquids are significant only as a group; their oppositions, *within* the group, though they are actualized and play their part in the linguistic structure, are not actualized in the style.

Conversely, the analytical categories applied can pull together under one label phenomena which are in fact totally different from one another in the poetic structure. A case in point is the plural. Jakobson and Lévi-Strauss rightly note its high frequency and its concurrence with important elements. Because a single grammatical category is applicable to every line of the poem, they see it as a key to the understanding of the sonnet; they quote a pronouncement of the poet that seems to give symbolic meaning to the plural: *Multitude, solitude: termes égaux et convertibles par le poète actif et fécond.* Better still, the authors see this mutual "convertibility" symbolized in [10]*solitudes,* where "solitude" as the word itself and "multitude" as the morpheme *-s* enjoy togetherness. This argument recalls their confusion of femaleness and feminine gender; they seem to assume that there is always a basic relationship between actual plurality (and what it symbolizes in Baudelaire's eyes) and plural morphemes. Needless to say, there are many exceptions to that general rule—and what is more, one of them occurs right here: [6]*ténèbres* is a conventional, meaningless plural; let us skip it, and also its rhyme companion [7]*funèbres.* We should probably discount all descriptive plurals, since they are dictated by nature and not the poet's choice: *mystiques* would drop out, cats having two *prunelles,* and also *reins.* We can keep *chats* and their human counterparts: collective singulars being available for groups, the plural may well have meaning. But *solitudes,* the pretext for this philosophical foray, will have to go: it is no paradox at all, just a hyperbole, a cliché where *solitudes* means "desert"—an emphatic plural stemming from the Latin. Baudelaire's quotation may apply elsewhere, certainly not here, and no interpretation of the sonnet can be drawn from it. The authors' mistake is understandable. In their search for a plural structure, they needed a unifying factor. The text yielded no sign that the data could be related, yet their common label demanded that they be so related. Faced with this dilemma, the authors must have gladly seized upon the coincidence between *solitudes* and Baudelaire's aphorism: the poet's mental obsession provided just the invariant required. Had all plural forms not been brought under the one label, there would have been no compulsion to find, at all costs, an equivalence value for every plural form.

But among these data lumped together because of their morphological similarity, there is a group of plurals set apart from the others because of their distribution: that is the plural feminine rhymes. These do form a stylistic structure, because their -*s* endings make the rhyme "richer" for the eye by increasing the number of its repeated components. In [1,4]*austères-sédentaires,* for instance, the *s* reinforces the visual similarity and offsets the spelling vagaries that spoil the transcription of /ɛ/. The way in which the -*s* is related to and functions in the rhyme system has nothing to do with its simultaneous function in the singular-plural opposition, where it carries a meaning: in the rhyme it works only as an eye-catcher. The interrelations of the -*s* rhymes within the conventional rhyme system are what gives them significance. Poetic convention demands, first, that the rhymes of the sonnet should form an invariable pattern alternating feminine and masculine rhymes; second, that this invariant alternation be combined with sound variants within each alternating series. The visual and aural implementation of the variant is constantly reinforced and constantly compels attention, thus strongly individualizing each stanza; this depends entirely upon the poet's creative fancy. The implementation of the invariant, on the contrary, is normally limited to the compulsory masculine-feminine alternation. By adding -*s* to the -*e*, Baudelaire personalizes, so to speak, what was an automatism, reemphasizes the opposition for the eye. A second constant element in the system of the sonnet as a whole gives more weight to the unifying factor in the rhymes, which more effectively countervails the centrifugal tendencies of each stanza to form an independent unit. Every line affected by this addition is thereby made to look longer, and the fact that such a line ends the sonnet contributes to its unity by emphasizing the final item and therefore the reader's consciousness of a terminal accord; since the word thus underlined happens to be *mystiques,* the combination of meaning and visual emphasis, accompanying it like an upbeat, make the end of the poem a point of departure for reverie and wonder. Jakobson and Lévi-Strauss point out that the feminine rhyme is orally actualized, despite the total disappearance of the unstressed end syllable in modern pronunciation, by the presence of a postvocalic sounded consonant in the rhyming syllable, and they remark, indeed, that this coincides with plural morphemes (pp. 7, 11); but they

see the plural as a parallel to the postvocalic consonant, that is, reinforcing each rhyme pair, separately, since that consonant varies and therefore structures only the stanza in which it occurs (/r, br, d, k/). In fact, the
invariable -s creates a frame that tightens the whole sonnet. This structure would not be overlooked if the term chosen did not also cover forms
that are grammatically identical but stylistically foreign to these -s
rhymes; [1]amoureux, [3]doux, [10]sphinx would not further obscure the operation of the -s ending; grammatical equivalence would not be equated
with stylistic equivalence.

    What I have just said should not be construed as a rejection of the
principle of equivalence: similarity in dissimilarity, dissimilarity in similarity, are apparent at all levels. But it seems evident that its pertinence
cannot be shown by using grammatical terminology, or any precon-
ceived, aprioristic frame. R. Jakobson chose grammar units to make this
exegesis and many others because grammar is the natural geometry of
language which superimposes abstract, relational systems upon the concrete, lexical material: hence grammar furnishes the analyst with
ready-made structural units. All parts of speech, in fact, may function
in parallelism and contrasts; the importance of pronouns, long neglected
by style analysts—pronouns, are, precisely, typical relational units—
comes out clearly in the first division of the poem. Jakobson seems to
think that any reiteration and contrast of a grammatical concept makes it
a poetic device, that the interrelationship of meter, morphological classes
and syntactic construction actualizes the structure and creates the poetic
effect.[5] There is no doubt that a linguistic actualization does take place,
but the question remains: are the linguistic and poetic actualizations
coextensive?

    The sonnet is rebuilt by the two critics into a "superpoem," inacces-
sible to the normal reader, and yet the structures described do not explain what establishes contact between poetry and reader. No
grammatical analysis of a poem can give us more than the grammar of
the poem.

The Poem as Response

    The literary scholar, especially of the humanist stripe, has always as-
sumed that grammar failed because it was incomplete, that the narrow,
rigorous methods of the *esprit de géométrie* could never catch the subtle,
indefinable *je ne sais quoi* that poetry is supposed to be made of. In fact the
opposite is true: the linguist sees all the data, and that is precisely the
reason he was prone, especially in pre-structuralist times, to define a
poetic utterance as abnormal, as language plus something else. The
whole idea of structure, of course, is that within the body of the text all

parts are bound together and that stylistically neutral components and active ones are interrelated in the same way as the marked and un-marked poles of any opposition. Our only solution is to observe and rearrange the data from a different angle. A proper consideration of the nature of the poetic phenomenon will give us the vantage point re-quired.

First of all, the poetic phenomenon, being linguistic, is not simply the message, the poem, but the whole act of communication. This is a very special act, however, for the speaker—the poet—is not present; any attempt to bring him back only produces interference, because what we know of him we know from history, it is knowledge external to the message, or else we have found it out by rationalizing and distorting the message. The message and the addressee—the reader—are indeed the only factors involved in this communication whose presence is neces-sary. As for the other factors—language (code), non-verbal context, means of keeping open the channel—, the appropriate language of ref-erence is selected from the message, the context is reconstituted from the message, contact is assured by the control the message has over the reader's attention, and depends upon the degree of that control. These special duties, and the esthetic emphasis characteristic of poetry demand that the message possess features corresponding to those functions. The characteristic common to such devices must be that they are designed to draw responses from the reader—despite any wanderings of his atten-tion, despite the evolution of the code, despite the changes in esthetic fashion.

The pertinent segmentation of the poem must therefore be based on these responses: they pinpoint in the verbal sequence the location of the devices that trigger them. Since literary criticism aims at informing and improving such responses, we seem to have a vicious circle. It is only apparent, however, for what is blurred in a response is its content, the subjective interpretation of that response, which depends on elements exterior to the act of communication. The response itself testifies objec-tively to the actuality of a contact. Thus two precautions absolutely must be taken: (1) empty the response of its content; I can then use all forms of reaction to the text—idiosyncrasy-oriented responses (positive or negative according to the reader's culture, era, esthetics, personality) and goal-oriented responses (those of the reader with nonliterary intent, who may be using the poem as a historical document, for purposes of linguistic analysis, etc.: such a reader will rationalize his responses to fit into his sphere of interest and its technical terminology); (2) multiply the response, to guard against physical interference with contact, such as the reader's fatigue or the evolving of the language since the time the poem was encoded.

This tool of analysis, this "superreader" in no way distorts the special act of communication under study: It simply explores that act more thoroughly by performing it over and over again. It has the enormous advantage of following exactly the normal reading process, of perceiving the poem as its linguistic shape dictates, along the sentence, starting at the beginning (whereas many critics use the end to comment on the start, and so destroy suspense; or else they use diagrams that modify the balance of the text's natural emphasis system—the chiasma-like division in the Jakobson and Lévi-Strauss analysis, or what they call diagonal or vertical correspondences); it has the advantage of screening pertinent structures and only pertinent structures. My superreader for "Les Chats" is composed of: to a limited extent, Baudelaire (correction of line 8, placing the sonnet in the ensemble of the collection); Gautier (his long paraphrasis of the sonnet, in his preface to the third edition of the *Fleurs*), and Laforgue (some echoes in *Sanglot de la Terre*, "La Première Nuit"); the translations of W. Fowlie, F. L. Freedman and F. Duke; as many critics as I could find, the more useful being those whose reason for picking out a line had nothing to do with the sonnet; Jakobson and Lévi-Strauss for those points in the text where they deviate from their method (when they are being faithful, their analysis scans everything with even hand and is therefore misleading); Larousse's *Dictionnaire du XIXème Siècle* for the entries which quote the sonnet; philological or textbook footnotes; informants such as students of mine and other souls whom fate has thrown my way.

Each point of the text that holds up the superreader is tentatively considered a component of the poetic structure. Experience indicates that such units are always pointed out by a number of informants who usually give divergent rationalizations. These units consist of lexical elements of the sentence interrelated by their contrasting characteristics. They also appear to be linked to one another by relations of opposition. The contrasts they create is what forces them upon the reader's attention; these contrasts result from their unpredictability within the context. This unpredictability is made possible by the fact that at every point in a sentence, the grammatical restrictions limiting the choice of the next word permit a certain degree of predictability. Predictability increases as the number of levels involved and the number of restrictions increase, which happens with any kind of recurrence, like parallelism in general and meter in particular—and where predictability increases, so does the effect of an unpredicted element. . . .

[In the lengthy and detailed analysis that follows, Riffaterre uses the first person plural ("we" "us"), the third person singular ("the reader"), and impersonal constructions ("it is now clear that") to refer to the reactions of a reader—presumably the superreader—moving through the poem line by line. To give a sense of the method and of the flavor of the analysis, I quote here a typical paragraph.—*Ed.*]

At this point, however, the importance of *frileux* and *sédentaires* gives by flashback a new orientation to our sense of the quatrain. The repeated identification *comme eux . . . comme eux* clinches the demonstration of identity between cats and their human counterparts. In this culminating phrase we might have expected adjectives in keeping with those that preceded, all laudatory; we might even have expected a climaxing allusion to certain glorious qualities common to both parties. Instead we get the mediocrity of *frileux* and *sédentaires*—a comic letdown; all the more galling because these are every bit as true as the preceding adjectives, though they ruin the image that has been built up. *Frileux* is fussy and oldmaidish; Baudelaire used it effectively in a parodic self-portrait, the satirical "Spleen I": *d'un fantôme frileux. Sédentaire* conjures up the image of the constipated stay-at-home, epitome of the unwholesome bourgeois. The reader takes in this surprise but has in mind the whole quatrain, so that *orgueil de la maison* still sounds complimentary, with perhaps a touch of parody in the *maison*, which narrowly limits the sphere of the fame, the scope of the glory: even thus does La Fontaine's fox cut his blandishments to the measure of the crow when he crowns him *phénix de ces bois*—but keeps the eyrie of the immortal bird in the neighborhood. Similarly, *mûre saison*, a conventional poetic substitute for *l'âge mûr*, may now be felt as a bit too elegiac, whereas without the twist in line 4 it would simply be the expected ornamental phrase needed to beautify everyday reality. Scholars, in the context and on the level of *amoureux*, are in danger of losing their dignity: their austere mien no longer impresses us, now that we see them as chilly homebodies. *Amoureux* is not, like *amants*, confined to serious or tragic contexts: the shock wave from line 4 destroys the synonymity with *amants* and actualizes the depreciatory or condescending connotations: nineteenth-century dictionaries rank *amoureux* below *amants; amoureux*, not *amants*, is the core of many mocking phrases like *amoureux transi;* and Baudelaire uses it elsewhere only to deride lovers (in the burlesque "La Lune offensée" their silly irresponsibility *sur leurs grabats prospères;* in "Hymne à la Beauté" where the irony is all his, as a comparison with the source makes clear their ungainly bed gymnastics: *L'amoureux pantelant incliné sur sa belle;* whereas his *amants* are never equivocal, always poetic). . . .

Notes

1. Roman Jakobson, "Linguistics and Poetics," in *Style in Language*, ed. T. A. Sebeok (Cambridge, Mass.: M.I.T. Press, 1960), pp. 350-77. See especially pages 358 ff.

2. Roman Jakobson, and Claude Lévi-Strauss, "Les Chats de Charles Baudelaire," *L'Homme* 2 (1962): 5-21.

3. A translation of the poem follows:

Cats

Fervent lovers and austere sages
Love equally, in their season of ripeness,
Cats, powerful and soft, pride of the household,
Who like them are easily chilled and like them sedentary.

Friends of knowledge and of sensual pleasure,
They seek out silence and the awfulness of shadows;
Erebus would have taken them as funereal coursers,
If they could bend their pride to servitude.

They assume, in their musings, the noble attitudes
Of great sphinxes stretched in the depth of solitudes,
Who seem to fall asleep in an endless dream;

Their fecund flanks are full of magic sparks,
And golden particles, like fine sand,
Bespangle dimly their mystical pupils.

Translated by Jane Tompkins and
Catherine Macksey

4. This structural role of the break is well documented: Malherbe condemned internal rhymes precisely because they had such effects.

5. Roman Jakobson, "Poetry of Grammar and Grammar of Poetry" (in Russian), *Poetics, Poetyka* (Warsaw, 1961), pp. 398 ff. See especially pp. 403 and 408-9.

4

CRITICISM AND THE EXPERIENCE OF INTERIORITY

Georges Poulet

I

At the beginning of Mallarmé's unfinished story *Igitur* there is the description of an empty room, in the middle of which, on a table, there is an open book. This seems to me the situation of every book, until someone comes and begins to read it. Books are objects. On a table, on shelves, in store windows, they wait for someone to come and deliver them from the their materiality, from their immobility. When I see them on display, I look at them as I would at animals for sale, kept in little cages, and so obviously hoping for a buyer. For—there is no doubting it—animals do know that their fate depends on a human intervention, thanks to which they will be delivered from the shame of being treated as objects. Isn't the same true of books? Made of paper and ink, they lie where they are put until the moment someone shows an interest in them. They wait. Are they aware that an act of man might suddenly transform their existence? They appear to be lit up with that hope. Read me, they seem to say. I find it hard to resist their appeal. No, books are not just objects among others.

This feeling they give me—I sometimes have it with other objects. I have it, for example, with vases and statues. It would never occur to me to walk around a sewing machine or to look at the under side of a plate. I am quite satisfied with the face they present to me. But statues make me want to circle around them, vases make me want to turn them in my hands. I wonder why. Isn't it because they give me the illusion that there

Reprinted from *The Structuralist Controversy: The Language of Criticism and the Sciences of Man*, edited by Richard A. Macksey and Eugenio Donato (Baltimore: The Johns Hopkins University Press, 1972), pp. 56–72.

is something in them which, from a different angle, I might be able to see? Neither vase nor statue seems fully revealed by the unbroken perimeter of its surfaces. In addition to its surfaces it must have an interior. What this interior might be, that is what intrigues me and makes me circle around them, as though looking for the entrance to a secret chamber. But there is no such entrance (save for the mouth of the vase, which is a true entrance since it gives access only to a little space to put flowers in). So the vase and the statue are closed. They oblige me to remain outside. We can have no true rapport—whence my sense of uneasiness.

So much for statues and vases. I hope books are not like them. Buy a vase, take it home, put it on your table or your mantel, and, after a while, it will allow itself to be made a part of your household. But it will be no less a vase, for that. On the other hand, take a book, and you will find it offering, opening itself. It is this openness of the book which I find so moving. A book is not shut in by its contours, is not walled-up as in a fortress. It asks nothing better than to exist outside itself, or to let you exist in it. In short, the extraordinary fact in the case of a book is the falling away of the barriers between you and it. You are inside it; it is inside you; there is no longer either outside or inside.

Such is the initial phenomenon produced whenever I take up a book, and begin to read it. At the precise moment that I see, surging out of the object I hold open before me, a quantity of significations which my mind grasps, I realize that what I hold in my hands is no longer just an object, or even simply a living thing. I am aware of a rational being, of a consciousness; the consciousness of another, no different from the one I automatically assume in every human being I encounter, except that in this case the consciousness is open to me, welcomes me, lets me look deep inside itself, and even allows me, with unheard-of license, to think what it thinks and feel what it feels.

Unheard of, I say. Unheard of, first, is the disappearance of the "object." Where is the book I held in my hands? It is still there, and at the same time it is there no longer, it is nowhere. That object wholly object, that thing made of paper, as there are things made of metal or porcelain, that object is no more, or at least it is as if it no longer existed, as long as I read the book. For the book is no longer a material reality. It has become a series of words, of images, of ideas which in their turn begin to exist. And where is this new existence? Surely not in the paper object. Nor, surely, in external space. There is only one place left for this new existence: my innermost self.

How has this come about? By what means, through whose intercession? How can I have opened my own mind so completely to what is usually shut out of it? I do not know. I know only that, while reading, I perceive in my mind a number of significations which have made themselves at home there. Doubtless they are still objects: images, ideas, words, objects of my thought. And yet, from this point of view, there is an enormous difference. For the book, like the vase, like the statue, like the table, was an object among others, residing in the external world: the world which objects ordinarily inhabit exclusively in their own society or each on its own, in no need of being thought by my thought; whereas, in this interior world where, like fish in an aquarium, words, images, and ideas disport themselves, these mental entities, in order to exist, need the shelter which I provide; they are dependent on my consciousness.

This dependence is at once a disadvantage and·an advantage. As I have just observed, it is the privilege of exterior objects to dispense with any interference from the mind. All they ask is to be let alone. They manage by themselves. But the same is surely not true of interior objects. By definition they are condemned to change their very nature, condemned to lose their materiality. They become images, ideas, words, that is to say purely mental entities. In sum, in order to exist as mental objects they must relinquish their existence as real objects. On the one hand, this is cause for regret. As soon as I replace my direct perception of reality by the words of a book, I deliver myself, bound hand and foot, to the omnipotence of fiction. I say farewell to what is, in order to feign belief in what is not. I surround myself with fictitious beings; I become the prey of language. There is no escaping this takeover. Language surrounds me with its unreality. On the other hand, the transmutation through language of reality into a fictional equivalent, has undeniable advantages. The universe of fiction is infinitely more elastic than the world of objective reality. It lends itself to any use: it yields with little resistance to the importunities of the mind. Moreover—and of all its benefits I find this the most appealing—this interior universe constituted by language does not seem radically opposed to the *me* who thinks it. Doubtless what I glimpse through the words are mental forms not divested of an appearance of objectivity. But they do not seem to be of another nature than my mind which thinks them. They are objects, but subjectified objects. In short, since everything has become part of my mind thanks to the intervention of language, the opposition between the subject and its objects has been considerably attenuated. And thus the greatest advantage of literature is that I am persuaded by it that I am free from my usual sense of incompatibility between my consciousness and its objects.

This is the remarkable transformation wrought in me through the act of reading. Not only does it cause the physical objects around me to disappear, including the very book I am reading, but it replaces those external objects with a congeries of mental objects in close *rapport* with my own consciousness. And yet the very intimacy in which I now live with my objects is going to present me with new problems. The most curious of these is the following: I am someone who happens to have as objects of his own thought, thoughts which are part of a book I am reading, and which are therefore the cogitations of another. They are the thoughts of another, and yet it is I who am their subject. The situation is even more astonishing than the one noted above. I am thinking the thoughts of another. Of course, there would be no cause for astonishment if I were thinking it as the thought of another. But I think it as my very own. Ordinarily there is the *I* which thinks, which recognizes itself (when it takes its bearings) in thoughts which may have come from elsewhere but which it takes upon itself as its own in the moment it thinks them. This is how we must take Diderot's declaration "Mes pensées sont *mes* catins" ("My thoughts are *my* whores"). That is, they sleep with everybody without ceasing to belong to their author. Now, in the present case things are quite different. Because of the strange invasion of my person by the thoughts of another, I am a self who is granted the experience of thinking thoughts foreign to him. I am the subject of thoughts other than my own. My consciousness behaves as though it were the consciousness of another.

This merits reflection. In a certain sense I must recognize that no idea really belongs to me. Ideas belong to no one. They pass from one mind to another as coins pass from hand to hand. Consequently, nothing could be more misleading than the attempt to define a consciousness by the ideas which it utters or entertains. But whatever these ideas may be, however strong the tie which binds them to their source, however transitory may be their sojourn in my own mind, so long as I entertain them I assert myself as subject of these ideas; I am the subjective principle for whom the ideas serve for the time being as the predications. Furthermore, this subjective principle can in no wise be conceived as a predication, as something which is discussed, referred to. It is I who think, who contemplate, who am engaged in speaking. In short it is never a *he* but an *I*.

Now what happens when I read a book? Am I then the subject of a series of predications which are not *my* predications? That is impossible, perhaps even a contradiction in terms. I feel sure that as soon as I think something, that something becomes in some indefinable way my own. Whatever I think is a part of *my* mental world. And yet here I am thinking a thought which manifestly belongs to another mental world, which is being thought in me just as though I did not exist. Already the notion is inconceivable and seems even more so if I reflect that, since every thought must have a subject to think it, this *thought* which is alien to me and yet in me, must also have in me a *subject* which is alien to me. It all happens, then, as though reading were the act by which a thought managed to bestow itself within me with a subject not myself. Whenever

I read, I mentally pronounce an *I*, and yet the *I* which I pronounce is not myself. This is true even when the hero of a novel is presented in the third person, and even when there is no hero and nothing but reflections or propositions: for as soon as something is presented as *thought,* there has to be a thinking subject with whom, at least for the time being, I identify, forgetting myself, alienated from myself. "Je est un autre," said Rimbaud. Another *I,* who has replaced my own, and who will continue to do so as long as I read. Reading is just that: a way of giving way not only to a host of alien words, images, ideas, but also to the very alien principle which utters them and shelters them.

The phenomenon is indeed hard to explain, even to conceive, and yet, once admitted, it explains to me what might otherwise seem even more inexplicable. For how could I explain, without such take-over of my innermost subjective being, the astonishing facility with which I not only understand but even *feel* what I read. When I read as I ought—that is without mental reservation, without any desire to preserve my independence of judgment, and with the total commitment required of any reader—my comprehension becomes intuitive and any feeling proposed to me is immediately assumed by me. In other words, the kind of comprehension in question here is not a movement from the unknown to the known, from the strange to the familiar, from outside to inside. It might rather be called a phenomenon by which mental objects rise up from the depths of consciousness into the light of recognition. On the other hand—and without contradiction—reading implies something resembling the apperception I have of myself, the action by which I grasp straightway what I think as being thought by a subject (who, in this case, is not I). Whatever sort of alienation I may endure, reading does not interrupt my activity as subject.

Reading, then, is the act in which the subjective principle which I call *I,* is modified in such a way that I no longer have the right, strictly speaking, to consider it as my *I.* I am on loan to another, and this other thinks, feels, suffers, and acts within me. The phenomenon appears in its most obvious and even naivest form in the sort of spell brought about by certain cheap kinds of reading, such as thrillers, of which I say, "It gripped me." Now it is important to note that this possession of myself by another takes place not only on the level of objective thought, that is with regard to images, sensations, ideas which reading affords me, but also on the level of my very subjectivity.

When I am absorbed in reading, a second self takes over, a self which thinks and feels for me. Withdrawn in some recess of myself, do I then silently witness this dispossession? Do I derive from it some comfort, or, on the contrary, a kind of anguish? However that may be, someone else holds the center of the stage, and the question which imposes itself,

which I am absolutely obliged to ask myself, is this: "Who is the usurper
who occupies the forefront? Who is this mind who alone all by himself
fills my consciousness and who, when I say *I,* is indeed that *I?*"

There is an immediate answer to this question, perhaps too easy an
answer. This *I,* who "thinks in me" when I read a book, is the *I* of the
one who writes the book. When I read Baudelaire or Racine, it is really
Baudelaire or Racine who thinks, feels, allows himself to be read within
me. Thus a book is not only a book, it is the means by which an author
actually preserves his ideas, his feelings, his modes of dreaming and
living. It is his means of saving his identity from death. Such an interpretation of reading is not false. It seems to justify what is commonly called
the biographical explication of literary texts. Indeed every word of literature is impregnated with the mind of the one who wrote it. As he makes
us read it, he awakens in us the analogue of what he thought or felt. To
understand a literary work, then, is to let the individual who wrote it
reveal himself to us *in* us. It is not the biography which explicates the
work, but rather the work which sometimes enables us to understand the
biography.

But biographical interpretation is in part false and misleading. It is
true that there is an analogy between the works of an author and the
experiences of his life. The works may be seen as an incomplete translation of the life. And further, there is an even more significant analogy
among all the works of a single author. Each of the works, however,
while I am reading it, lives in me its own life. The subject who is revealed
to me through my reading of it is not the author, either in the disordered
totality of his outer experiences, or in the aggregate, better organized,
and concentrated totality, which is the one of his writings. Yet the subject
which presides over the work can exist only in the work. To be sure,
nothing is unimportant for understanding the work, and a mass of biographical, bibliographical, textual, and general critical information is indispensable to me. And yet this knowledge does not coincide with the
internal knowledge of the work. Whatever may be the sum of the information I acquire on Baudelaire or Racine, in whatever degree of intimacy I may live with their genius, I am aware that this contribution does
not suffice to illuminate for me in its own inner meaning, in its formal
perfection, and in the subjective principle which animates it, the particular work of Baudelaire or of Racine the reading of which now absorbs
me. At this moment what matters to me is to live, from the inside, in a
certain identity with the work and the work alone. It could hardly be
otherwise. Nothing external to the work could possibly share the extraordinary claim which the work now exerts on me. It is there within
me, not to send me back, outside itself, to its author, nor to his other
writings, but on the contrary to keep my attention riveted on itself. It is
the work which traces in me the very boundaries within which this con-

sciousness will define itself. It is the work which forces on me a series of mental objects and creates in me a network of words, beyond which, for the time being, there will be no room for other mental objects or for other words. And it is the work, finally, which, not satisfied thus with defining the content of my consciousness, takes hold of it, appropriates it, and makes of it that *I* which, from one end of my reading to the other, presides over the unfolding of the work, of the single work which I am reading.

And so the work forms the temporary mental substance which fills my consciousness; and it is moreover that consciousness, the *I*-subject, the continued consciousness of what is, revealing itself within the interior of the work. Such is the characteristic condition of every work which I summon back into existence by placing my own consciousness at its disposal. I give it not only existence, but awareness of existence. And so I ought not to hesitate to recognize that so long as it is animated by this vital inbreathing inspired by the act of reading, a work of literature becomes at the expense of the reader whose own life it suspends a sort of human being, that it is a mind conscious of itself and constituting itself in me as the subject of its own objects.

II

The work lives its own life within me; in a certain sense, it thinks itself, and it even gives itself a meaning within me.

This strange displacement of myself by the work deserves to be examined even more closely.

If the work thinks itself in me, does this mean that, during a complete loss of consciousness on my part, another thinking entity invades me taking advantage of my unconsciousness in order to think itself without my being able to think it? Obviously not. The annexation of my consciousness by another (the other which is the work), in no way implies that I am the victim of any deprivation of consciousness. Everything happens, on the contrary, as though, from the moment I become a prey to what I read, I begin to share the use of my consciousness with this being whom I have tried to define and who is the conscious subject ensconced at the heart of the work. He and I, we start having a common consciousness. Doubtless, within this community of feeling, the parts played by each of us are not of equal importance. The consciousness inherent in the work is active and potent; it occupies the foreground; it is clearly related to its *own* world, to objects which are *its* objects. In opposition, I myself, although conscious of whatever it may be conscious of, play a much more humble role content to record passively all that is going on in me. A lag takes place, a sort of schizoid distinction between

what I feel and what the other feels; a confused awareness of delay, so
that the work seems first to think by itself, and then to inform me what it
has thought. Thus I often have the impression, while reading, of simply
witnessing an action which at the same time concerns and yet does not
concern me. This provokes a certain feeling of surprise within me. I am
a consciousness astonished by an existence which is not mine, but which I
experience as though it were mine. . . .

[In the intervening pages, Poulet explore varieties of the relationship between criticizing subject and criticized object in the work of six
French critics: Jacques Rivière, Jean-Pierre Richard, Maurice Blanchot,
Jean Starobinski, Marcel Raymond, and Jean Rousset. Poulet's focus in
each case is on the critic's capacity to link the objective aspects of the
work with the authorial subjectivity that sustains it. He concludes as
follows.—Ed.]

... In order to establish the interrelationship between subject and
object, which is the principle of all creative work and of the understanding of it, two ways, at least theoretically, are opened, one leading from
the objects to the subject, the other from the subject to the objects.
... Yet there is the risk of overlooking an important point. The aim of
criticism is not achieved merely by the understanding of the part played by
the subject in its interrelation with objects. When reading a literary work
there is a moment when it seems to me that the subject *present* in this
work disengages itself from all that surrounds it, and stands alone. Had I
not once the intuition of this, when visiting the Scuola di San Rocco in
Venice, one of the highest summits of art, where there are assembled so
many paintings of the same painter, Tintoretto? When looking at all
these masterpieces, brought there together and revealing so manifestly
their unity of inspiration, I had suddenly the impression of having
reached the common essence present in all the works of a great master,
an essence which I was not able to perceive, except when emptying my
mind of all the particular images created by the artist. I became aware of
a subjective power at work in all these pictures, and yet never so clearly
understood by my mind as when I had forgotten all their particular
figurations.

One may ask oneself: What is this subject left standing in isolation
after every examination of a literary work? Is it the individual genius of
the artist, visibly present in his work, yet having an invisible life independent of the work? Or is it, as Valéry thinks, an anonymous and
abstract consciousness presiding, in its aloofness, over the operations of
all more concrete consciousnesses? Whatever it may be, I am constrained
to acknowledge that all subjective activity present in a literary work is not
entirely explained by its relationship with forms and objects within the
work. There is in the work a mental activity profoundly engaged in
objective forms; and there is, at another level, forsaking all forms, a

subject which reveals itself to itself (and to me) in its transcendence relative to all which is reflected in it. At this point, no object can any longer express it; no structure can any longer define it; it is exposed in its ineffability and in its fundamental indeterminacy. Such is perhaps the reason why the critic, in his elucidation of works, is haunted by this transcendence of mind. It seems then that criticism, in order to accompany the mind in this effort of detachment from itself, needs to annihilate, or at least momentarily to forget, the objective elements of the work, and to elevate itself to the apprehension of a subjectivity without objectivity.

Translated by Catherine Macksey

5

THE READING PROCESS: A PHENOMENOLOGICAL APPROACH

Wolfgang Iser

I

The phenomenological theory of art lays full stress on the idea that, in considering a literary work, one must take into account not only the actual text but also, and in equal measure, the actions involved in responding to that text. Thus Roman Ingarden confronts the structure of the literary text with the ways in which it can be *konkretisiert* (realized).[1] The text as such offers different "schematised views"[2] through which the subject matter of the work can come to light, but the actual bringing to light is an action of *Konkretisation*. If this is so, then the literary work has two poles, which we might call the artistic and the esthetic: the artistic refers to the text created by the author, and the esthetic to the realization accomplished by the reader. From this polarity it follows that the literary work cannot be completely identical with the text, or with the realization of the text, but in fact must lie halfway between the two. The work is more than the text, for the text only takes on life when it is realized, and furthermore the realization is by no means independent of the individual disposition of the reader—though this in turn is acted upon by the different patterns of the text. The convergence of text and reader brings the literary work into existence, and this convergence can never be precisely pinpointed, but must always remain virtual, as it is not to be identified either with the reality of the text or with the individual disposition of the reader.

It is the virtuality of the work that gives rise to its dynamic nature, and this in turn is the precondition for the effects that the work calls

Reprinted from Wolfgang Iser, *The Implied Reader: Patterns in Communication in Prose Fiction from Bunyan to Beckett* (Baltimore: The Johns Hopkins University Press, 1974), pp. 274-94.

forth. As the reader uses the various perspectives offered him by the text in order to relate the patterns and the "schematised views" to one another, he sets the work in motion, and this very process results ultimately in the awakening of responses within himself. Thus, reading causes the literary work to unfold its inherently dynamic character. That this is no new discovery is apparent from references made even in the early days of the novel. Laurence Sterne remarks in *Tristram Shandy:* "no author, who understands the just boundaries of decorum and good breeding, would presume to think all: The truest respect which you can pay to the reader's understanding, is to halve this matter amicably, and leave him something to imagine, in his turn, as well as yourself. For my own part, I am eternally paying him compliments of this kind, and do all that lies in my power to keep his imagination as busy as my own."[3] Sterne's conception of a literary text is that it is something like an arena in which reader and author participate in a game of the imagination. If the reader were given the whole story, and there were nothing left for him to do, then his imagination would never enter the field, the result would be the boredom which inevitably arises when everything is laid out cut and dried before us. A literary text must therefore be conceived in such a way that it will engage the reader's imagination in the task of working things out for himself, for reading is only a pleasure when it is active and creative. In this process of creativity, the text may either not go far enough, or may go too far, so we may say that boredom and overstrain form the boundaries beyond which the reader will leave the field of play.

The extent to which the "unwritten" part of a text stimulates the reader's creative participation is brought out by an observation of Virginia Woolf's in her study of *Jane Austen:*

> Jane Austen is thus a mistress of much deeper emotion than appears upon the surface. She stimulates us to supply what is not there. What she offers is, apparently, a trifle, yet is composed of something that expands in the reader's mind and endows with the most enduring form of life scenes which are outwardly trivial. Always the stress is laid upon character. . . . The turns and twists of the dialogue keep us on the tenterhooks of suspense. Our attention is half upon the present moment, half upon the future. . . . Here, indeed, in this unfinished and in the main inferior story, are all the elements of Jane Austen's greatness.[4]

The unwritten aspects of apparently trivial scenes and the unspoken dialogue within the "turns and twists" not only draw the reader into the action but also lead him to shade in the many outlines suggested by the given situations, so that these take on a reality of their own. But as the reader's imagination animates these "outlines," they in turn will influence the effect of the written part of the text. Thus begins a whole dynamic process: the written text imposes certain limits on its unwritten implications in order to prevent these from becoming too blurred and hazy, but at the same time these implications, worked out by the reader's imagination, set the given situation against a background which endows it with far greater significance than it might have seemed to possess on its own. In this way, trivial scenes suddenly take on the shape of an "enduring form of life." What constitutes this form is never named, let alone explained in the text, although in fact it is the end product of the interaction between text and reader.

II

The question now arises as to how far such a process can be adequately described. For this purpose a phenomenological analysis recommends itself, especially since the somewhat sparse observations hitherto made of the psychology of reading tend mainly to be psychoanalytical, and so are restricted to the illustration of predetermined ideas concerning the unconscious. We shall, however, take a closer look later at some worthwhile psychological observations.

As a starting point for a phenomenological analysis we might examine the way in which sequent sentences act upon one another. This is of especial importance in literary texts in view of the fact that they do not correspond to any objective reality outside themselves. The world presented by literary texts is constructed out of what Ingarden has called *intentionale Satzkorrelate* (intentional sentence correlatives):

> Sentences link up in different ways to form more complex units of meaning that reveal a very varied structure giving rise to such entities as a short story, a novel, a dialogue, a drama, a scientific theory.... In the final analysis, there arises a particular world, with component parts determined in this way or that, and with all the variations that may occur within these parts—all this as a purely intentional correlative of a complex of sentences. If this complex finally forms a literary work, I call the whole sum of sequent intentional sentence correlatives the "world presented" in the work.[5]

This world, however, does not pass before the reader's eyes like a film. The sentences are "component parts" insofar as they make statements, claims, or observations, or convey information, and so establish various perspectives in the text. But they remain only "component parts"—they are not the sum total of the text itself. For the intentional correlatives disclose subtle connections which individually are less concrete than the statements, claims, and observations, even though these only take on their real meaningfulness through the interaction of their correlatives.

How is one to conceive the connection between the correlatives? It marks those points at which the reader is able to "climb aboard" the text.

He has to accept certain given perspectives, but in doing so he inevitably causes them to interact. When Ingarden speaks of intentional sentence correlatives in literature, the statements made or information conveyed in the sentence is already in a certain sense qualified: the sentence does not consist solely of a statement—which, after all, would be absurd, as one can only make statements about things that exist—but aims at something beyond what it actually says. This is true of all sentences in literary works, and it is through the interaction of these sentences that their common aim is fulfilled. This is what gives them their own special quality in literary texts. In their capacity as statements, observations, purveyors of information, etc., they are always indications of something that is to come, the structure of which is foreshadowed by their specific content.

They set in motion a process out of which emerges the actual content of the text itself. In describing man's inner consciousness of time, Husserl once remarked: "Every originally constructive process is inspired by pre-intentions, which construct and collect the seed of what is to come, as such, and bring it to fruition."[6] For this bringing to fruition, the literary text needs the reader's imagination, which gives shape to the interaction of correlatives foreshadowed in structure by the sequence of the sentences. Husserl's observation draws our attention to a point that plays a not insignificant part in the process of reading. The individual sentences not only work together to shade in what is to come; they also form an expectation in this regard. Husserl calls this expectation "pre-intentions." As this structure is characteristic of *all* sentence correlatives, the interaction of these correlatives will not be a fulfillment of the expectation so much as a continual modification of it.

For this reason, expectations are scarcely ever fulfilled in truly literary texts. If they were, then such texts would be confined to the individualization of a given expectation, and one would inevitably ask what such an intention was supposed to achieve. Strangely enough, we feel that any confirmative effect—such as we implicitly demand of expository texts, as we refer to the objects they are meant to present—is a defect in a literary text. For the more a text individualizes or confirms an expectation it has initially aroused, the more aware we become of its didactic purpose, so that at best we can only accept or reject the thesis forced upon us. More often than not, the very clarity of such texts will make us want to free ourselves from their clutches. But generally the sentence correlatives of literary texts do not develop in this rigid way, for the expectations they evoke tend to encroach on one another in such a manner that they are continually modified as one reads. One might simplify by saying that each intentional sentence correlative opens up a particular horizon, which is modified, if not completely changed, by succeeding sentences. While these expectations arouse interest in what is to come, the subsequent modification of them will also have a retrospective effect on what has already been read. This may now take on a different significance from that which it had at the moment of reading.

Whatever we have read sinks into our memory and is foreshortened. It may later be evoked again and set against a different background with the result that the reader is enabled to develop hitherto unforeseeable connections. The memory evoked, however, can never reassume its original shape, for this would mean that memory and perception were identical, which is manifestly not so. The new background brings to light new aspects of what we had committed to memory; conversely these, in turn, shed their light on the new background, thus arousing more complex anticipations. Thus, the reader, in establishing these inter-relations between past, present, and future, actually causes the text to reveal its potential multiplicity of connections. These connections are the product of the reader's mind working on the raw material of the text, though they are not the text itself—for this consists just of sentences, statements, information, etc.

This is why the reader often feels involved in events which, at the time of reading, seem real to him, even though in fact they are very far from his own reality. The fact that completely different readers can be differently affected by the "reality" of a particular text is ample evidence of the degree to which literary texts transform reading into a creative process that is far above mere perception of what is written. The literary text activates our own faculties, enabling us to recreate the world it presents. The product of this creative activity is what we might call the virtual dimension of the text, which endows it with its reality. This virtual dimension is not the text itself, nor is it the imagination of the reader: it is the coming together of text and imagination.

As we have seen, the activity of reading can be characterized as a sort of kaleidoscope of perspectives, preintentions, recollections. Every sentence contains a preview of the next and forms a kind of viewfinder for what is to come; and this in turn changes the "preview" and so becomes a "viewfinder" for what has been read. This whole process represents the fulfillment of the potential, unexpressed reality of the text, but it is to be seen only as a framework for a great variety of means by which the virtual dimension may be brought into being. The process of anticipation and retrospection itself does not by any means develop in a smooth flow. Ingarden has already drawn attention to this fact and ascribes a quite remarkable significance to it:

> Once we are immersed in the flow of *Satzdenken* (sentence-thought), we are ready, after completing the thought of one sentence, to think out the "continuation," also in the form of a sentence—and that is, in the form of a sentence that connects up with the sentence we have just thought through.

> In this way the process of reading goes effortlessly forward. But if by chance the following sentence has no tangible connection whatever with the sentence we have just thought through, there then comes a blockage in the stream of thought. This hiatus is linked with a more or less active surprise, or with indignation. This blockage must be overcome if the reading is to flow once more.[7]

The hiatus that blocks the flow of sentences is, in Ingarden's eyes, the product of chance, and is to be regarded as a flaw; this is typical of his adherence to the classical idea of art. If one regards the sentence sequence as a continual flow, this implies that the anticipation aroused by one sentence will generally be realized by the next, and the frustration of one's expectations will arouse feelings of exasperation. And yet literary texts are full of unexpected twists and turns, and frustration of expectations. Even in the simplest story there is bound to be some kind of blockage, if only because no tale can ever be told in its entirety. Indeed, it is only through inevitable omissions that a story gains its dynamism. Thus whenever the flow is interrupted and we are led off in unexpected directions, the opportunity is given to us to bring into play our own faculty for establishing connections—for filling in the gaps left by the text itself.[8]

These gaps have a different effect on the process of anticipation and retrospection, and thus on the "gestalt" of the virtual dimension, for they may be filled in different ways. For this reason, one text is potentially capable of several different realizations, and no reading can ever exhaust the full potential, for each individual reader will fill in the gaps in his own way, thereby excluding the various other possibilities; as he reads, he will make his own decision as to how the gap is to be filled. In this very act the dynamics of reading are revealed. By making his decision he implicitly acknowledges the inexhaustibility of the text; at the same time it is this very inexhaustibility that forces him to make his decision. With "traditional" texts this process was more or less unconscious, but modern texts frequently exploit it quite deliberately. They are often so fragmentary that one's attention is almost exclusively occupied with the search for connections between the fragments; the object of this is not to complicate the "spectrum" of connections, so much as to make us aware of the nature of our own capacity for providing links. In such cases, the text refers back directly to our own preconceptions—which are revealed by the act of interpretation that is a basic element of the reading process. With all literary texts, then, we may say that the reading process is selective, and the potential text is infinitely richer than any of its individual realizations. This is borne out by the fact that a second reading of a piece of literature often produces a different impression from the first. The reasons for this may lie in the reader's own change of circumstances, still; the text must be such as to allow this variation. On a second reading familiar occurrences now tend to appear in a new light and seem to be at times corrected, at times enriched.

In every text there is a potential time sequence which the reader must inevitably realize, as it is impossible to absorb even a short text in a single moment. Thus the reading process always involves viewing the text through a perspective that is continually on the move, linking up the different phases, and so constructing what we have called the virtual dimension. This dimension, of course, varies all the time we are reading. However, when we have finished the text, and read it again, clearly our extra knowledge will result in a different time sequence; we shall tend to establish connections by referring to our awareness of what is to come, and so certain aspects of the text will assume a significance we did not attach to them on a first reading, while others will recede into the background. It is a common enough experience for a person to say that on a second reading he noticed things he had missed when he read the book for the first time, but this is scarcely surprising in view of the fact that the second time he is looking at the text from a different perspective. The time sequence that he realized on his first reading cannot possibly be repeated on a second reading, and this unrepeatability is bound to result in modifications of his reading experience. This is not to say that the second reading is "truer" than the first—they are, quite simply, different: the reader establishes the virtual dimension of the text by realizing a new time sequence. Thus even on repeated viewings a text allows and, indeed, induces innovative reading.

In whatever way, and under whatever circumstances the reader may link the different phases of the text together, it will always be the process of anticipation and retrospection that leads to the formation of the virtual dimension, which in turn transforms the text into an experience for the reader. The way in which this experience comes about through a process of continual modification is closely akin to the way in which we gather experience in life. And thus the "reality" of the reading experience can illuminate basic patterns of real experience:

> We have the experience of a world, not understood as a system of relations which wholly determine each event, but as an open totality the synthesis of which is inexhaustible. . . . From the moment that experience—that is, the opening on to our *de facto* world—is recognized as the beginning of knowledge, there is no longer any way of distinguishing a level of *a priori* truths and one of factual ones, what the world must necessarily be and what it actually is.[9]

The manner in which the reader experiences the text will reflect his own disposition, and in this respect the literary text acts as a kind of mirror; but at the same time, the reality which this process helps to create is one that will be *different* from his own (since, normally, we tend to be bored by texts that present us with things we already know perfectly well ourselves). Thus we have the apparently paradoxical situation in which the reader is forced to reveal aspects of himself in order to experience a reality which is different from his own. The impact this reality makes on him will depend largely on the extent to which he himself actively provides the unwritten part of the text, and yet in supplying all the missing links, he must think in terms of experiences different from his own; indeed, it is only by leaving behind the familiar world of his own experience that the reader can truly participate in the adventure the literary text offers him.

III

We have seen that, during the process of reading, there is an active interweaving of anticipation and retrospection, which on a second reading may turn into a kind of advance retrospection. The impressions that arise as a result of this process will vary from individual to individual, but only within the limits imposed by the written as opposed to the unwritten text. In the same way, two people gazing at the night sky may both be looking at the same collection of stars, but one will see the image of a plough, and the other will make out a dipper. The "stars" in a literary text are fixed; the lines that join them are variable. The author of the text may, of course, exert plenty of influence on the reader's imagination—he has the whole panoply of narrative techniques at his disposal—but no author worth his salt will ever attempt to set the *whole* picture before his reader's eyes. If he does, he will very quickly lose his reader, for it is only by activating the reader's imagination that the author can hope to involve him and so realize the intentions of his text.

Gilbert Ryle, in his analysis of imagination, asks: "How can a person fancy that he sees something, without realizing that he is not seeing it?" He answers as follows:

> Seeing Helvellyn [the name of a mountain] in one's mind's eye does not entail, what seeing Helvellyn and seeing snapshots of Helvellyn entail, the having of visual sensations. It does involve the thought of having a view of Helvellyn and it is therefore a more sophisticated operation than that of having a view of Helvellyn. It is one utilization among others of the knowledge of how Helvellyn should look, or, in one sense of the verb, it is thinking how it should look. The expectations which are fulfilled in the recognition at sight of Helvellyn are not indeed fulfilled in picturing it, but the picturing of it is something like a rehearsal of getting them fulfilled. So far from picturing involving the having of faint sensations, or wraiths of sensations, it involves missing just what one would be due to get, if one were seeing the mountain.[10]

If one sees the mountain, then of course one can no longer imagine it, and so the act of picturing the mountain presupposes it absence. Similarly, with a literary text we can only picture things which are not there; the written part of the text gives us the knowledge, but it is the unwritten part that gives us the opportunity to picture things; indeed without the elements of indeterminacy, the gaps in the texts, we should not be able to use our imagination.[11]

The truth of this observation is borne out by the experience many people have on seeing, for instance, the film of a novel. While reading *Tom Jones,* they may never have had a clear conception of what the hero actually looks like, but on seeing the film, some may say, "That's not how I imagined him." The point here is that the reader of *Tom Jones* is able to visualize the hero virtually for himself, and so his imagination senses the vast number of possibilities; the moment these possibilities are narrowed down to one complete and immutable picture, the imagination is put out of action, and we feel we have somehow been cheated. This may perhaps be an oversimplification of the process, but it does illustrate plainly the vital richness of potential that arises out of the fact that the hero in the novel must be pictured and cannot be seen. With the novel the reader must use his imagination to synthesize the information given him, and so his perception is simultaneously richer and more private; with the film he is confined merely to physical perception, and so whatever he remembers of the world he had pictured is brutally cancelled out.

IV

The "picturing" that is done by our imagination is only one of the activities through which we form the "gestalt" of a literary text. We have already discussed the process of anticipation and retrospection, and to this we must add the process of grouping together all the different aspects of a text to form the consistency that the reader will always be in search of. While expectations may be continually modified, and images continually expanded, the reader will still strive, even if unconsciously, to fit everything together in a consistent pattern. "In the reading of images, as in the hearing of speech, it is always hard to distinguish what is given to us from what we supplement in the process of projection which is triggered off by recognition . . . it is the guess of the beholder that tests the medley of forms and colours for coherent meaning, crystallizing it into shape when a consistent interpretation has been found."[12] By grouping together the written parts of the text, we enable them to interact, we observe the direction in which they are leading us, and we project onto them the consistency which we, as readers, require. This "gestalt" must inevitably be colored by our own characteristic selection process. For it is not given by the text itself; it arises from the meeting between the written text and the individual mind of the reader with its own particular history of experience, its own consciousness, its own outlook. The "gestalt" is not the true meaning of the text; at best it is a configurative meaning; "comprehension is an individual act of seeing-things-together, and only that."[13] With a literary text such comprehension is inseparable from the reader's expectations, and where we have expectations, there too we have one of the most potent weapons in the writer's armory—illusion.

Whenever "consistent reading suggests itself . . . illusion takes over."[14] Illusion, says Northrop Frye, is "fixed or definable, and reality is best understood as its negation."[15] The "gestalt" of a text normally takes on (or, rather, is given) this fixed or definable outline, as this is essential to our own understanding, but on the other hand, if reading were to consist of nothing but an uninterrupted building up of illusions, it would be a suspect, if not downright dangerous, process: instead of bringing us into contact with reality, it would wean us away from realities. Of course, there is an element of "escapism" in all literature, resulting from this very creation of illusion, but there are some texts which offer nothing but a harmonious world, purified of all contradiction and deliberately excluding anything that might disturb the illusion once established, and these are the texts that we generally do not like to classify as literary. Women's magazines and the brasher forms of the detective story might be cited as examples.

However, even if an overdose of illusion may lead to triviality, this does not mean that the process of illusion-building should ideally be dispensed with altogether. On the contrary, even in texts that appear to resist the formation of illusion, thus drawing our attention to the cause of this resistance, we still need the abiding illusion that the resistance itself is the consistent pattern underlying the text. This is especially true of modern texts, in which it is the very precision of the written details which increases the proportion of indeterminacy; one detail appears to contradict another, and so simultaneously stimulates and frustrates our desire to "picture," thus continually causing our imposed "gestalt" of the text to disintegrate. Without the formation of illusions, the unfamiliar world of the text would remain unfamiliar; through the illusions, the experience offered by the text becomes accessible to us, for it is only the illusion, on its different levels of consistency, that makes the experience "readable." If we cannot find (or impose) this consistency, sooner or later we will put the text down. The process is virtually hermeneutic. The text provokes certain expectations which in turn we project onto the text in such a way that we reduce the polysemantic possibilities to a single interpretation in keeping with the expectations aroused, thus extracting an individual, configurative meaning. The polysemantic nature of the text and the illusion-making of the reader are opposed factors. If the illusion were complete, the polysemantic nature would vanish; if the polysemantic nature were all-powerful, the illusion would be totally destroyed. Both extremes are conceivable, but in the individual literary text we always find some form of balance between the two conflicting tendencies. The formation of illusions, therefore, can never be total, but it is this very incompleteness that in fact gives it its productive value.

With regard to the experience of reading, Walter Pater once observed: "For to the grave reader words too are grave; and the ornamental word, the figure, the accessory form or colour or reference, is rarely content to die to thought precisely at the right moment, but will inevitably linger awhile, stirring a long 'brainwave' behind it of perhaps quite alien associations."[16] Even while the reader is seeking a consistent pattern in the text, he is also uncovering other impulses which cannot be immediately integrated or will even resist final integration. Thus the semantic possibilities of the text will always remain far richer than any configurative meaning formed while reading. But this impression is, of course, only to be gained through reading the text. Thus the configurative meaning can be nothing but a *pars pro toto* fulfillment of the text, and yet this fulfillment gives rise to the very richness which it seeks to restrict, and indeed in some modern texts, our awareness of this richness takes precedence over any configurative meaning.

This fact has several consequences which, for the purpose of analysis, may be dealt with separately, though in the reading process they will all be working together. As we have seen, a consistent, configurative meaning is essential for the apprehension of an unfamiliar experience, which through the process of illusion-building we can incorporate in our own imaginative world. At the same time, this consistency conflicts with the many other possibilities of fulfillment it seeks to exclude, with the result that the configurative meaning is always accompanied by "alien associations" that do not fit in with the illusions formed. The first consequence, then, is the fact that in forming our illusions, we also produce at the same time a latent disturbance of these illusions. Strangely enough, this also applies to texts in which our expectations are actually fulfilled—though one would have thought that the fulfillment of expectations would help to complete the illusion. "Illusion wears off once the expectation is stepped up; we take it for granted and want more."[17]

The experiments in gestalt psychology referred to by Gombrich in *Art and Illusion* make one thing clear: "though we may be intellectually aware of the fact that any given experience *must* be an illusion, we cannot, strictly speaking, watch ourselves having an illusion."[18] Now, if illusion were not a transitory state, this would mean that we could be, as it were, permanently caught up in it. And if reading were exclusively a matter of producing illusion—necessary though this is for the understanding of an unfamiliar experience—we should run the risk of falling victim to a gross deception. But it is precisely during our reading that the transitory nature of the illusion is revealed to the full.

As the formation of illusions is constantly accompanied by "alien associations" which cannot be made consistent with the illusions, the reader constantly has to lift the restrictions he places on the "meaning" of the text. Since it is he who builds the illusions, he oscillates between involvement in and observation of those illusions; he opens himself to the unfamiliar world without being imprisoned in it. Through this process the reader moves into the presence of the fictional world and so experiences the realities of the text as they happen.

In the oscillation between consistency and "alien associations," between involvement in and observation of the illusion, the reader is bound to conduct his own balancing operation, and it is this that forms the esthetic experience offered by the literary text. However, if the reader were to achieve a balance, obviously he would then no longer be engaged in the process of establishing and disrupting consistency. And since it is this very process that gives rise to the balancing operation, we may say that the inherent nonachievement of balance is a prerequisite for the very dynamism of the operation. In seeking the balance we inevitably have to start out with certain expectations, the shattering of which is integral to the esthetic experience.

> Furthermore, to say merely that "our expectations are satisfied" is to be guilty of another serious ambiguity. At first sight such a statement seems to deny the obvious fact that much of our enjoyment is derived from surprises, from betrayals of our expectations. The solution to this paradox is to find some ground for a distinction between "surprise" and "frustration." Roughly, the distinction can be made in terms of the effects which the two kinds of experiences have upon us. Frustration blocks or checks activity. It necessitates new orientation for our activity, if we are to escape the *cul de sac*. Consequently, we abandon the frustrating object and return to blind impulse activity. On the other hand, surprise merely causes a temporary cessation of the exploratory phase of the experience, and a recourse to intense contemplation and scrutiny. In the latter phase the surprising elements are seen in their connection with what has gone before, with the whole drift of the experience, and the enjoyment of these values is then extremely intense. Finally, it appears that there must always be some degree of novelty or surprise in all these values if there is to be a progressive specification of the direction of the total act . . . and any aesthetic experience tends to exhibit a continuous interplay between "deductive" and "inductive" operations.[19]

It is this interplay between "deduction" and "induction" that gives rise to the configurative meaning of the text, and not the individual expectations, surprises, or frustrations arising from the different perspectives. Since this interplay obviously does not take place in the text itself, but can only come into being through the process of reading, we may conclude that this process formulates something that is unformulated in the text and yet represents its "intention." Thus, by reading we uncover the unformulated part of the text, and this very indeterminacy is the force that drives us to work out a configurative meaning while at the same time giving us the necessary degree of freedom to do so.

As we work out a consistent pattern in the text, we will find our "interpretation" threatened, as it were, by the presence of other possibilities of "interpretation," and so there arise new areas of indeterminacy (though we may only be dimly aware of them, if at all, as we are continually making "decisions" which will exclude them). In the course of a novel, for instance, we sometimes find that characters, events, and backgrounds seem to change their significance; what really happens is that the other "possibilities" begin to emerge more strongly, so that we become more directly aware of them. Indeed, it is this very shifting of perspectives that makes us feel that a novel is much more "true-to-life." Since it is we ourselves who establish the levels of interpretation and switch from one to another as we conduct our balancing operation, we ourselves impart to the text the dynamic lifelikeness which, in turn, enables us to absorb an unfamiliar experience into our personal world.

As we read, we oscillate to a greater or lesser degree between the building and the breaking of illusions. In a process of trial and error, we organize and reorganize the various data offered us by the text. These are the given factors, the fixed points on which we base our "interpretation," trying to fit them together in the way we think the author meant them to be fitted. "For to perceive, a beholder must *create* his own experience. And his creation must include relations comparable to those which the original producer underwent. They are not the same in any literal sense. But with the perceiver, as with the artist, there must be an ordering of the elements of the whole that is in form, although not in details, the same as the process of organization the creator of the work consciously experienced. Without an act of recreation the object is not perceived as a work of art."[20]

The act of recreation is not a smooth or continuous process, but one which, in its essence, relies on *interruptions* of the flow to render it efficacious. We look forward, we look back, we decide, we change our decisions, we form expectations, we are shocked by their nonfulfillment, we question, we muse, we accept, we reject; this is the dynamic process of recreation. This process is steered by two main structural components within the text: first, a repertoire of familiar literary patterns and recurrent literary themes, together with allusions to familiar social and historical contexts; second, techniques or strategies used to set the familiar against the unfamiliar. Elements of the repertoire are continually back-grounded or foregrounded with a resultant strategic overmagnification, trivialization, or even annihilation of the allusion. This defamiliarization of what the reader thought he recognized is bound to create a tension that will intensify his expectations as well as his distrust of those expecta-tions. Similarly, we may be confronted by narrative techniques that es-tablish links between things we find difficult to connect, so that we are forced to reconsider data we at first held to be perfectly straightforward. One need only mention the very simple trick, so often employed by novelists, whereby the author himself takes part in the narrative, thus establishing perspectives which would not have arisen out of the mere narration of the events described. Wayne Booth once called this the technique of the "unreliable narrator,"[21] to show the extent to which a literary device can counter expectations arising out of the literary text. The figure of the narrator may act in permanent opposition to the impressions we might otherwise form. The question then arises as to whether this strategy, opposing the formation of illusions, may be inte-grated into a consistent pattern, lying, as it were, a level deeper than our original impressions. We may find that our narrator, by opposing us, in fact turns us against him and thereby strengthens the illusion he appears to be out to destroy; alternatively, we may be so much in doubt that we begin to question all the processes that lead us to make interpretative decisions. Whatever the cause may be, we will find ourselves subjected to this same interplay of illusion-forming and illusion-breaking that makes reading essentially a recreative process.

We might take, as a simple illustration of this complex process, the incident in Joyce's *Ulysses* in which Bloom's cigar alludes to Ulysses's spear. The context (Bloom's cigar) summons up a particular element of the repertoire (Ulysses's spear); the narrative technique relates them to one another as if they were identical. How are we to "organize" these divergent elements, which, through the very fact that they are put to-gether, separate one element so clearly from the other? What are the prospects here for a consistent pattern? We might say that it is ironic—at least that is how many renowned Joyce readers have understood it.[22] In this case, irony would be the form of organization that integrates the material. But if this is so, what is the object of the irony? Ulysses's spear, or Bloom's cigar? The uncertainty surrounding this simple question al-ready puts a strain on the consistency we have established and, indeed, begins to puncture it, especially when other problems make themselves felt as regards the remarkable conjunction of spear and cigar. Various alternatives come to mind, but the variety alone is sufficient to leave one with the impression that the consistent pattern has been shattered. And even if, after all, one can still believe that irony holds the key to the mystery, this irony must be of a very strange nature; for the formulated text does not merely mean the opposite of what has been formulated. It may even mean something that cannot be formulated at all. The moment we try to impose a consistent pattern on the text, discrepancies are bound to arise. These are, as it were, the reverse side of the interpretative coin, an involuntary product of the process that creates discrepancies by trying to avoid them. And it is their very presence that draws us into the text, compelling us to conduct a creative examination not only of the text but also of ourselves.

This entanglement of the reader is, of course, vital to any kind of text, but in the literary text we have the strange situation that the reader cannot know what his participation actually entails. We know that we share in certain experiences, but we do not know what happens to us in the course of this process. This is why, when we have been particularly impressed by a book, we feel the need to talk about it; we do not want to get away from it by talking about it—we simply want to understand more clearly what it is in which we have been entangled. We have undergone an experience, and now we want to know consciously *what* we have experienced. Perhaps this is the prime usefulness of literary criticism—it helps to make conscious those aspects of the text which would otherwise remain concealed in the subconscious; it satisfies (or helps to satisfy) our desire to talk about what we have read.

The efficacy of a literary text is brought about by the apparent evocation and subsequent negation of the familiar. What at first seemed to be an affirmation of our assumptions leads to our own rejection of them, thus tending to prepare us for a re-orientation. And it is only when we have outstripped our preconceptions and left the shelter of the familiar that we are in a position to gather new experiences. As the literary text involves the reader in the formation of illusion and the simultaneous formation of the means whereby the illusion is punctured, reading reflects the process by which we gain experience. Once the reader is entangled, his own preconceptions are continually overtaken, so that the text becomes his "present" while his own ideas fade into the "past"; as soon as this happens he is open to the immediate experience of the text, which was impossible so long as his preconceptions were his "present."

V

In our analysis of the reading process so far, we have observed three important aspects that form the basis of the relationship between reader and text: the process of anticipation and retrospection, the consequent unfolding of the text as a living event, and the resultant impression of lifelikeness.

Any "living event" must, to a greater or lesser degree, remain open. In reading, this obliges the reader to seek continually for consistency, because only then can he close up situations and comprehend the unfamiliar. But consistency-building is itself a living process in which one is constantly forced to make selective decisions—and these decisions in their turn give a reality to the possibilities which they exclude, insofar as they may take effect as a latent disturbance of the consistency established. This is what causes the reader to be entangled in the text-"gestalt" that he himself has produced.

Through this entanglement the reader is bound to open himself up to the workings of the text and so leave behind his own preconceptions. This gives him the chance to have an experience in the way George Bernard Shaw once described it: "You have learnt something. That always feels at first as if you had lost something."[23] Reading reflects the structure of experience to the extent that we must suspend the ideas and attitudes that shape our own personality before we can experience the unfamiliar world of the literary text. But during this process, something happens to us.

This "something" needs to be looked at in detail, especially as the incorporation of the unfamiliar into our own range of experience has been to a certain extent obscured by an idea very common in literary discussion: namely, that the process of absorbing the unfamiliar is labeled as the *identification* of the reader with what he reads. Often the term "identification" is used as if it were an explanation, whereas in actual fact it is nothing more than a description. What is normally meant by "identification" is the establishment of affinities between oneself and someone outside oneself—a familiar ground on which we are able to experience the unfamiliar. The author's aim, though, is to convey the experience and, above all, an attitude toward that experience. Consequently, "identification" is not an end in itself, but a strategem by means of which the author stimulates attitudes in the reader.

This of course is not to deny that there does arise a form of participation as one reads; one is certainly drawn into the text in such a way that one has the feeling that there is no distance between oneself and the events described. This involvement is well summed up by the reaction of a critic to reading Charlotte Brontë's *Jane Eyre:* "We took up *Jane Eyre* one winter's evening, somewhat piqued at the extravagant commendations we had heard, and sternly resolved to be as critical as Croker. But as we read on we forgot both commendations and criticism, identified ourselves with Jane in all her troubles, and finally married Mr. Rochester about four in the morning."[24] The question is how and why did the critic identify himself with Jane?

In order to understand this "experience," it is well worth considering Georges Poulet's observations on the reading process. He says that books only take on their full existence in the reader.[25] It is true that they consist of ideas thought out by someone else, but in reading the reader becomes the subject that does the thinking. Thus there disappears the subject-object division that otherwise is a prerequisite for all knowledge and all observation, and the removal of this division puts reading in an apparently unique position as regards the possible absorption of new experiences. This may well be the reason why relations with the world of the literary text have so often been misinterpreted as identification. From the idea that in reading we must think the thoughts of someone else, Poulet draws the following conclusion: "Whatever I think is a part of *my* mental world. And yet here I am thinking a thought which manifestly belongs to another mental world, which is being thought in me just as though I did not exist. Already the notion is inconceivable and seems even more so if I reflect that, since every thought must have a subject to think it, this *thought* which is alien to me and yet in me, must also have in me a *subject* which is alien to me. . . . Whenever I read, I mentally pronounce an *I*, and yet the *I* which I pronounce is not myself."[26]

But for Poulet this idea is only part of the story. The strange subject that thinks the strange thought in the reader indicates the potential presence of the author, whose ideas can be "internalized" by the reader: "Such is the characteristic condition of every work which I summon back into existence by placing my consciousness at its disposal. I give it not only existence, but awareness of existence."[27] This would mean that consciousness forms the point at which author and reader converge, and at the same time it would result in the cessation of the temporary self-alienation that occurs to the reader when his consciousness brings to life the ideas formulated by the author. This process gives rise to a form of communication which, however, according to Poulet, is dependent on two conditions: the life-story of the author must be shut out of the work and the individual disposition of the reader must be shut out of the act of reading. Only then can the thoughts of the author take place subjectively in the reader, who thinks what he is not. It follows that the work itself must be thought of as a consciousness, because only in this way is there an adequate basis for the author-reader relationship—a relationship that can only come about through the negation of the author's own life-story and the reader's own disposition. This conclusion is actually drawn by Poulet when he describes the work as the self-presentation or materialization of consciousness: "And so I ought not to hesitate to recognize that so long as it is animated by this vital inbreathing inspired by the act of reading, a work of literature becomes (at the expense of the reader whose own life it suspends) a sort of human being, that it is a mind conscious of itself and constituting itself in me as the subject of its own objects."[28] Even though it is difficult to follow such a substantialist conception of the consciousness that constitutes itself in the literary work, there are, nevertheless, certain points in Poulet's argument that are worth holding onto. But they should be developed along somewhat different lines.

If reading removes the subject-object division that constitutes all perception, it follows that the reader will be "occupied" by the thoughts of the author, and these in their turn will cause the drawing of new "boundaries." Text and reader no longer confront each other as object and subject, but instead the "division" takes place within the reader himself. In thinking the thoughts of another, his own individuality temporarily recedes into the background, since it is supplanted by these alien thoughts, which now become the theme on which his attention is focussed. As we read, there occurs an artificial division of our personality, because we take as a theme for ourselves something that we are not. Consequently when reading we operate on different levels. For although we may be thinking the thoughts of someone else, what we are will not disappear completely—it will merely remain a more or less powerful virtual force. Thus, in reading there are these two levels—the alien "me" and the real, virtual "me"—which are never completely cut off from each other. Indeed, we can only make someone else's thoughts into an absorbing theme for ourselves, provided the virtual background of our own personality can adapt to it. Every text we read draws a different boundary within our personality, so that the virtual background (the real "me") will take on a different form, according to the theme of the text concerned. This is inevitable, if only for the fact that the relationship between alien theme and virtual background is what makes it possible for the unfamiliar to be understood.

In this context there is a revealing remark made by D. W. Harding, arguing against the idea of identification with what is read: "What is sometimes called wish-fulfilment in novels and plays can ... more plausibly be described as wish-formulation or the definition of desires. The cultural levels at which it works may vary widely; the process is the same.... It seems nearer the truth ... to say that fictions contribute to defining the reader's or spectator's values, and perhaps stimulating his desires, rather than to suppose that they gratify desire by some mechanism of vicarious experience."[29] In the act of reading, having to think something that we have not yet experienced does not mean only being in a position to conceive or even understand it; it also means that such acts of conception are possible and successful to the degree that they lead to something being formulated in us. For someone else's thoughts can only take a form in our consciousness if, in the process, our unformulated faculty for deciphering those thoughts is brought into play—a faculty which, in the act of deciphering, also formulates itself. Now since this formulation is carried out on terms set by someone else, whose thoughts are the theme of our reading, it follows that the formulation of our faculty for deciphering cannot be along our own lines of orientation.

Herein lies the dialectical structure of reading. The need to decipher gives us the chance to formulate our own deciphering capacity—i.e., we bring to the fore an element of our being of which we are not directly conscious. The production of the meaning of literary texts—which we discussed in connection with forming the "gestalt" of the text—does not merely entail the discovery of the unformulated, which can then be taken over by the active imagination of the reader; it also entails the possibility that we may formulate ourselves and so discover what had previously seemed to elude our consciousness. These are the ways in which reading literature gives us the chance to formulate the unformulated.

Translated by Catherine Macksey and Richard Macksey

Notes

1. Cf. Roman Ingarden, *Vom Erkennen des literarischen Kunstwerks* (Tübingen: Niemeyer, 1968), pp. 49 ff.

2. For a detailed discussion of this term see Roman Ingarden, *Das literarische Kunstwerk* (Tübingen: Niemeyer, 1960), pp. 270 ff.

3. Laurence Sterne, *Tristram Shandy* (London: Dent, 1956), p. 79.

4. Virginia Woolf, *The Common Reader*, First Series (London: Hogarth, 1957), p. 174.

5. Ingarden, *Vom Erkennen des literarischen Kunstwerks*, p. 29.

6. Edmund Husserl, *Zur Phänomenologie des inneren Zeitbewusstseins, Gesammelte Werke*, 22 vols. (The Hague: Nijhoff, 1966), 10:52.

7. Ingarden, *Vom Erkennen des literarischen Kunstwerks*, p. 32.

8. For a more detailed discussion of the function of "gaps" in literary texts see Wolfgang Iser, "Indeterminacy and the Reader's Response in Prose Fiction," in *Aspects of Narrative*, ed. J. Hillis Miller (New York: Columbia University Press, 1971), pp. 1–45.

9. Maurice Merleau-Ponty, *Phenomenology of Perception*, trans. Colin Smith (New York: Humanities Press, 1962), pp. 219–21.

10. Gilbert Ryle, *The Concept of Mind* (Harmondsworth, Great Britain: Penguin, 1968), p. 255.

11. Cf. Iser, "Indeterminacy," pp. 11 ff., 42ff.

12. E. H. Gombrich, *Art and Illusion: A Study in the Psychology of Pictoral Representation* (London: Phaidon Press, 1962), p. 204.

13. Louis O. Mink, "History and Fiction as Modes of Comprehension," *New Literary History* 1 (Spring, 1970):553.

14. Gombrich, *Art and Illusion*, p. 278.

15. Northrop Frye, *Anatomy of Criticism* (New York: Atheneum, 1967), pp. 169 ff.

16. Walter Pater, *Appreciations, With an Essay on Style* (London: Macmillan and Co., 1895), p. 15.

17. Gombrich, *Art and Illusion,* p. 54.

18. Ibid., p. 5.

19. B. Ritchie, "The Formal Structure of the Aesthetic Object," in *The Problems of Aesthetics,* ed. Eliseo Vivas and Murray Krieger (New York: Holt, Rinehart and Winston, 1965), pp. 230 ff.

20. John Dewey, *Art as Experience* (New York: Capricorn Books, 1958), p. 54.

21. Cf. Wayne C. Booth, *The Rhetoric of Fiction* (Chicago: University of Chicago Press, 1961), pp. 211 ff., 339 ff.

22. Richard Ellmann, "Ulysses, The Divine Nobody," in *Twelve Original Essays on Great English Novels,* ed. Charles Shapiro (Detroit: Wayne State University Press, 1960), p. 247, classified this particular allusion as "Mock-heroic."

23. George Bernard Shaw, *Major Barbara* (London: Penguin, 1964), p. 316.

24. William George Clark, review article in *Fraser's* (December, 1849), p. 692, quoted by Kathleen Tillotson, *Novels of the Eighteen-Forties* (Oxford: Clarendon Press, 1961), pp. 19 ff.

25. Cf. Georges Poulet, "Phenomenology of Reading," *New Literary History* 1 (Autumn 1969): 54.

26. Ibid., p. 56.

27. Ibid., p. 59.

28. Ibid.

29. D. W. Harding, "Psychological Processes in the Reading of Fiction," *British Journal of Aesthetics* 2 (April 1962): 144.

6

LITERATURE IN THE READER: AFFECTIVE STYLISTICS*

Stanley E. Fish

Meaning as Event

If at this moment someone were to ask, "what are you doing?" you
might reply, "I am reading," and thereby acknowledge the fact that
reading is an activity, something *you do*. No one would argue that the act
of reading can take place in the absence of someone who reads—how can
you tell the dance from the dancer?—but curiously enough when it
comes time to make analytical statements about the end product of reading (meaning or understanding), the reader is usually forgotten or ignored. Indeed in recent literary history he has been excluded by legislation. I refer, of course, to the *ex cathedra* pronouncements of Wimsatt
and Beardsley in their enormously influential article "The Affective Fallacy":

> The Affective Fallacy is a confusion between the poem and its *results* (what it
> *is* and what it *does*). . . . It begins by trying to derive the standards of criticism
> from the psychological effects of the poem and ends in impressionism and
> relativism. The outcome . . . is that the poem itself, as an object of specifically
> critical judgment, tends to disappear.[1]

In time, I shall return to these arguments, not so much to refute them as
to affirm and embrace them; but I would first like to demonstrate the
explanatory power of a method of analysis which takes the reader, as an
actively mediating presence, fully into account, and which, therefore,
has as its focus the "psychological effects" of the utterance. And I would

*This essay first appeared in *New Literary History* 2, no. 1 (Autumn 1970): 123-62.
Although I would no longer stand behind its every statement, it is here reprinted in full,
except for a small section on the *Phaedrus.*—Author's note. [The essay is reprinted as the
Appendix to *Self-Consuming Artifacts* (Berkeley: University of California Press, 1972)—*Ed.*]

like to begin with a sentence that does not open itself up to the questions
we usually ask.

> That Judas perished by hanging himself, there is no certainty in Scripture:
> though in one place it seems to affirm it, and by a doubtful word hath given
> occasion to translate it; yet in another place, in a more punctual description,
> it maketh it improbable, and seems to overthrow it.

Ordinarily, one would begin by asking "what does this sentence
mean?" or "what is it about?" or "what is it saying?" all of which preserve
the objectivity of the utterance. For my purposes, however, this particular sentence has the advantage of not saying anything. That is, you can't
get a fact out of it which could serve as an answer to any one of these
questions. Of course, this difficulty is itself a fact—of response; and it
suggests, to me at least, that what makes problematical sense as a statement makes perfect sense as a strategy, as an action made upon a reader
rather than as a container from which a reader extracts a message. The
strategy or action here is one of progressive decertainizing. Simply by
taking in the first clause of the sentence, the reader commits himself to
its assertion, "that Judas perished by hanging himself" (in constructions
of this type "that" is understood to be shorthand for "the *fact* that"). This
is not so much a conscious decision as it is an anticipatory adjustment to
his projection of the sentence's future contours. He knows (without giving cognitive form to his knowledge) that this first clause is preliminary
to some larger assertion (it is a "ground") and he must be in control of it
if he is to move easily and confidently through what follows; and in the
context of this "knowledge," he is prepared, again less than consciously,
for any one of several constructions:

> That Judas perished by hanging himself, *is* (an example for us all).
> That Judas perished by hanging himself, *shows* (how conscious he was of
> the enormity of his sin).
> That Judas perished by hanging himself, *should* (give us pause).

The range of these possibilities (and there are, of course, more than
I have listed) narrows considerably as the next three words are read,
"there is no." At this point, the reader is expecting, and even predicting,
a single word—"doubt"; but instead he finds "certainty"; and at that
moment the status of the fact that had served as his point of reference
becomes *un*certain. (It is nicely ironic that the appearance of "certainty"
should be the occasion for doubt, whereas the word "doubt" would have
contributed to the reader's certainty.) As a result, the terms of the
reader's relationship to the sentence undergo a profound change. He is
suddenly involved in a different kind of activity. Rather than following
an argument along a well-lighted path (a light, after all, has gone *out*), he
is now looking for one. The natural impulse in a situation like this, either

in life or in literature, is to go forward in the hope that what has been obscured will again become clear; but in this case going forward only intensifies the reader's sense of disorientation. The prose is continually opening, but then closing, on the possibility of verification in one direction or another. There are two vocabularies in the sentence; one holds out the promise of a clarification—"place," "affirm," "place," "punctual," "overthrow"—while the other continually defaults on that promise—"Though," "doubtful," "yet," "improbable," "seems"; and the reader is passed back and forth between them and between the alternatives—that Judas did or did not perish by hanging himself—which are still suspended (actually it is the reader who is suspended) when the sentence ends (trails off? gives up?). The indeterminateness of this experience is compounded by a superfluity of pronouns. It becomes increasingly difficult to tell what "it" refers to, and if the reader takes the trouble to retrace his steps, he is simply led back to "that Judas perished by hanging himself"; in short, he exchanges an indefinite pronoun for an even less definite (that is, certain) assertion.

Whatever is persuasive and illuminating about this analysis (and it is by no means exhaustive) is the result of my substituting for one question—what does this sentence mean?—another, more operational question—what does this sentence do? And what the sentence does is give the reader something and then take it away, drawing him on with the unredeemed promise of its return. An observation about the sentence as an utterance—its refusal to yield a declarative statement—has been transformed into an account of its experience (not being able to get a fact out of it). It is no longer an object, a thing-in-itself, but an *event*, something that *happens* to, and with the participation of, the reader. And it is this event, this happening—all of it and not anything that could be said about it or any information one might take away from it—that is, I would argue, the *meaning* of the sentence. (Of course, in this case there is no information to take away.)

This is a provocative thesis whose elaboration and defense will be the concern of the following pages, but before proceeding to it, I would like to examine another utterance which also (conveniently) says nothing:

> Nor did they not perceive the evil plight.

The first word of this line from *Paradise Lost* (I, 335) generates a rather precise (if abstract) expectation of what will follow: a negative assertion which will require for its completion a subject and a verb. There are then two "dummy" slots in the reader's mind waiting to be filled. This expectation is strengthened (if only because it is not challenged) by the auxiliary "did" and the pronoun "they." Presumably, the verb is not far behind. But in its place the reader is presented with a second negative, one that cannot be accommodated within his projection of the utterance's form. His progress through the line is halted and he is forced to come to terms with the intrusive (because unexpected) "not." In effect what the reader *does,* or is forced to do, at this point, is ask a question—did they or didn't they?—and in search of an answer he either rereads, in which case he simply repeats the sequence of mental operations, or goes forward, in which case he finds the anticipated verb, but in either case the syntactical uncertainty remains unresolved.

It could be objected that the solution to the difficulty is simply to invoke the rule of the double negative; one cancels the other and the "correct" reading is therefore "they did perceive the evil plight." But however satisfactory this may be in terms of the internal logic of grammatical utterances (and even in those terms there are problems),[2] it has nothing to do with the logic of the reading experience or, I would insist, with its meaning. That experience is a temporal one, and in the course of it the two negatives combine, not to produce an affirmative, but to prevent the reader from making the simple (declarative) sense which would be the goal of a logical analysis. To clean the line up is to take from it its most prominent and important effect—the suspension of the reader between the alternatives its syntax momentarily offers. What is a problem if the line is considered as an object, a thing-in-itself, becomes a *fact* when it is regarded as an occurrence. The reader's inability to tell whether or not "they" do perceive and his involuntary question (or its psychological equivalent) are events in his encounter with the line, and as events they are part of the line's *meaning,* even though they take place in the mind, not on the page. Subsequently, we discover that the answer to the question "did they or didn't they," is, "they did and they didn't." Milton is exploiting (and calling our attention to) the two senses of "perceive": they (the fallen angels) do perceive the fire, the pain, the gloom; physically they see it; however they are blind to the moral significance of their situation; and in that sense they do not perceive the evil plight in which they are. But that is another story.

Underlying these two analyses is a method, rather simple in concept, but complex (or at least complicated) in execution. The concept is simply the rigorous and disinterested asking of the question, what does this word, phrase, sentence, paragraph, chapter, novel, play, poem, *do?;* and the execution involves *an analysis of the developing responses of the reader in relation to the words as they succeed one another in time.* Every word in this statement bears a special emphasis. The analysis must be of the developing responses to distinguish it from the atomism of much stylistic criticism. A reader's response to the fifth word in a line or sentence is to a large extent the product of his responses to words one, two, three, and four. And by response, I intend more than the range of feelings (what Wimsatt and Beardsley call "the purely affective reports"). The category of response includes any and all of the activities provoked by a string of words: the projection of syntactical and/or lexical probabilities; their subsequent occurrence or non-occurrence; attitudes toward persons, or things, or ideas referred to; the reversal or questioning of those attitudes; and much more. Obviously, this imposes a great burden on the analyst who in his observations on any one moment in the reading experience must take into account all that has happened (in the reader's mind) at previous moments, each of which was in its turn subject to the accumulating pressures of its predecessors. (He must also take into account influences and pressures predating the actual reading experience—questions of genre, history, etc.—questions we shall consider later.) All of this is included in the phrase "in time." The basis of the method is a consideration of the *temporal* flow of the reading experience, and it is assumed that the reader responds in terms of that flow and not to the whole utterance. That is, in an utterance of any length, there is a point at which the reader has taken in only the first word, and then the second, and then the third, and so on, and the report of what happens to the reader is always a report of what has happened *to that point.* (The report includes the reader's set toward future experiences, but not those experiences.)

The importance of this principle is illustrated when we reverse the first two clauses of the Judas sentence: "There is no certainty that Judas perished by hanging himself." Here the status of the assertion is never in doubt because the reader knows from the beginning that it is doubtful; he is given a perspective from which to view the statement and that perspective is confirmed rather than challenged by what follows; even the confusion of pronouns in the second part of the sentence will not be disturbing to him, because it can easily be placed in the context of his initial response. There is no difference in these two sentences in the information conveyed (or not conveyed), or in the lexical and syntactical components,[3] only in the way these are received. But that one difference makes *all* the difference—between an uncomfortable, unsettling experience in which the gradual dimming of a fact is attended by a failure in perception, and a wholly self-satisfying one in which an uncertainty is comfortably certain, and the reader's confidence in his own powers remains unshaken, because he is always in control. It is, I insist, a difference in meaning.

The results (I will later call them advantages) of this method are fairly, though not exhaustively, represented in my two examples. Essentially what the method does is *slow down* the reading experience so that "events" one does not notice in normal time, but which do occur, are brought before our analytical attentions. It is as if a slow-motion camera with an automatic stop action effect were recording our linguistic experiences and presenting them to us for viewing. Of course the value of such a procedure is predicated on the idea of *meaning as an event,* something that is happening between the words and in the reader's mind, something not visible to the naked eye, but which can be made visible (or at least palpable) by the regular introduction of a "searching" question (what does this do?). It is more usual to assume that meaning is a function of the utterance, and to equate it with the information given (the message) or the attitude expressed. That is, the components of an utterance are considered either in relation to each other or to a state of affairs in the outside world, or to the state of mind of the speaker-author. In any and all of these variations, meaning is located (presumed to be imbedded) *in* the utterance, and the apprehension of meaning is an act of extraction.[4] In short, there is little sense of process and even less of the reader's actualizing participation in that process.

This concentration on the verbal object as a thing in itself and as a repository of meaning has many consequences, theoretical and practical. First of all, it creates a whole class of utterances, which, because of their alleged transparency, are declared to be uninteresting as objects of analysis. Sentences or fragments of sentences that immediately "make sense" (a deeply revealing phrase if one thinks about it) are examples of ordinary language; they are neutral and styleless statements, "simply" referring, or "simply" reporting. But the application to such utterances of the question "what does it do?" (which assumes that something is *always* happening) reveals that a great deal is going on in their production and comprehension (*every linguistic experience is affecting and pressuring*), although most of it is going on so close up, at such a basic, "preconscious" level of experience, that we tend to overlook it. Thus the utterance (written or spoken) "there is a chair" is at once understood as the report either of an existing state of affairs or of an act of perception (I see a chair). In either frame of reference, it makes immediate sense. To my mind, however, what is interesting about the utterance is the *sub rosa* message it puts out *by virtue of* its easy comprehensibility. Because it gives information directly and simply, it asserts (silently, but effectively) the "givability," directly and simply, of information; and it is thus an extension of the ordering operation we perform on experience whenever it is filtered through our temporal-spatial consciousness. In short, it *makes* sense, in exactly the way we make (i.e., manufacture) sense of whatever, if anything, exists outside us; and by making easy sense it tells us that sense can be easily made and that we are capable of easily making it. A whole document consisting of such utterances—a chemistry text or a telephone book—will be telling us that all the time; and *that*, rather than any reportable "content," will be its *meaning*. Such language can be called "ordinary" only because it confirms and reflects our ordinary understanding of the world and our position in it; but for precisely that reason it is *extra*ordinary (unless we accept a naive epistemology which grants us unmediated access to reality) and to leave it unanalyzed is to risk missing much of what happens—to us and through us—when we read and (or so we think) understand.

In short, the problem is simply that most methods of analysis operate at so high a level of abstraction that the basic data of the *meaning experience* are slighted and/or obscured. In the area of specifically literary studies, the effects of a naive theory of utterance meaning and of its attendant assumption of ordinary language can be seen in what is acknowledged to be the sorry state of the criticism of the novel and of prose in general. This is usually explained with reference to a distinction between prose and poetry, which is actually a distinction between ordinary language and poetic language. Poetry, it is asserted, is characterized by a high incidence of deviance from normal syntactical and lexical habits. It therefore offers the analyst-critic a great many points of departure. Prose, on the other hand (except for Baroque eccentrics like Thomas Browne and James Joyce) is, well, just prose, and just there. It is this helplessness before all but the most spectacular effects that I would remedy; although in one way the two examples with which this essay began were badly chosen, since they were analyses of utterances that are obviously and problematically deviant. This, of course, was a ploy to gain your attention. Assuming that I now have it, let me insist that the method shows to best advantage when it is applied to unpromising material. Consider for example this sentence (actually part of a sentence) from Pater's "Conclusion" to *The Renaissance,* which, while it is hardly the stuff of everyday conversation, does not, at first sight, afford much scope for the critic's analytical skill:

> That clear perpetual outline of face and limb is but an image of ours.

What can one say about a sentence like this? The analyst of style would, I fear, find it distressingly straightforward and nondeviant, a simple declarative of the form X is Y. And if he were by chance drawn to it, he would not be likely to pay very much attention to the first word—"That." It is simply there. But of course it is not simply there; it is *actively* there, doing something, and what that something is can be discovered by asking the question "what does it do?" The answer is obvious, right there in front of our noses, although we may not see it until we ask the question. "That" is a demonstrative, a word that points *out*, and as one takes it *in*, a sense of its referent (yet unidentified) is established. Whatever "that" is, it is outside, at a distance from the observer-reader; it is "pointable to" (pointing is what the word "that" does), something of substance and solidity. In terms of the reader's response, "that" generates an expectation that impels him forward, the expectation of finding out *what* "that" is. The word and its effect are the basic data of the meaning experience and they will direct our description of that experience because they direct the reader.

The adjective "clear" works in two ways; it promises the reader that when "that" appears, he will be able to see it easily, and, conversely, that it can be easily seen. "Perpetual" stabilizes the visibility of "that" even *before* it is seen and "outline" gives it potential form, while at the same time raising a question. That question—outline of what?—is obligingly answered by the phrase "of face and limb," which, in effect, fills the outline in. By the time the reader reaches the declarative verb "is"— which sets the seal on the objective reality of what has preceded it—he is fully and securely oriented in a world of perfectly discerned objects and perfectly discerning observers, of whom he is one. But then the sentence turns on the reader, and takes away the world it has itself created. With "but" the easy progress through the sentence is impeded (it is a split second before one realizes that "but" has the force of "only"); the declarative force of "is" is weakened and the status of the firmly drawn outline the reader has been pressured to accept is suddenly uncertain; "image" resolves that uncertainty, but in the direction of insubstantiality; and the now blurred form disappears altogether when the phrase "of ours" collapses the distinction between the reader and that which is (or was) "without" (Pater's own word). Now you see it (that), now you don't. Pater giveth and Pater taketh away. (Again this description of the reader's experience is an analysis of the sentence's meaning and if you were to ask, "but, what does it mean?" I would simply repeat the description.)

What is true of this sentence is true, I believe, of much of what we hold ourselves responsible for as critics and teachers of literature. There is more to it, that is, to its experience, than meets the casual eye. What is required, then, is a method, a machine if you will, which in its operation makes observable, or at least accessible, what goes on below the level of self-conscious response. Everyone would admit that something "funny" happens in the "Judas" sentence from Browne's *Religio Medici* and that there is a difficulty built into the reading and understanding of the line from *Paradise Lost;* but there is a tendency to assume that the Pater sentence is a simple assertion (whatever that is). It is, of course, nothing of the kind. In fact it is not an assertion at all, although (the promise of) an assertion is one of its components. It is an experience; it occurs; it does something; it makes us do something. Indeed, I would go so far as to say, in direct contradiction of Wimsatt-Beardsley, that what it does is what it means.

The Logic and Structure of Response

What I am suggesting is that there is no direct relationship between the meaning of a sentence (paragraph, novel, poem) and what its words mean. Or, to put the matter less provocatively, the information an utter-

ance gives, its message, is a constituent of, but certainly not to be identified with, its meaning. It is the experience of an utterance—*all* of it and
not anything that could be said about it, including anything I could
say—that *is* its meaning.

It follows, then, that it is impossible to mean the same thing in two
(or more) different ways, although we tend to think that it happens all
the time. We do this by substituting for our immediate linguistic experience an interpretation or abstraction of it, in which "it" is inevitably
compromised. We contrive to forget what has happened to us in our life
with language, removing ourselves as far as possible from the linguistic
event before making a statement about it. Thus we say, for example, that
"the book of the father" and "the father's book" mean the same thing,
forgetting that "father" and "book" occupy different positions of emphasis in our different experiences; and as we progress in this forgetting, we become capable of believing that sentences as different as these
are equivalent in meaning:

> This fact is concealed by the influence of language, moulded by science,
> which foists on us exact concepts as though they represented the immediate
> deliverances of experience.
>
> A. N. Whitehead

> And if we continue to dwell in thought on this world, not of objects in the
> solidity with which language invests them, but of impressions, unstable,
> flickering, inconsistent, which burn and are extinguished with our con-
> sciousness of them, it contracts still further.
>
> Walter Pater

It is (literally) tempting to say that these sentences make the same
point: that language which pretends to precision operates to obscure the
flux and disorder of actual experience. And of course they do, if one
considers them at a high enough level of generality. But as individual
experiences through which a reader lives, they are not alike at all, and
neither, therefore, are their meanings.

To take the Whitehead sentence first, it simply doesn't mean what it
says; for as the reader moves through it, he experiences the stability of
the world whose existence it supposedly denies. The word "fact" itself
makes an exact concept out of the idea of inexactness; and by referring
backward to find its referent—"the radically untidy ill-adjusted character of . . . experience"—the reader performs the characteristic action required of him by this sentence, the fixing of things in their places.

There is nothing untidy either in the sentence or in our experience
of it. Each clause is logically related to its predecessors and prepares the
way for what follows; and since our active attention is required only at
the points of relation, the sentence is divided *by us* into a succession of
discrete areas, each of which is dominated by the language of certainty.

Even the phrase "as though they represented" falls into this category, since its stress falls on "they represented" which then thrusts us forward to the waiting "deliverances of experience." In short, the sentence, in its action upon us, declares the tidy well-ordered character of actual experience, and that is its meaning.

At first the Pater sentence is self-subverting in the same way. The least forceful word in its first two clauses is "not," which is literally overwhelmed by the words that surround it—"world," "objects," "solidity," "language"; and by the time the reader reaches the "but" in "but of impressions," he finds himself inhabiting (dwelling in) a "world" of fixed and "solid" objects. It is of course a world made up of words, constructed in large part by the reader himself as he performs grammatical actions which reinforce the stability of its phenomena. By referring backwards from "them" to "objects," the reader accords "objects" a place in the sentence (whatever can be referred back to must be somewhere) and in his mind. In the second half of the sentence, however, this same world is unbuilt. There is still a backward dependence to the reading experience, but the point of reference is the word "impressions"; and the series which follows it—"unstable," "flickering," "inconsistent"—serves only to accentuate its *in*stability. Like Whitehead, Pater perpetrates the very deception he is warning against; but this is only one part of his strategy. The other is to break down (extinguish) the coherence of the illusion he has created. Each successive stage of the sentence is less exact (in Whitehead's terms) than its predecessors, because at each successive stage the reader is given less and less to hold on to; and when the corporeality of "this world" has wasted away to an "it" ("it contracts still further"), he is left with nothing at all.

One could say, I suppose, that at the least these two sentences gesture toward the same insight; but even this minimal statement makes me uneasy, because "insight" is another word that implies "there it is, I've got it." And this is exactly the difference between the two sentences: Whitehead lets you get "it" ("the neat, trim, tidy, exact world"), while Pater gives you the experience of having "it" melt under your feet. It is only when one steps back from the sentences that they are in any way equivalent; and stepping back is what an analysis in terms of doings and happenings does not allow.

The analysis of the Pater sentence illustrates another feature of the method, its independence of linguistic logic. If a casual reader were asked to point out the most important word in the second clause—"not of objects in the solidity with which language invests them"—he would probably answer "not," because as a logical marker "not" controls everything that follows it. But as one component in an experience, it is hardly controlling at all; for as the clause unfolds, "not" has less and less a claim on our attention and memories; working against it, and finally overwhelming it, as we saw, is an unbroken succession of more forceful words. My point, of course, is that in an analysis of the sentence as a thing in itself, consisting of words arranged in syntactological relationships, "not" would figure prominently, while in an experiential analysis it is noted chiefly for its weakness.

The case is even clearer and perhaps more interesting in this sentence from one of Donne's sermons:

> And therefore as the mysteries of our religion, are not the objects of our reason, but by faith we rest on God's decree and purpose, (it is so, O God, because it is thy will it should be so) so God's decrees are ever to be considered in the manifestation thereof.

Here the "not"—again logically controlling—is subverted by the very construction in which it is imbedded; for that construction, unobtrusively, but nonetheless effectively, pressures the reader to perform exactly those mental operations whose propriety the statement of the sentence—what it is saying—is challenging. That is, a paraphrase of the material before the parenthesis might read—"Matters of faith and religion are not the objects of our reason"; but the simple act of taking in the words "And therefore" involves us unavoidably in reasoning about matters of faith and religion; in fact so strong is the pull of these words that our primary response to this part of the sentence is one of anticipation; we are waiting for a "so" clause to complete the logically based sequence begun by "And therefore as." But when that "so" appears, it is not at all what we had expected, for it is the "so" of divine fiat—it is so O God because it is thy will it should be so—of a causality more real than any that can be observed in nature or described in a natural (human) language. The speaker, however, completes his "explaining" and "organizing" statement as if its silent claim to be a window on reality were still unquestioned. As a result the reader is alerted to the inadequacy of the very process in which he is (through the syntax) involved, and at the same time he accepts the necessity, for limited human beings, of proceeding within the now discredited assumptions of that process.

Of course, a formalist analysis of this sentence would certainly have discovered the tension between the two "so's," one a synonym for therefore, the other shorthand for "so be it," and might even have gone on to suggest that the relationship between them is a mirror of the relationship between the mysteries of faith and the operations of reason. I doubt, however, that a formalist analysis would have brought us to the point where we could see the sentence, and the mode of discourse it represents, as a self-deflating joke ("thereof" mocks "therefore"), to which the reader responds and of which he is a victim. In short, and to repeat myself, to consider the utterance apart from the consciousness receiving it is to risk missing a great deal of what is going on. It is a risk which analysis in terms of "doings and happenings"[5] works to minimize.

Another advantage of the method is its ability to deal with sentences (and works) that don't mean anything, in the sense of not making sense. Literature, it is often remarked (either in praise or with contempt), is largely made up of such utterances. (It is an interesting comment, both on Dylan Thomas and the proponents of a deviation theory of poetic language, that their examples so often are taken from his work.) In an experiential analysis, the sharp distinction between sense and nonsense, with the attendant value judgments and the talk about truth content, is blurred, because the place where sense is made or not made is the reader's mind rather than the printed page or the space between the covers of a book. For an example, I turn once again, and for the last time, to Pater: "This at least of flame-like, our life has, that it is but the concurrence, renewed from moment to moment, of forces parting sooner or later on their ways."

This sentence deliberately frustrates the reader's natural desire to organize the particulars it offers. One can see, for instance, how different its experience would be if "concurrence of forces" were substituted for "concurrence, renewed from moment to moment, of forces." The one allows and encourages the formation of a physical image which has a spatial reality; the mind imagines (pictures) separate and distinct forces converging, in an orderly fashion, on a center where they form a new, but still recognizable and manageable (in a mental sense) force; the other determinedly prevents that image from forming. Before the reader can respond fully to "concurrence," "renewed" stops him by making the temporal status of the motion unclear. Has the concurrence already taken place? Is it taking place now? Although "from moment to moment" answers these questions, it does so at the expense of the assumptions behind them; the phrase leaves no time for anything so formal and chartable as a "process." For "a moment," at "of forces," there is a coming together; but in the next moment, the moment when the reader takes in "parting," they separate. Or do they? "Sooner or later" upsets this new attempt to find pattern and direction in "our life" and the reader is once more disoriented, spatially and temporally. The final deterrent to order is the plural "ways," which prevents the mind's eye from traveling down a single path and insists on the haphazardness and randomness of whatever it is that happens sooner or later.

Of course this reading of the sentence (that is, of its effects) ignores its status as a logical utterance. "Concurrence, renewed from moment to moment, of forces" is meaningless as a statement corresponding to a state of affairs in the "real" world; but its refusal to mean in that discursive way creates the experience that is its meaning; and an analysis of that experience rather than of logical content is able to make sense of one kind—experiential sense—out of nonsense.

A similar (and saving) operation can be performed on units larger than the sentence. . . . Whatever the size of the unit, the focus of the method remains the reader's experience of it, and the mechanism of the method is the magic question, "what does this ——— do?" Answering it, of course, is more difficult than it would be for a single sentence. More variables creep in, more responses and more different kinds of responses have to be kept track of; there are more contexts which regulate and modulate the temporal flow of the reading experience. Some of these problems will be considered below. For the present, let me say that I have usually found that what might be called the basic experience of a work (do *not* read basic meaning) occurs at every level. . . .

The Affective Fallacy Fallacy

In the preceding pages I have argued the case for a method of analysis which focuses on the reader rather than on the artifact, and in what remains of this essay I would like to consider some of the more obvious objections to that method. The chief objection, of course, is that affective criticism leads one away from the "thing itself" in all its solidity to the inchoate impressions of a variable and various reader. This argument has several dimensions to it, and will require a multidirectional answer.

First, the charge of impressionism has been answered, I hope, by some of my sample analyses. If anything, the discriminations required and yielded by the method are too fine for even the most analytical of tastes. This is in large part because in the category of response I include not only "tears, prickles," and "other psychological symptoms,"[6] but all the precise mental operations involved in reading, including the formulation of complete thoughts, the performing (and regretting) of acts of judgment, the following and making of logical sequences; and also because my insistence on the cumulative pressures of the reading experience puts restrictions on the possible responses to a word or a phrase.

The larger objection remains. Even if the reader's responses can be described with some precision, why bother with them, since the more palpable objectivity of the text is immediately available ("the poem itself, as an object of specifically critical judgment, tends to disappear"). My reply to this is simple. The objectivity of the text is an illusion, and moreover, a dangerous illusion, because it is so physically convincing. The illusion is one of self-sufficiency and completeness. A line of print or a page or a book is so obviously *there*—it can be handled, photographed, or put away—that it seems to be the sole repository of whatever value and meaning we associate with it. (I wish the pronoun could be avoided, but in a way *it* makes my point.) This is, of course, the unspoken assumption behind the word "content." The line or page or book *contains*—everything.

The great merit (from this point of view) of kinetic art is that it forces you to be aware of "it" as a changing object—and therefore no "object" at all—and also to be aware of yourself as correspondingly changing. Kinetic art does not lend itself to a static interpretation because it refuses to stay still and doesn't let you stay still either. In its operation it makes inescapable the actualizing role of the observer. Literature is a kinetic art, but the physical form it assumes prevents us from seeing its essential nature, even though we so experience it. The availability of a book to the hand, its presence on a shelf, its listing in a library catalogue—all of these encourage us to think of it as a stationary object. Somehow when we put a book down, we forget that while we were reading, *it* was moving (pages turning, lines receding into the past) and forget too that *we* were moving with it.

A criticism that regards "the poem itself as an object of specifically critical judgment" extends this forgetting into a principle; it transforms a temporal experience into a spatial one; it steps back and in a single glance takes in a whole (sentence, page, work) which the reader knows (if at all) only bit by bit, moment by moment. It is a criticism that takes as its (self-restricted) area the physical dimensions of the artifact and within these dimensions it marks out beginnings, middles, and ends, discovers frequency distributions, traces out patterns of imagery, diagrams strata of complexity (vertical of course), all without ever taking into account the relationship (if any) between its data and their affective force. Its question is what goes into the work rather than what does the work go into. It is "objective" in exactly the wrong way, because it determinedly ignores what is objectively true about the *activity* of reading. Analysis in terms of doings and happenings is on the other hand truly objective because it recognizes the fluidity, "the movingness," of the meaning experience and because it directs us to where the action is—the active and activating consciousness of the reader.

But what reader? When I talk about the responses of "the reader," am I not really talking about myself, and making myself into a surrogate for all the millions of readers who are not me at all? Yes and no. Yes in the sense that in no two of us are the responding mechanisms exactly alike. No, if one argues that because of the uniqueness of the individual, generalization about response is impossible. It is here that the method can accommodate the insights of modern linguistics, especially the idea of "linguistic competence," "the idea that it is possible to characterize a linguistic system that every speaker shares."[7] This characterization, if it were realized, would be a "competence model," corresponding more or less to the internal mechanisms which allow us to process (understand) and produce sentences that we have never before encountered. It would be a spatial model in the sense that it would reflect a system of rules preexisting, and indeed making possible, any actual linguistic experience.

The interest of this for me is its bearing on the problem of specifying

response. If the speakers of a language share a system of rules that each
of them has somehow internalized, understanding will, in some sense, be
uniform; that is, it will proceed in terms of the system of rules all speakers share. And insofar as these rules are constraints on production—
establishing boundaries within which utterances are labeled "normal,"
"deviant," "impossible," and so on—they will also be constraints on the
range, and even the direction, of response; that is, they will make response, to some extent, predictable and normative. Thus the formula, so
familiar in the literature of linguistics, "Every native speaker will recognize. . . ."

A further "regularizing" constraint on response is suggested by what
Ronald Wardhaugh, following Katz and Fodor, calls "semantic competence," a matter less of an abstract set of rules than of a backlog of
language experience which determines probability of choice and therefore of response. "A speaker's semantic knowledge," Wardhaugh con-
tends,

> is no more random than his syntactic knowledge . . . ; therefore, it seems
> useful to consider the possibility of devising, for semantic knowledge, a set
> of rules similar in form to the set used to characterize syntactic knowledge.
> Exactly how such a set of rules should be formulated and exactly what it
> must explain are to a considerable extent uncertain. At the very least the
> rules must characterize some sort of norm, the kind of semantic knowledge
> that an ideal speaker of the language might be said to exhibit in an ideal set
> of circumstances—in short, his semantic competence. In this way the rules
> would characterize just that set of facts about English semantics that all
> speakers of English have internalized and can draw upon in interpreting
> words in novel combinations. When one hears or reads a new sentence, he
> makes sense out of that sentence by drawing on both his syntactic and his
> semantic knowledge. The semantic knowledge enables him to know what
> the individual words mean and how to put these meanings together so that
> they are compatible. (P. 90)
>
> The resulting description could then be said to be a representation of the
> kind of system that speakers of a language have somehow internalized and
> that they draw upon in interpreting sentences. (P. 92)

Wardhaugh concedes that the "resulting description" would resemble
rather than be equivalent to the system actually internalized, but he
insists that "What is really important is the basic principle involved in the
total endeavor, the principle of trying to formalize in as explicit a way as
possible the semantic knowledge that a mature listener or reader brings
to his task of comprehension and that underlies his actual behavior in
comprehension" (p. 92). (Interestingly enough, this is a good description
of what Empson tries to do, less systematically of course, in *The Structure
of Complex Words*.) Obviously the intersection of the two systems of
knowledge would make it possible to further restrict (make predictable

and normative) the range of response; so that one could presume (as I have) to describe a reading experience in terms that would hold for all speakers who were in possession of both competences. The difficulty is that at present we do not have these systems. The syntactic model is still under construction and the semantic model has hardly been proposed. (Indeed, we will need not a model, but models, since "the semantic knowledge that a mature . . . reader brings to his task of comprehension" will vary with each century or period.[8]) Nevertheless, the incompleteness of our knowledge should not prevent us from hazarding analyses on the basis of what we presently know about what we know.

Earlier, I offered this description of my method: "an analysis of the developing responses of the reader to the words as they succeed one another on the page." It should now be clear that the developing of those responses takes place within the regulating and organizing mechanism, preexisting the actual verbal experience, of these (and other) competences. Following Chomsky, most psychologists and psycholinguists insist that understanding is more than a linear processing of information.[9] This means, as Wardhaugh points out, that "sentences are not just simple left to right sequences of elements" and that "sentences are not understood as a result of adding the meaning of the second to that of the first, the third to the first two, and so on" (p. 54). In short, something other than itself, something existing outside its frame of reference, must be modulating the reader's experience of the sequence.[10] In my method of analysis, the temporal flow is monitored and structured by everything the reader brings with him, by his competences; and it is by taking these into account as they interact with the temporal left to right reception of the verbal string, that I am able to chart and project *the* developing response.

It should be noted however that my category of response, and especially of meaningful response, includes more than the transformational grammarians, who believe that comprehension is a function of deep structure perception, would allow. There is a tendency, at least in the writings of some linguists, to downgrade surface structure—the form of actual sentences—to the status of a husk, or covering, or veil; a layer of excrescences that is to be peeled away or penetrated or discarded in favor of the kernel underlying it. This is an understandable consequence of Chomsky's characterization of surface structure as "misleading" and "uninformative"[11] and his insistence (somewhat modified recently) that deep structure alone determines meaning. Thus, for example, Wardhaugh writes that "Every surface structure is interpretable only by reference to its deep structure" (p. 49) and that while "the surface structure of the sentence provides clues to its interpretation, the interpretation itself depends on a correct processing of these clues to reconstruct all the elements and relationships of the deep structure." Presumably the "correct processing," that is, the uncovering of the deep structure and the extraction of deep meaning, is the only goal, and whatever stands in the way of that uncovering is to be tolerated, but assigned no final value. Clues, after all, are sometimes misleading and give rise to "mistakes."

> For example, we sometimes anticipate words in a conversation or text only to discover ourselves to be wrong, or we do not wait for sentences to be completed because we assume we know what their endings will be.... Many of the mistakes students make in reading are made because the students have adopted inappropriate strategies in their processing. (Pp. 137–38)

In my account of reading, however, the temporary adoption of these inappropriate strategies is itself a response to the strategy of an author; and the resulting mistakes are part of the experience provided by that author's language, and therefore part of its meaning. Deep structure theorists, of course, deny that differences in meaning can be located in surface forms. And this for me vitiates the work of Richard Ohmann, who does pay attention to the temporal flow, but only so that he can uncover beneath it the deep structure, which, he assumes, is really doing the work.

The key word is, of course, experience. For Wardhaugh, reading (and comprehension in general) is a process of extraction. "The reader is required to get the meaning from the print in front of him" (p. 139). For me, reading (and comprehension in general) is an event, no part of which is to be discarded. In that event, which is the actualization of meaning, the deep structure plays an important role, but it is not every-thing; for we comprehend not in terms of the deep structure alone, but in terms of a *relationship* between the unfolding, in time, of the surface structure and a continual checking of it against our projection (always in terms of surface structure) of what the deep structure will reveal itself to be; and when the final discovery has been made and *the* deep structure is perceived, all the "mistakes," the positing, on the basis of incomplete evidence, of deep structures that failed to materialize, will not be can-celed out. They have been experienced; they have existed in the mental life of the reader; they *mean*. (This is obviously the case in our experi-ence of the line "Nor did they not perceive the evil plight.")

All of which returns us to the original question. Who is *the* reader? Obviously, my reader is a construct, an ideal or idealized reader; some-what like Wardhaugh's "mature reader" or Milton's "fit" reader, or to use a term of my own, *the* reader is the *informed* reader. The informed reader is someone who

1. is a competent speaker of the language out of which the text is built up.

2. is in full possession of "the semantic knowledge that a mature ... listener brings to his task of comprehension." This in-

cludes the knowledge (that is, the experience, both as a producer and comprehender) of lexical sets, collocation probabilities, idioms, professional and other dialects, etc.

   3. has *literary* competence.

That is, he is sufficiently experienced as a reader to have internalized the properties of literary discourses, including everything from the most local of devices (figures of speech, etc.) to whole genres. In this theory, then, the concerns of other schools of criticism—questions of genre, conventions, intellectual background, etc.—*become redefined in terms of potential and probable response,* the significance and value a reader can be expected to attach to the idea "epic," or to the use of archaic language, or to anything.

   The reader, of whose responses I speak, then, is this informed reader, neither an abstraction, nor an actual living reader, but a hybrid—a read reader (me) who does everything within his power to make himself informed. That is, I can with some justification project my responses into those of "the" reader because they have been modified by the constraints placed on me by the assumptions and operations of the method: (1) the conscious attempt to become the informed reader by making my mind the repository of the (potential) responses a given text might call out and (2) the attendant suppressing, insofar as that is possible, of what is personal and idiosyncratic and 1970ish in my response. In short, the informed reader is to some extent processed by the method that uses him as a control. Each of us, if we are sufficiently responsible and self-conscious, can, in the course of employing the method become the informed reader and therefore be a more reliable reporter of his experience.

   (Of course, it would be easy for someone to point out that I have not answered the charge of solipsism, but merely presented a rationale for a solipsistic procedure; but such an objection would have force only if a better mode of procedure were available. The one usually offered is to regard the work as a thing in itself, as an object; but as I have argued above, this is a false and dangerously self-validating objectivity. I suppose that what I am saying is that I would rather have an acknowledged and controlled subjectivity than an objectivity which is finally an illusion.)

   In its operation, my method will obviously be radically historical. The critic has the responsibility of becoming not one but a number of informed readers, each of whom will be identified by a matrix of political, cultural, and literary determinants. The informed reader of Milton will not be the informed reader of Whitman, although the latter will necessarily comprehend the former. This plurality of informed readers implies a plurality of informed reader aesthetics, or no aesthetic at all. A method of analysis that yields a (structured) description of response has built into it an *operational* criterion. The question is not how good it is, but how does it work; and both question and answer are framed in terms of local conditions, which include local notions of literary value.

This raises the problem of the consideration of local beliefs as a possible basis of response. If a reader does not share the central concerns of a work, will he be capable of fully responding to it? Wayne Booth has asked that question: "But is it really true that the serious Catholic or atheist, however sensitive, tolerant, diligent, and well-informed about Milton's beliefs he may be, enjoys *Paradise Lost* to the degree possible to one of Milton's contemporaries and co-believers, of equal intelligence and sensitivity?"[12] The answer, it seems to me, is no. There are some beliefs that cannot be momentarily suspended or assumed. Does this mean, then, that *Paradise Lost* is a lesser work because it requires a narrowly defined ("fit") reader? Only if we hold to a universal aesthetic in the context of which value is somehow correlated with the number of readers who can experience it fully, irrespective of local affiliations. My method allows for no such aesthetic and no such fixings of value. In fact it is oriented *away* from evaluation and toward description. It is difficult to say on the basis of its results that one work is better than another or even that a single work is good or bad. And more basically, it doesn't permit the evaluation of literature as literature, as apart from advertising or preaching or propaganda or "entertainment." As a report of a (very complex) stimulus-response relationship, it provides no way to distinguish between literary and other effects, except, perhaps, for the components which go into one or the other; and no one, I assume, will assent to a "recipe" theory of literary difference. For some this will seem a fatal limitation of the method. I welcome it, since it seems to me that we have for too long, and without notable results, been trying to determine what distinguishes literature from ordinary language. If we understood "language," its constituents and its operations, we would be better able to understand its subcategories. The fact that this method does not begin with the assumption of literary superiority or end with its affirmation, is, I think, one of its strongest recommendations.

This is not to say that I do not evaluate. The selection of texts for analysis is itself an indication of a hierarchy in my own tastes. In general I am drawn to works which do not allow a reader the security of his normal patterns of thought and belief. It would be possible, I suppose, to erect a standard of value on the basis of this preference—a scale on which the most unsettling of literary experiences would be the best (perhaps literature is what disturbs our sense of self-sufficiency, personal and linguistic)—but the result would probably be more a reflection of a personal psychological need than of a universally true aesthetic.

Three further objections to the method should be considered if only because they are so often made in my classes. If one treats utterances, literary or otherwise, as strategies, does this not claim too much for the conscious control of their producer-authors? I tend to answer this question by begging it, by deliberately choosing texts in which the evidence of control is overwhelming. (I am aware that to a psychoanalytic critic, this principle of selection would be meaningless, and indeed, impossible.) If pressed I would say that the method of analysis, apart from my own handling of it, does not require the assumption either of control or of intention. One can analyze an effect without worrying about whether it was produced accidentally or on purpose. (However I always find myself worrying in just this way, especially when reading Defoe.) The exception would be cases where the work includes a statement of intention ("to justify the ways of God to man"), which, because it establishes an expectation on the part of a reader, becomes a part of his experience. This, of course, does not mean that the stated intention is to be believed or used as the basis of an interpretation, simply that it, like everything else in the text, draws a response, and, like everything else, it must be taken into account.

The second objection also takes the form of a question. If there is a measure of uniformity to the reading experience, why have so many readers, and some equally informed, argued so well and passionately for differing interpretations? This, it seems to me, is a pseudo-problem. Most literary quarrels are not disagreements about response, but about a response to a response. What happens to one informed reader of a work will happen, within a range of nonessential variation, to another. It is only when readers become literary critics and the passing of judgment takes precedence over the reading experience, that opinions begin to diverge. The act of interpretation is often so removed from the act of reading that the latter (in time the former) is hardly remembered. The exception that proves the rule, and my point, is C. S. Lewis, who explained his differences with Dr. Leavis in this way: "It is not that he and I see different things when we look at *Paradise Lost*. He sees and hates the very same things that I see and love."

The third objection is a more practical one. In the analysis of a reading experience, when does one come to the point? The answer is, "never," or, no sooner than the pressure to do so becomes unbearable (psychologically). Coming to the point is the goal of a criticism that believes in content, in extractable meaning, in the utterance as a repository. Coming to the point fulfills a need that most literature deliberately frustrates (if we open ourselves to it), the need to simplify and close. Coming to the point should be resisted, and in its small way, this method will help you to resist.

Other Versions, Other Readers

Some of what I have said in the preceding pages will be familiar to students of literary criticism. There has been talk of readers and re-

sponses before and I feel some obligation at this point both to acknowledge my debts and to distinguish my method from others more or less
like it.[13]

One begins of course with I. A. Richards, whose principal article of
faith sounds very much like mine:

> The belief that there is such a quality or attribute, namely Beauty, which
> attaches to the things which we rightly call beautiful, is probably inevitable
> for all reflective persons at a certain stage of their mental development.
>
> Even among those who have escaped from this delusion and are well
> aware that we continually talk as though things possess qualities, when what
> we ought to say is that they cause effects in us of one kind or another, the
> fallacy of "projecting" the effect and making it a quality of its cause tends to
> recur....
>
> Whether we are discussing music, poetry, painting, sculpture or architec-
> ture, we are forced to speak as though certain physical objects . . . are what
> we are talking about. And yet the remarks we make as critics do not apply to
> such objects but to states of mind, to experiences.[14]

This is obviously a brief for a shift of analytical attention away from the
work as an object to the response it draws, the experience it generates;
but the shift is, in Richards's theory, preliminary to *severing* one from the
other, whereas I would insist on their precise interaction. He does this by
distinguishing sharply between scientific and emotive language:

> A statement may be used for the sake of the *reference* true or false, which it
> causes. This is the *scientific* use of language. But it may also be used for the
> sake of the effects in emotion and attitude produced by the reference it
> occasions. This is the *emotive* use of language. The distinction once clearly
> grasped is simple. We may either use words for the sake of the references
> they promote, or we may use them for the sake of the attitudes and emotions
> which ensue. (P. 267)

But may we? Isn't it the case, rather, that in any linguistic experience
we are internalizing attitudes and emotions, even if the attitude is the
pretension of no attitude and the emotion is a passionate coldness?
Richards's distinction is too absolute and in his literary theorizing it
becomes more absolute still. Referential language, when it appears in
poetry, is not to be attended to as referential in any sense. Indeed, it is
hardly to be attended to at all. This is in general the thesis of *Science and
Poetry:*[15]

> The intellectual stream is fairly easy to follow; it follows itself, so to speak;
> but it is the less important of the two. In poetry it matters only as a *means.*
> (P. 13)
>
> A good deal of poetry and even some great poetry exists (e.g., some of
> Shakespeare's Songs and, in a different way, much of the best of Swinburne)
> in which the sense of the words can be *almost* entirely missed or neglected
> without loss. (Pp. 22–23)

Most words are ambiguous as regards their plain sense, especially in poetry. We can take them as we please in a variety of senses. The sense we are
pleased to choose is the one which most suits the impulses already stirred
through the form of the verse.... Not the strictly logical sense of what is said,
but the tone of voice and the occasion are the primary factors by which we
interpret. (P. 23)

It is never what a poem *says* which matters, but what it *is*. (P. 25)

Well what is it? And what exactly is the "form of the verse" which is
supposed to displace our interest in and responsibility to the sense? The
answers to these questions, when they come, are disturbing: the cognitive structure of poetic (read literary) language is a conduit through
which a reader is to pass untouched and untouching on his way to the
impulse which was the occasion of the poem in the first place:

The experience itself, the tide of impulses sweeping through the mind, is
the source and the sanction of the words ... to a suitable reader ... the
words will reproduce in his mind a similar play of interests putting him for
the while into a similar situation and leading to the same response.

Why this should happen is still somewhat of a mystery. An extraordinarily intricate concourse of impulses brings the words together. Then in
another mind the affair in part reverses itself, the words bring a similar
concourse to impulses. (Pp. 26–27)

Declining to identify message with meaning, Richards goes too far and
gives the experience of decoding (or attempting to decode) the message
no place in the actualization of meaning. From feeling to words to feeling, the passage should be made with as little attention as possible to the
sense, which is usually "fairly easy to follow" (disposable, like a straw). In
fact, attention to the sense can be harmful, if one takes it too seriously.
Assertions in poetry are "pseudo-statements": "A pseudo-statement is a
form of words which is justified entirely by its effect in releasing or
organizing our impulses and attitudes (due regard being had for the
better or worse organizations of these *inter se*); a statement, on the other
hand, is justified by its truth, i.e., its correspondence ... with the fact to
which it points" (p. 59). This would be unexceptionable, were Richards
simply warning against applying the criterion of truth-value to statements in poetry; but he seems to mean that we should not experience
them as statements at all, even in the limited universe of a literary discourse. That is, very little corresponding to cognitive processes should be
going on in our minds when we read poetry, lest the all-important re-
lease of impulses be impaired or blocked. Contradictions are not to be
noted or worried about. Logical arguments need not be followed too
closely ("the relevant consequences are ... to be arrived at by a partial
relaxation of logic"). But while this may be the response called forth by
some poetry (and prose), it is by no means universally true that in reading literature we are always relieved of our responsibility to logic and

argument. Very often, and even when the sense is "fairly easy to follow," cognitive processes—calculating, comparing, deducting, etc.—form the largest part of our response to a work, and any description of its effects must take this into account. Richards arbitrarily limits the range of meaningful response to feelings (impulses and attitudes) and of course here I cannot follow him. (In seventeenth-century literature, for example, the impact of a work often depends on the encouragement and manipulation of ratiocinative patterns of response.)

The range of response is further narrowed when Richards argues for a hierarchy of experiences. What is the best life one can live, he asks? "The best life . . . which we can wish for our friend will be one in which as much as possible of himself is engaged (as many of his impulses as possible). The more he lives and the less he thwarts himself the better. . . . And if it is asked, what does such life feel like . . . the answer is that it feels like and is the experience of poetry" (p. 33). The best poetry then is the poetry that gives the most impulses, with the greatest intensity, and, presumably, with the least ratiocinative interference. It is hardly surprising, given this theory of poetic value, that Richards is not really interested in the sequence of the reading experience. His analysis of reading a poem (*Principles*, chapter XVI) is spatial, in terms of isolated word-impulse relationships, exactly what we might expect from an aesthetic which regards the ligatures of thought as a kind of skeletal container, holding the experience in, but not forming any considerable part of it.

Richards's theories and his prejudices weigh heavily on his protocols and account, in part, for their miserable performance in *Practical Criticism*.[16] They begin, not with a sense of responsibility to language in all of its aspects, but with a license and, indeed, an obligation to ignore some of them. They are simply reporting on the impulses and attitudes they experience while reading, presumably under the influence of Richards's anticognitive bias. It is ironic and unfortunate that the case against analysis in terms of reader response is often made by referring to the example of a group of readers whose idea of response was disastrously narrow, and whose sensitivity to language was restricted to only one of its registers. If *Practical Criticism* makes any case, it is a case for the desirability of my informed reader; for it shows what happens when people who have never thought about the language they use every day are suddenly asked to report precisely on their experience of poetry, and even worse, are asked to do so in the context of an assumption of poetic "difference." . . .

Finally, I come to Michael Riffaterre whose work has only recently been called to my attention. Mr. Riffaterre *is* concerned with the reader's developing responses, and insists on the constraints imposed on response by the left to right sequence of a temporal flow, and he objects, as

I do, to methods of analysis that yield descriptions of the observable features of an utterance without reference to their reception by the reader. In a reply to a reading by Jakobson and Levi-Strauss of Baudelaire's "Les Chats," Riffaterre makes his position on these points very clear.[17] The systems of correspondences yielded by a structuralist analysis are not necessarily perceived or attended to by the reader; and the resulting data, encased as they often are in formidable spatial schematizations, often prevent us from looking at what is going on in the act of comprehension. The question, Riffaterre insists, is "whether unmodified structural linguistics is relevant at all to the analysis of poetry" (p. 202). The answer, it seems to me, is yes and no. Clearly we must reject any claims made for a direct relationship between structurally derived descriptions and meaning; but it does not follow for me, as it does for Riffaterre, that the data of which such descriptions consist are therefore irrelevant:

> The authors' method is based on the assumption that any structural system they are able to define in the poem is necessarily a poetic structure. Can we not suppose, on the contrary, that the poem may contain certain structures that play no part in its function and effect as a literary work of art, and that there may be no way for structural linguists to distinguish between these unmarked structures and those that are literarily active? Conversely, there may well be strictly poetic structures that cannot be recognized as such by an analysis not geared to the specificity of poetic language. (P. 202)

Here the basis for both my agreement and disagreement with Riffaterre is clear. He is a believer in two languages, ordinary and poetic, and therefore in two structures of discourse and two kinds of response; and he believes, consequently, that analysis should concern itself with "turning up" features, of language, structure and response, that are specifically poetic and literary.

> Poetry is language, but it produces effects that language in everyday speech does not consistently produce; a reasonable assumption is that the linguistic analysis of a poem should turn up specific features, and that there is a casual relationship between the presence of these features in the text and our empirical feeling that we have before us a poem. . . . In everyday language, used for practical purposes, the focus is usually upon the situational context, the mental or physical reality referred to. . . . In the case of verbal art, the focus is upon the message as an end in itself, not just as a means. . . . (P. 200)

This is distressingly familiar deviationist talk, with obvious roots in Mukarovsky's distinction between standard language and poetic language and in Richards's distinction between scientific and emotive language. Riffaterre's conception of the relation between standard and poetic language is more flexible and sophisticated than most, but nevertheless his method shares the weakness of its theoretical origins, the a priori assumption that a great deal doesn't count. Deviation theories always narrow the range of meaningful response by excluding from consideration features or effects that are not poetic; and in Riffaterre's version, as we shall see, the range of poetic effects is disastrously narrow, because he restricts himself only to that which is called to a reader's attention in the most spectacular way.

For Riffaterre, stylistic study is the study of SDs or stylistic devices which are defined as those mechanisms in the text which "prevent the reader from inferring or predicting any important feature. For predictability may result in superficial reading; unpredictability will compel attention: the intensity of reception will correspond to the intensity of the message."[18] Talking about style then is talking about moments in the reading experience when attention is compelled because an expectation has been disappointed by the appearance of an unpredictable element. The relationship between such moments and other moments in the sequence which serve to highlight them is what Riffaterre means by the "stylistic context":

> The stylistic context is a linguistic *pattern suddenly broken by an element which was unpredictable,* and the contrast resulting from this interference is the stylistic stimulus. The rupture must not be interpreted as a dissociating principle. The stylistic value of the contrast lies in the relationship it establishes between the two clashing elements; no effect would occur without their association in a sequence. In other words, the stylistic contrasts, like other useful oppositions in language, create a structure. (P. 171)

Riffaterre is more interesting than other practitioners of "contrast" stylistics because he locates the disrupted pattern in the context rather than in any preexisting and exterior norm. For if "in the style norm relationship we understood the norm pole to be universal (as it would be in the case of the linguistic norm), we could not understand how a deviation might be an SD on some occasions and on others, not" ("Criteria," p. 169). This means, as he points out in "Stylistic Context,"[19] that one can have the pattern *Context-SD starting new context—SD:* "The SD generates a series of SDs of the same type (e.g., after an SD by archaism, proliferation of archaisms); the resulting saturation causes these SDs to lose their contrast value, destroys their ability to stress a particular point of the utterance and reduces them to components of a new context; this context in turn will permit new contrasts." In the same article (pp. 208-9) this flexible and changing relationship is redefined in terms of microcontext ("the context which creates the opposition constituting the SD") and macrocontext ("the context which modifies this opposition by reinforcing or weakening it"). This enables Riffaterre to talk about the relationship between local effects and a series of local effects which in its entirety or duration determines to some extent the impact of its members; but the principle of contextual norm, and its advantages, remains the same.

Those advantages are very real; attention is shifted away from the message to its reception, and therefore from the object to the reader. (Indeed in a later article Riffaterre calls for a "separate linguistics of the decoder" and argues that SF, the impact made on the reader, "prevails consistently over referential function," especially in fiction.[20]) No fixed and artificial inventory of stylistic devices is possible, since in terms of contextual norms anything can be a stylistic device. The temporal flow of the reading experience is central and even controlling; it literally locates, with the help of the reader, the objects of analysis. The view of language and of comprehension is nonstatic; the context and SDs are moving and shifting; the reader is moving with them and, through his responses, creating them, and the critic is moving too, placing his analytic apparatus now here, now there.

All of this, however, is vitiated for me by the theory of language and style in the context (that word again) of which the methodology operates. I refer of course to the positing of two kinds of language and the resulting restriction of meaningful or interesting response to effects of surprise and disruption. Riffaterre is very forthright about this:

> *Stylistic facts can be apprehended only in language, since that is their vehicle;* on the other hand, *they must have a specific character,* since other*wise they could not be distinguished from linguistic facts.* . . .
>
> It is necessary to gather first all those elements which present stylistic features, and secondly, to subject to linguistic analysis only these, to the exclusion of all others (which are stylistically irrelevant). Then and only then will the confusion between style and language be avoided. For this sifting, preliminary to analysis, we must find specific criteria to delineate the distinctive features of style. . . .
>
> *Style* is understood as an emphasis (expressive, affective, or aesthetic) added to the information conveyed by the linguistic structure, without alteration of meaning. Which is to say that language expresses and that style stresses.[21]

"Stylistic facts"—"Linguistic facts," "stylistically irrelevant," "distinctive features of style," "emphasis . . . added to the information . . . without alteration of meaning." This is obviously more than a distinction, it is a hierarchy in which the lower of the two classes is declared uninteresting and, what is more important, *inactive.* That is, the stress of style is doing something and is therefore the proper object of attention, while the expression, the encoding and decoding of information, the meaning, is just there, and need not be looked into very closely. (Language expresses, style stresses.) One could quarrel with this simply on the basis of its radical separation of style and meaning, and with its naive equation of meaning with information; but for my purposes it is enough to point out the implications for the specifying and analyzing of response. Underlying Riffaterre's theorizing is the assumption that for long stretches of language, in both ordinary and literary discourse, there is no response worth talking about because nothing much is happening. (Minimal decoding, minimal response.)

This assumption is reflected at every level of his operation. It is the basis of his distinction between what is and what is not a literary structure. It is the basis too, of the context-SD relationship that obtains once a literary structure has been identified. That relationship is, as Riffaterre says, one of "binary opposition" in which "the poles cannot be separated."[22] Of course these are variable, not fixed, poles; but within their individual relationships one is always doing nothing but preparing the way (passively) for the other, for the "big moment" when the contextual pattern is disrupted and attention is compelled (that is, response occurs). And finally, it is the basis of Riffaterre's use of the reader as a locating device. Since all the features yielded by a linguistic analysis are not poetically active, there must be a way of isolating those features that are; and since these are the features that disrupt pattern and compel attention, we shall locate them by attending to the responses of actual readers, whether they are readers in our classroom-laboratory or readers who have left us a record of their experience in footnotes or articles. Riffaterre's reader is a composite reader (either the "average reader" or "superreader"), not unlike my informed reader. The difference, of course, is that his experience is considered relevant only at those points where it becomes unusual or "effortful." "Each point of the text that holds up the superreader is tentatively considered a component of the poetic structure. Experience indicates that such units are always pointed out by a number of informants."[23]

I am less bothered by the idea of a super-reader than by what happens to his experience in the course of a Riffaterrian analysis. It, too, will become binary in structure, a succession of highlighted moments alternating with and created by intervals of contextual norm, more cyclical than linear, and of course, in a large part of it, nothing will be happening. At one point in his reading of "Les Chats," Riffaterre comes upon the line *"Ils cherchent le silence"* and here is what he has to say:

> Informants unanimously ignore *Ils cherchent le silence*. Undoubtedly *cherchent* is the poetic or high-tone substitute for *rechercher* or *aimer*, but this is no more than the normal transformation of prose into verse: the device marks genre, as do verse and stanza, setting the context apart from everyday contexts. It is expected and not surprising.[24]

In other words, nobody noticed it or had any trouble with it; it's perfectly ordinary; therefore it's not doing anything and there's nothing to say about it.

Even when Mr. Riffaterre finds something to talk about, his method does not allow him to do much with it. This analysis of a sentence from *Moby Dick* is a case in point:

> "And heaved and heaved, still unrestingly heaved the black sea, as if its vast tides were a conscience. . . ." We have here a good example of the extent to which decoding can be controlled by the author. In the above instance it is difficult for the reader not to give his attention to each meaningful word. The decoding cannot take place on a minimal basis because the initial position of the verb is unpredictable in the normal English sentence, and so is its repetition. The repetition has a double role of its own, independent of its unpredictability: it creates the rhythm, and its total effect is similar to that of explicit speech. The postponement of the subject brings unpredictability to its maximum point; the reader must keep in mind the predicate before he is able to identify the subject. The "reversal" of the metaphor is still another example of contrast with the context. The reading speed is reduced by these hurdles, attention lingers on the representation, the stylistic effect is created.[25]

"Stylistic effect is created." But to what end? What does one do with the SDs or with their convergence once they have been located by the informer-reader? One cannot go from them to meaning, because meaning is independent of them; they are stress. ("Stress" occupies the same place in Riffaterre's affections as does "impulse" in Richards's and they represent the same narrowing of response.) We are left with a collection of stylistic effects (of a limited type), and while Mr. Riffaterre does not claim transferability for them, he does not claim anything else either, and their interest is to me at least an open question. (I should add that Riffaterre's analysis of "Les Chats" is brilliant and persuasive, as is his refutation of the Jakobson-Lévi-Strauss position. It is an analysis, however, which depends on insights his own method could not have generated. He will not thank me for saying so, but Mr. Riffaterre is a better critic than his theory would allow.)

The difference between Riffaterre and myself can be most conveniently located in the concept of "style." The reader may have wondered why in an essay subtitled, "Affective Stylistics," the word has been so little used. The reason is that my insistence that everything counts and that something (analyzable and significant) is always happening, makes it impossible to distinguish, as Riffaterre does, between "linguistic facts" and "stylistic facts." For me, a stylistic fact is a fact of response, and since my category of response includes everything, from the smallest and least spectacular to the largest and most disrupting of linguistic experiences, everything is a stylistic fact, and we might as well abandon the word since it carries with it so many binary hostages (style *and*—).

This, of course, commits me to a monistic theory of meaning; and it is usually objected to such theories that they give no scope to analysis.

But my monism permits analysis, because it is a monism of effects, in which meaning is a (partial) product of the utterance-object, but not to be identified with it. In this theory, the message the utterance carries—usually one pole of a binary relationship in which the other pole is style—is in its operation (which someone like Richards would deny) one more effect, one more drawer of response, one more constituent in the meaning experience. It is simply not *the* meaning. Nothing is.

Perhaps, then, the word "meaning" should also be discarded, since it carries with it the notion of message or point. The meaning of an utterance, I repeat, is its experience—all of it—and that experience is immediately compromised the moment you say anything about it. It follows, then, that we shouldn't try to analyze language at all. The human mind, however, seems unable to resist the impulse to investigate its own processes; but the least (and probably the most) we can do is proceed in such a way as to permit as little distortion as possible.

Conclusion

From controversy, I descend once more to the method itself and to a few final observations.

First, strictly speaking, it is not a method at all, because neither its results nor its skills are transferable. Its results are not transferable because there is no fixed relationship between formal features and response (reading has to be done every time); and its skills are not transferable because you can't hand it over to someone and expect him at once to be able to use it. (It is not portable.) It is, in essence, a language-sensitizing device, and as the "ing" in sensitizing implies, its operation is long term and never ending (never coming to the point). Moreover, its operations are interior. It has no mechanism, except for the pressuring mechanism of the assumption that more is going on in language than we consciously know; and, of course, the pressure of this assumption must come from the individual whose untrained sensitivity it is challenging. Becoming good at the method means asking the question "what does that . . . . . do?" with more and more awareness of the probable (and hidden) complexity of the answer; that is, with a mind more and more sensitized to the workings of language. In a peculiar and unsettling (to theorists) way, it is a method which processes its own user, who is also its only instrument. It is self-sharpening and what it sharpens is *you*. In short, it does not organize materials, but transforms minds.

For this reason, I have found it useful as a teaching method, at every level of the curriculum. Characteristically I begin a course by putting some simple sentences on the board (usually "He is sincere" and "Doubtless, he is sincere") and asking my students to answer the question, "what does that . . . . . do?" The question is for them a new one and they always reply by answering the more familiar question, "what does . . . . . mean?" But the examples are chosen to illustrate the insufficiency of this question, an insufficiency they soon prove from their own classroom experience; and after a while they begin to see the value of considering effects and begin to be able to think of language as an experience rather than as a repository of extractable meaning. After that, it is a matter of exercising their sensitivities on a series of graduated texts—sentences of various kinds, paragraphs, an essay, a poem, a novel—somewhat in the order represented by the first section of this paper. And as they experience more and more varieties of effect and subject them to analysis, they also learn how to recognize and discount what is idiosyncratic in their own responses. Not incidentally, they also become incapable of writing uncontrolled prose, since so much of their time is spent discovering how much the prose of other writers controls them, and in how many ways. There are, of course, devices—the piecemeal left to right presentation of texts via a ticker-tape method, the varying of the magic question (what would have happened were a word not there or somewhere else?)—but again the area of the method's operation is interior and its greatest success is not the organizing of materials (although that often occurs), but the transforming of minds.

In short, the theory, both as an account of meaning and as a way of teaching, is full of holes; and there is one great big hole right in the middle of it, which is filled, if it is filled at all, by what happens inside the user-student. The method, then, remains faithful to its principles; it has no point of termination; it is a process; it talks about experience and is an experience; its focus is effects and its result is an effect. In the end the only unqualified recommendation I can give it is that it works.

Notes

1. William Wimsatt, Jr., and Monroe Beardsley, *The Verbal Icon: Studies in the Meaning of Poetry* (Lexington: University Press of Kentucky, 1954), p. 21.

2. Thus the line could not read: "They did not not perceive," which is not the same as saying they did perceive. (The question is still open.) One could also argue that "nor" is not really a negative.

3. Of course, "That" is no longer read as "the fact that," but this is because the order of the clauses has resulted in the ruling out of that possibility.

4. This is not true of the Oxford school of ordinary language philosophers (Austin, Grice, Searle), who discuss meaning in terms of hearer-speaker relationships and intention-response conventions, i.e., "situational meaning."

5. I borrow this phrase from P. W. Bridgman, *The Way Things Are* (Cambridge, Mass.: Harvard University Press, 1959).

6. Wimsatt and Beardsley, *The Verbal Icon*, p. 34.

7. Ronald Wardhaugh, *Reading: A Linguistic Perspective* (New York: Harcourt, Brace and World, 1969), p. 60.

8. That is to say, there is a large difference between the two competences. One is uniform through human history, the other different at different points in it.

9. Noam Chomsky, *Syntactic Structures* (The Hague: Mouton, 1957), pp. 21-24.

10. See Wardhaugh, *Reading*, p. 55: "Sentences have a 'depth' to them, a depth which grammatical models such as phrase structure models and generative-transformational models attempt to represent. These models suggest that if a left-to-rightness principle is relevant to sentence processing, it must be a left-to-rightness of an extremely sophisticated kind that requires processing to take place concurrently at several levels, many of which are highly abstract: phonological or graphological, structural, and semantic."

11. Noam Chomsky, *Language and Mind* (New York: Harcourt, Brace, and World, 1968), p. 32.

12. Wayne C. Booth, *The Rhetoric of Fiction* (Chicago: University of Chicago Press, 1961), p. 139.

13. What follows is by no means exhaustive; it is selective in three directions. First I arbitrarily exclude, and therefore lump together in one undifferentiated mass, all those whose models of production and comprehension are primarily spatial; all those who are more interested in what goes into a work than what goes into and out of the reader; all those who offer top to bottom rather than left to right analyses; statisticians of style (Curtis Hayes, Josephine Miles, John Carroll), descriptive linguists (Halliday and Company), formalist-structuralists (Roman Jakobson, Roland Barthes), and many more. (In the longer study to which this essay is preliminary, these men and women will be considered and discriminated.) I am also selective in my discussion of psychologically oriented critics; and within that selection I must make further apologies for considering their work only in relation to my own methodological concerns, which are on the whole narrower and less ambitious than theirs. In short, with the possible exception of Michael Riffaterre, I shall do less than justice to my predecessors.

14. I. A. Richards, *Principles of Literary Criticism* (1924; reprint ed., New York: Harcourt, Brace and Co., 1959), pp. 20-22.

15. I. A. Richards, *Science and Poetry* (New York: W. W. Norton and Co., 1926).

16. I. A. Richards, *Practical Criticism: A Study of Literary Judgment* (1929; reprint ed., New York: Harcourt, Brace & Co., 1935).

17. Michael Riffaterre, "Describing Poetic Structures: Two Approaches to Baudelaire's 'Les Chats,'" *Yale French Studies* 36-37 (1966): 200-242 (chapter 3 in this volume).

18. Michael Riffaterre, "Criteria for Style Analysis," *Word* 15 (April 1959): 158.

19. Michael Riffaterre, "Stylistic Context," *Word* 16 (August 1960).

20. Michael Riffaterre, "The Stylistic Function," *Proceedings of the Ninth International Congress of Linguistics* (Cambridge, 1962), pp. 320-21.

21. Riffaterre, "Criteria for Style Analysis," pp. 154-155.

22. Riffaterre, "Stylistic Context," p. 207.

23. Riffaterre, "Describing Poetic Structures," pp. 215-16.

24. Ibid., p. 223.

25. Riffaterre, "Criteria for Style Analysis," pp. 172-73.

7

LITERARY COMPETENCE

Jonathan Culler

> To understand a sentence means
> to understand a language. To
> understand a language means to
> be master of a technique.
>
> Wittgenstein

When a speaker of a language hears a phonetic sequence, he is able to give it meaning because he brings to the act of communication an amazing repertoire of conscious and unconscious knowledge. Mastery of the phonological, syntactic and semantic systems of his language enables him to convert the sounds into discrete units, to recognize words, and to assign a structural description and interpretation to the resulting sentence, even though it be quite new to him. Without this implicit knowledge, this internalized grammar, the sequence of sounds does not speak to him. We are nevertheless inclined to say that the phonological and grammatical structure and the meaning are *properties* of the utterance, and there is no harm in that way of speaking so long as we remember that they are properties of the utterance only with respect to a particular grammar. Another grammar would assign different properties to the sequence (according to the grammar of a different language, for example, it would be nonsense). To speak of the structure of a sentence is necessarily to imply an internalized grammar that gives it that structure.

We also tend to think of meaning and structure as properties of literary works, and from one point of view this is perfectly correct: when the sequence of words is treated *as a literary work* it has these properties.

But that qualification suggests the relevance and importance of the linguistic analogy. The work has structure and meaning because it is read in a particular way, because these potential properties, latent in the object itself, are actualized by the theory of discourse applied in the act of reading. "How can one discover structure without the help of a methodological model?" asks Barthes (*Critique et vérité*, p. 19). To read a text as literature is not to make one's mind a *tabula rasa* and approach it without preconceptions; one must bring to it an implicit understanding of the operations of literary discourse which tells one what to look for.

Anyone lacking this knowledge, anyone wholly unacquainted with literature and unfamiliar with the conventions by which fictions are read, would, for example, be quite baffled if presented with a poem. His knowledge of the language would enable him to understand phrases and sentences, but he would not know, quite literally, what to *make* of this strange concatenation of phrases. He would be unable to read it *as* literature—as we say with emphasis to those who would use literary works for other purposes—because he lacks the complex "literary competence" which enables others to proceed. He has not internalized the "grammar" of literature which would permit him to convert linguistic sequences into literary structures and meanings.

If the analogy seems less than exact it is because in the case of language it is much more obvious that understanding depends on mastery of a system. But the time and energy devoted to literary training in schools and universities indicate that the understanding of literature also depends on experience and mastery. Since literature is a second-order semiotic system which has language as its basis, a knowledge of language will take one a certain distance in one's encounter with literary texts, and it may be difficult to specify precisely where understanding comes to depend on one's supplementary knowledge of literature. But the difficulty of drawing a line does not obscure the palpable difference between understanding the language of a poem, in the sense that one could provide a rough translation into another language, and understanding the poem. If one knows French, one can translate Mallarmé's "Salut," but that translation is not a thematic synthesis—it is not what we would ordinarily call "understanding the poem"—and in order to identify various levels of coherence and set them in relation to one another under the synoptic heading or theme of the "literary quest" one must have considerable experience of the conventions for reading poetry.

The easiest way to grasp the importance of these conventions is to take a piece of journalistic prose or a sentence from a novel and set it down on the page as a poem. The properties assigned to the sentence by a grammar of English remain unchanged, and the different meanings which the text acquires cannot therefore be attributed to one's knowledge of the language but must be ascribed to the special conventions for reading poetry which lead one to look at the language in new ways, to make relevant properties of the language which were previously unexploited, to subject the text to a different series of interpretive operations. But one can also show the importance of these conventions by measuring the distance between the language of a poem and its critical interpretation—a distance bridged by the conventions of reading which comprise the institution of poetry.

Anyone who knows English understands the language of Blake's "Ah! Sun-flower":

> Ah, Sun-flower, weary of time,
> Who countest the steps of the Sun,
> Seeking after that sweet golden clime
> Where the traveller's journey is done:
>
> Where the Youth pined away with desire,
> And the pale Virgin shrouded in snow
> Arise from their graves, and aspire
> Where my Sun-flower wishes to go.

But there is some distance between an understanding of the language and the thematic statement with which a critic concludes his discussion of the poem: "Blake's dialectical thrust at asceticism is more than adroit. You do not surmount Nature by denying its prime claim of sexuality. Instead you fall utterly into the dull round of its cyclic aspirations."[1] How does one reach this reading? What are the operations which lead from the text to this representation of understanding? The primary convention is what might be called the rule of significance: read the poem as expressing a significant attitude to some problem concerning man and/or his relation to the universe. The sunflower is therefore given the value of an emblem and the metaphors of "counting" and "seeking" are taken not just as figurative indications of the flower's tendency to turn toward the sun but as metaphorical operators which make the sunflower an instance of the human aspirations compassed by these two lines. The conventions of metaphorical coherence—that one should attempt through semantic transformations to produce coherence on the levels of both tenor and vehicle—lead one to oppose time to eternity and to make "that sweet golden clime" both the sunset which marks the closure of the daily temporal cycle and the eternity of death when "the traveller's journey is done". The identification of sunset and death is further justified by the convention which allows one to inscribe the poem in a poetic tradition. More important, however, is the convention of thematic unity, which forces one to give the youth and virgin of the second stanza a role which justifies choosing them as examples of aspiration; and since the semantic feature they share is a repression of sexuality, one must find a way of integrating that with the rest of the poem. The curious syntactic structure, with three clauses each depending on a "where," provides a way of doing this:

> The Youth and the Virgin have denied their sexuality to win the allegorical abode of the conventionally visualized heaven. Arriving there, they arise from their graves to be trapped in the same cruel cycle of longings; they are merely at the sunset and aspire to go where the Sun-flower seeks his rest, which is precisely where they already are.[2]

Such interpretations are not the result of subjective associations. They are public and can be discussed and justified with respect to the conventions of reading poetry—or, as English allows us to say, of *making* sense. Such conventions are the constituents of the institution of literature, and in this perspective one can see that it may well be misleading to speak of poems as harmonious totalities, autonomous natural organisms, complete in themselves and bearing a rich immanent meaning. The semiological approach suggests, rather, that the poem be thought of as an utterance that has meaning only with respect to a system of conventions which the reader has assimilated. If other conventions were operative its range of potential meanings would be different.

Literature, as Genette says, "like any other activity of the mind, is based on conventions of which, with some exceptions, it is not aware" (*Figures*, p. 258). One can think of these conventions not simply as the implicit knowledge of the reader but also as the implicit knowledge of authors. To write a poem or a novel is immediately to engage with a literary tradition or at the very least with a certain idea of the poem or the novel. The activity is made possible by the existence of the genre, which the author can write against, certainly, whose conventions he may attempt to subvert, but which is none the less the context within which his activity takes place, as surely as the failure to keep a promise is made possible by the institution of promising. Choices between words, between sentences, between different modes of presentation, will be made on the basis of their effects; and the notion of effect presupposes modes of reading which are not random or haphazard. Even if the author does not think of readers, he is himself a reader of his own work and will not be satisfied with it unless he can read it as producing effects. One would find very strange the notion of a poet saying, "when I reflect on the sunflower I have a particular feeling, which I shall call 'p' and which I think can be connected with another feeling which I shall call 'q'," and then writing "if p then q" as a poem on the sunflower. This would not be a poem because even the poet himself cannot read the meanings in that series of signs. He can take them as referring to the feelings in question, but that is very much another matter. His text does not explore, evoke or even make use of the feelings, and he will be unable to read it as if it did. To experience any of the satisfactions of having written a poem he must create an order of words which he can read according to the conventions of poetry: he cannot simply assign meaning but must make possible, for himself and for others, the production of meaning.

"Every work," wrote Valéry, "is the work of many things besides an author"; and he proposed that literary history be replaced by a poetics which would study "the conditions of the existence and development of literature." Among all the arts, it is "the one in which convention plays the greatest role," and even those authors who may have thought their works due only to personal inspiration and the application of genius

> had developed, without suspecting it, a whole system of habits and notions which were the fruit of their experience and indispensable to the process of production. However little they might have suspected all the definitions, all the conventions, the logic and the system of combinations that composition presupposes, however much they believed that they owed nothing but to the instant itself, their work necessarily called into play all these procedures and these inevitable operations of the mind.[3]

The conventions of poetry, the logic of symbols, the operations for the production of poetic effects, are not simply the property of readers but the basis of literary forms. However, for a variety of reasons it is easier to study them as the operations performed by readers than as the institutional context taken for granted by authors. The statements authors make about the process of composition are notoriously problematic, and there are few ways of determining what they are taking for granted. Whereas the meanings readers give to literary works and the effects they experience are much more open to observation. Hypotheses about the conventions and operations which produce these effects can therefore be tested not only by their ability to account for the effects in question but by their ability, when applied to other poems, to account for the effects experienced in those cases. Moreover, when one is investigating the process of reading one can make alterations in the language of a text so as to see how this changes literary effects, whereas that kind of experimentation is not possible if one is investigating the conventions assumed by authors, who are not available to give their reactions to the effects of proposed alterations in their texts. As the example of transformational grammar suggests, the best way of producing a formal representation of the implicit knowledge of both speakers and hearers is to present sentences to oneself or to colleagues and then to formulate rules which account for the hearers' judgments about meaning, well-formedness, deviance, constituent structure, and ambiguity.

To speak, therefore, as I shall do, of literary competence as a set of conventions for reading literary texts is in no way to imply that authors are congenital idiots who simply produce strings of sentences, while all the truly creative work is done by readers who have artful ways of processing these sentences. Structuralist discussions may seem to promote such a view by their failure to isolate and praise an author's "conscious art," but the reason is simply that here, as in most other human activities of any complexity, the line between the conscious and the unconscious is highly variable, impossible to identify, and supremely uninteresting. "*When* do you know how to play chess? All the time? or just while you are making a move? And the *whole* of chess during each move?"[4] When driving a car is it consciously or unconsciously that you keep to the correct side of the road, change gears, apply the brakes, dip the head-lights? To ask of what an author is conscious and of what unconscious is as fruitless as to ask which rules of English are consciously employed by speakers and which are followed unconsciously. Mastery may be largely unconscious or it may have reached a stage of highly self-conscious theoretical elaboration, but it is mastery in both cases. Nor does one in any way impugn the author's talent in speaking of his mastery as an ability to construct artifacts which prove extremely rich when subjected to the operations of reading.

The task of a structuralist poetics, as Barthes defines it, would be to make explicit the underlying system which makes literary effects possible. It would not be a "science of contents" which, in hermeneutic fashion, proposed interpretations for works,

> but a science of the conditions of content, that is to say of forms. What interests it will be the variations of meaning generated and, as it were, capable of being generated by works; it will not interpret symbols but describe their polyvalency. In short, its object will not be the full meanings of the work but on the contrary the empty meaning which supports them all. (*Critique et vérité*, p. 57)

In this sense structuralism effects an important reversal of perspective, granting precedence to the task of formulating a comprehensive theory of literary discourse and assigning a secondary place to the interpretation of individual texts. Whatever the benefits of interpretation to those who engage in it, within the context of poetics it becomes an ancillary activity—a way of using literary works—as opposed to the study of literature itself as an institution. To say that is in no way to condemn interpretation, as the linguistic analogy should make perfectly evident. Most people are more interested in using language to communicate than in studying the complex linguistic system which underlies communication, and they need not feel that their interests are threatened by those who make the study of linguistic competence a coherent and autonomous discipline. Similarly, a structuralist poetics would claim that the study of literature involves only indirectly the critical act of placing a work in situation, reading it as a gesture of a particular kind, and thus giving it a meaning. The task is rather to construct a theory of literary discourse which would account for the possibilities of interpretation, the "empty meanings" which support a variety of full meanings but which do not permit the work to be given just any meaning.

This would not need to be said if interpretive criticism had not tried to persuade us that the study of literature means the elucidation of individual works. But in this cultural context it is important to reflect on what has been lost or obscured in the practice of an interpretive criticism which treats each work as an autonomous artifact, an organic whole whose parts all contribute to a complex thematic statement. The notion that the task of criticism is to reveal thematic unity is a post-Romantic concept, whose roots in the theory of organic form are, at the very least, ambiguous. The organic unity of a plant is not easily translated into thematic unity, and we are willing to admit that the botanical gaze be allowed to compare one plant with another, isolating similarities and differences, or to dwell on formal organization without immediately invoking some teleological purpose or thematic unity. Nor has discourse on literature always been so imperiously committed to interpretation. It used to be possible, in the days before the poem became pre-eminently the act of an individual and emotion recollected in tranquillity, to study its interaction with norms of rhetoric and genre, the relation of its formal features to those of the tradition, without feeling immediately compelled to produce an interpretation which would demonstrate their thematic relevance. One did not need to move from poem to world but could explore it within the institution of literature, relating it to a tradition and identifying formal continuities and discontinuities. That this should have been possible may tell us something important about literature or at least lead us to reflect on the possibility of loosening interpretation's hold on critical discourse.

Such loosening is important because if the analyst aims at understanding how literature works he must, as Northrop Frye says, set about "formulating the broad laws of literary experience, and in short writing as though he believed that there is a totally intelligible structure of knowledge attainable about poetry, which is not poetry itself, or the experience of it, but poetics" (*Anatomy of Criticism*, p. 14). Few have put the case for poetics more forcefully than Frye, but in his perspective, as this quotation shows, the relationship between poetry, the experience of poetry and poetics remains somewhat obscure, and that obscurity affects his later formulations. His discussions of modes, symbols, myths and genres lead to the production of taxonomies which capture something of the richness of literature, but the status of his taxonomic categories is curiously indeterminate. What is their relation to literary discourse and to the activity of reading? Are the four mythic categories of Spring, Summer, Autumn and Winter devices for classifying literary works or categories on which the experience of literature is based? As soon as one asks why these categories are to be preferred to those of other possible taxonomies it becomes evident that there must be something implicit in Frye's theoretical framework which needs to be made explicit.

The linguistic model provides a slight reorientation which makes apparent what is needed. Study of the linguistic system becomes theoretically coherent when we cease thinking that our goal is to specify the properties of objects in a corpus and concentrate instead on the task of formulating the internalized competence which enables objects to have the properties they do for those who have mastered the system. To discover and characterize structures one must analyse the system which assigns structural descriptions to the objects in question, and thus a literary taxonomy should be grounded on a theory of reading. The relevant categories are those which are required to account for the range of acceptable meanings which works can have for readers of literature.

The notion of literary competence or of a literary system is, of course, anathema to some critics, who see in it an attack on the spontaneous, creative and affective qualities of literature. Moreover, they might argue, the very concept of literary competence, which carries the presumption that we can distinguish between competent and incompetent readers, is objectionable for precisely those reasons which lead one to propose it: the postulation of a norm for "correct" reading. In other human activities where there are clear criteria for success and failure, such as playing chess or climbing mountains, we can speak of competence and incompetence, but the richness and power of literature depend, precisely, on the fact that it is not an activity of this kind and that appreciation is varied, personal, and not subject to the normative legislation of self-styled experts.

Such arguments, however, would seem to miss the point. None would deny that literary works, like most other objects of human attention, can be enjoyed for reasons that have little to do with understanding and mastery—that texts can be quite blatantly misunderstood and still be appreciated for a variety of personal reasons. But to reject the notion of misunderstanding as a legislative imposition is to leave unexplained the common-experience of being shown where one went wrong, of grasping a mistake and seeing why it was a mistake. Though acquiescence may occasionally be disgruntled yielding to a higher authority, none would maintain that it was always thus; more often one feels that one has indeed been shown the way to a fuller understanding of literature and a better grasp of the procedures of reading. If the distinction between understanding and misunderstanding were irrelevant, if neither party to a discussion believed in the distinction, there would be little point to discussing and arguing about literary works and still less to writing about them.

Moreover, the claims of schools and universities to offer literary training cannot be lightly dismissed. To believe that the whole institution of literary education is but a gigantic confidence trick, would strain even a determined credulity, for it is, alas, only too clear that knowledge of a language and a certain experience of the world do not suffice to make someone a perceptive and competent reader. That achievement requires acquaintance with a range of literature and in many cases some form of guidance. The time and effort devoted to literary education by generations of students and teachers creates a strong presumption that there is something to be learned, and teachers do not hesitate to judge their pupil's progress towards a general literary competence. Most would claim, no doubt with good reason, that their examinations are designed not simply to determine whether their students have read various set works but to test their acquisition of an ability.

"Everyone who has seriously studied literature," Northrop Frye maintains, "knows that the mental process involved is as coherent and progressive as the study of science. A precisely similar training of the mind takes place, and a similar sense of the unity of the subject is built up" (*ibid.*, pp. 10–11). If that seems overstated it is no doubt because what is explicit in the teaching of science usually remains implicit in the teaching of literature. But it is clear that study of one poem or novel facilitates the study of the next: one gains not only points of comparison but a sense of how to read. One develops a set of questions which experience shows to be appropriate and productive and criteria for determining whether they are, in a given case, productive; one acquires a sense of the possibilities of literature and how these possibilities may be distinguished. We may speak, if we like, of extrapolating from one work to another, so long as we do not thereby obscure the fact that the process of extrapolation is precisely what requires explanation. To account for extrapolation, to explain what are the formal questions and distinctions whose relevance the student learns, would be to formulate a theory of literary competence. If we are to make any sense at all of the process of literary education and of criticism itself we must, as Frye argues, assume the possibility of "a coherent and comprehensive theory of literature, logically and scientifically organized, some of which the student unconsciously learns as he goes on, but the main principles of which are as yet unknown to us" (p. 11).

It is easy to see why, from this perspective, linguistics offers an attractive methodological analogy: a grammar, as Chomsky says, "can be regarded as a theory of a language," and the theory of literature of which Frye speaks can be regarded as the "grammar" or literary competence which readers have assimilated but of which they may not be consciously aware. To make the implicit explicit is the task of both linguistics and poetics, and generative grammar has placed renewed emphasis on two fundamental requirements for theories of this kind: that they state their rules as formal operations (since what they are investigating is a kind of intelligence they cannot take for granted intelligence used in applying rules but must make them as explicit as possible) and that they be testable (they must reproduce, as it were, attested facts about semiotic competence).

Can this step be taken in literary criticism? The major obstacle would seem to be that of determining what will count as evidence about literary competence. In linguistics it is not difficult to identify facts that an adequate grammar must account for: though one may need to speak of "degrees of grammaticalness" one can produce lists of sentences which are incontestably well-formed and sentences which are unquestionably deviant. Moreover, we have a sufficiently strong intuitive sense of paraphrase relations to be able to say roughly what a sentence means for speakers of a language. In the study of literature, however, the situation is considerably more complex. Notions of "well-formed" or "intelligible" literary works are notoriously problematic, and it may be difficult to secure agreement about what should count as a proper "understanding" of a text. That critics should differ so widely in their interpretations might seem to undermine any notion of a general literary competence.

But in order to overcome this apparent obstacle we have only to ask what we want a theory of literature to account for. We cannot ask it to account for the "correct" meaning of a work since we manifestly do not believe that for each work there is a single correct reading. We cannot ask it to draw a clear line between the well-formed and the deviant work if we believe that no such line exists. Indeed, the striking facts that do require explanation are how it is that a work can have a variety of meanings but not just any meaning whatsoever or how it is that some works give an impression of strangeness, incoherence, incomprehensibility. The model does not imply that there must be unanimity on any particular count. It suggests only that we must designate a set of facts, of whatever kind, which seem to require explanation and then try to construct a model of literary competence which would account for them.

The facts can be of many kinds: that a given prose sentence has different meanings if set down as a poem, that readers are able to recognize the plot of a novel, that some symbolic interpretations of a poem are more plausible than others, that two characters in a novel contrast with one another, that *The Waste Land* or *Ulysses* once seemed strange and now seems intelligible. Poetics bears, as Barthes says, not so much on the work itself as on its intelligibility (*Critique et vérité*, p. 62) and therefore problematic cases—the work which some find intelligible and others incoherent, or the work which is read differently in two different periods—furnish the most decisive evidence about the system of operative conventions. Any work can be made intelligible if one invents appropriate conventions: the most obscure poem could be interpreted if there were a convention which permitted us to replace every lexical item by a word beginning with the same letter of the alphabet and chosen according to the ordinary demands of coherence. There are numerous other bizarre conventions which might be operative if the institution of literature were different, and hence the difficulty of interpreting some works provides evidence of the restricted nature of the conventions actually in force in a culture. Moreover, if a difficult work later becomes intelligible it is because new ways of reading have been developed in order to meet what is the fundamental demand of the system: the demand for sense. A comparison of old and new readings will shed light on the change in the institution of literature.

As in linguistics, there is no automatic procedure for obtaining information about competence, but there is no dearth of facts to be explained.[5] To take surveys of the behavior of readers would serve little purpose, since one is interested not in performance itself but in the tacit knowledge or competence which underlies it. Performance may not be a direct reflection of competence, for behavior can be influenced by a host of irrelevant factors: I may not have been paying attention at a given moment, may have been led astray by purely personal associations, may have forgotten something important from an earlier part of the text, may have made what I would recognize as a mistake if it were pointed out to me. One's concern is with the tacit knowledge that recognition of a mistake would show rather than with the mistake itself, and so even if one were to take surveys one would still have to judge whether particular reactions were in fact a direct reflection of competence. The question is not what actual readers happen to do but what an ideal reader must know implicitly in order to read and interpret works in ways which we consider acceptable, in accordance with the institution of literature.

The ideal reader is, of course, a theoretical construct, perhaps best thought of as a representation of the central notion of acceptability. Poetics, Barthes writes, "will describe the logic according to which meanings are engendered in ways that can be *accepted* by man's logic of symbols, just as the sentences of French are *accepted* by the linguistic intuitions of Frenchmen" (*Critique et vérité*, p. 63). Though there is no automatic procedure for determining what is acceptable, that does not matter, for one's proposals will be sufficiently tested by one's readers' acceptance or rejection of them. If readers do not accept the facts one sets out to explain as bearing any relation to their knowledge and experience of literature, then one's theory will be of little interest; and therefore the analyst must convince his readers that meanings or effects which he is attempting to account for are indeed appropriate ones. The meaning of a poem within the institution of literature is not, one might say, the immediate and spontaneous reaction of individual readers but the meanings which they are willing to accept as both plausible and justifiable when they are explained. "Ask yourself: How does one *lead* anyone to comprehension of a poem or of a theme? The answer to this tells us how meaning is to be explained here."[6] The paths by which the reader is led to comprehension are precisely those of the logic of literature: the effects must be related to the poem in such a way that the reader sees the connection to be just in terms of his own knowledge of literature.

One cannot therefore emphasize too strongly that every critic, whatever his persuasion, encounters the problems of literary competence as soon as he begins to speak or write about literary works, and that he takes for granted notions of acceptability and common ways of reading. The critic would not write unless he thought he had something new to say about a text, yet he assumes that his reading is not a random and idiosyncratic phenomenon. Unless he thinks that he is merely recounting to others the adventures of his own subjectivity, he claims that his interpretation is related to the text in ways which he presumes his readers will accept once those relations are pointed out: either they will accept his interpretation as an explicit version of what they intuitively felt or they will recognize from their own knowledge of literature the justice of the operations that lead the critic from text to interpretation. Indeed, the possibility of critical argument depends on shared notions of the acceptable and the unacceptable, a common ground which is nothing other than the procedures of reading. The critic must invariably make decisions about what can in fact be taken for granted, what must be explicitly defended, and what constitutes an acceptable defence. He must show his readers that the effects he notices fall within the compass of an implicit logic which they are presumed to accept; and thus he deals in his own practice with the problems which a poetics would hope to make explicit.

William Empson's *Seven Types of Ambiguity* is a work from a nonstructuralist tradition which shows considerable awareness of the problems of literary competence and illustrates just how close one comes to a structuralist formulation if one begins to reflect on them. Even if Empson were content to present his work as a display of ingenuity in discovering ambiguities, his enterprise would still be governed by conceptions of plausibility. But of course he wants to make broader claims for his analysis and finds that to do so entails a position very like that recommended above:

> I have continually employed a method of analysis which jumps the gap between two ways of thinking; which produces a possible set of alternative meanings with some ingenuity, and then says it is grasped in the preconsciousness of the reader by a native effort of the mind. This must seem very dubious; but then the facts about the apprehension of poetry are in any case very extraordinary. Such an assumption is best judged by the way it works in detail. (P. 239)

Poetry has complex effects which are extremely difficult to explain, and the analyst finds that his best strategy is to assume that the effects he sets out to account for have been conveyed to the reader and then to postulate certain general operations which might explain these effects and analogous effects in other poems. To those who protest against such assumptions one might reply, with Empson, that the test is whether one succeeds in accounting for effects which the reader accepts when they are pointed out to him. The assumption is in no way dangerous, for the analyst "must convince the reader that he knows what he is talking about"—make him see the appropriateness of the effects in question— and "must coax the reader into seeing that the cause he names does, in fact, produce the effect which is experienced; otherwise they will not seem to have anything to do with each other" (p. 249). If the reader is brought to accept both the effects in question and the explanation he will have helped to validate what is, in essence, a theory of reading. "I have claimed to show how a properly-qualified mind works when it reads the verses, how those properly-qualified minds have worked which have not at all understood their own working" (p. 248). Such claims about literary competence are not to be verified by surveys of readers' reactions to poems but by readers' assent to the effects which the analyst attempts to explain and the efficacy of his explanatory hypotheses in other cases.

It is Empson's self-awareness and outspokenness as much as his brilliance which make his work invaluable to students of poetics; he has little respect for the critical piety that meanings are always implicitly and objectively present in the language of the poem, and thus he can attend to the operations which produce meanings. Discussing the translation of a Chinese fragment,

> Swiftly the years, beyond recall.
> Solemn the stillness of this spring morning.

he notes that

> these lines are what we should normally call poetry only by virtue of their compactness; two statements are made as if they were connected, and the reader is forced to consider their relations for himself. The reason why these facts should have been selected for a poem is left for him to invent; he will invent a variety of reasons and order them in his own mind. This, I think, is the essential fact about the poetical use of language. (P. 25)

This is indeed an essential fact, and one should hasten to point out what it implies: reading poetry is a rule-governed process of producing meanings; the poem offers a structure which must be filled up and one therefore attempts to invent something, guided by a series of formal rules derived from one's experience of reading poetry, which both make possible invention and impose limits on it. In this case the most obvious feature of literary competence is the intent at totality of the interpretive process: poems are supposed to cohere, and one must therefore discover a semantic level at which the two lines can be related to one another. An obvious point of contact is the contrast between "swiftly" and "stillness," and there is thus a primary condition on "invention": any interpretation should succeed in making thematic capital out of this opposition. Moreover, "years" in the first sentence and "this morning" in the second, both located in the dimension of time, provide another opposition and point of contact. The reader might hope to find an interpretation which relates these two pairs of contrasts. If this is indeed what happens it is no doubt because the experience of reading poetry leads to implicit recognition of the importance of binary oppositions as thematic devices: in interpreting a poem one looks for terms which can be placed on a semantic or thematic axis and opposed to one another.

The resulting structure or "empty meaning" suggests that the reader try to relate the opposition between "swiftly" and "stillness" to two ways of thinking about time and draw some kind of thematic conclusion from the tension between the two sentences. It seems eminently possible to produce in this way a reading which is "acceptable" in terms of poetic logic. On the one hand, taking a large panoramic view, we can think of the human life-span as a unit of time and of the years as passing swiftly; on the other, taking the moment of consciousness as the unit, we can think of the difficulty of experiencing time except discontinuously, of the stillness of a clock's hand when one looks at it. "Swiftly the years" implies a vantage point from which one can consider the passage of time, and the swiftness of passage is compensated for by what Empson calls "the answering stability of self-knowledge" implicit in this view of life (p. 24). "This morning" implies other mornings—a discontinuity of experience reflected in the ability to separate and name—and hence an instability which makes "stillness" the more valued. This process of binary structuring, then, can lead one to find tension within each of the lines as well as between the two lines. And since thematic contrasts should be related to opposed values we are led to think about the advantages and disadvantages of these two ways of conceiving of time. A variety of conclusions are of course possible. The claim is not that competent readers would agree on an interpretation but only that certain expectations about poetry and ways of reading guide the interpretive process and impose severe limitations on the set of acceptable or plausible readings.

Empson's example indicates that as soon as one reflects seriously on the status of critical argument and the relation of interpretation to text one approaches the problems which confront poetics, in that one must justify one's reading by locating it within the conventions of plausibility defined by a generalized knowledge of literature. From the point of view of poetics, what requires explanation is not the text itself so much as the possibility of reading and interpreting the text, the possibility of literary effects and literary communication. To account for the notions of acceptability and plausibility on which criticism relies is, as J.-C. Gardin emphasizes, the primary task of the systematic study of literature.

> This is in any case the only sort of objective that a "science" may set for itself, even if it be a science of literature: the regularities unveiled by natural phenomena correspond, in the literary field, to certain convergences of perception for members of a given culture. ("Semantic analysis procedures in the sciences of man," p. 33)

But one should stress that even if the analyst showed little explicit interest in notions of acceptability and merely set out to explain in a systematic way his own reading of literature, the results would be of considerable moment for poetics. If he began by noting his own interpretations and reactions to literary works and succeeded in formulating a set of explicit rules which accounted for the fact that he produced these interpretations and not others, one would then possess the basis of an account of literary competence. Adjustments could be made to include other readings which seemed acceptable and to exclude any readings which seemed wholly personal and idiosyncratic, but there is every reason to expect that other readers would be able to recognize substantial portions of their own tacit knowledge in his account. To be an experienced reader of literature is, after all, to have gained a sense of what can be done with literary works and thus to have assimilated a system which is largely interpersonal. There is little reason to worry initially about the validity of the facts which one sets out to explain; the only risk one runs is that of wasting one's time. The important thing is to start by isolating a set of facts and then to construct a model to account for them, and though structuralists have often failed to do this in their own practice, it is at least implicit in the linguistic model: "Linguistics can give literature the generative model which is the principle of all science, since it is a matter of making use of certain rules to explain particular results" (Barthes, *Critique et vérité*, p. 58).

Since poetics is essentially a theory of reading, critics of every persuasion who have tried to be explicit about what they are doing have made some contribution to it and indeed in many cases have more to offer than structuralists themselves. What structuralism does provide is a reversal of critical perspective and a theoretical framework within which the work of other critics can be organized and exploited. Granting precedence to the task of formulating a theory of literary competence and relegating critical interpretation to a secondary role, it leads one to reformulate as conventions of literature and operations of reading what others might think of as facts about various literary texts. Rather than say, for example, that literary texts are fictional, we might cite this as a

convention of literary interpretation and say that to read a text as literature is to read it as fiction. Such a reversal may, at first sight, seem trivial,
but to restate propositions about poetic or novelistic discourse as procedures of reading is a crucial reorientation for a number of reasons,
wherein lie the revitalizing powers of a structuralist poetics.

First of all, to stress literature's dependence on particular modes of
reading is a firmer and more honest starting point than is customary in
criticism. One need not struggle, as other theorists must, to find some
objective property of language which distinguishes the literary from the
non-literary but may simply start from the fact that we can read texts as
literature and then inquire what operations that involves. The operations will, of course, be different for different genres, and here by the
same model we can say that genres are not special varieties of language
but sets of expectations which allow sentences of a language to become
signs of different kinds in a second-order literary system. The same
sentence can have a different meaning depending on the genre in which
it appears. Nor is one upset, as a theorist working on the distinctive
properties of literary language must be, by the fact that the boundaries
between the literary and the non-literary or between one genre and
another change from age to age. On the contrary, change in modes of
reading offers some of the best evidence about the conventions operative
in different periods.

Second, in attempting to make explicit what one does when reading
or interpreting a poem one gains considerably in self-awareness and
awareness of the nature of literature as an institution. As long as one
assumes that what one does is natural it is difficult to gain any understanding of it and thus to define the differences between oneself and
one's predecessors or successors. Reading is not an innocent activity. It is
charged with artifice, and to refuse to study one's modes of reading is to
neglect a principal source of information about literary activity. By seeing literature as something animated by special sets of conventions one
can attain more easily a sense of its specificity, its peculiarity, its difference, shall we say, from other modes of discourse about the world.
Those differences lie in the work of the literary sign: in the ways in
which meaning is produced.

Third, a willingness to think of literature as an institution composed
of a variety of interpretive operations makes one more open to the most
challenging and innovatory texts, which are precisely those that are difficult to process according to received modes of understanding. An
awareness of the assumptions on which one proceeds, an ability to make
explicit what one is attempting to do, makes it easier to see where and
how the text resists one's attempts to make sense of it and how, by its
refusal to comply with one's expectations, it leads to that questioning of
the self and of ordinary social modes of understanding which has always
been the result of the greatest literature. My readers, says the narrator at

the end of *A la recherche du temps perdu*, will become "les propres lecteurs d'eux-mêmes": in my book they will read themselves and their own limits. How better to facilitate a reading of oneself than by trying to make explicit one's sense of the comprehensible and the incomprehensible, the significant and the insignificant, the ordered and the inchoate. By offering sequences and combinations which escape our accustomed grasp, by subjecting language to a dislocation which fragments the ordinary signs of our world, literature challenges the limits we set to the self as a device or order and allows us, painfully or joyfully, to accede to an expansion of self. But that requires, if it is to be fully accomplished, a measure of awareness of the interpretive models which inform one's culture. Structuralism, because of its interest in the adventures of the sign, has been exceedingly open to the revolutionary work, finding in its resistance to the operations of reading confirmation of the fact that literary effects depend on these conventions and that literary evolution proceeds by displacement of old conventions of reading and the development of new.

And so, finally, structuralism's reversal of perspective can lead to a mode of interpretation based on poetics itself, where the work is read against the conventions of discourse and where one's interpretation is an account of the ways in which the work complies with or undermines our procedures for making sense of things. Though it does not, of course, replace ordinary thematic interpretations, it does avoid premature foreclosure—the unseemly rush from word to world—and stays within the literary system for as long as possible. Insisting that literature is something other than a statement about the world, it establishes, finally, an analogy between the production or reading of signs in literature and in other areas of experience and studies the ways in which the former explores and dramatizes the limitations of the latter. In this kind of interpretation the meaning of the work is what it shows the reader, by the acrobatics in which it involves him, about the problems of his condition as *homo significans*, maker and reader of signs. The notion of literary competence thus comes to serve as the basis of a reflexive interpretation. . . .

Notes

1. Harold Bloom, *The Visionary Company: A Reading of English Romantic Poetry* (New York: Doubleday, 1961), p. 42.

2. Ibid.

3. Paul Valéry, *Oeuvres*, ed. Jean Hytier, 2 vols. (Paris: Bibliothèque de la Pléiade, 1957–1960), 2:629 and 1:1439–41.

4. Ludwig Wittgenstein, *Philosophical Investigations*, trans. G.E.M. Anscombe (New York: Macmillan, 1953), p. 59.

5. See Noam Chomsky, *Aspects of the Theory of Syntax* (Cambridge: M.I.T. Press, 1965), p. 19.

6. Wittgenstein, *Philosophical Investigations*, p. 144.

8

UNITY   IDENTITY   TEXT   SELF

Norman N. Holland

My title has big words, but my essay aims into the white spaces between those big words. Those spaces suggest to me the mysterious openness and receptivity of literature. Somehow, all kinds of people from different eras and cultures can achieve and re-achieve a single literary work, replenishing it by infinitely various additions of subjective to objective. As it turns out, however, to explore the white spaces we need first to bound them, that is, to define the four big words. Then the spaces will—more or less—take care of themselves.

First, *text*. Simply, the words-on-the-page that formalists and "New" critics have been talking about for the last several decades. Evidently, the meaning of the term is so obvious there is scarcely a literary handbook that troubles to mention it. It is just what the writer wrote or, to take the word back to its etymological root, *texere* (to weave), what he wove, as in a textile, or what he made, as in words like archi*tect*. In this sense, the writer's emblem is the badger, Old High German *dahs,* an animal who builds; thus, the critic's symbol would be that animal specially bred for ferreting out badgers, the *dachshund,* like so many of my colleagues, long of nose and low of belly.

The notion of literary *unity* involves a good deal more. It first occurs in the *Phaedrus* in connection with oratory, when Socrates argues that a speech should be put together "like a living creature . . . not headless or footless." Aristotle, in a famous passage of the *Poetics,* required that all the arts "must imitate . . . a whole, the structural union of the parts being such that, if any one of them is displaced or removed, the whole will be disjointed and disturbed." And in another famous passage he asked that narratives and, by implication, other works of literature "resemble a living organism in all its unity."[1]

Reprinted by permission of the Modern Language Association of America from *PMLA* 90 (1975): 813–22.

The idea has, of course, passed through many versions, of which the most energizing came from the German Romantic critics and Coleridge, leading to such emphases and even overextensions of the zoological metaphor as this elegant phrasing by Henry James in "The Art of Fiction": "A novel is a living thing, all one and continuous, like any other organism, and in proportion as it lives will it be found, I think, that in each of the parts there is something of each of the other parts."[2] Our own time is both more analytical and more professional. We heed statements like this by Northrop Frye in a standard handbook for graduate students, suggesting that the first task of the academic critic is to "see the whole design of the work as a unity . . . a simultaneous pattern radiating out from a center" or "central theme," "the unity to which everything else must be relevant."[3]

I find that I arrive at this unity by grouping the particular details of a work together under certain themes, then grouping those particular themes together until I arrive at a few basic terms which constitute a central theme. For example, I might say, "*Hamlet* is a play about the split between the purity of symbolic action and the physicality of real action." Such a theme is not necessarily unique—that is, someone else might arrive at a different theme from mine or, alternatively, I might find that this theme would help me grasp the unity of some other play besides *Hamlet*. All that is implied by the idea of a central theme is that it helps one particular person grasp the unity of one particular work.

Such a theme as this one for *Hamlet* is highly abstract, yet one can quickly move up or down the hierarchy of generality it sets up. One can go from an abstract word in the theme, like "physicality," to the particulars it subsumes, like Gertrude's sensuality or the gravediggers' jokes. One can relate such a detail of speech as the doubling of words in phrases like "the gross and scope of mine opinion," "the expectancy and rose of the fair state," or "you . . . that are but mutes or audience to this act" to a very general term in the theme such as "split" which would link the hendiadys, the "figure of twins" as Puttenham called it, to splittings of characters like Laertes and Ophelia, Horatio and Fortinbras, or the scarcely distinguishable Rosencrantz and Guildenstern whose duality will hardly bear justification but a thematic one.

As I describe this method of successive abstraction, of induction and deduction around a few general polarities, I realize I am making it sound much more regular and fixed than it is. Obviously, the process is as intuitive and imaginative as it is rational. Each reader groups the details of the play into themes that he thinks important, and if he chooses to press on to a highly condensed central theme it will surely be something that matters to him. Nevertheless, most professional critics assure us that there are right and wrong, better and worse readings, and they insist, often quite fiercely, that the themes and other literary entities they discover have an "objective" validity. Certainly, readings of literary works for their unity can be compared in an almost quantitative way as to how effectively they bring the details of the play into convergence around some central theme. Even more important, however, we compare readings by the extent to which we *feel* we share them. There is, then, a deep question here as to whether literary unities are "subjective" or "objective" or, more exactly, how the subjective and objective parts of a reading for unity interrelate. I think our analysis of the four terms, unity, identity, text, self—will help answer it.

Our second term, *unity*, I realize, has become altogether familiar, even routine, to literary critics. I have lingered with it, though, because it has an important and largely unrecognized use in psychology—not, however, for the first of our two psychological terms: *self*. That is, as the psychological handbooks say, more of a commonsense term than a psychological one—an interesting dichotomy that! It is more easily defined by exclusion, as "one's 'own person' as contrasted with 'other persons' and objects outside [one]self." It is thus "the real total person of an individual, including both his body and his psyche." Freud, for example, sometimes spoke of a *Gesamt-Ich* in contrast to *das Ich* proper, the intrapsychic ego.[4]

The more complex psychological term is *identity*. Erik Erikson, who has done more to make it a byword in and out of psychoanalysis than anyone else, has suggested that it comprises four meanings, any or all of which may be—must be—considered a possibility in any given use: the individual's awareness of the continuity of his existence in space and time and his recognition of others' awareness of his existence; more, his awareness of the continuity in the style of his individuality and its existence and the coincidence of his personal style with his meaning for significant others in his immediate community. Obviously, such a concept is both rich and ambiguous. Indeed, Nathan Leites has recently devoted much of a book to arguing that the word *identity* has been used and abused to the point where it has ceased to have any clear meaning left; that the older word "character" would do just as well.[5]

I would like to restore meaning to the word by turning to the most precise of the modern theorists of identity, Heinz Lichtenstein.[6] When we describe the "character" or "personality" of another person, Lichtenstein shows, we abstract an invariant from "the infinite sequence of bodily and behavioral transformations during the whole life of an individual." That is, we can be precise about individuality by conceiving of the individual as living out variations on an identity theme much as a musician might play out an infinity of variations on a single melody. We discover that underlying theme by abstracting it from its variations.

From a developmental point of view, Lichtenstein holds that such a theme is actually "in" the individual. Out of the newborn child's inheritance of potentialities, its mother-person actuates a specific way of being, namely, being the child that fits this particular mother. The mother thus imprints on the infant, not a specific identity or even a sense of its own identity, but a "primary identity," itself irreversible but capable of infinite variation. This primary identity stands as an invariant which provides all the later transformations of the individual, as he develops, with an unchanging inner form or core of continuity.

Identity in this developmental sense shows up most graphically, perhaps, in the series of photographs that picture magazines publish at the deaths of famous people. Here is the future President toddling at two, here are his pictures in school and college yearbooks, here as he first began to appear in the news, then the sixty-year-old smiling public man, and finally, "Last scene of all" is "mere oblivion, sans teeth, sans eyes, sans taste, sans everything." And yet, if we look closely we can read back from the careworn visage of the old man at the end and at the height of his career to the soft features of the toddler, finding the same structure, expressions, and frame. In this way, too, identity is like a musical theme on which variations are played: not the notes themselves but their structural relationship to one another remains constant through a lifetime of transformations.

In the developed adult, I can assume such an invariant identity theme (whether or not it coincides with an actual primary identity imprinted in infancy), and by means of it grasp an unchanging essence, a "personality" or "character," that permeates the millions of ego choices that constitute the visible human before me, ever changing and different, yet ever continuous with what went before. I can abstract, from the choices in the life I see, facts as visible as the words on a page, various subordinate patterns and themes until I arrive at one central, unifying pattern in that life which is the invariant sameness, the "identity theme" of the individual living it. In other words, just as I can arrive at a *unity* for the series of choices that is *Hamlet* by means of a central, unifying theme, so I can arrive an an *identity* for a particular self by means of a centering identity theme. And again, it may not be unique: the same identity theme may describe several different people, just as a single literary theme might describe several different texts.

In short, within our four terms, *identity* quite resembles *unity*, so much so that once having defined *unity, identity, text,* and *self,* we can fill in the white spaces between them as follows: unity/identity = text/self. Now my title reads: "*Unity* is to *identity* as *text* is to *self*," or, by a familiar algebraic transposition, "*Unity* is to *text* as *identity* is to *self*." Or you could say, "*Identity* is the *unity* I find in a *self* if I look at it as though it were a *text*."

Now this seems a reasonable enough proportion, I think, something very close to applying the Aristotelian idea of essence both to literary texts and to people. Thus, Aristotle says in his first definition of the term: "What is soul? . . . It is substance in the sense which corresponds to the definitive formula of a thing's essence. That means it is 'the essential whatness' of a body."[7] In more modern terms, we can think of *text* and *self* as data and *unity* and *identity* as constructs drawn from the data. Or we can think of *unity* and *identity* as expressing only sameness or continuity while *text* and *self* show difference or change, or, more exactly, *both* sameness *and* difference, *both* continuity *and* change.

In that sense, *unity* and *identity* are relatively fixed and *text* and *self* relatively variable, as, for example, when I read a novel and decide fairly quickly, within fifty pages or so, what its theme is, although its outcome is as yet quite unknown to me. The same thing happens in human development: one can discern identity, a personal style, within the second or third year of life, yet it is impossible to tell, looking at the three-year-old child, even the simplest things about the adult he will become, whether he will marry, have children, what his profession will be, his health, his location, or any of the most obvious passport data. Because we arrive at identity by considering events apart from their position in time, identity is a purely synchronic concept; it does not help us look diachronically through a life in time and make predictions or retrodictions. Rather, identity defines what the individual brings from old experiences to new ones, and it is the newness of experiences, both those from the world without and those from the biological and emotional world within, by which the individual creates the variations which are his life lived in historical time.

Therefore, the tidy little equation I have offered you, this mathematical neatness matching literary criticism to psychology, must mercifully give way before the essential humanity of both disciplines. *Unity* and *identity*, on the one hand, belong to an entirely different order of factuality from *text* and *self* on the other. *Text* and *self* are very close to experience, while *unity* and *identity* represent quite abstract principles drawn from the experience of *text* or *self*. We sometimes assume, as Aristotle did, that essences such as unity and identity inhere in the physical beings they describe, like a DNA code, but whether or not that is true in some final sense, it is we who have to uncover or decode the surface manifestations to arrive at the informing principle of the text or person. And when I do so, I engage in an act that becomes part of the historical self which grows out of and expresses my own identity theme. To put it another way, when I arrive at the unity in a literary text or the identity theme of a personality I am studying, I do so in a way that is characteristic for me—for my identity theme. And so do you. Otherwise we would all agree about the themes of novels or our understanding of human beings and there would be—o horribile dictu!—no need for *PMLA* or any other forum in which people work out their differing interpretations of texts, selves, and the other events we experience in the world.

Thus, the neat little equation I offered you is not neat at all. The ratio, unity to text, equals the ratio, identity to self, but the terms on the right side of the equation cannot be eliminated from the left side. The unity we find in literary texts is impregnated with the identity that finds that unity. This is simply to say that my reading of a certain literary work will differ from yours or his or hers. As readers, each of us will bring different kinds of external information to bear. Each will seek out the particular themes that concern him. Each will have different ways of making the text into an experience with a coherence and significance that satisfies.

Further, when you actually collect and compare these variations among interpretations, they turn out to be very much larger than one would have expected. For instance, at Buffalo's Center for the Psychological Study of the Arts, I was analyzing readers' taped remarks on Faulkner's "A Rose for Emily." The story contains the following clause describing Colonel Sartoris: "he who fathered the edict that no Negro woman should appear on the streets without an apron." Three readers singled out the word "fathered" for comment. Sandra said: "It's a great little touch of ironic humor . . . using these heroic terms to describe such a petty and obvious extension of bigotry." " 'Fathered,' " said Saul, "is the word you're asking about, I suspect. . . . Sponsored. It means practically the same as 'sponsored,' I think, although I suppose you could talk about paternalism and stuff." "I react to the term, 'fathered the edict,' " said Sebastian when I read him the passage. "That was a strange phrase to use—like fathering the edict seems to in some way be fathering the women, to be fathering that state of affairs. So it implied for me the sexual intercourse that took place between whites and Negroes."[8]

Obviously, since the text presents just the one word "fathered," one cannot explain by means of the text alone why one reader would find that word heroic, another neutral and abstract, and a third sexual. To be sure, differences in age, sex, nationality, class, or reading experience will contribute to differences in interpretation. Yet it is a familiar experience in the world of literary or clinical interpretation to find people similar in age, sex, nationality, class, and interpretive skill nevertheless differing radically over particular interpretations. And one finds the opposite situation: people superficially different agreeing on interpretations. Certainly, the hundreds of psychological experiments inconclusively correlating such variables with interpretation give little hope that they will provide an answer. At the Center for the Psychological Study of the Arts, we have found that we can explain such differences in interpretation by examining differences in the personalities of the interpreters. More precisely, *interpretation is a function of identity*, specifically, identity conceived as variations upon an identity theme.

Merely to state that idea, however, requires an immediate warding off of misunderstandings. The assertion that all interpretations express the identity themes of the people making the interpretations is a statement of fact, not an ethical plea for interpretive Liberty Halls. Nor does that factual statement logically or in any other way imply that all interpretations work equally well as interpretations for people other than the interpreter. On the contrary, I and, I feel sure, you distinguish different readings of a text or personality "objectively" by how much and how directly they seem to us to bring the details of a text or a self into convergence around a centering theme. We also compare them as to whether they "feel right" or "make sense." That is, do we feel we could use them to organize and make coherent our own experience of that text or person?

If, as a factual matter, interpretation is a function of identity, can we be more precise about that function? Recently, at this Center, we have been able to tease out three strands and trace a single overall principle, a figure in the carpet, if you will; in all, four principles that govern the relationship between character or personality or identity and the creation and re-creation of literary and other experiences.[9] Although I present them sequentially, obviously they all go on together.

The overarching principle is: identity re-creates itself, or, to put it another way, style—in the sense of personal style—creates itself. That is, all of us, as we read, use the literary work to symbolize and finally to replicate ourselves. We work out through the text our own characteristic patterns of desire and adaptation. We interact with the work, making it part of our own psychic economy and making ourselves part of the literary work—as we interpret it. For, always, this principle prevails: identity re-creates itself. Then, within that general principle, we can isolate three specific modalities.

First, adaptations must be matched; and, therefore, we interpret the new experience in such a way as to cast it in the terms of our characteristic ways of coping with the world. That is, each of us will find in the literary work the kind of thing we characteristically wish or fear the most. Therefore, to respond, we need to be able to re-create from the literary work our characteristic strategies for dealing with those deep fears and wishes. Imagine, for example, several individuals, all of whom perceive the central desire and danger in their worlds as authority figures. One of these people might characteristically deal with those loved and feared authorities by establishing alternatives in response to their demands; and he might therefore respond to, say, *Hamlet* in terms of the opportunities he found in the play for such alternatives: for him, dualisms, split characters, or the interplay of multiple plots would be primary. Another person might characteristically cope with the authority figures he both fears and is attracted to by establishing limits and qualifications on their authority: he might relate therefore to *Hamlet* by discovering and stressing irony and occasional farce, Osric, Polonius, the gravediggers, and, in general, the contradictions and counterbalance of "purposes mistook/Fall'n on th' inventors' heads." Still another person might customarily deal with authority by total compliance, and he might respond to the tragedy by seeking out and accepting, totally, uncritically, with a gee-gosh, the authority of its author.

The point in this crucial phase of response is that any individual shapes the materials the literary work offers him—including its author—to give him what he characteristically both wishes and fears, and that he also constructs his characteristic way of achieving what he wishes and defeating what he fears. Because his psychological defenses are brought into play, this matching has to take place with considerable exactitude. That is, unless the defense mechanisms are bribed into tranquility, the individual wards off the experience entirely. The defenses, at least, must be matched very closely.

I am, however, talking about much more than defenses: I mean to include the whole, large system by which the individual achieves pleasure in the world and avoids unpleasure, his characteristic pattern of defense mechanisms, methods of coping, or adaptive strategies, including his systems of symbols and values. In the largest sense, I am talking about his whole identity theme considered from the point of view of defense and adaptation. But to the extent the defense mechanisms in a strict sense are included, this matching acts like a shibboleth. The individual can accept the literary work only to the extent he exactly re-creates with it a verbal form of his particular pattern of defense mechanisms and, in a broader sense, the particular system of adaptive strategies that he keeps between himself and the world. This matching is therefore crucial. Without it the individual blocks out the experience. With it the other phases of response take place.

Once someone has taken into himself through his adaptive strategies some literary work, as he has made it fit those strategies, then he derives from it fantasies of the particular kind that yield him pleasure—and he does so very easily indeed. In our observations of readers, the matching of defenses must be very exact, but they can very freely adapt literary works to yield the gratifications of fantasy. Fantasies move in the same "direction" as the continuing pressure from our drives for gratification, while defenses and adaptations have to oppose and redirect those pressures. Hence one matching—the fit to the adaptive strategy—must be quite tight, while the other can be very loose, because the fantasy content we conventionally locate in the literary work is really created by the reader from the literary work to express his own drives.

It is this fantasy content that most psychoanalytic studies of particular works of literature, beginning with Freud's discovery of Hamlet's oedipus complex, purport to discover. Such studies, however, raise a difficult question: How is it that readers of widely differing personalities as well as different genders, ages, and cultures can all get pleasure from the same fantasy? Conversely, how can one individual with one dominant mode of fantasy take pleasure in a great range of literary works with widely varying unconscious content? The same man can enjoy the homosexual theme of *Death in Venice* and the intrusive, thrusting masculinity of a Hemingway or Mark Twain. And he can go on to enjoy Scott Fitzgerald's need to be frustrated by a dominant woman and Sylvia Plath's anger at the womanly roles forced upon her. How can one person enjoy such a spectrum? How can many different people from many different cultures and eras enjoy it?

The answer, I believe, is that different readers can all gain pleasure from the same fantasy and one reader can gain pleasure from many different fantasies because *all* readers create from the fantasy seemingly "in" the work fantasies to suit their several character structures. Each reader, in effect, re-creates the work in terms of his own identity theme. First, he shapes it so it will pass through the network of his adaptive and defensive strategies for coping with the world. Second, he re-creates from it the particular kind of fantasy and gratification he responds to.

Finally, a third modality completes the individual's re-creation of his identity or life-style from the literary work. Fantasies that boldly represent the desires of the adult or the more bizarre imaginings of the child will ordinarily arouse guilt and anxiety. Thus, we usually feel a need to transform raw fantasy into a total experience of esthetic, moral, intellectual, or social coherence and significance.[10] Most typically, we seek our own particular version of the esthetic unity Plato and Aristotle first described, but we use other ways as well: comparing this experience to others, associating to it, bringing one's knowledge or expertise to bear, evaluating it, placing it in a tradition, treating it as an encoded message to be decoded, and all the other strategies of professional, amateur, and vulgar literary criticism. All serve to synthesize the experience and make it part of the mind's continuing effort to balance the pressures of the drives for gratification, the restraints of conscience and reality, and one's inner need to avoid emotional and cognitive dissonance. In short, we put the work together at an intellectual or esthetic level as we do in terms of fantasy or defense—according to the same overarching principle: identity re-creates itself.

This description of the way identity finds unity is, I realize, both abstract and long. To ameliorate the length, I can offer a simple mnemonic, the square root sign we learned in school: $\sqrt{}$. We can think of our three steps as the left end of the sign, the bottom tip, and the right end. The small horizontal portion on the left images the tight, narrow process of filtering the literary work through the defensive aspect of one's identity. Once in, the literary experience drops down to "deep," unconscious levels (like the day-residue from which a dream is made) and there becomes transformed into the unconscious wish associated with this person's particular identity theme, a fantasy pushing for gratification, pressing upward toward coherence and significance. And it is at this higher level that we talk about artistic experience to others, passing the work through from left to right and from primitive, "lower" modes of enjoyment to "higher" appreciations. If you prefer a verbal mnemonic for the *defense-fantasy-transformation* model of the literary experience, the best acronym I can find is DEFT (not, I would insist, "daft").

A mnemonic may help compress the length of the description; it does nothing, of course, for its abstractness. To try to overcome that I would like to talk about one particular reader; and to demonstrate, in so brief a space as this, how one person's identity re-creates itself through literary and other experiences, I have picked a reader well known through his writings, but whom, for the time being, I would like to leave nameless. Let me identify him for you, not by a sketch or portrait, but only by his X-ray, that is, his identity theme. I would like you then to read, not his imaginative works, which you probably know, but informal remarks that reveal the way he constructs his experience of the world, of science, say, or poetry, fiction, politics, and himself. Compare that to his identity theme and, when you come to recognize him, to those of his literary works you know.

As I look over his writings and the facts of his life, this man seems to me to have seen his world as something huge, threatening, unknown, and chaotic, but nevertheless something he could identify with or even master by treating small things (notably words) as magical symbols for those large unknowns. That is, he polarized his world into the big unknown and the familiar small, the big being potentially destructive in aggressive or sexual ways, and the small serving as a way his ego would either master or become part of the big powers. I can put his identity theme (as I see it) in somewhat more precise terms this way: *to be in touch with, to create, and to restrain huge unknown forces of sex and aggression by smaller symbols: words or familiar objects.* Or, more briefly, *to manage great, unmanageable unknowns by means of small knowns.*

As we shall see, one can move from this very abstract formulation to the particular details of the man's life, much as if we were going from a central theme for *Hamlet* to particular details of text. Notice, too, how this statement of an identity theme involves polarities: great and small, known and unknown, creation and restraint, manageable and unmanageable. Such dualisms reflect the paradoxical combinations of love and hate or wish and fear that underlie all human development, permeating every later experience. Notice the way this man in particular finds such polarities in experience and then deals with them by playing off symbols against one another.

For example, in a letter to his daughter after his wife's death, he characterized himself in terms of such a balancing: "No matter how humorous I am, I am sad. I am a jester about sorrow." He saw other writers the same way. "The style is the man," he quoted.

> Rather say the style is the way the man takes himself; and to be at all charming or even bearable, the way is almost rigidly prescribed. If it is with outer humor, it is with inner seriousness. Neither one alone without the other under it will do.

In fact, as if to carry this balance out, our writer was known to his friends for his anger and rages—he himself called them "my Indian vindictiveness"—but he was known to the public for his folksiness and his gentle, proverbial humor and irony. All his life he needed to make himself into a legend this way, often falsifying the actual facts to do so. "Don't trust me too far ... don't trust me on my life" was his repeated caution to scholars and biographers. It was as though he needed to put on myth like a mask to help him, not just with his public image but with his far deeper need to cope with an important polarity in himself between the manageable and the unmanageable. The small, cozy mannerisms served to deal with the large, aggressive forces within.

His literary tastes carried out the same defensive strategy. Among his favorite reading he included the *Odyssey* (as I see it, the escape and homecoming rather than the deadlock and entanglement of the grander *Iliad*); Poe and Emerson (both of whom deal with efforts to master supernatural forces by natural ones); and such romances as *The Last of the Mohicans, The Prisoner of Zenda,* and *The Jungle Book.* Romances matched the way he created an exaggerated need for courage as a reaction against the unmanageable in himself. He would set up heroes and worship them, and he constantly tried to build himself up into the sturdy stoicism he admired. Thus, he was especially fond of Kipling; and, he said, "*Robinson Crusoe* is never quite out of my mind. I never tire of being shown how the limited can make snug in the limitless. *Walden* has something of the same fascination. Crusoe was cast away; Thoreau was self-cast away. Both found themselves sufficient."

The same defensive strategy, using the tangible or limited to stand off the unknown and unlimited, emerged as his intellectual style when he came to evaluate science or philosophy.

> Greatest of all attempts to say one thing in terms of another is the philosophical attempt to say matter in terms of spirit, or spirit in terms of matter, to make the final unity. That is the greatest attempt that ever failed. We stop just short there. But it is the height of poetry, the height of all thinking, the height of all poetic thinking, that attempt to say matter in terms of spirit and spirit in terms of matter. It is wrong to call anybody a materialist simply because he tries to say spirit in terms of matter, as if that were a sin. ... The only materialist—be he poet, teacher, scientist, politician, or statesman—is the man who gets lost in his material without a gathering metaphor to throw it into shape and order. He is the lost soul.

He saw science, too, as an attempt to achieve such a gathering metaphor and, given his attitude toward superior forces, he was not about to allow that it was any different from poetry as a way of managing the big unknowns. Thus he said of Einstein's theory, "Wonderful, yes, wonderful but no better as a metaphor than you or I might make for ourselves before five o'clock." And in more general terms: "Isn't science just an extended metaphor; its aim to describe the unknown in terms of the known? Isn't it a kind of poetry, to be treated as plausible material, not as cold fact?"

He himself took over an idea of Emerson's, that "the world is a temple whose walls are covered with emblems, pictures and commandments of the Deity . . . there is no fact in nature which does not carry the whole sense of nature." That is a nice way of putting it. A rival poet, however, wrote of a man,

> To whom every grass-blade's a telephone wire,
> With Heaven as central and electrifier.
> He has only to ring up the switch-board and hear
> A poem lightly pattering into his ear.[11]

That's a bit nasty, but is it really inaccurate?

Our writer himself often implied that poetry was his way of getting in touch with and managing the great unmanageables. "I believe in what the Greeks called synecdoche: the philosophy of the part for the whole; skirting the hem of the goddess. All that an artist needs is samples." "I started calling myself a Synecdochist when others called themselves Imagists or Vorticists. Always, always a larger significance. A little thing touches a larger thing." "I am a mystic," he told a reporter. "I believe in symbols." And so he should, for by manipulating symbols he achieved not only great poetry and national acclaim but the warding off of his deepest fears. "Every poem is an epitome of the great predicament; a figure of the will braving alien entanglements." "When in doubt there is always form for us to go on with. Anyone who has achieved the least form to be sure of it, is lost to the larger excruciations." For him, a poem took on a life and direction of its own, culminating in a sense of mastery or at least an attempt at it:

> The figure a poem makes. It begins in delight and ends in wisdom. . . . It begins in delight, it inclines to the impulse, it assumes direction with the first line laid down, it runs a course of lucky events, and ends in a clarification of life—not necessarily a great clarification, such as sects and cults are founded on, but in a momentary stay against confusion.

Finally, I can comprehend this man as a unity. By seeing him centered around an identity theme, I can interrelate what he says about his own writing, the writing of others, or the relation of science to poetry or matter to spirit. I can, in fact, achieve Yeats's "fancy that there is some one Myth for every man, which, if we but knew it, would make us understand all he did and thought."[12] I can understand why Robert Frost's commitment to synecdoche went along with a fondness for Rudyard Kipling or why a man who enjoys "being shown how the limited can make snug in the limitless" would also feel "All than an artist needs is samples."

Through the concept of identity as an identity theme and variations upon it, I can bring together intellectually the way this particular individual construed experiences of all kinds. But more than that, I can reach him empathically as well. Once I could feel teased, even a bit annoyed, by the cuteness in a remark like

I never dared be radical when young
For fear it would make me conservative when old.

Now, I hear in it another note: the need to hold at bay the fear and dare of politics in 1936 by balancing off opposed symbols. I can delight in his description of poetry, for example: "The figure is the same as for love. Like a piece of ice on a hot stove the poem must ride on its own melting." Yet that image of the small object harried by its dangerous and hostile environment (and as a figure of love!) reminds me of the pain Robert Frost knew alongside the marvels of wit and irony that enabled him to tolerate it.[13]

I can share empathically the unity and continuity this man created in his life because, by the very act of experiencing his identity, I mingle this characteristic style with my own. Indeed, the only way one can ever discover unity in texts or identity in selves is by creating them from one's own inner style, for we are all caught up in the general principle that identity creates and re-creates itself as each of us discovers and achieves the world in his own mind. Whenever, as a critic, I engage a writer or his work, I do so through my own identity theme. My act of perception is also an act of creation in which I partake of the artist's gift. I find in myself what Freud called the writer's "innermost secret; the essential *ars poetica*," that is, the ability to break through the repulsion associated with "the barriers that rise between each single ego and the others."[14]

In doing so, I close a dualism that has dominated systematic thought since Descartes: the belief that the reality and meaning of the external world exist alone, independent of the perceiving self, and that therefore true knowledge requires the splitting of the knower from the known.[15] I am suggesting that a larger law subsumes this seventeenth-century epistemology and points rather to experiencing as an in-gathering and in-mixing of self and other as described by Whitehead or Bradley or Dewey or Cassirer or Langer or Husserl. The Cartesian cleaving of res extensa from res cogitans is a historical and personal strategy governed by a still more all-encompassing principle; and the psychoanalytic psychologist can give precision to what the philosophers adumbrated: *interpretation re-creates identity,* considered specifically as defense, fantasy, and ego style.

As Basil Willey urged some forty years ago,[16] seventeenth-century science itself came into being as a result of a deep psychological change in the kind of assurance people sought from explanations.

> For example, the spots on the moon's surface might be due, theologically, to the fact that it was God's will they should be there; scientifically they might be "explained" as the craters of extinct volcanoes. The newer explanation may be said, not so much to contain "more" truth than the older, as to supply the *kind* of truth which was now demanded. An event was "explained" . . . when its history had been traced and described.

"Interest was now directed to the *how,* the manner of causation, not its *why,* its final cause."

In our own time, we the successors of Freud, Marx, and Durkheim find ourselves amidst cultural anthropology, transactional psychology, the discovery of absolute limits to mathematical axiomatization, the Whorf-Sapir hypothesis in linguistics, relativity, randomness, and uncertainty even in the "hard" sciences, and many other relativizing discoveries, most important for our purposes, psychoanalytic psychology. Psychoanalysis enables us to go *through* science, as it were, to a psychological principle that itself explains science: any way of interpreting the world, even physics, meets human needs, for interpretation is a human act. From a medieval *why* to the *how* that underlay the three great centuries of classical science, we proceed to a psychoanalytic *to whom.* Willey might have been anticipating it when he said, "One cannot . . . define 'explanation' absolutely; one can only say that it is a statement which satisfies the demands of a particular time or place." Or, I would say, person. The claim of objectivity can take the form of experiment in psychology, formalism in literary criticism, or even the universal DEFT principle relating identity to interpretation here put forward. Whatever form it takes, any such toehold into objectivity makes it possible for some human being to feel he has protected his self against falling into some Other, human or inhuman, a fear to which the nonlegendary Robert Frost was no stranger, nor am I. Nor, I suspect, is any literary critic.

I began with assurance, but I sense that I must end with reassurance. Please recognize that in establishing an inextricable proportionality among unity, identity, text, and self, and so denying claims of objectivity that would separate them, I am not positing an isolated, solipsistic self. Just the opposite, in fact. I said I would try to fill in the white spaces in my enigmatic title. Let me now reassure you that I am indeed filling them in, and you are too, and all people are, all the time—including the hardest of "hard" scientists. Every time a human being reaches out,

across, or by means of symbols to the world, he reenacts the principles
that define that mingling of self and other, the creative and relational
quality of all our experience, not least the writing and reading of literature.

Notes

1. Plato, *Phaedrus,* 264C; Aristotle, *Poetics,* Section 8 and 1459a20.

2. Henry James, "The Art of Fiction," in *The Great Critics: An Anthology of Literary
Criticism,* ed. James H. Smith and Edd Winfield Parks, 3rd edition (New York: W. W.
Norton & Co., 1951), p. 661.

3. Northrop Frye, "Literary Criticism," in *The Aims and Methods of Scholarship in
Modern Languages and Literature,* ed. James Thorpe (New York: Modern Language Association, 1963), p. 65.

4. Burness E. Moore and Bernard D. Fine, eds., *A Glossary of Psychoanalytic Terms and
Concepts* (New York: American Psychoanalytic Association, 1967), p. 65.

5. Erik Erikson, *Identity: Youth and Crisis* (New York: Norton, 1968), p. 50. Nathan
Leites, *The New Ego: Pitfalls in Current Thinking about Patients in Psychoanalysis* (New York:
Science House, 1971), chapters 8 and 9.

6. Heinz Lichtenstein, "Identity and Sexuality: A Study of Their Interrelationship in
Man," *Journal of the American Psychoanalytic Association* 9 (1961): 179–260; idem, "The
Dilemma of Human Identity: Notes on Self-Transformation, Self-Objectivation and
Metamorphosis," *Journal of the American Psychoanalytic Association* 11 (1963): 173–223; idem,
"The Role of Narcissism in the Emergence and Maintenance of a Primary Identity,"
International Journal of Psycho-Analysis 45 (1964): 49–56; idem, "Toward a Metapsychologi-
cal Definition of the Concept of Self," *International Journal of Psycho-Analysis* 46 (1965):
117–28.

7. Aristotle, *De Anima,* Section 2, 1.412b11, trans. J. A. Smith in *Introduction to Aristotle,* ed. Richard McKeon (New York: Random House, 1947), p. 172.

8. The responses of readers to this story are reported and analyzed in detail in my *5
Readers Reading* (New Haven: Yale University Press, 1975). In "A Letter to Leonard,"
Hartford Studies in Literature 5 (1973): 9–30, I have described how these larger-than-
expected differences make the usual explanation of the variability of literary response
inadequate. It is usually said that the literary text embodies norms for an infinite number
of experiences which its several readers each partially achieve. One can explain the very
many and very different readings of a text more economically (or more Occamically),
however, by saying the differences come from the very many and very different readers
rather than from the text which, after all, remains the same and is demonstrably not
infinite.

Incidentally, it is the close analysis of what readers actually say about what they read
that differentiates, on the one hand, the work of what has been called the "Buffalo school
of psychoanalytic critics" or the literary use of communication theory by Elemer Hankiss in
Budapest from, on the other hand, the "affective stylistics" of Stanley E. Fish or more
philosophical statements on response by Wolfgang Iser and Hans Robert Jauss of the
Universität Konstanz. Compare, e.g., this essay of Hankiss, "Shakespeare's *Hamlet:* The
Tragedy in the Light of Communication Theory," *Acta Litteraria Academiae Scientiarum
Hungaricae* 12 (1970): 297–312, with Fish, "Literature in the Reader: Affective Stylistics,"
New Literary History 2, no. 1 (Autumn 1970): 123–62 (chapter 6 in this volume), Iser,
"Indeterminacy and the Reader's Response in Prose Fiction," in *Aspects of Narrative,* ed. J.
Hillis Miller (New York: Columbia University Press, 1971), pp. 1–45, or Jauss, "Literary

History as a Challenge to Literary Theory," trans. Elizabeth Benzinger, *New Literary History* 2 (Autumn 1970): 7–37.

9. These principles are evidenced and more fully stated in my *Poems in Persons: An Introduction to the Psychoanalysis of Literature* (New York: Norton, 1973) and *5 Readers Reading.*

10. I have described at length this transformational process and the way the reader uses materials from the literary work to achieve it in *The Dynamics of Literary Response* (New York: Oxford University Press, 1968), chapters 1–6.

11. Amy Lowell, *A Critical Fable* (Boston: Houghton, 1922), p. 22.

12. William Butler Yeats, "At Stratford-on-Avon," *Ideas of Good and Evil* (London: A. H. Bullen, 1903), p. 162.

13. My first quotation is from a letter to Lesley Frost Francis, 1 March 1939, *Family Letters of Robert and Elinor Frost,* ed. Arnold Grade (Albany: State University of New York Press, 1972), p. 210. Most of the rest come from the first two volumes of the Lawrance Thompson biography, *Robert Frost: The Early Years, 1874–1915* (New York: Holt, 1966) and *Robert Frost: The Years of Triumph, 1915–1938* (New York: Holt, 1970). "The style is the man" (vol. 2, p. 421). Reading tastes (vol. 1, p. 549). "Greatest of all attempts" (vol. 2, pp. 694 and 364). Two remarks on science (vol. 2, pp. 649–50). Emerson (vol. 1, pp. 70–71). Synecdoche (vol. 2, p. 693). "I am a mystic" (vol. 1, p. 550). "Every poem is an epitome" (vol. 1, p. xxii). Quotations that use the phrase, "The Figure a Poem Makes," are from that essay, preface to the 1939 and succeeding editions of his collected poems. "I never dared be radical" is from the poem "Precaution" (1936).

While this essay was in manuscript, C. Barry Chabot published a searching and convincing—and conformatory—formulation of Frost's central theme: the created as a wall against a giant invader ("The 'Melancholy Dualism' of Robert Frost," *Review of Existential Psychology and Psychiatry* 13 (1974): 42–56.

14. Sigmund Freud, "Creative Writers and Day-Dreaming," *Standard Edition of the Complete Psychological Works of Sigmund Freud,* ed. James Strachey, 24 vols. (London: Hogarth, 1959), 9:153.

15. In this paragraph, I am drawing on ideas developed in an essay by Murray Schwartz, "The Space of Psychological Criticism," *Hartford Studies in Literature* 5 (1973): x–xxi.

16. Basil Willey, *The Seventeenth-Century Background: Studies in the Thought of the Age in Relation to Poetry and Religion* (1934; reprint ed., Garden City: Doubleday, 1953), pp. 12–14.

9

EPISTEMOLOGICAL ASSUMPTIONS IN THE STUDY OF RESPONSE

David Bleich

When interpretation is conceived as motivated resymbolization, the idea of response, which otherwise has an inapplicably wide range of minimal meanings, becomes specifiable in experience. Generally, response is a peremptory perceptual act that translates a sensory experience into consciousness. The sensory experience has become part of the sense of self, and in this way, we have identified it. Identification always takes place automatically and may thus often be erroneous; a configuration of lights on a country road at night may be identified at first either as a stopped vehicle nearby or a town in the distance. The identification is a peremptory act; subsequently, its truth value may or may not be determined by different sorts of interpretation, depending on the motive created by the original identification.

Consider the responses, and their respective consequences, to two different real objects. I am at a dinner table with another person, who interrupts my conversation by saying, "Could you pass the salt, please." My visual identification of the salt is my response, and its consequence is the motor act of passing it. The latter act did not interpret or resymbolize my response but, rather, removed the idea of the salt from consciousness so that my conversation could continue. The response of identification was the most complex level of intellection I reached in that parenthetical behavior. But suppose I am in the country, and I identify in the distance Mt. Rainier, which, like the salt, is a real object and registers in consciousness in the same way. I may not take note of it and may direct my attention to something else, so that I remove the identification from consciousness just as I did with the salt. Since I am not so

Reprinted from David Bleich, *Subjective Criticism* (Baltimore: The Johns Hopkins University Press, 1978), pp. 97–133.

disposed, I think about the mountain, and this entails a series of deliberate reviews of the scene. My motive for having directed consciousness in this way is found in the fact that my original identification was *evaluative;* it was not simply "Mt. Rainier" that I saw, but it was "the magnificent Mt. Rainier." Because there was no situational motive to regulate my response in advance, my evaluation of the scene is automatically attached to my identification of it. This means that I have peremptorily converted the real mountain into a symbolic mountain, since it is now primarily a function of my self-awareness. In this instance, the response is an act of symbolization; if I then conceptualize the symbolization, I will have interpreted my perceptual experience of the mountain. I will not, however, have interpreted the mountain, whose status as a real object is no longer relevant to me. When there is no prior motivational constraint on my perceptual initiatives, response will be an act of evaluative symbolization, which is the only basis on which an interpretation may proceed.

This conception of response and its connection to interpretation becomes especially useful in the efforts to understand the mental handling of aesthetic experience. When we decide that an object is aesthetic, it means that we have cleared the motivational ground by the simple act of confronting the object. The universally agreed-upon boundaries of the aesthetic object represent a collective declaration that the perceptual symbolization of the object will be the ground for all further discussion of it and that, furthermore, this object is no longer "real"—that is, for example, Michelangelo's *Moses* is no longer a block of stone in the shape of a seated man, but is a symbolic representation of something. The object of attention is not the item itself but is the response of those who observe it. The assumption derived from the objective paradigm that all observers have the same perceptual response to a symbolic object creates the illusion that the object is real and that its meaning must reside in it. The assumption of the subjective paradigm is that collective similarity of response can be determined only by each individual's announcement of his response and subsequent communally motivated negotiative comparison. This assumption is validated by the ordinary fact that when each person says what he sees, each statement will be substantially different. The response must therefore be the starting point for the study of aesthetic experience.

In one sense, response has occupied this fundamental position for a long time. Aristotle, for example, defined tragedy as that sort of drama to which the audience's response is pity and fear, where such feelings mark the evaluative identification of the dramatic experience. By similar reasoning, the mere description of a work as comic or of a character as pathetic shows how response defines what we perceive. But because of the paradigmatic imperative to keep the symbolic object objectively real, the ensuing critical discussion is always characterized by the respondents' arbitrary shifts from their own responses to the assumed factualities of the object. Ultimately, regardless of the actual shape of the discussion, its conclusions are automatically taken to apply as if the symbolic object were a real object. But because such conclusions are always contestable, interpretatively formulated knowledge has less authority than mathematically formulated knowledge. The epistemological assumptions of the subjective paradigm equalize these authorities by conceiving any knowledge as having been deliberately sought and by relating its authority to the motives of those who seek it. More importantly, subjective epistemology is a framework through which the *study* of both response and interpretation may be actively integrated with the *experience* of response and interpretation, thereby transforming knowledge from something to be acquired into something that can be synthesized on behalf of oneself and one's community.

In spite of the considerable interest in the act of reading that the language and literature professions now have, there is uncertainty regarding just how to conceive a reader's response. Two recent essays— Cary Nelson's "Reading Criticism" and Eugene R. Kintgen's "Reader Response and Stylistics"—help articulate the problem.[1] Nelson poses the question by observing that in the prefaces to several important critical treatises, the authors present disclaimers or apologies for their strong voice, and he infers that this relatively unconscious convention shows that even the most accomplished critics are not certain about the nature and authority of the knowledge they are proposing. He traces this epistemological problem to "the collective professional illusion of objectivity" and proposes in his concluding remarks the abandonment of this illusion:

> If we can forgo the collective professional illusion of objectivity and learn to be somewhat iconoclastic about what we write, the practice and evaluation of criticism will become unashamedly exciting. Both the reading and the writing of criticism will be energized by an inquiry into the dynamics of critical language. For the study of criticism is necessarily also the study of ourselves as critics, just as the study of literature is also the study of ourselves as readers. Those critics who can (or must) risk themselves in their writing not only give us a glimpse of their own inwardness, they also let us see ourselves from a new vantage point. Perhaps that self-reflexiveness, like the self-reflexiveness of this essay, can now be welcomed.[2]

In this formulation, Nelson seeks to enlarge the traditional purview of critical discourse by including, in subsequent critical efforts, the individual critic-reader's awareness of his own purposes, motives, and feelings. This is the principle of the "involved observer" [explored in some philosophical dimension in chapter 1 of *Subjective Criticism—Ed.*]. Pursuant to this principle, the critic-reader, instead of apologizing for the appearance of motives where they were not consciously intended, attempts to articulate his motives for knowledge as the rationale for his declaration of knowledge.

In answering responses to his essay, Nelson elaborates his own motives: "Though 'Reading Criticism' was motivated partly by a need to understand my own critical practice, it would be false for me to suggest I could have written it in some more overtly confessional form. In the process of reading, rereading, and writing about other critics, I learned a good deal about myself as a critic. This is one of the rewards of studying other critics: the benefits of pure self-reflection are not the same."[3] This passage brings out the complex difficulties in the problem of studying response. The personal need of the critic-reader for self-understanding is definitely a guiding factor in the search for knowledge; yet simply to "confess" one's own motives is not satisfying either to the individual or to others in his community. Thus, Nelson's work clarifies the problem of response to some degree: How shall subjective feelings and motives be converted into publicly negotiable issues, and what knowledge does this conversion yield?

Eugene R. Kintgen's essay discusses the connection between the problem of response and the study of language. Attention to language, he points out, necessarily involves attention to style, which, in turn, cannot be understood without reference to the reader's perception of and response to language. He observes that "it is apparent that there may be no simple relation between the linguistic stimulus and our response to it, and . . . it is thus futile to attempt to account for response merely by isolating certain linguistic configurations." Furthermore, linguistic description may actually inhibit understanding of response: "It may be that the better a description is from a linguistic point of view, the less likely it is to reflect subjective processes."[4] Kintgen is one of a number of linguists who have begun to question whether formal linguistic description leads to the kind of knowledge demanded by many observers' intuitive experiences of language. He is relatively unique in this group in his tendency to understand the response to language and the response to literature as the same problem.

Kintgen's intuition of how to explain language is analogous to Nelson's of explaining literature and criticism. The intuition is that when a person uses language—either as a listener, reader, or speaker—the explanation and/or interpretation of such use is not an objective matter of formalizing a set of facts, but a subjective matter of becoming aware of how one's own participation in the study of language and literature shapes the construction of knowledge.

That the organized inquiry of the last few decades into literary response has emerged from the pedagogical community testifies that increasing numbers of literature students have intuited the inseparability of their knowledge from their experience. Yet the attempts of these students to develop some knowledge of response have met with repeated frustration, which can be ascribed to the inadequacy—or lack, in some instances—of the epistemological assumptions that prevailed in their work. Particularly, either of two main sets of assumptions were used. The first is largely objective, in that the response to a work of literature is isolated as an object of study and treated either as an independently analyzable item or as a member of a class of responses that is analyzed statistically. The second set conceives of response as the outcome of a relationship or transaction between a reader and a text, where the text is considered a real object. Although the results of both approaches have been problematical, the various research plans and their authors' judgments of their value suggest how subjective thinking may be most productively integrated into our present efforts.[5]

About twenty years ago, James R. Squire undertook to study the reading responses of fifty-two ninth and tenth graders because, "for the teacher of English, the study of literature must involve not only consideration of the literary work itself, but also concern for the way in which students respond to a literary work."[6] The rationale for Squire's work, as well as for dozens of similar studies begun at about the same time and still being conducted, is that attention to the text is not enough; attention to response is necessary. The atmosphere of this aim is pragmatic: textually oriented pedagogy was conceived as, in one way or another, ineffective. Many teachers believed that if they understood response, it would make the teaching of literature more successful, by whatever standards of success one applied.

Squire called *response* whatever a student said while he was reading a short story; he divided the stories into segments and recorded the remarks of each reader immediately after reading each segment. As a group, the resulting protocols were analyzed statistically. Each statement in each response was placed into one of the following categories: literary judgment, interpretation, narration, association, self-involvement, prescriptive judgment, and miscellaneous. The analysis showed that interpretations formed by far the largest group of statements. He further found that interpretive cogency was "generally unrelated to the intelligence and reading ability of the subjects."[7] Finally he saw that there were discernible correspondences between statements of self-involvement and those of literary judgment—that is, the same readers tended to have both sorts of statements in their responses.

Squire did not say why he thought interpretation was the predominating category, nor why he thought self-involvement and judgment seemed to go together. He did say that the independence of interpretive cogency from intelligence and reading ability reflected badly on the usefulness of the standardized tests he used to measure the latter two items. If, however, interpretation is conceived as a natural consequence of motivationally governed language experience, both its predominance as a reaction to literature and its independence of testable skills are explained. Interpretation is naturally motivated and is a more general and determining mental function than reading skill or test performance. Furthermore, if response is necessarily evaluative, deeper self-involvement brings with it more pronounced value judgments. In general, Squire observes, his statistical analysis suggests "that although certain group tendencies are observable in the reading reactions of adolescents, individual variation is caused by the unique influence of abilities, predispositions, and experiential background of each reader"[8]—that is to say, the reactions are subjective.

Squire directed part of his study toward this consideration. He investigated the personal backgrounds of thirteen of his subjects and obtained detailed information "through school counselors, conferences with teachers and individuals, and from a trained classroom observer who maintained a running anecdotal record of the behavior and comments of each student during his English class." Unfortunately, he felt unable to work with the results of this investigation: "The case studies of 13 readers revealed certain additional evidence indicating ways in which personal characteristics influence literary responses. However, the complexity of the relationships and the individual variation tend to prevent any easy generalization. Moreover, the problem of obtaining clear-cut, easily interpreted evidence is compounded by the difficulty of developing precise measures both of the responses and of personal traits."[9] The epistemological standards of precise measurement and easily interpretable evidence prevented Squire from making use of the elaborate materials he had compiled. His intuitive attentions to response and its subjective character were ultimately inhibited by his sense that there was no way to extract conclusive knowledge from the natural sources and manifestations of response and interpretation. As a result, Squire concluded that "literary analysis" remained the pedagogical goal and response only a possible subordinate function.[10]

James R. Wilson's study of the reading of novels by college freshmen, conducted about nine years after Squire's, used the same research structure—fifty-four readers responding to three novels each, with the responses statistically analyzed using Squire's categories—but investigated more fully the depth-studies of nine of the subjects. The results of the statistical analyses repeated Squire's finding regarding the predominating role of interpretation in students' responses and further suggested that classroom discussion of responses increased the readers' interpretive fluency. Wilson's more consequential observations, however, came out of the depth-studies. First, he says, although some responses "were unsophisticated or evasive, . . . fragmentary or partial . . . it would have been difficult to demonstrate that these interpretations were misinterpretations based on misreadings or on stock responses." This conclusion was reached in the course of Wilson's conscious attempt to test Squire's claim that his readers often misinterpreted and distorted the work. Wilson's finding was not ultimately contrary to Squire's; it was simply the result of closer study and less restrictive epistemological assumptions: "Even obvious misinterpretations caused by vocabulary deficiencies or by failure to finish reading the novel—and these were rarely found—involve complicated issues. On the one hand, what are the boundaries of valid interpretation? . . . On the other hand, is literature a 'structure of norms'? . . . An instrumental definition of interpretation might have bypassed these critical cruxes, but the findings suggested that an analysis of received responses was more useful.[11] Because Wilson was not certain what constitutes validity in interpretation, he was able to find complexity and value in a variety of readings and was even willing to allow the subjective source of failures of skill and discipline to enter as an ethically and psychologically legitimate aspect of a reader's interpretation. Attention to response, Wilson's work suggests, is therefore more relevant to literary study than the use of standards of interpretive accuracy.

Wilson's sense of the responses' significance led to his considering further Squire's observation regarding the connection between self-involvement and evaluative judgments. In discerning a "complex" relationship "between self-involvement and quality of interpretation," Wilson speculates that "an initial self-involvement is necessary for effective interpretational processes. Perhaps most subjects can begin to concern themselves only with questions which have personal importance. That is to say, interpretation may be a secondary predicative process, impossible without initial self-involvement." Although this is admittedly only a speculation, it accommodates Squire's observation, enlarges it to include interpretation, and thereby articulates the proposition discussed in the foregoing two chapters: interpretation is *predicated* on response. Wilson is generally less satisfied with the results of the statistical survey than was Squire, and seems to place more emphasis on the implications of the individuality of each interpretation. His protocols suggested that when there was what he deemed a "high degree of interpretational adequacy," "it seemed to unify rather than separate the processes of empathy and analysis."[12] By and large, in the context of Wilson's research, this last observation is anomalous, since it speaks against dividing the response into categories and in favor of viewing each response as a unified mental act describable mainly in connection with the respondent and only superficially in connection with other responses. More than Squire, Wilson is aware of the magnitude of this anomaly, but, again, because of the epistemological inhibition, his only recourse was to articulate it as a guideline or useful expectation for the college instructor of literature.

The work of Alan Purves, which began some years after Wilson's and still continues, proposes response study as the central feature of literary pedagogy in high school and college curricula. He has edited a series of volumes, *Responding*, which serve as texts for the response-centered curriculum he proposed some years ago.[13] The context of his proposals is the same as those of Squire and Wilson, namely, the intuition about the importance of any reader's response to literature and the creation of pragmatic plans to elicit response from and discuss it with student readers from the seventh grade through the university. Purves's epistemology is similar to Wilson's, but less responsive than Wilson's to the complexity of the issue, and thus less attentive to the subjective experience of reading.

The conceptual grounding of Purves's work is an elaborate system of classification originally designed to identify any element of all likely written manifestations of response to literature.[14] The system began as a refinement of those used by Squire and Wilson, but it became a categorical definition of the possibilities of response. The categories are engagement (or involvement), perception, interpretation, and evaluation. In the classroom, these become areas in which the teacher consciously seeks to improve student performance. Purves conceives of engagement and evaluation as being regulated by the reader and his community, while perception and interpretation are regulated by the text: "These two, the literary work and the individual who responds to it, can be used, I think, as the foci for any statements that that individual can make about a work, and these two theoretical foci could well serve as educational foci."[15] Toward the purpose of developing knowledge in the future, Purves suggests an analogous division of effort: "The next direction in research, thus, might well be exploration into the complex system of literary response. Such exploration might well employ the case-study technique of exploring many aspects of the responses of a few individuals. This technique should be combined with multivariate analysis, multidimensional scaling, partition analysis, and other more sophisticated statistical treatments."[16] In Purves's work, the attention to response is very great, while the conception of knowledge is unchanged from that of the Newtonian scientists; at best, in fact, there is no epistemology at all, as is manifested in the application of existing research techniques without a sense of how to use the knowledge they produce. For example, in order to use the four categories as developed, each class's response distribution has to be obtained, and then each category of response becomes an occasion for developing objective knowledge: presumably, a student sees that he is only involving himself but not interpreting, so that interpretation becomes the subject that he has to "learn." The pedagogical action in this instance is no different from that used when a student is required to "learn" literature. If a student should ask *why* he should now learn interpretation, the only answer he can get is that "studies show that response should (do, have to) include all four categories." Ultimately, the authority for developing knowledge is objective and prescriptive rather than subjective or self-generating. Correspondingly, organized research tries to collect larger, more statistically significant groups of responses and studies them with more complex mathematical techniques. Yet if individual response is not governed by actuarial findings, such findings serve no purpose: a reader's unique questions cannot be answered with statistical knowledge.

Purves's concrete proposals for classroom functioning show the consequences of the lack of epistemology. In the response-centered curriculum, he explains, "the teacher works to elicit the fullest possible response. At some points the teacher must be dogged about asking, 'Why?' 'What do you mean?' 'Tell us more.' 'I don't understand.' "[17] While these questions are consistent with attention to subjective response, the pedagogical issue is in the difficulty of dealing with the answers. Unless a teacher understands the kind of knowledge such questions can develop, there are no means of pursuing the discussion they begin.[18] The "fullness" of response is defined objectively from the categories, rather than subjectively from the personality orientation of the reader at that time. The handling of a reader's efforts at self-knowledge, on the other hand, uses language that refers back to the motivational basis of the reading experience. Without such a language, the answers to the above questions can be perceived only as information-giving rather than as acts of personal synthesis. Purves's program represents the limit of what can be achieved in the study of response without revising the commonsense attitude that both the responding subject and the aesthetic object may be conceived as real objects.

In several efforts to study response, these assumptions have undergone important changes, though they have not involved a shift to a new paradigm. There are elements assignable to either paradigm in the studies, but they are better characterized as aparadigmatic because their attention is on the single anomalous experience of response, with a view toward discovering what it will take to understand it. This group of studies acknowledges the active role of the reader—his status as a subject rather than an object—in developing his response, and it conceives this response as the outcome, or expression of, the reader's relationship with the author or the text or both. The text is conceived as either a real object or a person, but not as a symbolic object. These assumptions represent a renunciation of the search for mathematically formulatable knowledge, but they do not embody an alternative epistemology.

About forty years ago, D. W. Harding proposed that the response situation is analogous to the gossip situation: "The playwright, the novelist, the song-writer and the film-producing team are all doing the same thing as the gossip. . . . Each invites his audience to agree that the experience he portrays is possible and interesting, and that his attitude to it, implicit in his portrayal, is fitting." Although in gossip, "the roles of the entertainer and audience are passed backwards and forwards from one person to another," the basic condition of the onlooker defines the listener in gossip and the audience in art.[19] In this way, Harding defines the response circumstance as overtaking a central aspect of a conversational circumstance.

Pursuing this line of thought about twenty-five years later, Harding articulated his proposal more exactly. He restates the original idea by saying that "the mode of response made by the reader of a novel can be regarded as an extension of the mode of response made by an onlooker at actual events." Within this response (to art), two factors are fundamental: "imaginative or empathic insight into other living things, mainly other people," and "evaluation of the participants and what they do and suffer, an evaluation that I would relate in further analysis to his structure of interests and sentiments." Harding thus relates cognition and evaluation as codefining features of response, as I discussed earlier in the chapter. Harding then allows that the correspondent of the gossip-reader is not a collection of real people "but only *personae* created by the author for the purpose of communication."[20] Therefore, rather than further defining response by the symbolic character of its occasion, Harding returns to the original gossip model and defines response as part of a communication situation, this time with the author. Harding reaches the same intellectual destination through his attention to response that Hirsch reached through his attention to interpretation. Neither considers the symbolic nature of the work of art as the factor that most determines either response or interpretation. In spite of Harding's claim that authors communicate their own satisfaction more than meaning, he ultimately argues that "understanding in the reader and intelligibility in the author are essential to literature and involve obligations in both."[21] This view, like Hirsch's, diminishes both the psychological range and the defining function of subjective action in response and interpretation.

Like Harding, and at about the same time, Louise Rosenblatt tried to reach a new understanding of response by reconceiving the reading situation with special emphasis on the action of the reader: "Fundamentally, the process of understanding a work implies a recreation of it, an attempt to grasp completely the structured sensations and concepts through which the author seeks to convey the quality of his sense of life. Each must make a new synthesis of these elements with his own nature, but it is essential that he evoke those components of experience to which the text actually refers."[22] Rosenblatt departs from the views of Hirsch

and Harding when, after acknowledging the author's original creation of the text, she directs her attention to the reader's resynthesis not
of the author's experience but of the meanings denoted in the text. The
idea she uses to conceptualize this process is the literary transaction,
which she explains in this way: "*Transaction* is used . . . in the way that
one might refer to the interrelationship between the *knower* and what is
known." She is thus led to the distinction between "*the text*, the sequence
of printed or voiced symbols, and *the literary work* (*the poem, the novel,*
etc.), which results from the conjunction of a reader and a text."[23] This
definition of the work is the keynote of Rosenblatt's basic outlook, which
includes the idea of communication between author and reader but
considers it only a subordinate function of the reader's subjective
action—the knower's synthesis of the known.

    She points out in this connection that many facts—social, biographi-
cal, formal—may be adduced as knowledge about literature but "all such
facts are expendable unless they demonstrably help to clarify or enrich
individual experiences of specific novels, poems, or plays." Meanwhile,
the reader defines this experience by bringing "to the work personality
traits, memories of past events, present needs and preoccupations, a
particular mood of the moment and a particular physical condition.
These and many other elements in a never-to-be-duplicated combination determine his response to the peculiar contribution of the text."[24]
Each reading of a text, according to these considerations, is actually a
different poem, a term which "should designate an involvement of both
reader and text." A reading experience is an involved transaction, and
this constitutes the work. Therefore, if we seek to "know" a poem, "we
cannot simply look at the text and predict" it; rather, "a reader or
readers with particular attributes must be postulated: e.g., the author-
as-reader as he is creating the text, or as he reads it years later; a contemporary of the author with similar or different background of education and experience; other individuals living in specific places, times and
milieus."[25] These formulations amount to the claim that no work even
exists unless someone is reading it, that no matter when a text is studied
it has to be conceived as a function of some reader's mind, and that,
inversely, it cannot be described "without reference to the . . . reader."[26]
As an operational principle, this is one of the bases of subjective criticism.

    Rosenblatt's thinking represents the formulation, for the first time,
of an intellectual attitude that can accommodate response, in its full
dimensions, in the organized study of literature. Her proposals, like
those of Richards and Harding, were first presented several decades
ago, but they only began receiving attention less than a decade ago. In
the intervening years, a different outlook prevailed, that of the highly
objectivist New Criticism. This history strongly documents the existence

of the thought-paradigm developments [discussed in chapter 1 of *Subjective Criticism—Ed.*]. Only after the objective paradigm had run its course in critical and literary study did the subjective forms of thought become viable.

Rosenblatt's work, informed though it is by subjective attitudes and interests, is most problematical in its exclusive conceptual attention to literary matters. Because, for her, the special connection between a reader and a text is not given as a local manifestation of a general paradigmatic shift, the basic rationale for recognizing this connection is pragmatic. The main authority she claims is moral—it is for the good of the student to inquire into his idiosyncratic literary experience. While this argument is acceptable, it is also rejectable because many believe the contrary—namely, that on a purely pragmatic basis it may be just as important to read carefully as to respond fully. In fact, Rosenblatt believes this latter argument, since in many phases of her discussion she cautions against straying too far from the "experience to which the text actually refers."[27]

The idea of a transaction between reader and text entails, in her treatise, an equal respect for both. She argues that as the reader's response develops, it is successively altered and limited by the text rather than by a new perception of it. The assumption behind this argument is the active nature of the text. It is true that there is often an illusion that a text acts on a reader, but it can hardly be the case that a text actually does act on the reader. The subjective paradigm, in emphasizing the distinction between real objects, symbolic objects, and subjects (i.e., people), holds that only subjects are capable of initiating action and that the most fundamental form of that action is the motivated division of experience into those three classes. The distinction a subject feels between himself and the symbols he uses is the basis of sanity and conscious functioning. Symbols are the subjective correlatives of experience, just as the name *myself* is the symbol of the feeling and awareness of self. Because the reader is actually dealing with his symbolization of the text, knowledge of the reading experience has to begin with that subjective dialectic. The most that a reader can do with the real object, the text, is to see it. Readers of the same text will agree that their sensorimotor experience of the text is the same. They may also agree that the nominal meaning of the words is the same for each of them. Beyond these agreements, the only consensus about a text is on its role as a symbolic object, which means that further discussion of this text is predicated on each reader's symbolization and resymbolization of it. These two actions by the reader convert the text into a literary work. Therefore, discussion of the work must refer to the subjective syntheses of the reader and not to the reader's interaction with the text.

The issue of how to conceive the act of reading if major importance is attributed to response is most recently discussed in the work of Norman N. Holland. Although his view of the problem is different from Rosenblatt's in several key aspects, his underlying conception of reading is very similar: "Literary criticism . . . takes as its subject matter, not a text, but the transaction between a reader and a text. . . . The true focus of criticism has to be the relation between oneself and the text."[28] Holland claims that his formulations differ from Rosenblatt's because "she simply concluded that the text's causal role in the transaction equaled the perceiver's." But while Holland does not use the idea of causality to explain the role of the text,[29] he nevertheless claims that its objectivity is significant: "Every reader has available to him . . . the words-on-the-page, that is, the promptuary (a store of structured language) . . . which . . . includes constraints on how one can put its contents together."[30] Under the subjective paradigm the epistemological role of these constraints is trivial: they function as any real object functions, since they can be changed by subjective action. For Holland, they are not trivial, as can be seen from how he derived the idea of transaction.

Holland says that a literary work is the same as a "transitional object," as first defined by D. W. Winnicott. Reading is the handling of such an object: "Reading provides us with a potential space in which the distinction between 'in here' and 'out there' blurs as we ingest the external world into our ongoing psychological processes. The world of things and people presents itself to us as transitional objects that are both found reality and created symbol."[31] The transitional object is Winnicott's conceptualization of the blanket, teddy bear, or similar item an infant becomes attached to as he makes the transition from sensorimotor intelligence to representational intelligence. Sometimes this object clearly represents the child's self; at other times it is a "friend" or something "objective." Emotionally, such objects are always very important to the infant, and they are usually not susceptible to the same treatment other toys get. Whatever the "essence" of such objects, they seem to play a major role in the child's development of the capacity for symbol-making; this might have been the role played by Helen Keller's two dolls in her acquisition of language. The objects are said to exist in "potential space" because it is usually not possible to observe exactly what they mean to children at any given moment. According to our perception, the object could be subjective or objective, or both, for the child; but the main fact is that an observer cannot tell. Thus, the general term *potential space* becomes useful simply to denote the phenomenon for discourse.

With regard to reading, however, the concept complicates our thinking unnecessarily. While reading, the reader converts his sensory perception of the words into an imaginary context or system that is clearly within the purview of his own subjectivity. Unlike the transitional infant, the reader already has a well-established sense of just which objects are real and which are symbolic. The words are real, but the thoughts in his mind that bear those words are symbols or conceptions. Neither a reader nor an observer of a reader can confuse the reader's conception of this experience with any real object. There is no need, therefore, to define a special space in which to locate the "union of reader and text."[32] The symbolization of the text and the interpretive resymbolization, if any, are both located in the reader's mind.

A two-year-old knows the difference between reality and "pretend." That is, he knows how to alternate his perspective from objective to subjective. From that age onward the instances are extremely rare when a person cannot thus alternate his perspective; it can happen during inebriation, delirium, or psychosis. But except under such circumstances, the condition of being conscious is identical with being able to alternate perspectives. The defining difference between the consciousness of a linguistic person and a prelinguistic infant is that in the former there is never a blur between real objects and symbolic objects, or between either of these and people (subjects). There is no sane, conscious person who does not make a decisive distinction between "things and people," or between what is in his imagination and what is not. When there is doubt, as when one hears noises of uncertain origin, special attention is given immediately to remove the uncertainty. Finally, at any moment during the watching of a film or the reading of a book we are capable of deliberately switching our perspective from "I am watching Donald Duck" to "I am watching a picture of Donald Duck." Because the distinction in me between "in here" and "out there" is as clear in mind as ever, I know that the "text" of Donald Duck did not amuse me, but my way of perceiving and understanding it did.

Considerably more than Rosenblatt's, Holland's way of conceiving the reading and response experiences aims, as did Whitehead's, to "struggle back to some sort of objectivist position." In this cause, Holland observes that "Whitehead properly understood" supports the principle that "*one cannot separate subjective and objective perspectives.*"[33] Holland presents the idea of subjectivity just as Whitehead did, as an instance of solipsism where the mere existence of tables and chairs is denied. The palpability of ordinary real objects is Holland's main argument that subjectivity and objectivity are merged not simply in the reading experience but in all experience. This means that Holland takes the standard of reality to reside in these real objects. He thus believes that this reality is "added" to subjective experience, though he no longer believes that subjective experience can be "subtracted" from objective reality.[34] The ubiquitous potential space is the result of this addition, and the "real" reality is where the two perspectives are inseparable. The experiential consequence of this fusion, he argues, is that one no longer need trouble to distinguish between what we say is objective and what we say is subjective, since all experience, in potential space, is "transactive." For Holland, the mentation involved in the way we relate to stones, books, and people is identical: we transact them. In Holland's view, verbal meaning in a text constrains response in the same way that a stone constrains one's foot; the objectivity of each is recognized as independent and *then* it is "added" to oneself. From the viewpoint of subjective epistemology, there is a different sort of motive at work when we handle these three types of experience, and in each instance the motive is located unambiguously in the subject or in the community of subjects. . . . [In material that has been omitted here, Bleich continues by criticizing at length and in detail Holland's experimental methodology in *5 Readers Reading* on the grounds that it is an extension of the objectivist epistemology that governs his conception of the text—*Ed.*]

Consistent with the functional shrinkage of relationships, motives, and affect as defining features of response in Holland's work is the general dynamic conception of it as a reiterative process; the "one overarching idea" that sums up the four principles is "style seeks itself."[35] The basic motive for any response is the person's need to replicate his personality style. Holland claims that as a matter of epistemological principle, "tenacity, not negotiation, is the human style, for we use the ideas we hold to re-create our very identities."[36] This attitude is as defensible as any other sort of conservatism: there is sense in declaring the inertial character of personality, and there is sense in understanding certain behaviors as features of this character. But in which context is this sort of understanding appropriate? In the act of declaring that "style seeks itself," Holland defines the context of its application as any one where it appears that style does not seek itself. Thus, when a person perceives an experience as, in some important way, a departure from the normal run of experience, he would, if he accepts this principle, have to understand the new experience as a repetition of previous experiences: the act of resymbolization would be consciously directed toward denying the novelty of the experience. The idea of novelty loses its meaning altogether.

But there is a more serious consequence than the loss of novelty. If the act of self-enlightenment is only an act of self-replication, the idea that consciousness is an organ of self-enhancement has to be discarded. The defining characteristic of consciousness is its ability to take deliberate initiatives to improve the lot of the individual. This involves a continuing series of complex alterations of one's self-image and the conscious pursuit of experience that will facilitate greater psychological and social adaptability. If a person decides that he will begin a regimen of jogging, for example, it does not constitute an explanation of this act to say that it replicates his identity. But it is an explanation to adduce a motive for his attempt to *change* his preexisting self-image or lifestyle. By the same reasoning, it can hardly constitute an explanation of a new reading experience to translate the new configuration of perceptions, feelings, and interpretations into the ever-present identity theme. The search for an explanation is, to begin with, an act motivated by the desire to enlarge or enhance the sense of self at that time, and not by the desire to retain that sense exactly as before; in fact, the continuing process of growth defines any new act of ideation as a contribution to that process. The motive for perceiving the self-replication of certain behaviors appears only in therapy, where the experience of past disharmonies has produced a painful present that needs alleviation. But the ordinary engagement of self in new experiences has not such therapeutic motive; it proceeds from the natural impulse to articulate a new sense of self more commensurate with the most recent life circumstances. Style seeking itself, like the identity theme, cannot be a principle that explains response.

Early in this chapter, I claimed that the study of response and interpretation and the experience of them are part of the same activity. My discussion of the epistemological problems in the various approaches to response study held this claim as an implicit evaluative standard which proceeds from the subjective principle that the observer is part of the observed while the observed is defined by the observer. In his recent work, Stanley Fish reached the same standard by following established critical and pedagogical assumptions to their logical conclusions, just as Bridgman reached a subjective viewpoint by logically extending operationalism.

Fish began by considering the familiar question of how to understand and teach literary style. His normal habit of study was that taught by New Critics—scrupulously close reading of literature. The first important fact that he came upon was that every time he read another word in a poem, or another group of words, his *whole sense* of the poem changed. Although at first tempted to say that this change is to be understood as an action of the text, he soon conceived the source of the action as his own linguistic and literary experience. He thus observed:

> The objectivity of the text is an illusion, and moreover, a dangerous illusion, because it is so physically convincing. The illusion is one of self-sufficiency and completeness. A line of print or a page or a book is so obviously *there*—it can be handled, photographed, or put away—that it seems to be the sole repository of whatever value and meaning we associate with it. (I wish the pronoun could be avoided, but in a way *it* makes my point.) This is of course the unspoken assumption behind the word "content." The line or page or book *contains*—everything.[37]

In his awareness of his own language as well as of the accepted language of criticism ("content"), Fish shows that when we symbolize a symbolic object as a real object, the result is an illusion. This passage also implies what I would state explicitly—that the motive for maintaining this illusion is the comfort in the palpability of an item which, in its definitive functions, is imaginary. Fish does suggest parenthetically that "perhaps literature is what disturbs our sense of self-sufficiency, personal and linguistic." His conviction about the authenticity of this circumstance leads to the decisive shift of attitude: "I would rather have an acknowledged and controlled subjectivity than an objectivity which is finally an illusion."[38]

The subjective assumption was necessitated by several considerations regarding the nature of language. One of these is the widely accepted distinction between literary and ordinary language. Among critics, Fish states, literary language occupied a special position as intrinsically other than everyday language. Among linguists, everyday language was taken as a common denominator the explanation of which in terms of formal rules was believed to describe any manifestation of language. But because semantic aspects of any language system are "a motivating force in that system," whether literary or ordinary, the "objectively descriptive language unattached to situations and purposes that was traditionally at the center of linguistic philosophy is shown to be a fiction."[39] Language as a separate phenomenon cannot be so investigated because it necessarily includes the "realm of values, intentions, and purposes,"[40] the sources of which are always in the users of language:

> Literature is still a category, but it is an open category, not definable by fictionality, or by a disregard of propositional truth, or by a statistical predominance of tropes and figures, but simply by what we decide to put into it. The difference lies not in the language but in ourselves. Only such a view, I believe, can accommodate and reconcile the two intuitions that have for so long kept linguistic and literary theory apart; the intuition that there *is* a class of literary utterances, and the intuition that any piece of language can become a member of that class.[41]

The openness of linguistic categories places the authority for their definition in subjective initiative. With regard to symbolic objects, intuitions are definitive, in that a shared intuition objectifies the literary status of, say, *Hamlet*, but the lack of such sharing withholds this status from *Captain Marvel:* "All aesthetics, then, are local and conventional rather than universal, reflecting a collective decision as to what will count as literature, a decision that will be in force only so long as a community of readers or believers (it is very much an act of faith) continues to abide by it."[42] Fish's affirmation of the intuition that sees language and literature as commonly rooted in subjective choice over the intuition that separates the two as different objects results from a crisis in the development of knowledge. In both criticism and linguistics, the dependency of knowledge on varying degrees of communal faith had, under the influence of positivism, been devalued. The subjective assumption renders both areas of knowledge responsible to each other and, mainly, to the fact that language governs all forms of ideation in these disciplines.

Fish portrays the crisis of interpretive knowledge in criticism as originating in the objective indeterminacy of verbal meanings of key passages in many prominent works. Any word available to multiple contradictory meanings "transfers the pressure of judgment to us."[43] The functional role of an interpretive problem in the act of reading is to produce awareness of the equivalence of reading and interpretation. Even though the occasions which instigate such awareness do not occur at every word read, they nevertheless imply the generality of the reader's constructive action in any form of interpretation:

> What I am suggesting is that formal units are always a function of the interpretive model one brings to bear; they are not "in" the text, and I would make the same argument for intentions. That is, intention is no more embodied "in" the text than are formal units; rather an intention, like a formal unit, is made when perceptual or interpretive closure is hazarded; it is verified by an interpretive act, and I would add, it is not verifiable in any other way. . . . intention is known when and only when it is recognized; it is recognized as soon as you decide about it; you decide about it as soon as you make a sense; and you make a sense . . . as soon as you can.[44]

In this view, any literary judgment has to be understood as part of the critic's definable perspective. Thus, only two readers who agree that there will be such a thing as an extractable author's intention will perceive this intention. The authority for such a perception lies only in the influence of that interpretive community which claims that perspective, which is its accepted way of making a sense of what it reads. Aside from this community's choice of perspective, there is no authority for claiming the objectivity of the author's intention in the text. For any community, "the choice is never between objectivity and interpretation but between interpretation that is unacknowledged as such and an interpretation that is at least aware of itself."[45] Thus, Fish shifts the standard of interpretation from illusory objectivities to communally declared awareness. This means that interpretations can be authorized by subjective resymbolization and intersubjective negotiation, and by nothing else.

Although Fish believes that this is the only view of interpretation that can be held with full integrity—that is, with no illusions or other superstitious claims—he suggests two problems which follow from it: first, there seems no way to "prove" that one is a member of a particular interpretive community, and second, one cannot finally identify the object of interpretation. From the perspective of the subjective paradigm, these are not problems, however. Fish actually solved the first problem himself. He says, "You will agree with me (that is, understand) only if

you already agree with me."[46] This is the definition of a community—
people who already agree with one another—and this fact is immediately
obvious to a third party. Proof does not enter the question. On a less
immediate level a community is founded on similarities of *concern*, where
agreement is not always necessary except of what is of common interest.
If this is not obvious, it is always negotiated until it is; if the negotiation is
unsuccessful, the community dissolves. Conversely, the sheer con-
tinuance of the community means that negotiations have thus far been
successful. In any case, the simple "knowing" that one is in a community
on the part of two or more people defines that community.

The second problem is solved by conceiving interpretation as resymbolization of the interpreter's *response*. Although the fact of response
is implicit in Fish's understanding of language, it does not enter into his
conception of interpretation. If the object of interpretation is thought to
be either the text or nothing, then it is not possible to name that object.
But response, like a text, is a symbolic object and may be understood to
be the text as immediately and evaluatively perceived. Fish indicates his
own tendency to give special attention to line endings, and his subsequent reasonings accrue from this perceptual habit.[47] Therefore, it is
no contradiction of his argument to say that he likes to interpret his
perceptions of line endings in seventeenth-century poetry. I identify
Fish's symbolization of his texts—his perceptual stress on line endings—
as his response, and I identify his resymbolization of his response—the
judgment that ambiguous line endings make a special demand on him
the reader—as his interpretation. He then interprets his interpretation
in the ways I have just discussed. The immediate motive for the interpretation is the response; however, to propose a motive for the response
requires a more personal interaction with Fish. In the present context,
this latter motive is not germane. Fish's logic of interpretation is consistent with the logic I outlined in the previous chapter. Fish's conception
of interpretation is consistent with the present understanding of both
response and interpretation as instances of subjective symbol-formation.
To include response in the general notion of interpretation is to establish
a means both to acknowledge and control the subjective perspective that
is now needed for further thought.

The consequences of this orientation of thought, which has governed my own efforts over the past decade (as well as, in part, the recent
work of Fish, Kintgen, and Nelson) are suggested in studies by Susan
Elliott and Thornton Jordan of their own responses. These two inquiries
aim less to produce "insight" in the traditional critical sense than to
document how a proposal of knowledge about language and literature
may be systematically authorized through deliberate attention to response. As with the work of Squire, Wilson, Purves, and Rosenblatt, the
work of Elliott and Jordan grew from the increasing difficulty of using

New Critical insight in pedagogical communities. The general result of the subjective attitude makes knowledge seem more reliable because it is not conceived as a real object or "thing" and because it allows each community to authorize its own knowledge with its own experiences.

Susan Elliott's study "Fantasy behind Play" (1973)[48] is an examination of the critical reaction and her own responses to Harold Pinter's *The Birthday Party, The Caretaker,* and *The Homecoming.* She explores reviewers' and scholars' comments about these plays and takes special note of their complaints that traditional literary comprehension is usually frustrated by study of the plays. Counting herself among those readers with the same complaint, Elliott presents and discusses her own free-associative response statements with the aim of further defining for herself the emotional character of, and reasons for, her general attitude toward the plays. Her detailed analyses of both the criticism and her responses produce the conclusion that her involvement in each play yields a similar feeling in her—the "odd man out" syndrome, in which she feels socially ostracized and sexually impotent. These feelings, in turn, explain her sense of intellectual frustration. That is, because she peremptorily sees the plays as occasion in which she is ostracized and impotent, she objectifies these feelings by saying *the plays* are irrational, incomprehensible, or absurd. Insofar as other readers are rendering similar judgments, sometimes with similar personal justifications, Elliott is proposing knowledge about the community of Pinter readers *to* this community, and she is authorizing her proposals by presenting her responses in detailed, organized forms.

In the conclusion to this study, Elliott reports the following observation, which she calls a "most amazing experience":

> In the midst of seeing Pinter's most recent play, *Old Times,* for the first time in . . . 1971, I felt myself powerfully rejecting it and saying in great disappointment, "Pinter didn't make it this time. How awful this is!" I felt terribly depressed after seeing the production. After hours of argument with my husband about what it was about, I suddenly recognized my problem. On the surface, the play had me stymied; I was puzzled. This had never before occurred to me so long after an experience of Pinter. Usually I had it "all figured out." I say that I was puzzled "on the surface" because later, after setting down some thoughts that came to mind about the play, and reading it once it was published, I understood some of my essential identifications with the characters and my emotional involvement in their situations. To be brief, they recalled some rather painful and disturbing associations to adolescence and made quite evident to me a recurrent theme of my responses to the plays studied here, the "odd man out" symdrome in my psychic life. Since that recognition of my subjective relationship to the play, I have re-read it several times, taught it to three undergraduate classes, seen it in two more productions, and enjoyed most of these experiences immensely.[49]

It is of particular interest in this report that Elliott's experience of the new play appeared to her at first uninfluenced by her previous lengthy involvement in the other plays and in Pinter criticism in general. Her knowledge of her patterns of response to the previous plays could not predict the response to the new work. On the one hand, it was "predictable" that Elliott would be puzzled by the new play as she had been by the others; on the other hand, it was also "predictable" that she would *not* be puzzled, owing to her awareness of how she had responded in the past. Her remark "Pinter didn't make it this time" suggests that she was significantly aware of her previous Pinter experiences as she watched this play. This fact strongly implies the determining influence of the respondent's *current* state of mind. The evaluation of that state begins with the recording of the response—"setting down some thoughts that came to mind about the play"—and then considering them in retrospect, which, in this instance, did involve reading the play as well as viewing it. The subsequent decision that she perceived the play in terms of a previously known psychological syndrome—the "odd man out syndrome"—is not a revelation about the inevitability of a certain response to Pinter in Elliott, but a formulation of how she understands her present concern with this author's work. Both the character of the response and Elliott's subsequent comprehension of it are local and must be understood by the rest of us not as a definition of her character but as a statement of her commitment to this group of works and to the community of those similarly committed.

Once the interpretations of Pinter are grounded in this psychological perspective, the proposals of how others understand and react to Pinter's work are authorized for negotiation. Instead of proposing a thought in the form "This is how Pinter is," Elliott says, "This is how I see his work." The former statement constitutes "an objectivity which is finally an illusion"; the latter is an "acknowledged and controlled subjectivity."

Thornton Jordan's use of a similar epistemology in the study of his response to the Joseph story in *Genesis* suggests certain consequential connections between language and interpretation and makes it possible to conceive of alternatives to the logical analyses of language currently used by linguists. After recording his perception of, and feelings about, the Joseph story, Jordan's retrospective analysis of his work yields the following observations: "The sense of double emotions, often ambivalent, is the dominant emotional chord of my response. . . . I let my ambivalent feelings influence my estimation of Joseph. . . . While I see his anger as a source of strength, I judge his patience, obedience, and sense of duty as 'inhuman.'" Jordan observes that in general, when he likes Joseph, it is for strengths Jordan claims for himself, and when he rejects him, it is for weaknesses he eschews in himself. He traces these feelings to his handling of his ongoing relationship with his father: "My sense of mission towards my father was founded on the double feelings of sensitive concern for his feelings and my own guilt for my mother's death."[50] These formulations of the motives guiding the response as a whole then become an explanatory principle for a prominent language pattern in the response statement: specifically, "ambivalence is characteristic of my style in this particular paper, as in the following examples":

(1) Joseph is envied *not only* because he is the favorite *but* because he is a tattletale, and he reveals his dream of superiority to his brothers.

(2) *On the one hand,* his retention of anger is a source of strength; *on the other,* his patience and obedience are inhuman.

(3) As I attempted to run away from home, I was *both* scared *and* angry.

(4) I chose my career *partly* from desire, *partly* as a gesture of anger.

(5) There were two motives for my choices: *one to pursue* a career on my own terms, *the other to bring my father* to recognize me.

(6) In emotional exile I felt the *double feeling* of resentment and longing.

(7) *I was angry and pained* at my parents' decision, *but* I characteristically. . . .

(8) *I felt like* an alien . . . *but* did well.

(9) *I recognize* the advantage of Joseph's withholding resent, *yet* I resent it.[51]

As an objective set of sentences bearing a semantic pattern, this is not very different from the hundreds of analogous ones extracted from novels and studied in the scholarly literature of stylistics. But the epistemological status of this set is considerably different because it was written by Jordan in one motivational context and then interpreted by him in a subsequent context, itself created by the first one. The succession of motives defines Jordan's interpretive authority in much the same way as Freud's interpretation of his own dreams became authoritative: the meanings for the sentences are defined, not in the act of writing them, but in the process of interpretation. The sentences have a nominal meaning independent of Jordan's judgment, but only in the sense that other speakers of English identify them as English sentences. Any view of a language sample beyond trivial functional identification must involve interpretation and, therefore, the motives and subjectivity of the interpreter. To propose a meaning for this set of sentences is to propose knowledge about Jordan and his community of cosubjects. Such proposals are more satisfyingly understood in psychological, rather than logical, formulations.

The doubleness Jordan indicates in the nine sentences quoted above appears in a variety of grammatical forms, sometimes through the juxtaposition of clauses, other times in two parts of the same predicate. As studies in stylistics have repeatedly shown, it is practically impossible to draw conclusions about language from a direct comparison of syntax

and semantics, even though the intuition persists that they are systematically related.[52] Jordan's psychological considerations, however, help to
validate this intuition. His idea of doubleness is derived from his knowledge of ambivalent feelings toward his father that are connected with his
conception of himself and his perception of Joseph. In their varying
grammatical forms, the sentences reflect these feelings. If the sentences
are analyzed logically, the same value would be applied, say, to all main
clauses. If they are analyzed motivationally, each articulation of doubleness is the primary psychological initiative that determines how the
structure of each sentence is defined. Sentence 4, for example, is made
up of two parts: "I chose my career," and "partly from desire, partly as a
gesture of anger." The two parts of sentence 5 are on either side of the
colon. Sentence 6 divides into two parts between "felt" and "the." Each of
these pairs is a semantic, as opposed to grammatical, predication. The
pair of ambivalent feelings in the semantic "predicate" is a personal
comment on a variety of local topics. In sentences such as 2, 7, and 8, the
predicate appears by itself as an instance of a full-sentence presentation
of what Jordan considers the main feeling of the response. Because
there is a prior psychological subject for these predicates, they are similar in psychological import to sentences 4, 5, and 6. In these latter sentences, the phrases "I chose my career," "There were two motives for my
choices," and "In emotional exile I felt" presuppose an analogy between
the speaker and Joseph. This analogy, which may be provisionally formulated as "the fact that I identify with Joseph" or "I perceive myself as I
perceive Joseph," is the prior psychological subject for sentences 2, 7,
and 8. Furthermore, the phrases "Joseph is envied" in sentence 1 and
"As I attempted to run away from home" in sentence 3 are also specific
new instances of the main prior psychological subject.

This prior subject is Jordan's *perception* of the text, or the text as he
perceives it. Each full sentence written in response to this perception
represents a different psychological initiative taken with the main perception, a different resymbolization of the original perception of the
text—the original symbolization. Jordan's thoughts at the time of response concerned an analogy between this story and his own experience
with his father and the extent to which this analogy is tenable for him.
Accordingly, the response may be understood as a subjective dialectic
between Jordan's identification with Joseph and his identification with
(or distance from) his father. When the subjects and predicates of the
sentences are understood as discussed above, each sentence manifests
this dialectic, which, in turn, constitutes the meaning of the sentences
most relevant to Jordan's context of presentation. The advantage of
understanding the response this way is that the interpretation is immediately seen as a subjective presentation. There is no need to claim
that the Joseph story is "about" ambivalent feelings of sons toward
fathers, since it is obvious that this describes *Jordan's* experience of the

story. More importantly, however, the language of the presentation is not subject to arbitrary confusion. The variety of predications given by each of the nine sentences are different dimensions in which the basic response motive is the organizing principle of self-expression for Jordan, and a principle of interpretation for his cosubjects to use, even with individual sentences and phrases.[53]

Undoubtedly, Jordan's sentences are describable with transformational rules to some extent; semantically, they do not seem obscure. The epistemological question is, How explanatory can logically formulated rules be in a consequential, knowledge-making context such as this? Even if every detail of the nine sentences is accounted for formally, it will not explain how or why *Jordan* made these sentences. Logical explanations have been most convincing in coping with mechanical phenomena and least convincing with psychological events. Alternatively, motivated behavior cannot be explained by finding a way to deny the presence of motives either in the behavior or in the explanation; behavior that always involves a subject—in this instance, language behavior—is most easily understood through motivational or subjective explanations.

Most of the sentences used to demonstrate the operation of linguistic rules are specifically stipulated to be unmotivated—that is, unrelated to the speaker and to his context of utterance. These sentences—such as the well-known "John is eager to please"—have only a trivial semantic: the nominal meaning is never in doubt. The concept of competence defines sentences by their formulation alone and thus defines out of consideration the only contexts in which language has any consequence to begin with—when individuals use it to deal with one another and with themselves. In the so-called steady-state functioning of language, the abstract form of sentences is shared by two or more speakers to the extent that this form is simply not a factor in the sentence exchange; it therefore cannot constitute an explanation of the language events. If the concept of competence is conceived as "capability of performance," it is determined by perusal of the range of sentences everyone already speaks, and nothing has been explained. If *competence* refers to "permissibility of performance," *permissibility* can only mean "that which the speaking situation permits," since each speaker is perfectly capable of changing rules arbitrarily and saying what he pleases. Speaking situations constrain speech to certain formalities and habits in order that we may isolate the unique and personal features of each contribution. The mutual perception of one another's unique contributions is the matter to be explained in any language situation. If this is the case, the formal abstraction of each speaker's sentences must be a subfeature of the motives which define the teleology of the speech situation, and the motives cannot be a subfeature of the abstractions.[54]

The practice of formulating response statements is a means for making a language experience (hearing, speaking, reading, or writing) available for conversion into knowledge. A response can acquire meaning only in the context of a predecided community (two or more people) interest in knowledge. These are the circumstances in which Jordan reached the knowledge he claimed. Aware of an identity element in himself as a teacher, Jordan entered class with the conscious purpose of reading and responding in cooperation with the others in the class. He collected a group of response statements, one of which is his own. It is not immediately clear what he or anyone else has learned, nor is it obvious how to coordinate the responses with one another. At this point, the subjective conception of language and interpretation governs the procedural options by posing the question "What do I, Mr. Jordan, a member of this pedagogical community, want to know?" To develop knowledge, the first step is not to consult the data, like an empiricist, or to consult an abstraction, like a rationalist. Rather, one *decides,* as in everyday life, what one would like to know. Jordan's attempt to characterize his own self-knowledge, like Elliott's, then makes it possible for the classroom community to negotiate that formulation in a direction of common interest. Jordan proposed both interpretive knowledge of the reading experience—knowledge of his own language habits in that response—and provisional knowledge regarding the connections between response, interpretation, and linguistic style. The main point is that response cannot be one particular object or thing that each person produces as just another learning activity; rather, it is an expression of, and declaration of, self in a local context reflecting a set of local choices, motives, and interests in knowledge.

Most of the negative receptions to response studies can be traced to an abiding sense that *any* means of making subjective experiences public necessarily leads to psychological danger, intellectual disarray, and pedagogical anarchy; some proponents of subjective pedagogy have even supported a certain degree of anarchy as a valuable principle.[53] Yet it seems obvious to me that such pitfalls are the common risks of any social initiative that involves new thinking.

The connection between knowledge of language and literature and the formation of interpretive communities originates in the common social purpose of pedagogy. Kuhn has suggested that the usual conception of science as a monolith of truth was created by the transformation of scientific knowledge into textbook knowledge, which stresses unambiguous presentation of accepted formalisms. This fact points less to a defect in the establishment of knowledge than to a normal circumstance of its use and, more importantly, to its origin in personal and interpersonal motivation. In addition to its undisputed utilitarian function (say, of healing the sick), knowledge formation is a natural psychological function, and it takes place in the minds of young people and adults regardless of whether they go to school. Like the infantile process of language acquisition, subsequent contexts of knowledge formation are always communal, even if a particular individual forms knowledge in opposition to his community. Part of the communal contribution to new knowledge is to facilitate the dialectical process that leads to this knowledge. The activity of developing knowledge is as phylogenetically founded as the formation of new families.

When knowledge is no longer conceived as objective, the purpose of pedagogical institutions from the nursery through the university is to synthesize knowledge rather than to pass it along: schools become the regular agency of subjective initiative. Because language use and the interpretive practices that follow from it underlie the processes of understanding, the pedagogical situations in which consciousness of language and literature is exercised establish the pattern of motives a student will bring to bear in his own pursuit of knowledge. For the development of subjective knowledge, motivation has to become a consciously articulable experience, and the configuration of classroom relationships—between student and student and between teacher and student—themselves have to motivate such articulation. This involves a definition of the purpose, authority, and scope of the subjective classroom.

Notes

1. Cary Nelson, "Reading Criticism," *PMLA* 91 (October 1976): 801–15; and Eugene R. Kintgen, "Reader Response and Stylistics," *Style* 11 (Winter 1977): 1–18.

2. Nelson, "Reading Criticism," p. 813.

3. Cary Nelson, "Forum," *PMLA* 92 (March 1977): 311.

4. Kintgen, "Reader Response," pp. 10–11.

5. The material that I am about to review will not include the contributions of the European school of Rezeptionsästhetik, which has produced considerable work by Ingarden, Jauss, Iser, Groeben, and others. This work has been reviewed recently by Rien Segers in "Readers, Text, and Author: Some Implications of Rezeptionsästhetik," *Yearbook of Comparative and General Literature*, no. 24 (1975): 15–23. Most of the European studies differ in a fundamental way from those discussed here, for these European writers aim mainly at presenting models of the reader without studying specific responses of specific readers and without inquiring into their own mental processes as readers. A study with purposes different from my own would probably provide a more suitable context to investigate this work in detail and to take into account its variety of theoretical formulations about the "aesthetics of reception."

6. James R. Squire, *The Responses of Adolescents While Reading Four Short Stories* (Urbana, Ill.: National Council of Teachers of English, 1964), p. 1. The study was begun about eight years before it was published.

7. Ibid., p. 51.

8. Ibid., p. 50.

9. Ibid., pp. 15–27.

10. Ibid., p. 54. Here is a specific sense in which Squire conceives literary analysis: "Techniques which enable the teacher to offer help in how to interpret at times when the

interpretations are being made may increase the effectiveness of instruction in literary analysis. A teacher may read a portion of a story to a class, for example, and then ask students to predict the behavior of the characters on the basis of the segment presented. A comparison of the responses of students with the actual events in the remaining portion of the story could enable the teacher to deal concretely with such problems as plausibility and objectivity in interpretation." While this technique may be of interest, it remains no different from traditional means of teaching in its ultimate measurement of interpretive efficacy by assuming the psychological norm of the text. Thus, a student who did not guess the correct ending would have to consider his guess valid, even though this guess might well contain an important degree of truth value for that reader.

11. James R. Wilson, *Responses of College Freshmen to Three Novels* (Urbana, Ill.: National Council of Teachers of English, 1966), pp. 39, 40.

12. Ibid., p. 38.

13. Alan C. Purves, ed. *How Porcupines Make Love: Notes on a Response-Centered Curriculum* (Lexington, Mass.: Xerox Publishing Co., 1972).

14. The classification system was first proposed in Alan C. Purves and Victoria Rippère, *Elements of Writing About a Literary Work: A Study of Responses to Literature* (Urbana, Ill.: National Council of Teachers of English, 1968).

15. Ibid., p. 64. Purves's conception of the text as a regulative norm may be seen in his view of the act of perceiving a work of literature: "When the student examines his statement of perception, he has recourse only to the text . . . and he can prove the validity of his statement by showing that the data are sufficient" (p. 61). As I have already discussed in some detail in *Readings and Feelings: An Introduction to Subjective Criticism* (Urbana, Ill.: National Council of Teachers of English, 1975), a reader's perception of the text is of pedagogical interest far more in its idiosyncratic dimension than in its correspondence to the text, which can never be exact. I further discuss this matter in chapter 5 of *Subjective Criticism* (Baltimore: The Johns Hopkins University Press, 1978).

16. Alan C. Purves and Richard Beach, *Literature and the Reader: Research in Response to Literature, Reading Interests, and the Teaching of Literature* (Urbana, Ill.: National Council of Teachers of English, 1972), p. 37.

17. Purves, *How Porcupines Make Love*, p. 48.

18. In the "Readers' Response to Literature" session at the November 1976 convention of the National Council of Teachers of English in Chicago, the presentation by Walter Slatoff was "On Responding to Readers' Responses," and that of Richard Adler was "They Read; They Respond. Then What?" As Slatoff's title suggests, his approach is informal; he encourages responses, but lacking any epistemological teleology, finds it difficult to integrate and define the authority he feels he has as a teacher; once he asserts this authority, the collection and discussion of response begins deferring altogether to him, and the class assumes a traditional format. Adler reported how he, by and large, followed Purves's technique and likewise defined his pedagogical authority in the traditional manner. It is particularly noteworthy in these two instances that epistemology is shown to be decisively tied to how each teacher conceives his classroom authority. The work of Fish, Elliott, and Jordan, discussed later in this essay, helps to enlighten this issue.

19. D. W. Harding, "The Role of the Onlooker," *Scrutiny* 6 (December 1937): 257.

20. D. W. Harding, "Psychological Processes in the Reading of Fiction," *British Journal of Aesthetics* 2 (April 1962): 147.

21. D. W. Harding, "Reader and Author," *Experience into Words: Essays on Poetry* (London: Chatto and Windus, 1963), p. 173. In fact, Harding argues that the author's communication of his satisfaction depends on his meaning. This view of meaning is the same as Hirsch's: when "we depart too far from any meaning that the work could possibly have had for its author, . . . we lose the possibility of sharing in his satisfaction with the finished work" (p. 168). If, however, the reader's satisfaction and his meaning are not

identified with the author's, the range of possible experience from reading is much wider and regulated by the reader's responsibility to himself and his community.

22. Louise M. Rosenblatt, *Literature as Exploration* (1938; revised and rpt., New York: Noble, 1968), p. 113.

23. Ibid., p. 27n. These views are also discussed in idem, "The Poem as Event," *College English* 26, no. 2 (November 1964): 123–28.

24. Rosenblatt, *Literature as Exploration*, pp. 27, 30–31.

25. Rosenblatt, "The Poem as Event," p. 127.

26. Rosenblatt, *Literature as Exploration*, p. 29.

27. Ibid., p. 113. Throughout Rosenblatt's treatise, there are formulations that imply an objective distinction between adequate and inadequate interpretation: "The attainment of a sound vision of the work will require the disengagement of the passing or irrelevant from the fundamental and appropriate elements in his response to the text. What was there in his state of mind that led to a distorted or partial view of the work?" (p. 79). As soon as there is a sense of "sound vision" or "distorted" perception, the ideal of objective correctness is implicitly invoked, and any student knows this. Rosenblatt subsequently speaks of the need to attain "an undistorted vision of the work of art" and argues that "the student should be led to discover that some interpretations are more defensible than others" (p. 115). I think that students already know that they can defend certain views better than other views, and that their task is to come to terms with the niggling suspicion that the teacher's interpretation is somehow always more defensible than their own. The universal facts of perceptual distortion and idiosyncratic interpretation come across in Rosenblatt's argument as immoral or inadequate features of mental functioning rather than definitive features that seek conscious cultivation in school. The idea of "transaction" is a rationalization for the contradiction between the habitual belief in objective interpretation and the new-found sense of the reader's defining activity. I will discuss this matter further in connection with both Rosenblatt and Norman N. Holland.

28. Norman N. Holland, *5 Readers Reading* (New Haven: Yale University Press, 1975), p. 248.

29. Norman N. Holland, "The New Paradigm: Subjective or Transactive?" *New Literary History* 7, no. 2 (Winter 1976): 345n. Rosenblatt did not discuss causality either, and she reached the same conclusion Holland did, but considerably before him. Rosenblatt did not invoke an epistemological paradigm; Holland did not either before Professor Ralph Cohen invited the essay cited above in response to my essay, "The Subjective Paradigm in Science, Psychology, and Criticism," which appears in the same issue of *New Literary History*. Holland claims his paradigm to be that "*one cannot separate subjective and objective perspectives*" (p. 339; italics in original). This circumstance cannot be paradigmatic because it *states* that no paradigm is in effect. Holland conceptualizes the aparadigmatic state by claiming mental life takes place in "potential space," as I discuss in the text. This space is the same as the one-year-old's "transitional space," which the infant has not yet divided up into objective and subjective perceptions. Applied to adult life, this idea denies the obvious and fundamental fact that one can systematically vary one's perspective from objective to subjective and that one does this as a matter of everyday behavior. From the standpoint of the subjective paradigm, any perspective as well as the possibilities for new perspectives are determined by subjective capacities for perception and cognition. The claim for inseparable perspectives amounts to a declaration of the chaotic nature of the human mind; epistemologically, our demand is to distinguish sensibly among perspectives, rather than to deny the problem by declaring no distinction possible.

Heinrich Henel ("Forum," *PMLA* 91, no. 2 [March 1976]: 293–94) has a similar view of Holland's formulations. He first observes that Holland's essay "UNITY IDENTITY TEXT SELF" (*PMLA* 90, no. 5 [October 1975]: 813–22 [chapter 8 in this volume—*Ed.*]) "is so full of hedges, equivocations, and contradictions that it is difficult to take issue with him." After detailing these difficulties, he concludes: "What actually happened is that Holland's objective criterion, which he mentions only to brush it aside, triumphed at least in this instance." Although my overall viewpoint is not Henel's, I agree with his perception of Holland's work. I believe there are so many hedges and so many evidences of the "objective criterion" because there is an out-and-out rejection of the whole epistemological question: "one cannot separate" the two perspectives. The hedges appear when Holland contradicts his declaration, and then arbitrarily and silently separates his perspectives and retains the right to claim an absolute objective perspective for himself.

30. Holland, *5 Readers Reading*, p. 286. Earlier, he had explained: "Yet the words can't be just anything. Miss Emily [in "A Rose for Emily"], we have noted, cannot be an Eskimo—at least not without doing violence to the text. The writer creates opportunities for projection but he also sets constraints on what the reader can or cannot project into the words-on-the-page and how he can or cannot combine them. The reader can violate these stringencies, of course, but if he does so, he loses the possibility of sharing with others and winning their support for his lonely and idiosyncratic construct" (pp. 219-20). This argument is identical to Hirsch's with regard to the author's determinate meaning. It is not a matter of dispute or interpretation whether Emily is an Eskimo or a salesgirl. But if someone *says* Emily is an Eskimo, this is an act of interpretation that can easily have meaning to an Eskimo. Holland is assuming that Emily *is* this or that; there are interpretations of *Hamlet* that *say* Hamlet is a woman; everyone understands that such interpretations are given over and above his putative designation as a man, since no one disputes the nominal designation. From a subjective standpoint, there is truth value in any such seriously-given reading, and to moralistically claim violations of the text is only an attempt to say that one's own objectification is more authoritative than someone else's. At the same time, the text cannot thus be understood as constraining, except in a trivial sense. The prior agreement by a community of readers to accept *this* text transfers all constraining action to the community and its motives in handling its language.

31. Ibid., pp. 287-88. The idea of the transitional object was invented to make a distinction between infantile and adult mental experience. To say, as Holland does, that experiencing in general takes place in this way cancels the understanding that Winnicott originally brought.

32. Ibid., p. 290.

33. Holland, "The New Paradigm," pp. 342, 339; italics in the original.

34. Terms like *add* and *substract,* as well as the mathematical metaphors of function he uses in the essay cited above, further suggest the objectivist orientation of Holland's thinking.

35. Holland, *5 Readers Reading*, p. 113.

36. Holland, "The New Paradigm," p. 342. This claim is about as consequential as the familiar religious ones that say that man is basically good (or evil or guilty or sinful) and then derive ethical imperatives from the claim.

37. Stanley E. Fish, "Literature in the Reader: Affective Stylistics," *New Literary History* 2, no. 1 (Autumn 1970): 140.

38. Ibid., pp. 147, 146.

39. Stanley E. Fish, "How Ordinary Is Ordinary Language?" *New Literary History* 5, no. 1 (Autumn 1973): 50.

40. Ibid., p. 51.

41. Ibid., p. 52. I would put the argument thus: since language and literature are, when objects of study, symbolic, their status depends on semantics, values, intentions, and purposes; therefore, the principles of subjectivity and motivation, rather than those of objective explanation, are to be used.

42. Ibid. If we understand *aesthetics* to mean "knowledge of language and literature," this statement describes the intersubjective negotiation that develops such knowledge.

43. Stanley E. Fish, "Interpreting the *Variorum*," *Critical Inquiry* 2, no. 2 (Spring 1976): 468 (chapter 10 in this volume). The implication of this transfer is that "it is the structure of the reader's experience rather than any structures available on the page that should be the object of description" (p. 468). To change priorities from the text to one's own experience of the text is a consequence of the shift to the subjective paradigm. If this shift is not made, we are in the contradictory positions of both Rosenblatt and Holland, which affirm the objectivity of both the text and the reader's experience, and the experience becomes just another text. But if this experience is a *priority*, then the subsequent knowledge has a new character altogether, as Fish claims.

44. Ibid., p. 478.

45. Ibid., p. 480.

46. Ibid., p. 485.

47. Ibid., p. 479.

48. Ph.D. diss., Indiana University, 1973.

49. Ibid., p. 542.

50. Thornton F. Jordan, "Report on Teaching Subjective Criticism of Literature," unpublished essay, p. 23.

51. Ibid., p. 25.

52. Kintgen, "Reader Response," has reviewed some of these studies, as has Stanley E. Fish in "What Is Stylistics and Why Are They Saying Such Terrible Things About It?" in *Approaches to Poetics*, ed. Seymour Chatman (New York: Columbia University Press, 1973), pp. 109–52.

53. Although it is obviously necessary to advance a proposal such as this in a full-length discussion, the purpose here is to distinguish between two epistemological attitudes. Particularly, I understand the epistemology of formalist criticism to be the same as the epistemology of transformational (that is, formalist) linguistics; if the epistemological paradigm is shifted to subjectivity, it is much easier to see how the study of literature and the study of language involve the same forms of thought and the same criteria of explanation. Both require an epistemological principle that *explains both experience and explanation as one shifts from one to the other.*

54. As George Greenfield has argued (unpublished essay, Department of English, Indiana University, April 1977), unique phenomena are, as a matter of principle, not susceptible to either of the traditional rationalist or empiricist forms of explanation. This is one of the reasons both aesthetics and language have eluded systematic explanation. If it is accepted that both art and language (in their common status as symbolic objects) are, in experience, unique phenomena, then either no explanation or subjective explanations apply.

55. For example, Barrett John Mandel, *Literature and the English Department* (Urbana, Ill.: National Council of Teachers of English, 1970), describes the sense in which a completely open-ended classroom can be successful: there are no set meeting hours, no exams, no set reading lists, and every item of work is initiated by students. Only pragmatic objections to such procedures are admissable; but these objections—such as a range of applicability, class size, existing requirements, teaching motives of the instructors, and so on—have to be summarily denied if Mandel's proposals are to go into effect. Mandel does successfully deny them, but the problem of how to authorize knowledge remains untreated, except in individual student reports that they "learned something important."

10

INTERPRETING THE *VARIORUM*

Stanley E. Fish

I

The first two volumes of the Milton *Variorum Commentary* have now appeared, and I find them endlessly fascinating. My interest, how-ever, is not in the questions they manage to resolve (although these are many) but in the theoretical assumptions which are responsible for their occasional failures. These failures constitute a pattern, one in which a host of commentators—separated by as much as two hundred and seventy years but contemporaries in their shared concerns—are lined up on either side of an interpretive crux. Some of these are famous, even infamous: what is the two-handed engine in *Lycidas?* what is the meaning of Haemony in *Comus?* Others, like the identity òf whoever or whatever comes to the window in *L'Allegro,* line 46, are only slightly less notorious. Still others are of interest largely to those who make editions: matters of pronoun referents, lexical ambiguities, punctuation. In each instance, however, the pattern is consistent: every position taken is supported by wholly convincing evidence—in the case of *L'Allegro* and the coming to the window there is a persuasive champion for every proper noun within a radius of ten lines—and the editorial procedure always ends either in the graceful throwing up of hands, or in the recording of a disagreement between the two editors themselves. In short, these are problems that apparently cannot be solved, at least not by the methods traditionally brought to bear on them. What I would like to argue is that they are not *meant* to be solved, but to be experienced (they signify), and that con-sequently any procedure that attempts to determine which of a number of readings is correct will necessarily fail. What this means is that the commentators and editors have been asking the wrong questions and

Reprinted from *Critical Inquiry* 2 (Spring 1976): 465–85 by permission of The Univer-sity of Chicago Press. © 1976 by The University of Chicago.

that a new set of questions based on new assumptions must be formulated. I would like at least to make a beginning in that direction by
examining some of the points in dispute in Milton's sonnets. I choose the
sonnets because they are brief and because one can move easily from
them to the theoretical issues with which this paper is finally concerned.

Milton's twentieth sonnet—"Lawrence of virtuous father virtuous
son"—has been the subject of relatively little commentary. In it the poet
invites a friend to join him in some distinctly Horatian pleasures—a neat
repast intermixed with conversation, wine, and song; a respite from
labor all the more enjoyable because outside the earth is frozen and the
day sullen. The only controversy the sonnet has inspired concerns its
final two lines:

> Lawrence of virtuous father virtuous son,
>   Now that the fields are dank, and ways are mire,
>   Where shall we sometimes meet, and by the fire
>   Help waste a sullen day; what may be won
> 5 From the hard season gaining; time will run
>   On smoother, till Favonius reinspire
>   The frozen earth; and clothe in fresh attire
>   The lily and rose, that neither sowed nor spun.
>   What neat repast shall feast us, light and choice,
> 10   Of Attic taste, with wine, whence we may rise
>   To hear the lute well touched, or artful voice
> Warble immortal notes and Tuscan air?
>   He who of those delights can judge, and spare
>   To interpose them oft, is not unwise.[1]

The focus of the controversy is the word "spare," for which two readings
have been proposed: leave time for and refrain from. Obviously the
point is crucial if one is to resolve the sense of the lines. In one reading
"those delights" are being recommended—he who can leave time for
them is not unwise; in the other, they are the subject of a warning—he
who knows when to refrain from them is not unwise. The proponents of
the two interpretations cite as evidence both English and Latin syntax,
various sources and analogues, Milton's "known attitudes" as they are
found in his other writings, and the unambiguously expressed sentiments of the following sonnet on the same question. Surveying these
arguments, A. S. P. Woodhouse roundly declares: "It is plain that all the
honours rest with" the meaning "refrain from" or "forbear to." This
declaration is followed immediately by a bracketed paragraph initialed
D. B. for Douglas Bush, who, writing presumably after Woodhouse has
died, begins "In spite of the array of scholarly names the case for 'forbear to' may be thought much weaker, and the case for 'spare time for'

much stronger, than Woodhouse found them."² Bush then proceeds to review much of the evidence marshaled by Woodhouse and to draw from it exactly the opposite conclusion. If it does nothing else, this curious performance anticipates a point I shall make in a few moments: evidence brought to bear in the course of formalist analyses—that is, analyses generated by the assumption that meaning is embedded in the artifact—will always point in as many directions as there are interpreters; that is, not only will it prove something, it will prove anything.

It would appear then that we are back at square one, with a controversy that cannot be settled because the evidence is inconclusive. But what if that controversy is *itself* regarded as evidence, not of an ambiguity that must be removed, but of an ambiguity that readers have always experienced? What, in other words, if for the question "what does 'spare' mean?" we substitute the question "what does the fact that the meaning of 'spare' has always been an issue mean"? The advantage of this question is that it can be answered. Indeed it has already been answered by the readers who are cited in the *Variorum Commentary*. What these readers debate is the judgment the poem makes on the delights of recreation; what their debate indicates is that the judgment is blurred by a verb that can be made to participate in contradictory readings. (Thus the important thing about the evidence surveyed in the *Variorum* is not how it is marshaled, but that it could be marshaled at all, because it then becomes evidence of the equal availability of both interpretations.) In other words, the lines first generate a pressure for judgment—"he who of those delights can judge"—and then decline to deliver it; the pressure, however, still exists, and it is transferred from the words on the page to the reader (the reader is "he who"), who comes away from the poem not with a statement, but with a responsibility, the responsibility of deciding when and how often—if at all—to indulge in "those delights" (they remain delights in either case). This transferring of responsibility from the text to its readers is what the lines ask us to do—it is the essence of their experience—and in my terms it is therefore what the lines *mean*. It is a meaning the *Variorum* critics attest to even as they resist it, for what they are laboring so mightily to do by fixing the sense of the lines is to give the responsibility back. The text, however, will not accept it and remains determinedly evasive, even in its last two words, "not unwise." In their position these words confirm the impossibility of extracting from the poem a moral formula, for the assertion (certainly too strong a word) they complete is of the form, "He who does such and such, of him it cannot be said that he is unwise"; but of course neither can it be said that he is wise. Thus what Bush correctly terms the "defensive" "not unwise" operates to prevent us from attaching the label "wise" to any action, including *either* of the actions—leaving time for or refraining from—represented by the ambiguity of "spare." Not only is the pressure of judgment taken off the poem, it is taken off the activity the poem at first pretended to judge. The issue is finally not the moral status of "those delights"—they become in seventeenth-century terms "things indifferent"—but on the good or bad uses to which they can be put by readers who are left, as Milton always leaves them, to choose and manage by themselves.

Let us step back for a moment and see how far we've come. We began with an apparently insoluble problem and proceeded, not to solve it, but to make it signify; first by regarding it as evidence of an experience and then by specifying for that experience a meaning. Moreover, the configurations of that experience, when they are made available by a reader-oriented analysis, serve as a check against the endlessly inconclusive adducing of evidence which characterizes formalist analysis. That is to say, any determination of what "spare" means (in a positivist or literal sense) is liable to be upset by the bringing forward of another analogue, or by a more complete computation of statistical frequencies, or by the discovery of new biographical information, or by anything else; but if we first determine that everything in the line before "spare" creates the expectation of an imminent judgment, then the ambiguity of "spare" can be assigned a significance in the context of that expectation. (It disappoints it and transfers the pressure of judgment to us.) That context is experiential, and it is within its contours and constraints that significances are established (both in the act of reading and in the analysis of that act). In formalist analyses the only constraints are the notoriously open-ended possibilities and combination of possibilities that emerge when one begins to consult dictionaries and grammars and histories; to consult dictionaries, grammars, and histories is to assume that meanings can be specified independently of the activity of reading; what the example of "spare" shows is that it is in and by that activity that meanings—experiential, not positivist—are created.

In other words, it is the structure of the reader's experience rather than any structures available on the page that should be the object of description. In the case of Sonnet XX, that experiential structure was uncovered when an examination of formal structures led to an impasse; and the pressure to remove that impasse led to the substitution of one set of questions for another. It will more often be the case that the pressure of a spectacular failure will be absent. The sins of formalist-positivist analysis are primarily sins of omission, not an inability to explain phenomena, but an inability to see that they are there because its assumptions make it inevitable that they will be overlooked or suppressed. Consider, for example, the concluding lines of another of Milton's sonnets, "Avenge O Lord thy slaughtered saints."

Avenge O Lord thy slaughtered saints, whose bones
   Lie scattered on the Alpine mountains cold,
   Even them who kept thy truth so pure of old
   When all our fathers worshipped stocks and stones,
5 Forget not: in thy book record their groans
   Who were thy sheep and in their ancient fold
   Slain by the bloody Piedmontese that rolled
   Mother with infant down the rocks. Their moans
The vales redoubled to the hills, and they
10   To heaven. Their martyred blood and ashes sow
   O'er all the Italian fields where still doth sway
The triple Tyrant: that from these may grow
   A hundredfold, who having learnt thy way
   Early may fly the Babylonian woe.

In this sonnet, the poet simultaneously petitions God and wonders aloud about the justice of allowing the faithful—"Even them who kept thy truth"—to be so brutally slaughtered. The note struck is alternately one of plea and complaint, and there is more than a hint that God is being called to account for what has happened to the Waldensians. It is generally agreed, however, that the note of complaint is less and less sounded and that the poem ends with an affirmation of faith in the ultimate operation of God's justice. In this reading, the final lines are taken to be saying something like this: From the blood of these martyred, O God, raise up a new and more numerous people, who, by virtue of an early education in thy law, will escape destruction by fleeing the Babylonian woe. Babylonian woe has been variously glossed;[3] but whatever it is taken to mean it is always read as part of a statement that specifies a set of conditions for the escaping of destruction or punishment; it is a warning to the reader as well as a petition to God. As a warning, however, it is oddly situated since the conditions it seems to specify were in fact met by the Waldensians, who of all men most followed God's laws. In other words, the details of their story would seem to undercut the affirmative moral the speaker proposes to draw from it. It is further undercut by a reading that is fleetingly available, although no one has acknowledged it because it is a function, not of the words on the page, but of the experience of the reader. In that experience, line 13 will for a moment be accepted as a complete sense unit and the emphasis of the line will fall on "thy way" (a phrase that has received absolutely no attention in the commentaries). At this point "thy way" can refer only to the way in which God has dealt with the Waldensians. That is, "thy way" seems to pick up the note of outrage with which the poem began, and if we continue to so interpret it, the conclusion of the poem will be a grim one indeed: since by this example it appears that God rains down punishment indiscriminately, it would be best perhaps to withdraw from the arena of his service, and thereby hope at least to be safely out of the line of fire. This is not the conclusion we carry away, because as line 14 unfolds, another reading of "thy way" becomes available, a reading in which "early" qualifies "learnt" and refers to something the faithful should do (learn thy way at an early age) rather than to something God has failed to do (save the Waldensians). These two readings are answerable to the pulls exerted by the beginning and ending of the poem: the outrage expressed in the opening lines generates a pressure for an explanation, and the grimmer reading is answerable to that pressure (even if it is also disturbing); the ending of the poem, the forward and upward movement of lines 10–14, creates the expectation of an affirmation, and the second reading fulfills that expectation. The criticism shows that in the end we settle on the more optimistic reading—it feels better—but even so the other has been a part of our experience, and because it has been a part of our experience, it *means*. What it means is that while we may be able to extract from the poem a statement affirming God's justice, we are not allowed to forget the evidence (of things seen) that makes the extraction so difficult (both for the speaker and for us). It is a difficulty we experience in the act of reading, even though a criticism which takes no account of that act has, as we have seen, suppressed it.

II

In each of the sonnets we have considered, the significant word or phrase occurs at a line break where a reader is invited to place it first in one and then in another structure of syntax and sense. This moment of hesitation, of semantic or syntactic slide, is crucial to the experience the verse provides, but, in a formalist analysis, that moment will disappear, either because it has been flattened out and made into an (insoluble) interpretive crux, or because it has been eliminated in the course of a procedure that is incapable of finding value in temporal phenomena. In the case of "When I consider how my light is spent," these two failures are combined.

> When I consider how my light is spent,
>   Ere half my days, in this dark world and wide,
>   And that one talent which is death to hide,
>   Lodged with me useless, though my soul more bent
> 5 To serve therewith my maker, and present
>   My true account, lest he returning chide,
>   Doth God exact day-labour, light denied,
>   I fondly ask; but Patience to prevent
>   That murmur, soon replies, God doth not need
> 10 Either man's work or his own gifts, who best
>   Bear his mild yoke, they serve him best, his state
>   Is kingly. Thousands at his bidding speed
>   And post o'er land and ocean without rest:
>   They also serve who only stand and wait.

The interpretive crux once again concerns the final line: "They also serve who only stand and wait." For some this is an unqualified acceptance of God's will, while for others the note of affirmation is muted or even forced. The usual kinds of evidence are marshaled by the opposing parties, and the usual inconclusiveness is the result. There are some areas of agreement. "All the interpretations," Woodhouse remarks, "recognize that the sonnet commences from a mood of depression, frustration [and] impatience."[4] The object of impatience is a God who would first demand service and then take away the means of serving, and the oft noted allusion to the parable of the talents lends scriptural support to the accusation the poet is implicitly making: you have cast the wrong servant into unprofitable darkness. It has also been observed that the syntax and rhythm of these early lines, and especially of lines 6–8, are rough and uncertain; the speaker is struggling with his agitated thoughts and he changes directions abruptly, with no regard for the line as a unit of sense. The poem, says one critic, "seems almost out of control."[5]

The question I would ask is "whose control?"; for what these formal descriptions point to (but do not acknowledge) is the extraordinary number of adjustments required of readers who would negotiate these lines. The first adjustment is the result of the expectations created by the second half of line 6—"lest he returning chide." Since there is no full stop after "chide," it is natural to assume that this will be an introduction to reported speech, and to assume further that what will be reported is the poet's anticipation of the voice of God as it calls him, to an unfair accounting. This assumption does not survive line 7—"Doth God exact day-labour, light denied"—which rather than chiding the poet for his inactivity seems to rebuke him for having expected that chiding. The accents are precisely those heard so often in the Old Testament when God answers a reluctant Gideon, or a disputatious Moses, or a self-justifying Job: do you presume to judge my ways or to appoint my motives? Do you think I would exact day-labor, light denied? In other words, the poem seems to turn at this point from a questioning of God to a questioning of that questioning; or, rather, the reader turns from the one to the other in the act of revising his projection of what line 7 will say and do. As it turns out, however, that revision must itself be revised because it had been made within the assumption that what we are hearing is the voice of God. This assumption falls before the very next phrase "I fondly ask," which requires not one, but two adjustments. Since the speaker of line 7 is firmly identified as the poet, the line must be reinterpreted as a continuation of his complaint—Is that the way you operate, God, denying light, but exacting labor?—but even as that interpretation emerges, the poet withdraws from it by inserting the adverb "fondly," and once again the line slips out of the reader's control.

In a matter of seconds, then, line 7 has led four experiential lives, one as we anticipate it, another as that anticipation is revised, a third when we retroactively identify its speaker, and a fourth when that speaker disclaims it. What changes in each of these lives is the status of the poet's murmurings—they are alternately expressed, rejected, reinstated, and qualified—and as the sequence ends, the reader is without a firm perspective on the question of record: does God deal justly with his servants?

A firm perspective appears to be provided by Patience, whose entrance into the poem, the critics tell us, gives it both argumentative and metrical stability. But in fact the presence of Patience in the poem finally assures its continuing instability by making it impossible to specify the degree to which the speaker approves, or even participates in, the affirmation of the final line: "They also serve who only stand and wait." We know that Patience to prevent the poet's murmur soon replies (not soon enough however to prevent the murmur from registering), but we do not know when that reply ends. Does Patience fall silent in line 12, after "kingly"? or at the conclusion of line 13? or not at all? Does the poet appropriate these lines or share them or simply listen to them, as we do? These questions are unanswerable, and it is because they remain unanswerable that the poem ends uncertainly. The uncertainty is not in the statement it makes—in isolation line 14 is unequivocal—but in our inability to assign that statement to either the poet or to Patience. Were the final line marked unambiguously for the poet, then we would receive it as a resolution of his earlier doubts; and were it marked for Patience, it would be a sign that those doubts were still very much in force. It is marked for neither, and therefore we are without the satisfaction that a firmly conclusive ending (in *any* direction) would have provided. In short, we leave the poem unsure, and our unsureness is the realization (in our experience) of the unsureness with which the affirmation of the final line is, or is not, made. (This unsureness also operates to actualize the two possible readings of "wait": wait in the sense of expecting, that is waiting for an opportunity to serve actively; or wait in the sense of waiting *in* service, a waiting that is itself fully satisfying because the impulse to self-glorifying action has been stilled.)

The question debated in the *Variorum Commentary* is, how far from the mood of frustration and impatience does the poem finally move? The answer given by an experiential analysis is that you can't tell, and the fact that you can't tell is responsible for the uneasiness the poem has always inspired. It is that uneasiness which the critics inadvertently acknowledge when they argue about the force of the last line, but they are unable to make analytical use of what they acknowledge because they have no way of dealing with or even recognizing experiential (that is, temporal) structures. In fact, more than one editor has eliminated those structures by punctuating them out of existence: first by putting a full

stop at the end of line 6 and thereby making it unlikely that the reader
will assign line 7 to God (there will no longer be an expectation of
reported speech), and then by supplying quotation marks for the sestet
in order to remove any doubts one might have as to who is speaking.
There is of course no warrant for these emendations, and in 1791
Thomas Warton had the grace and honesty to admit as much. "I have,"
he said, "introduced the turned commas both in the question and answer, not from any authority, but because they seem absolutely necessary
to the sense."[6]

III

Editorial practices like these are only the most obvious manifestations of the assumptions to which I stand opposed: the assumption that
there *is* a sense, that it is embedded or encoded in the text, and that it
can be taken in at a single glance. These assumptions are, in order,
positivist, holistic, and spatial, and to have them is to be committed both
to a goal and to a procedure. The goal is to settle on a meaning, and the
procedure involves first stepping back from the text, and then putting
together or otherwise calculating the discrete units of significance it
contains. My quarrel with this procedure (and with the assumptions that
generate it) is that in the course of following it through, the reader's
activities are at once ignored and devalued. They are ignored because
the text is taken to be self-sufficient—everything is *in* it—and they are
devalued because when they are thought of at all, they are thought of as
the disposable machinery of extraction. In the procedures I would urge,
the reader's activities are at the center of attention, where they are regarded, not as leading to meaning, but as *having* meaning. The meaning
they have is a consequence of their not being empty; for they include the
making and revising of assumptions, the rendering and regretting of
judgments, the coming to and abandoning of conclusions, the giving and
withdrawing of approval, the specifying of causes, the asking of questions, the supplying of answers, the solving of puzzles. In a word, these
activities are interpretive—rather than being preliminary to questions of
value they are at every moment settling and resettling questions of
value—and because they are interpretive, a description of them will also
be, and without any additional step, an interpretation, not after the fact,
but of the fact (of experiencing). It will be a description of a moving field
of concerns, at once wholly present (not waiting for meaning, but constituting meaning) and continually in the act of reconstituting itself.

As a project such a description presents enormous difficulties, and
there is hardly time to consider them here;[7] but it should be obvious
from my brief examples how different it is from the positivist-formalist

project. Everything depends on the temporal dimension, and as a consequence the notion of a mistake, at least as something to be avoided, disappears. In a sequence where a reader first structures the field he inhabits and then is asked to restructure it (by changing an assignment of speaker or realigning attitudes and positions) there is no question of priority among his structurings; no one of them, even if it is the last, has privilege; each is equally legitimate, each equally the proper object of analysis, because each is equally an event in his experience.

The firm assertiveness of this paragraph only calls attention to the questions it avoids. Who is this reader? How can I presume to describe his experiences, and what do I say to readers who report that they do not have the experiences I describe? Let me answer these questions or rather make a beginning at answering them in the context of another example, this time from Milton's *Comus*. In line 46 of *Comus* we are introduced to the villain by way of a genealogy:

> Bacchus that first from out the purple grape,
> Crushed the sweet poison of misused wine.

In almost any edition of this poem, a footnote will tell you that Bacchus is the god of wine. Of course most readers already know that, and because they know it, they will be anticipating the appearance of "wine" long before they come upon it in the final position. Moreover, they will also be anticipating a negative judgment on it, in part because of the association of Bacchus with revelry and excess, and especially because the phrase "sweet poison" suggests that the judgment has already been made. At an early point then, we will have both filled in the form of the assertion and made a decision about its moral content. That decision is upset by the word "misused"; for what "misused" asks us to do is transfer the pressure of judgment from wine (where we have already placed it) to the abusers of wine, and therefore when "wine" finally appears, we must declare it innocent of the charges we have ourselves made.

This, then, is the structure of the reader's experience—the transferring of a moral label from a thing to those who appropriate it. It is an experience that depends on a reader for whom the name Bacchus has precise and immediate associations; another reader, a reader for whom those associations are less precise will not have that experience because he will not have rushed to a conclusion in relation to which the word "misused" will stand as a challenge. Obviously I am discriminating between these two readers and between the two equally real experiences they will have. It is not a discrimination based simply on information, because what is important is not the information itself, but the action of the mind which its possession makes possible for one reader and impossible for the other. One might discriminate further between them by noting that the point at issue—whether value is a function of objects and actions or of intentions—is at the heart of the seventeenth-century debate over "things indifferent." A reader who is aware of that debate will not only *have* the experience I describe; he will recognize at the end of it that he has been asked to take a position on one side of a continuing controversy; and that recognition (also a part of his experience) will be part of the disposition with which he moves into the lines that follow.

It would be possible to continue with this profile of the optimal reader, but I would not get very far before someone would point out that what I am really describing is the intended reader, the reader whose education, opinions, concerns, linguistic competences, etc. make him capable of having the experience the author wished to provide. I would not resist this characterization because it seems obvious that the efforts of readers are always efforts to discern and therefore to realize (in the sense of becoming) an author's intention. I would only object if that realization were conceived narrowly, as the single act of comprehending an author's purpose, rather than (as I would conceive it) as the succession of acts readers perform in the continuing assumption that they are dealing with intentional beings. In this view discerning an intention is no more or less than understanding, and understanding includes (is constituted by) all the activities which make up what I call the structure of the reader's experience. To describe that experience is therefore to describe the reader's efforts at understanding, and to describe the reader's efforts at understanding is to describe his realization (in two senses) of an author's intention. Or to put it another way, what my analyses amount to are descriptions of a succession of decisions made by readers about an author's intention; decisions that are not limited to the specifying of purpose but include the specifying of every aspect of successively intended worlds; decisions that are precisely the shape, because they are the content, of the reader's activities.

Having said this, however, it would appear that I am open to two objections. The first is that the procedure is a circular one. I describe the experience of a reader who in his strategies is answerable to an author's intention, and I specify the author's intention by pointing to the strategies employed by that same reader. But this objection would have force only if it were possible to specify one independently of the other. What is being specified from either perspective are the conditions of utterance, of what could have been understood to have been meant by what was said. That is, intention and understanding are two ends of a conventional act, each of which necessarily stipulates (includes, defines, specifies) the other. To construct the profile of the informed or at-home reader is at the same time to characterize the author's intention and vice versa, because to do either is to specify the *contemporary* conditions of utterance, to identify, by becoming a member of, a community made up of those who share interpretive strategies.

The second objection is another version of the first: if the content of the reader's experience is the succession of acts he performs in search of an author's intentions, and if he performs those acts at the bidding of the text, does not the text then produce or contain everything—intention *and* experience—and have I not compromised my antiformalist position? This objection will have force only if the formal patterns of the text are assumed to exist independently of the reader's experience, for only then can priority be claimed for them. Indeed, the claims of independence and priority are one and the same; when they are separated it is so that they can give circular and illegitimate support to each other. The question "do formal features exist independently?" is usually answered by pointing to their priority: they are "in" the text before the reader comes to it. The question "are formal features prior?" is usually answered by pointing to their independent status: they are "in" the text before the reader comes to it. What looks like a step in an argument is actually the spectacle of an assertion supporting itself. It follows then that an attack on the independence of formal features will also be an attack on their priority (and vice versa), and I would like to mount such an attack in the context of two short passages from *Lycidas*.

The first passage (actually the second in the poem's sequence) begins at line 42:

> The willows and the hazel copses green
> Shall now no more be seen,
> Fanning their joyous leaves to thy soft lays.
>   [Ll. 42–44]

It is my thesis that the reader is always making sense (I intend "making" to have its literal force), and in the case of these lines the sense he makes will involve the assumption (and therefore the creation) of a completed assertion after the word "seen," to wit, the death of Lycidas has so affected the willows and the hazel copses green that, in sympathy, they will wither and die (will no more be seen by *anyone*). In other words at the end of line 43 the reader will have hazarded an interpretation, or performed an act of perceptual closure, or made a decision as to what is being asserted. I do not mean that he has done four things, but that he has done one thing the description of which might take any one of four forms—making sense, interpreting, performing perceptual closure, deciding about what is intended. (The importance of this point will become clear later.) Whatever he has done (that is, however we characterize it) he will undo it in the act of reading the next line; for here he discovers that his closure, or making of sense, was premature and that he must make a new one in which the relationship between man and nature is exactly the reverse of what was first assumed. The willows and the hazel copses green will in fact be seen, but they will not be seen by Lycidas. It is he who will be no more, while they go on as before, fanning their joyous leaves to someone else's soft lays (the whole of line 44 is now perceived as modifying and removing the absoluteness of "seen"). Nature is not sympathetic, but indifferent, and the notion of her sympathy is one of those "false surmises" that the poem is continually encouraging and then disallowing.

The previous sentence shows how easy it is to surrender to the bias of our critical language and begin to talk as if poems, not readers or interpreters, did things. Words like "encourage" and "disallow" (and others I have used in this paper) imply agents, and it is only "natural" to assign agency first to an author's intentions and then to the forms that assumedly embody them. What really happens, I think, is something quite different: rather than intention and its formal realization producing interpretation (the "normal" picture), interpretation creates intention and its formal realization by creating the conditions in which it becomes possible to pick them out. In other words, in the analysis of these lines from *Lycidas* I did what critics always do: I "saw" what my interpretive principles permitted or directed me to see, and then I turned around and attributed what I had "seen" to a text and an intention. What my principles direct me to "see" are readers performing acts; the points at which I find (or to be more precise, declare) those acts to have been performed become (by a sleight of hand) demarcations *in* the text; those demarcations are then available for the designation "formal features," and as formal features they can be (illegitimately) assigned the responsibility for producing the interpretation which in fact produced them. In this case, the demarcation my interpretation calls into being is placed at the end of line 42; but of course the end of that (or any other) line is worth noticing or pointing out only because my model *demands* (the word is not too strong) perceptual closures and therefore locations at which they occur; in that model this point will be one of those locations, although (1) it needn't have been (not every line ending occasions a closure) and (2) in another model, one that does not give value to the activities of readers, the possibility of its being one would not have arisen.

What I am suggesting is that formal units are always a function of the interpretative model one brings to bear; they are not "in" the text, and I would make the same argument for intentions. That is, intention is no more embodied "in" the text than are formal units; rather an intention, like a formal unit, is made when perceptual or interpretive closure is hazarded; it is verified by an interpretive act, and I would add, it is not verifiable in any other way. This last assertion is too large to be fully considered here, but I can sketch out the argumentative sequence I would follow were I to consider it: intention is known when and only when it is recognized; it is recognized as soon as you decide about it; you decide about it as soon as you make a sense; and you make a sense (or so my model claims) as soon as you can.

Let me tie up the threads of my argument with a final example from
Lycidas:

He must not float upon his wat'ry bier
Unwept . . .

[LI. 13–14]

Here the reader's experience has much the same career as it does in lines
42–44: at the end of line 13 perceptual closure is hazarded, and a sense is
made in which the line is taken to be a resolution bordering on a promise: that is, there is now an expectation that something will be done about
this unfortunate situation, and the reader anticipates a call to action,
perhaps even a program for the undertaking of a rescue mission. With
"Unwept," however, that expectation and anticipation are disappointed,
and the realization of that disappointment will be inseparable from the
making of a new (and less comforting) sense: nothing will be done;
Lycidas will continue to float upon his wat'ry bier, and the only action
taken will be the lamenting of the fact that no action will be efficacious,
including the actions of speaking and listening to this lament (which in
line 15 will receive the meretricious and self-mocking designation
"melodious tear"). Three "structures" come into view at precisely the
same moment, the moment when the reader having resolved a sense
unresolves it and makes a new one; that moment will also be the moment
of picking out a formal pattern or unit, end of line / beginning of line,
and it will also be the moment at which the reader having decided about
the speaker's intention, about what is meant by what has been said, will
make the decision again and in so doing will make another intention.

   This, then, is my thesis: that the form of the reader's experience,
formal units, and the structure of intention are one, that they come into
view simultaneously, and that therefore the questions of priority and
independence do not arise. What does arise is another question: what
produces *them?* That is, if intention, form, and the shape of the reader's
experience are simply different ways of referring to (different perspectives on) the same interpretive act, what is that act an interpretation *of?* I
cannot answer that question, but neither, I would claim, can anyone else,
although formalists try to answer it by pointing to patterns and claiming
that they are available independently of (prior to) interpretation. These
patterns vary according to the procedures that yield them: they may be
statistical (number of two-syllable words per hundred words),
grammatical (ratio of passive to active constructions, or of right-
branching to left-branching sentences, or of anything else); but whatever
they are I would argue that they do not lie innocently in the world but
are themselves constituted by an interpretive act, even if, as is often the
case, that act is unacknowledged. Of course, this is as true of my analyses
as it is of anyone else's. In the examples offered here I appropriate the
notion "line ending" and treat it as a fact of nature; and one might

conclude that as a fact it is responsible for the reading experience I
describe. The truth I think is exactly the reverse: line endings exist by
virtue of perceptual strategies rather than the other way around. Historically, the strategy that we know as "reading (or hearing) poetry" has
included paying attention to the line as a unit, but it is precisely that
attention which has made the line as a unit (either of print or of aural
duration) available. A reader so practiced in paying that attention that he
regards the line as a brute fact rather than as a convention will have a
great deal of difficulty with concrete poetry; if he overcomes that difficulty, it will not be because he has learned to ignore the line as a unit but
because he will have acquired a new set of interpretive strategies (the
strategies constitutive of "concrete poetry reading") in the context of
which the line as a unit no longer exists. In short, what is noticed is what
has been *made* noticeable, not by a clear and undistorting glass, but by an
interpretive strategy.

   This may be hard to see when the strategy has become so habitual
that the forms it yields seem part of the world. We find it easy to assume
that alliteration as an effect depends on a "fact" that exists independently of any interpretive "use" one might make of it, the fact that words
in proximity begin with the same letter. But it takes only a moment's
reflection to realize that the sameness, far from being natural, is en-
forced by an orthographic convention; that is to say, it is the product of
an interpretation. Were we to substitute phonetic conventions for orthographic ones (a "reform" traditionally urged by purists), the supposedly "objective" basis for alliteration would disappear because a
phonetic transcription would require that we distinguish between the
initial sounds of those very words that enter into alliterative relationships; rather than conforming to those relationships the rules of spelling
make them. One might reply that, since alliteration is an aural rather
than a visual phenomenon when poetry is heard, we have unmediated
access to the physical sounds themselves and hear "real" similarities. But
phonological "facts" are no more uninterpreted (or less conventional)
than the "facts" of orthography; the distinctive features that make articulation and reception possible are the product of a system of differences
that must be *imposed* before it can be recognized; the patterns the ear
hears (like the patterns the eye sees) are the patterns its perceptual habits
make available.

   One can extend this analysis forever, even to the "facts" of grammar.
The history of linguistics is the history of competing paradigms each of
which offers a different account of the constituents of language. Verbs,
nouns, cleft sentences, transformations, deep and surface structures,
semes, rhemes, tagmemes—now you see them, now you don't, depending on the descriptive apparatus you employ. The critic who confidently
rests his analyses on the bedrock of syntactic descriptions is resting on an

interpretation; the facts he points to *are* there, but only as a consequence of the interpretive (man-made) model that has called them into being.

The moral is clear: the choice is never between objectivity and interpretation but between an interpretation that is unacknowledged as such and an interpretation that is at least aware of itself. It is this awareness that I am claiming for myself, although in doing so I must give up the claims implicitly made in the first part of this paper. There I argue that a bad (because spatial) model had suppressed what was really happening, but by my own declared principles the notion "really happening" is just one more interpretation.

IV

It seems then that the price one pays for denying the priority of either forms or intentions is an inability to say how it is that one ever begins. Yet we do begin, and we continue, and because we do there arises an immediate counter-objection to the preceding pages. If interpretive acts are the source of forms rather than the other way around, why isn't it the case that readers are always performing the same acts or a random succession of forms? How, in short, does one explain these two "facts" of reading?: (1) the same reader will perform differently when reading two "different" (the word is in quotation marks because its status is precisely what is at issue) texts; and (2) different readers will perform similarly when reading the "same" (in quotes for the same reason) text. That is to say, both the stability of interpretation among readers and the variety of interpretation in the career of a single reader would seem to argue for the existence of something independent of and prior to interpretive acts, something which produces them. I will answer this challenge by asserting that both the stability and the variety are functions of interpretive strategies rather than of texts.

Let us suppose that I am reading *Lycidas*. What is it that I am doing? First of all, what I am not doing is "simply reading," an activity in which I do not believe because it implies the possibility of pure (that is, disinterested) perception. Rather, I am proceeding on the basis of (at least) two interpretive decisions: (1) that *Lycidas* is a pastoral and (2) that it was written by Milton. (I should add that the notions "pastoral" and "Milton" are also interpretations; that is they do not stand for a set of indisputable, objective facts; if they did, a great many books would not now be getting written.) Once these decisions have been made (and if I had not made these I would have made others, and they would be consequential in the same way), I am immediately predisposed to perform certain acts, to "find," by looking for, themes (the relationship between natural processes and the careers of men, the efficacy of poetry or of any other action), to confer significances (on flowers, streams, shepherds, pagan deities), to mark out "formal" units (the lament, the consolation, the turn, the affirmation of faith, etc.). My disposition to perform these acts (and others; the list is not meant to be exhaustive) constitutes a set of interpretive strategies, which, when they are put into execution, become the large act of reading. That is to say, interpretive strategies are not put into execution after reading (the pure act of perception in which I do not believe); they are the shape of reading, and because they are the shape of reading, they give texts their shape, making them rather than, as it is usually assumed, arising from them. Several important things follow from this account:

1. I did not have to execute this particular set of interpretive strategies because I did not have to make those particular interpretive (pre-reading) decisions. I could have decided, for example, that *Lycidas* was a text in which a set of fantasies and defenses find expression. These decisions would have entailed the assumption of another set of interpretive strategies (perhaps like that put forward by Norman Holland in *The Dynamics of Literary Response*) and the execution of that set would have made another text.

2. I could execute this same set of strategies when presented with texts that did not bear the title (again a notion which is itself an interpretation) *Lycidas, A Pastoral Monody.* . . . I could decide (it is a decision some have made) that *Adam Bede* is a pastoral written by an author who consciously modeled herself on Milton (still remembering that "pastoral" and "Milton" are interpretations, not facts in the public domain); or I could decide, as Empson did, that a great many things not usually considered pastoral were in fact to be so read; and either decision would give rise to a set of interpretive strategies, which, when put into action, would *write* the text I write when reading *Lycidas*. (Are you with me?)

3. A reader other than myself who, when presented with *Lycidas*, proceeds to put into execution a set of interpretive strategies similar to mine (how he could do so is a question I will take up later), will perform the same (or at least a similar) succession of interpretive acts. He and I then might be tempted to say that we agree about the poem (thereby assuming that the poem exists independently of the acts either of us performs); but what we really would agree about is the way to write it.

4. A reader other than myself who, when presented with *Lycidas* (please keep in mind that the status of *Lycidas* is what is at issue), puts into execution a different set of interpretive strategies will perform a different succession of interpretive acts. (I am assuming, it is the article of my faith, that a reader will always execute some set of interpretive strategies and therefore perform some succession of interpretive acts.) One of us might then be tempted to complain to the other that we could not possibly be reading the same poem (literary criticism is full of such

complaints) and he would be right; for each of us would be reading the poem he had made.

The large conclusion that follows from these four smaller ones is that the notions of the "same" or "different" texts are fictions. If I read *Lycidas* and *The Waste Land* differently (in fact I do not), it will not be because the formal structures of the two poems (to term them such is also an interpretive decision) call forth different interpretive strategies but because my predisposition to execute different interpretive strategies will *produce* different formal structures. That is, the two poems are different because I have decided that they will be. The proof of this is the possibility of doing the reverse (that is why point 2 is so important). That is to say, the answer to the question "why do different texts give rise to different sequences of interpretive acts?" is that *they don't have to,* an answer which implies strongly that "they" don't exist. Indeed it has always been possible to put into action interpretive strategies designed to make all texts one, or to put it more accurately, to be forever making the same text. Augustine urges just such a strategy, for example, in *On Christian Doctrine* where he delivers the "rule of faith" which is of course a rule of interpretation. It is dazzlingly simple: everything in the Scriptures, and indeed in the world when it is properly read, points to (bears the meaning of) God's love for us and our answering responsibility to love our fellow creatures for His sake. If only you should come upon something which does not at first seem to bear this meaning, that "does not literally pertain to virtuous behavior or to the truth of faith," you are then to take it "to be figurative" and proceed to scrutinize it "until an interpretation contributing to the reign of charity is produced." This then is both a stipulation of what meaning there is and a set of directions for finding it, which is of course a set of directions—of interpretive strategies—for making it, that is, for the endless reproduction of the same text. Whatever one may think of this interpretive program, its success and ease of execution are attested to by centuries of Christian exegesis. It is my contention that any interpretive program, any set of interpretive strategies, can have a similar success, although few have been as spectacularly successful as this one. (For some time now, for at least three hundred years, the most successful interpretive program has gone under the name "ordinary language.") In our own discipline programs with the same characteristic of always reproducing one text include psychoanalytic criticism, Robertsonianism (always threatening to extend its sway into later and later periods), numerology (a sameness based on the assumption of innumerable fixed differences).

The other challenging question—"why will different readers execute the same interpretive strategy when faced with the 'same' text?"—can be handled in the same way. The answer is again that *they don't have to,* and my evidence is the entire history of literary criticism. And again this answer implies that the notion "same text" is the product of the possession by two or more readers of similar interpretive strategies.

But why should this ever happen? Why should two or more readers ever agree, and why should regular, that is, habitual, differences in the career of a single reader ever occur? What is the explanation on the one hand of the stability of interpretation (at least among certain groups at certain times) and on the other of the orderly variety of interpretation if it is not the stability and variety of texts? The answer to all of these questions is to be found in a notion that has been implicit in my argument, the notion of *interpretive communities*. Interpretive communities are made up of those who share interpretive strategies not for reading (in the conventional sense) but for writing texts, for constituting their properties and assigning their intentions. In other words these strategies exist prior to the act of reading and therefore determine the shape of what is read rather than, as is usually assumed, the other way around. If it is an article of faith in a particular community that there are a variety of texts, its members will boast a repertoire of strategies for making them. And if a community believes in the existence of only one text, then the single strategy its members employ will be forever writing it. The first community will accuse the members of the second of being reductive, and they in turn will call their accusers superficial. The assumption in each community will be that the other is not correctly perceiving the "true text," but the truth will be that each perceives the text (or texts) its interpretive strategies demand and call into being. This, then, is the explanation both for the stability of interpretation among different readers (they belong to the same community) and for the regularity with which a single reader will employ different interpretive strategies and thus make different texts (he belongs to different communities). It also explains why there are disagreements and why they can be debated in a principled way: not because of a stability in texts, but because of a stability in the makeup of interpretive communities and therefore in the opposing positions they make possible. Of course this stability is always temporary (unlike the longed for and timeless stability of the text). Interpretive communities grow larger and decline, and individuals move from one to another; thus while the alignments are not permanent, they are always there, providing just enough stability for the interpretive battles to go on, and just enough shift and slippage to assure that they will never be settled. The notion of interpretive communities thus stands between an impossible ideal and the fear which leads so many to maintain it. The ideal is of perfect agreement and it would require texts to have a status independent of interpretation. The fear is of interpretive anarchy, but it would only be realized if interpretation (text making) were completely random. It is the fragile but real consolidation of interpretive communities that allows us to talk to one another, but with no hope or fear of ever being able to stop.

In other words interpretive communities are no more stable than texts because interpretive strategies are not natural or universal, but *learned*. This does not mean that there is a point at which an individual has not yet learned any. The ability to interpret is not acquired; it is constitutive of being human. What is acquired are the ways of interpreting and those same ways can also be forgotten or supplanted, or complicated or dropped from favor ("no one reads that way anymore"). When any of these things happens, there is a corresponding change in texts, not because they are being read differently, but because they are being written differently.

The only stability, then, inheres in the fact (at least in my model) that interpretive strategies are always being deployed, and this means that communication is a much more chancy affair than we are accustomed to think it. For if there are no fixed texts, but only interpretive strategies making them; and if interpretive strategies are not natural, but learned (and are therefore unavailable to a finite description), what is it that utterers (speakers, authors, critics, me, you) do? In the old model utterers are in the business of handing over ready made or prefabricated meanings. These meanings are said to be encoded, and the code is assumed to be in the world independently of the individuals who are obliged to attach themselves to it (if they do not they run the danger of being declared deviant). In my model, however, meanings are not extracted but made and made not by encoded forms but by interpretive strategies that call forms into being. It follows then that what utterers do is give hearers and readers the opportunity to make meanings (and texts) by inviting them to put into execution a set of strategies. It is presumed that the invitation will be recognized, and that presumption rests on a projection on the part of a speaker or author of the moves *he* would make if confronted by the sounds or marks he is uttering or setting down.

It would seem at first that this account of things simply reintroduces the old objection; for isn't this an admission that there is after all a formal encoding, not perhaps of meanings, but of the directions for making them, for executing interpretive strategies? The answer is that they will only *be* directions to those who already have the interpretive strategies in the first place. Rather than producing interpretive acts, they are the product of one. An author hazards his projection, not because of something "in" the marks, but because of something he assumes to be in his reader. The very existence of the "marks" is a function of an interpretive community, for they will be recognized (that is, made) only by its members. Those outside that community will be deploying a different set of interpretive strategies (interpretation cannot be withheld) and will therefore be making different marks.

So once again I have made the text disappear, but unfortunately the problems do not disappear with it. If everyone is continually executing interpretive strategies and in that act constituting texts, intentions, speakers, and authors, how can any one of us know whether or not he is a member of the same interpretive community as any other of us? The answer is that he can't, since any evidence brought forward to support the claim would itself be an interpretation (especially if the "other" were an author long dead). The only "proof" of membership is fellowship, the nod of recognition from someone in the same community, someone who says to you what neither of us could ever prove to a third party: "we know." I say it to you now, knowing full well that you will agree with me (that is, understand) only if you already agree with me.

Notes

1. All references are to *The Poems of John Milton,* ed. John Carey and Alastair Fowler (London: Longmans, 1968).

2. A. S. P. Woodhouse and Douglas Bush, eds. *A Variorum Commentary on the Poems of John Milton,* Vol. 2, p. 2 (New York: Columbia University Press, 1972), p. 475.

3. It is first of all a reference to the city of iniquity from which the Hebrews are urged to flee in Isaiah and Jeremiah. In Protestant polemics Babylon is identified with the Roman Church whose destruction is prophesied in the book of Revelation. And in some Puritan tracts, Babylon is the name for Augustine's earthly city, from which the faithful are to flee inwardly in order to escape the fate awaiting the unregenerate. See Woodhouse and Bush, *Variorum Commentary,* pp. 440–41.

4. Ibid., p. 469.

5. Ibid., p. 457.

6. *Poems Upon Several Occasions, English, Italian, and Latin, with Translations, by John Milton,* ed. Thomas Warton (London, 1791), p. 352.

7. See my *Surprised by Sin: The Reader in* Paradise Lost (London and New York: St. Martin's Press, 1967); *Self-Consuming Artifacts: The Experience of Seventeenth-Century Literature* (Berkeley: University of California Press, 1972); "What Is Stylistics and Why Are They Saying Such Terrible Things About It?" in *Approaches to Poetics,* ed. Seymour Chatman (New York: Columbia University Press, 1973), pp. 109–52; "How Ordinary Is Ordinary Language?" in *New Literary History* 5, no. 1 (Autumn 1973): 41–54; "Facts and Fictions: A Reply to Ralph Rader," *Critical Inquiry* 1 (June 1975): 883–91.

11

THE INTERPRETER'S SELF:
PEIRCE ON THE CARTESIAN "SUBJECT"

Walter Benn Michaels

... we have the right to say that the world is a construction. Not to say that it is *my* construction, for in that way "I" am as much "my" construction as the world is. ...

—T. S. Eliot, *Knowledge and Experience*

One of the most interesting aspects of the American response to the French structuralist and deconstructive criticism of the last ten years has been the way in which the polemical force of the Continental movement has been so notably skewed in translation. In retrospect, at least, it seems fairly obvious that the "critique of representation" derived from the Saussurean notions of the arbitrariness of the sign and hence the systematic and differential character of meaning could hardly have appeared as revolutionary to American literary criticism as it once did to the French. It was, after all, a fundamental tenet of the New Criticism that *literary* language, at least, is "non-referential" (i.e., that it can be understood neither as the representation of an hypostasized author's intention nor as the representation of an external and prior "reality") and so, to the extent that "deconstructive discourse" can be appropriately characterized as a discourse which "undermines the referential status of the language being deconstructed," we might all claim, if we felt like it, to have been deconstructors some twenty years *avant la lettre*. What is interesting, of course, is that we haven't felt like it. In fact, the existence of these apparently shared assumptions has made little or no impression on American critics who have been instead quick to react negatively to another aspect of deconstructive theory altogether, what they take to be its implicit subjectivism. Thus we have debates like that

Reprinted from the *Georgia Review* 31 (Summer 1977): 383–402 by permission of the author and the *Georgia Review*.

between Hillis Miller (writing in *Diacritics*) and M. H. Abrams (responding in *Critical Inquiry*)—the confrontation of journals has perhaps some
iconic significance of its own—in which Miller accuses Abrams of interpretive naiveté, the assumption that texts have "a single unequivocal
meaning," and Abrams replies that he is not so naive as all that—he, in
fact, believes that "all complex passages are in some degree ambiguous,"
but, he goes on to say, unless one accepts the possibility of some meanings being "determinate and determinable," the very notion of literary
history becomes an impossibility. Thus, he says, his own interpretive
assumptions are that

> the authors cited (in *Natural Supernaturalism*) wrote, not in order to present a
> verbal stimulus . . . to the play of the reader's interpretive ingenuity, but in
> order to be understood. To do so they had to obey the communal norms of
> their language so as to turn them to their own innovative uses. The sequence
> of sentences these authors wrote were designed to have a core of determi-
> nate meanings; and though the sentences allow a certain degree of interpre-
> tive freedom . . . the central core of what they undertook to communicate
> can usually be understood by a competent reader who knows how to apply
> the norms of the language and literary form employed by the writer. The
> reader has various ways to test whether his understanding is an "objective"
> one, but the chief way is to make his interpretation public, and so permit it to
> be confirmed or falsified by the interpretations of other competent readers
> who subscribe to the same assumptions about the possibility of determinable
> communication.

This passage raises a great many theoretical issues, but I think it can
be seen that they are all grounded in the central opposition between
what Abrams calls "determinate communication" on the one hand, and
what he calls "interpretive freedom" on the other, and that this opposition is itself a function of Abrams's sense of the radically subjective
potential of the self and his conviction of the necessity to restrict that
potential. Abrams, of course, suggests himself that the two elements
which I have described as opposed are in fact complementary—the
virtue of his model is thus that it is neither completely univocal nor
completely equivocal, rather it allows for a "core" of determinate or
agreed-upon meanings and what legal theorists call a "penumbra" of
more problematic meanings, about which it is appropriate for literary
critics to debate. (In this sense, Abrams's distinctions correspond fairly
closely to E. D. Hirsch's well-known division between "meaning" and
"significance.") It is worth noting, however, that the complementarity
between Abrams's two areas of meaning can be maintained only by
thinking of them as hierarchical, that is, by granting a clear primacy to
determinate meaning. This is because determinate meaning, to be determinate, must be understood to exist independent of any interpreter.

The reader is encouraged to exercise what Abrams calls his "interpretive ingenuity" only after the "core" of meaning has been determined; subjectivity comes into play only as a kind of afterthought.

Abrams does not, however, merely insist upon the primacy of determinate meaning; he suggests at least three different strategies for locating and guaranteeing it. One is the invocation of authorial intention ("the sequence of sentences these authors wrote were designed to have a core of determinate meaning"), a second is the appeal to the linguistic reality of the text itself ("the norms of the language and literary form"), the third is the appeal to the professional competence of trained readers. This eclecticism seems a little peculiar at first glance but in fact it is rather acute. Its peculiarity is the curious way in which it homogenizes critical approaches that are usually understood to be in competition with each other. Thus the battle over the "intentional fallacy," for example, is completely neutralized by a model which insists simultaneously on the need to discover an author's intentions and on the communal and normative status of the text itself. Or, to take another example, the claims of French structuralism (at least as translated by Jonathan Culler) are understood to be perfectly congruent with, if not identical to, those of the New Critics as well as the Chicago school. But if it's this process of homogenization which is so peculiar, it's the very same process which is so acute. For what Abrams seems to be implying here is that such distinctions between critical schools are comparatively trivial, and what he seems to offer us in their place is a rather compelling account of the recent history of Anglo-American literary criticism, which now appears as a series of strategies designed to guarantee the existence and availability of determinate meanings, strategies made necessary by the fear of subjectivity, of the individual interpreter's self. By this account, then, determinate meaning may come from the author (in which case the text is understood to mean what the author intended it to mean), it may be located in the text itself (the text means what it says), or it may be a function of "literary competence" (the text means what the community of professional readers says it means)—the only thing that matters is that the meaning be determinate, not subject to the whims of individual readers. If there were no determinate meanings, the interpreter's freedom could make of a text anything it wanted, and this absolute relativism would at the least make a solipsistic mockery of literary criticism and at worst give sanction to a thoroughgoing and destructive moral skepticism. The enemy, as E. D. Hirsch puts it, are "cognitive atheists"; since they do not believe in the possibility of "objective knowledge in the humanities," they feel free to impose their own subjective interpretations on any and all texts—they offer us only the unacceptable proposition that any text can have any meaning that any one of us wants it to have.

This suspicion of the individual self is by no means unprecedented

in American criticism and philosophy. The problem of the self was central to the development of American Pragmatism and, in fact, one of the
time-honored ways of distinguishing between the Pragmatism of William
James and that of Charles Sanders Peirce is by pointing out that James,
in the words of Ralph Barton Perry, "proclaimed the supreme value of
those strivings which are unique in every individual, and whose authentic quality is revealed to him alone," whereas Peirce, and later Josiah
Royce, "emphasized the community, both as a reality and an ideal," with
Royce, in moments of extreme enthusiasm, going almost so far as to
equate individualism with original sin. In pointing toward Royce and
Peirce, however, we don't merely indicate a high-water mark in American mistrust of the self, rather we identify a series of historical
moments—Peirce's readings of Descartes in 1868 and then again in
1877–78, Royce's reading of Peirce some thirty-five years later in
1913—in which the questions of interpretation and the self are explicitly
linked and in which some of the "interpretive assumptions" announced
by Abrams are subjected to a rigorous and sustained investigation. It is
primarily with the first of these moments, the appearance in 1868 of the
essays entitled "Questions Concerning Certain Faculties Claimed for
Man" and "Some Consequences of Four Incapacities," that I am concerned here.

   For the literary critic to speak of these essays as Peirce's "readings" of
Descartes may be, however, a little misleading, since they sound not so
much like readings as like an all-out attack in which Descartes, as the
"father of modern philosophy," is held directly responsible for the sins
of his many children. Peirce identifies in particular four aspects of the
"spirit of Cartesianism" which mark it as distinctively modern and
nefarious: first, its teaching that "philosophy must begin with universal
doubt; whereas scholasticism had never questioned fundamentals"; second, its teaching that "the ultimate test of certainty is to be found in the
individual consciousness; whereas scholasticism had rested on the testimony of the sages and of the Catholic Church"; third, its rejection of
the "multiform argumentation of the Middle Ages" in favor of "a single
thread of inference depending often upon inconspicuous premises";
and fourth, its rendering "absolutely inexplicable" numerous
phenomena, unless, he notes, "to say that 'God made them so' is to be
regarded as an explanation." Against these positions, Peirce offers four
theses of his own: that "we cannot begin with complete doubt"—
Descartes's "initial scepticism" is not "real doubt" at all but "mere self-
deception"; that "to make single individuals absolute judges of truth is
most pernicious" because "we individuals cannot reasonably hope to
attain the ultimate philosophy we pursue; we can only seek it for the
community of philosophers"; that "philosophy ought to . . . proceed only
from tangible premises that can be subjected to careful scrutiny, and to

trust rather to the multitude and variety of its arguments than to the conclusiveness of any one"; and last, that the supposition of "some absolutely inexplicable, unanalyzable ultimate" rests on an epistemological confusion which completely invalidates it.

It will be seen even from this synopsis that Peirce's disagreements with Descartes are major and that they have their foundations not only in his studies of logic but in his understanding of scientific method as a model for all philosophical thought. He seems to emphasize in particular two closely related aspects of this method, each of which has found its way, under a somewhat different guise, into the ideogram of interpretive assumptions that I have characterized as typical of contemporary American literary theory. Where Descartes found certainty through introspection, for example, Peirce insists that the determination of the real cannot be left to what he calls private "idiosyncrasy." Rather, "the real . . . is that which sooner or later, information and reasoning would finally result in, and which is therefore independent of the vagaries of you and me." The "real" here is like Abrams's "core of determinate meaning," your vagaries and mine are what Abrams calls "interpretive freedom." And this definition of the real is not only public, it is progressive: where the Cartesian method of systematic doubt requires every investigator to set aside the results achieved by his predecessors and start over again for himself, the very notion of the sciences clearly requires the possibility of cumulative knowledge—were the study of physics, say, to begin again with each new physicist, it would never get much beyond the rudimentary stages. And this too, of course, finds its echo in contemporary literary theory, in the desire to identify for literary criticism what Jonathan Culler calls "a progressive, interpersonal body of knowledge," something more than the record of merely individual exercises of the self.

But to understand both the force and the limitation of these analogies, we have to look more closely at some of Peirce's central arguments against Descartes and in particular, I think, at precisely this project of the systematic doubt which Descartes himself thought of as the methodological cornerstone of his philosophy. This is an aspect of Peirce's critique which is not given much weight by some historians of philosophy. What Peirce claimed, as I have already noted, was that Cartesian doubt was not "real." "Some philosophers," he writes, "have imagined that to start an inquiry it was only necessary to utter a question or set it down upon paper, and have even recommended us to begin our studies with questioning everything. But the mere putting of a proposition into the interrogative form does not stimulate the mind to any struggle after belief. There must be a real and living doubt, and without this all discussion is idle." Now at least one commentator has claimed that this objection misunderstands the whole point of Cartesian doubt, but it is worth noticing that this question of the reality of Descartes's doubt, even if it may be in some sense misguided, was not new with Peirce; it had been raised by some of Descartes's earliest critics, and from at least two perspectives. Pierre Gassendi, for example, understood and agreed with what he took to be the purpose of Descartes's programmatic skepticism, the freeing of the philosopher's mind from every "prejudice," but he criticized Descartes for not distinguishing clearly enough between a feeling of uncertainty and the belief that everything which we know is false. This latter assertion, even if temporary, leads to unconvincing excess; "Say what you will," he wrote,

> no one will be convinced that you have convinced yourself that none of the things you have learned are true, and that your senses, or a dream, or God, or an evil spirit have imposed on you. Would it not have been better and more consonant with philosophical candour and the love of truth to state the actual facts in a straightforward and simple manner, rather than to incur the possible objection of having recourse to an artifice, of eagerness for verbal trickery and seeking evasions?

Gassendi's complaints are like Peirce's then, at least insofar as he found Descartes's procedure unconvincing, mere "verbal trickery," but there were if anything many more objections from the opposite position. What worried the theologian Anton Arnauld, for instance, was not the unconvincing character of Descartes's skepticism but rather the possibility that certain readers would find it too convincing, and hence he suggested that the first *Meditation* be "equipped with a slight preface in which it is pointed out that the doubt entertained about these matters is not really serious." Descartes replied that since the *Meditations* were to be published in Latin, they would be read "only by intellectual and educated persons" who would presumably understand the circumstances of his skepticism and so avoid being seduced by it. In this, however, he was overly sanguine; the *Meditations* were soon translated into French and Arnauld's suggestions were soon escalated by other critics into outright accusations of impiety, and so in 1647 (some six years after the publication of the *Meditations*) Descartes decided to answer these charges at greater length.

His defense was essentially a literary one. "What could be more unjust," he writes, "than to attribute to a writer opinions which he states only to the end that he may refute them?" "I enunciated the objections (to the existence of God, the credibility of sense data, etc.) as though they were my own" only "to suit the style of 'meditations' which I judged the style best fitted for unfolding arguments." This defense is strikingly like Flaubert's in the famous obscenity trial of *Madame Bovary*—God exists, Emma dies, each story ends by affirming the moral order it only seemed to question. In the case of *Madame Bovary,* the prosecutor's reply to this line of argument was that "a moral conclusion could not excuse lascivious details"; if it did, then one could describe any immorality, "every orgy imaginable," he says, and get off the legal hook merely by having one's heroine die in disgrace at the end. The prosecutor insists, in other words, on the temporal dimension of the text, and accuses Flaubert himself of what we might call premature thematizing. And Descartes, in reply to his critics, also adopts a thematic reading of the *Meditations*—the doubt, he says, was never real, it was only a literary convention. From this point of view, then, Descartes's defense is Peirce's accusation. "No one," Peirce says, "who follows the Cartesian method will ever be satisfied until he has formally recovered all those beliefs that in form he has given up." This is an account to which, as we have just seen, Descartes himself was more than willing to subscribe. The question which remains is why Peirce and some of his readers have found this explanation so damning while Descartes and his readers (Gassendi, for example) found the narrative of the doubt to be at worst a literary mistake, "not consonant with philosophic candour."

To begin to answer this question, it is necessary to rehearse for a minute the plot of that first *Meditation*. It opens on an autobiographical note; the author recalls discovering some time ago the many "false beliefs" that he had from "his earliest youth admitted as true," and he remembers his determination eventually to rid himself of all unsure opinions and "commence to build anew from the foundation." Being acutely aware, however, of the difficulty of such a project, he has put it off until now when, on the one hand, he is "mature" enough to manage such a great enterprise, and, on the other hand, young enough to devote to it all the time and energy that will be necessary:

> Today . . . since very opportunely for the plan I have in view I have delivered my mind from every care (and am happily agitated by no passions), and since I have procured for myself an assured leisure in a peaceable retirement, I shall at last seriously and freely address myself to the general upheaval of all my former opinions.

The purpose of this paragraph is merely to set the stage for the virtuoso display of doubt to follow. But it may be that we can get some sense of what Peirce found so troubling—without examining the doubts themselves—by paying attention to the state of mind which is said to have produced them. For surely that is in some sense what is most remarkable about this whole first *Meditation*. Its author sits himself next to his fireplace, attired, he tells us, in a dressing gown; having delivered his mind from every care, he has no worries; being happily agitated by no passions, he has no desires; having procured for himself an assured leisure in a peaceable retirement, he is free from the demands of life in the world, free that is, to philosophize. In other words, having estab-

lished a kind of philosophical vacuum, a neutral space in which what
Descartes calls the philosopher's "unprejudiced" self can function, he is
free to begin doubting. Peirce's question will be: What can it mean for
such a self to doubt? How can a man so comfortable address himself to
the general upheaval of all his opinions? Or put another way, What is the
status of this philosopher's self and his philosophical space?

That such a notion of neutrality is essential to Descartes's understanding of philosophy is, I think, unquestionable. In each of the three
sets of introductory notes to the *Meditations,* the "Dedication to the Doc-
tors of the Sorbonne," the "Preface to the Reader," and the "Synopsis,"
he speaks of philosophy as a study demanding "a mind wholly free of
prejudices, and one which can be easily detached from the affairs of the
sense." One purpose these repetitions no doubt serve is that of a ritualis-
tic appeal to the reader to keep an open mind, but they serve also to
define, for Descartes, the place where philosophy is to begin, and to
characterize the readers and writers who are to begin it. Philosophical
inquiry and the philosophical self are required to begin context-free.
The systematic doubt itself is understood as a technique for suspending
context, a way of gaining access to essentials which are obscured by the
intrusion of the world. Thus when Peirce writes that "we cannot begin
with complete doubt. We must begin with all the prejudices that we
actually have when we enter upon the study of philosophy," he is not
only questioning the reality of Cartesian doubt, he is putting forward an
alternative account of philosophy and of the philosophical self, one
which poses an explicit challenge to the related values of autonomy and
neutrality.

Now nothing, of course, has been more common than for certain
types of empiricist philosophers, beginning with Gassendi, to question
the validity of the systematic doubt. And insofar as we can locate Peirce
too within the empiricist tradition, it is not surprising that he, like Gassendi, should be skeptical of Descartes's skepticism. There is however, a
crucial difference between them. Gassendi was uncertain about the efficacy of Cartesian doubt—he suspected Descartes of having been seduced
by the temptation of literary artifice into substituting a new prejudice for
an old one—but he acquiesced completely in the goal of neutrality. "I
agree with your plan of freeing the mind from every prejudice," he
wrote Descartes, and Descartes wrote back, Of course—who could ever
"pretend there was any fault to find with this?" Peirce too is skeptical
about the doubt, but it is with the plan and the goal that he takes real
issue. And this objection is not primarily an empiricist one, since it takes
the form not of an argument for the validity of sense data but of an
argument against a notion of the self which, in Peirce's view, Descartes
and the British empiricists held in common.

Peirce's own account of the self is a subject not much examined;

most of his commentators have read these 1868 essays primarily as attacks on the doctrine of intuition and so have tended to regard the question of the self as an altogether subsidiary one. And those writers who have discussed it have been generally dismayed by Peirce's not uncharacteristic refusal to be clear on the subject. Justin Buchler writes, for example, "I do not know what Peirce means by 'self,' but it is not unlikely that in 1868 he would, if pressed, have given an empirical account." This potential empiricism seems a little less likely to me than to Professor Buchler but it is a point not easily resolved and I think we can get some sense at least of what Peirce felt was at stake in the question of the self by placing his account in opposition to Descartes's. He deals most straightforwardly with this issue in his response to the second of the "Questions Concerning Certain Faculties." The question is "Whether we have an intuitive self-consciousness." By intuition, Peirce means "a cognition not determined by a previous cognition," that is, a direct knowledge of the thing itself, what he calls elsewhere "the transcendental object." By self-consciousness he means "a knowledge of ourselves," and furthermore of "our personal selves." "Pure apperception," he says, "is the self assertion of the ego; the self-consciousness here meant is the recognition of my private self." The point of the argument that follows is that we don't have any such faculty of introspection, that our notion of our selves is produced by inference not by intuition; it is in the process of elaborating this argument that Peirce is most explicit about the self.

The argument takes the form of a narrative of the growth of self-consciousness in children. When they are very young, he says, they don't seem to have any, that is "they manifest powers of thought" long before they have any sense of the "I" that is thinking. Take, for example, the case of a child who decides to move a table. "Does he think of himself as desiring or only of the table as fit to be moved?" "That he has the latter thought," Peirce says, "is beyond question; that he has the former must . . . remain an arbitrary and baseless supposition." When the child actually succeeds in moving the table, this way of thinking is obviously confirmed, but even if he is unsuccessful, he has learned, Peirce implies, only that tables aren't fit to be moved, not that he can't move one. But take the example of a child who "hears it said that the stove is hot." It isn't, the child says; but he touches it and gets burned. "Thus," Peirce writes, "he becomes aware of ignorance and it is necessary to suppose a self in which this ignorance can inhere." We may wonder what makes this example different from the first—why doesn't the child learn simply that stoves are hot as he did that tables can (or cannot) be moved? Why does he learn about the self? The difference between the two examples is the introduction, into the second, of language, which can assert a relation between the child and the stove which he can first agree to or deny and then test. Thus, when he touches the stove, he learns not only that it is hot but that he didn't know it was hot. "So," Peirce says, "testimony gives the first dawning of self-consciousness."

As an argument against intuitive self-consciousness, the point of the story is clear—the child discovers his self not by intuition but by hypothesis, the self is necessary to explain the phenomena of ignorance and error. And "Ignorance and error," Peirce says "are all that distinguish our private selves from the absolute *ego* of pure apperception." But the intervention of language is if anything even more crucial in our attempt to make sense of what kind of thing the self is for Peirce. For one of the next questions he asks in this essay is "Whether we can think without signs," and since, he says, the only argument that we can is the unproven assertion "that thought must precede every sign," he concludes that we can't. If then, we can have in the first place no direct knowledge of the self, that is to say, if we can know it only as an inference or thought, and if, in the second place all our thoughts are signs, it follows in the third place that we can only know the self as a sign. And if furthermore, we accept Peirce's principle "that the absolutely incognizable (unknowable) does not exist," then we must go on to say not merely that we can only know the self as a sign, but that the self is a sign, or, as Peirce rather dramatically puts it, "the word or sign that man uses *is* the man himself."

Now this, as the eminent Peirce scholar Murray G. Murphey says, is a "rather surprising thesis," and it is one which Peirce himself never developed very fully and which the Pragmatism of James and Dewey either left strictly alone or treated with extreme caution. In fact, the only major American philosopher to take it seriously was Josiah Royce in *The Problem of Christianity*. But the contrast between the Peirceian notion of the self and the Cartesian one is illuminating. For Descartes, the self is primary—it can be known directly, and its existence is the single privileged certainty; for Peirce the self is derived—it can only be known by inference from the existence of ignorance and error. For Descartes the self is neutral—"unprejudiced," it begins by believing in nothing except its own existence; for Peirce the self is always committed—it cannot begin by calling into question all its beliefs, for these beliefs, these "prejudices," "are things that it does not occur to us can be questioned." For Descartes the self is autonomous—this is simply to say again that it is primary, it exists independent of any external constraints; for Peirce the self is a sign—it is itself "external," like all signs, it "must address itself to some other, must determine some other, since that is the essence of a sign." These others constitute the sign system, what Peirce calls "reality," what Royce will call the "community of interpretation."

The distinctive character of this reading of Descartes can be shown most clearly, I think, by comparing it briefly to another, perhaps better-known reading—Husserl's in his *Cartesian Meditations*. Husserl begins by lamenting the loss of the "radical" spirit of Cartesianism and calling for its renewal, a second "Cartesian overthrow" in response to the "demand for a philosophy aiming at the ultimate conceivable freedom from prejudice, shaping itself with actual autonomy according to ultimate evidences it has itself produced, and therefore absolutely self-responsible." This exhortation is accompanied, however, by a warning—in embracing the "impulse" of the original Cartesian *Meditations,* we must be careful "not to adopt their content," we must avoid above all the "seductive aberrations, into which Descartes and later thinkers strayed." And what are these seductive aberrations? Fundamentally, it turns out, Descartes himself succumbed to prejudice, in the form of the Scholastic assumptions uncovered by Gilson and Koyré, but more importantly in the wrong turn which converts the *ego* into a "*substantia cogitans,* a separate human *mens sive animus.*" Descartes imagined, Husserl writes, that with the *cogito* he had "rescued a little *tag-end of the world . . .* and that now the problem [was] to infer the rest of the world by rightly conducted arguments, according to principles innate in the ego." But Husserl's ego, the reduced or transcendental ego, "is not a piece of the world . . . [and] neither the world nor any worldly object is a piece of [the] ego." Thus Husserl characterizes the ego as "disinterested," "a non-participant onlooker." Husserl's strategy is one of ritual purification: first to demonstrate the prejudices implicit in the Cartesian construction of the unprejudiced and then to exorcize them.

What is perhaps most interesting about this way of reading Descartes is that it is, in principle, infinitely repeatable, and it has, in fact, been repeated, most recently by Derrida, who uncovers Husserl's prejudices as Husserl had uncovered Descartes's. Husserl, Derrida says, "puts out of play all constituted knowledge, he insists on the necessary absence of presuppositions," but, Derrida goes on to ask, "do not phenomenological necessity, the rigor and subtlety of Husserl's analysis, the exigencies to which it responds . . . nonetheless conceal a metaphysical presupposition?" And his own procedure is to identify this metaphysical presupposition, and to delineate its workings at the heart of the Husserlian project of ridding philosophy of any prior metaphysics. What is always left problematic is the status of the deconstructive ground, but my real point here is that this Derridean or Husserlian move, deconstructing the unprejudiced by uncovering the prejudice it conceals, is exactly the move that Peirce does *not* make. When, in 1868, he attacks Descartes, it is not for concealing prejudices, but for imagining a category of the unprejudiced, and when, in a curious way, he modifies this attack in 1877–78, it is not a phenomenological or reduced version of the *cogito* that he returns to but the somewhat confused and troublesome account in *Meditation* III of the "clear and distinct ideas."

It is in this third *Meditation* that Descartes puts forward his first proof of the existence of God. He begins with a discussion of those ideas which are so vivid to us, so "clear and distinct," that we do not doubt their veracity. And yet, it must be acknowledged that if there were a God who was also a "deceiver," those clear and distinct ideas might still prove false. Hence we must determine whether or not there is a God and whether or not He is a deceiver. To this end, Descartes distinguishes between what he considers to be two different classes of ideas—those which could have been produced by the mind and those which could not. Most ideas, Descartes reminds us, light, color, sounds, taste, etc., fall into the first class and so their actual existence is uncertain. The second class, on the other hand, turns out to contain basically only one idea, that of "a substance that is infinite . . . independent, all-knowing, all powerful, and by which I myself and everything else, if anything else does exist, have been created." This "infinite" substance is, of course, God, and the idea of this substance cannot come from within me since I myself am finite. It may be argued that I have no real idea of the infinite except as a negation of the finite, but how could it be possible, Descartes replies, "that I should know that I doubt and desire, that is to say, that something is lacking to me, and that I am not quite perfect, unless I had within me some idea of a being more perfect than myself, in comparison with which I should recognize the deficiencies of my nature?" Therefore, if I have a clear and distinct idea of an infinite or perfect being, it cannot come from within me (since I myself am neither infinite nor perfect), and since it cannot come from within me, it must come from that being himself, God, who must therefore exist.

Particularly in the schematic form in which I have given it here, the problem with this argument is fairly clear, and it is put very cogently by the theologian Arnauld when he calls attention to the apparent circularity of Descartes's reasoning. According to Descartes, "the only secure reason we have for believing that what we clearly and distinctly perceive is true is the fact that God exists," Arnauld says. "But we can be sure that God exists, only because we clearly and evidently perceive that; therefore prior to being certain that God exists, we should be certain that whatever we clearly and evidently believe is true." Thus we have what has become famous as the Cartesian circle: the objection that in proving the existence of God, Descartes relies upon the truth of the clear and distinct ideas, a truth which is itself only guaranteed by the existence of God. This objection, if admitted, is fatal to the whole Cartesian project of relocating all knowledge on the indubitable ground of the *cogito,* and that Peirce was prepared to admit the objection is clear from his comment in "How to Make Our Ideas Clear" where he says that "the distinction between an idea *seeming* clear and really being so, never occurred" to Descartes. This is simply to say that the only guarantee for Descartes that an idea which seems clear will really be clear is the existence of a

God who is no deceiver, and if the existence of such a God cannot be proved without circularity, then the distinction breaks down.

What Peirce does next, however, is rather dramatic and unexpected; for instead of repudiating the Cartesian circularity, he embraces it. It marks for him "the most essential point of the Cartesian philosophy, which is that to accept propositions that seem perfectly evident to us is a thing that, whether it be logical or illogical, we cannot help doing." Peirce himself says no more about his altered perspective on Descartes, but his single comment serves to point out a curious phenomenon—the first three *Meditations* seem to contain at least two different versions of the self, and what both unites them and distinguishes them is the constitutive role of doubt. Doubt as a particular instance of thought in general establishes the primacy of the *cogito*—even when I doubt my own existence, I am thinking, and if I am thinking, I exist—and the systematic doubt serves, as we have already seen, to affirm the "unprejudiced" character of the self whose existence is proved. But in the proof of the existence of God in *Meditation* III, the fact of doubt is used to demonstrate not that I am self-sufficient but rather that "something is lacking to me." The self of this *Meditation* is derived, not primary, and it is associated with error and inadequacy. So when Peirce accepts or even embraces the Cartesian circle, he is embracing not the error in logic but the alternate notion of a self which is no longer neutral, no longer context-free.

A further reading of these essays of 1877 and 1878 would involve locating Peirce's remarks on Descartes more precisely in the context of his attempt to develop a coherent theory of doubt and belief, a problem which would in turn require us to explore from a slightly altered viewpoint the status of the longstanding opposition between literature and philosophy. In the form of questions like "Can we understand a poem without believing it?" this opposition was to play a major role in Anglo-American literary criticism of the first half of the twentieth century. For T. S. Eliot, for example, the very existence of literature depended on a "yes" answer, depended, that is, on the possibility of our freely deployed skepticism (a possibility about which Eliot himself was to grow increasingly skeptical). And in this context, we may begin to see more clearly what is at stake in Gassendi's complaint that the Cartesian doubt is merely literary, "an artifice," "not consonant with philosophic candour." Peirce's eventual understanding of belief as habit calls these distinctions between literature and philosophy, between reading and believing, into question, even though the question itself will only be asked by Eliot, who will have learned how to ask it from Royce.

Royce's place in this tradition is clearly central and because of its centrality at least potentially controversial. What I want to suggest on the one hand is that Royce's very late work involved a significant use and extension of Peirce's very early work, and on the other hand, that Royce's *The Problem of Christianity* played a crucial, albeit indirect, role in the subsequent development of at least one strain of American literary theory. The first of these claims is potentially controversial because it calls into question the more or less canonical opposition between Royce's Idealism and the Pragmatism of William James, a dichotomy which places Peirce firmly on the side of the Pragmatists and hence in opposition to Royce. The second claim is potentially controversial because it dissents from the fairly common view of Royce as a philosophical dead-end, one of a group of nineteenth-century neo-Hegelians (including, among others, F. H. Bradley at Oxford and J. M. E. McTaggart at Cambridge) whose general philosophical stance now seems, as A. J. Ayer has put it, "so palpably untenable that it is hard for us to understand how they could ever have been taken seriously." In tracing a line from Peirce to Royce to Eliot, I propose first a reading of Peirce which sees him as something other than a forerunner of James, Bertrand Russell, and G. E. Moore, and further propose that Ayer's hopeful report of the death of Anglo-American Idealism was, as usual, greatly exaggerated. What we might want to say instead is that Peirce and Royce (Eliot studied with Royce at Harvard in 1913–14) helped to create a context in which it was possible for Eliot to read Bradley, and that Eliot derived from these figures a fundamentally Idealist theory of interpretation which, along with the New Critical attempt to repress that Idealism, has had some important consequences for our understanding of literary theory.

This counterhistory of American theories of interpretation raises questions, however, which go beyond the scope of this essay, limited as it is to Peirce's theory of the self. But this theory of the self has its own consequences for literary criticism and points its own morals, and perhaps the most important of these morals is that the problem of the reader's subjectivity is, at least from Peirce's standpoint, a false problem. It is false because it relies upon precisely the notion of self (and hence of interpretation) which Peirce was at such pains to attack in Descartes. What Abrams, Hirsch, Culler, et al. fear is a situation in which the reader will be allowed or encouraged to grant his unconstrained subjective responses the status of "meaning." Their model of interpretation is the nineteenth-century scientistic model of the autonomous reader or observer confronting an autonomous text or data. If all goes well, the reader suspends his prejudices and interprets the texts correctly. If all doesn't go well, the reader enforces his prejudices and makes the text over in their image. From Peirce's standpoint, however, neither of these alternatives is feasible because the model they are derived from is mistaken. In rejecting the Cartesian goal of neutrality, he rejects on the one hand a notion of the self free to assert its subjectivity without constraint and on the other hand a notion of the self wiped clean of prejudice and ready to accept determinate meaning. These two positions are simply the flip sides of the context-free self, active and passive; one generates any interpretation it pleases, the other denies that it interprets at all.

In this light, we can also see that the recently heralded substitution of a "subjective paradigm" for the worn-out "objective paradigm" leaves the model comparatively unchanged, at least with respect to the status of the self. Unlike Abrams or Hirsch, David Bleich will deny the "autonomy of what is 'out there.'" "An observer is a subject," he writes, "and his means of perception define the essence of the object and even its existence to begin with. . . . Knowledge is not a parent, a spouse, or a God; it is the subjective construction of our minds, which are more accessible to us than anything else." But the assertion that our minds are "more accessible to us than anything else" is exactly what Peirce's account of the self denies. Instead he suggests that our minds are accessible to us in *exactly the same way* that everything else is. The self, like the world, is a text. Hence the notion of an autonomous unconstituted subject is just as problematic (and for the same reasons) as the autonomous and unconstituted world. From a Peirceian standpoint, Bleich's (and Norman Holland's) "subjectivist" understanding of the self is exactly the same as Abrams's and Hirsch's. The only difference is that Bleich and Holland like what they see and Abrams and Hirsch don't.

In Peirce's view, then, the self is already embedded in a context, the community of interpretation or system of signs. The rhetoric of the community of interpretation emphasizes the role readers play in constituting texts, while the rhetoric of the self as sign in a system of signs emphasizes the role texts play in constituting consciousness—the strategy in each case is to collapse the distinction between the interpreter and what he interprets. "Every cognition," Peirce writes, "involves something represented, or that of which we are conscious, and some action or passion of the self whereby it becomes represented." And elsewhere, "the content of consciousness, the entire phenomenal manifestation of mind, is a sign resulting from inference," and since "every thought is an *external* sign . . . man [himself] is an external sign." This is to say not only that the self interprets but that the self is an interpretation, that we are neither as data-bound nor as fancy-free as the neo-Cartesian models suggest, because the self is in principle a compromise. Principled compromises are themselves not very satisfactory constructions—they deprive us of too many pleasures. We can't simply insist on our principles and say that meaning is either subjective or objective, in the reader or in the text, but we can't compromise them either and say there's a little bit of meaning in the reader and a little in the text, put them both together and you get literary criticism. The most we can say is that we can choose our interpretations but we can't choose our range of choices. There are no text-derived canons of interpretation which prevent the self from doing what it wants, there is only our convictions that what the self wants has already been constituted by canons of interpretation.

In elaborating this early Pragmatic account of the self, it may seem finally that what I have done is to push the semiotic deconstruction of the subject back another sixty or seventy years. And in a certain sense that is true and, I think, necessary, since readers who are astonishingly eager to see shattered or social selves in novels and poems are a good deal more reluctant to acknowledge the consequences of such a deconstruction for their own relations to texts, and it is precisely with this relation that I have been concerned. But Peirce was not interested in eliminating the subject; in fact, in his terms the Structuralist liquidation of the self appears as simply another way of establishing neutrality, a process of formalization which denies the reciprocally constitutive effects he *was* interested in. It is these effects which are the beginning of a Pragmatism that locates its origin not in the empty moment before constitution or in the reified world after but in the act of constitution itself.

What Peirce tells the literary critic, then, is not only that reading is constitutive but that readers have themselves been constituted, and hence that the critic's pose of neutrality is as fictitious as the philosopher's. To call this neutrality fictitious, however, is not to suggest that it should be scrapped and replaced with *real* neutrality. The point is rather that neutrality itself is a fiction, perhaps the enabling fiction of philosophy, and that the literary critic, whose avowed subject is fictions, need not find this embarrassing. His taxonomies are mythologies, his descriptions evaluations, but they are none the worse for that. The mistake is to imagine an alternative—a self before interpretation or a text after.

12

THE READER IN HISTORY:
THE CHANGING SHAPE
OF LITERARY RESPONSE

Jane P. Tompkins

It is apparent that although theorists of reader-oriented criticism disagree on many issues, they are united in one thing: their opposition to the belief that meaning inheres completely and exclusively in the literary text. This opposition, which ranges from timid qualifications of the doctrine of textual autonomy to frontal assaults on the idea of objectivity itself,[1] seems to represent a concerted attack on the foundation of the New Critical endeavor—"the poem itself as an object of specifically critical judgment."[2] In the literature of the reader-response movement, this attack sometimes claims for itself the status of a critical revolution: formalism is pronounced dead, and the responses of individual readers are declared the true object of literary study. In short, reader-response critics define their work as a radical departure from New Critical principles, but I believe that a closer look at the theory and practice of these critics will show that they have not revolutionized literary theory but merely transposed formalist principles into a new key.

The essential similarity between New Criticism and reader-response criticism is obscured by the great issue that seems to divide them: whether meaning is to be located in the text or in the reader. The location of meaning, however, is only an issue when one assumes that the specification of meaning is the aim of the critical act. Thus, although New Critics and reader-oriented critics do not locate meaning in the same place, both schools assume that to specify meaning is criticism's ultimate goal. This assumption not only joins these polemically opposed movements, it binds them together in opposition to a long history of critical thought in which the specification of meaning is not a central concern. But the difference in assumptions that separates twentieth-century literary studies from most previous critical thought has been concealed by the fact that the same terms have been used throughout centuries of critical discussion to refer

201

to practices that are not at all alike. On initial inspection, for instance, contemporary reader-response criticism seems to have much in common with classical literary theories. Classical commentaries on literature, after all, exhibit an overwhelming preoccupation with audience response. Plato, Aristotle, Horace, and Longinus all discuss literature primarily in terms of its effects upon an audience. However, if one looks closely at what ancient writers mean when they speak of audience reaction, one soon discovers that it is not at all what Wolfgang Iser, Stanley Fish, Michael Riffaterre, and their contemporaries have in mind. In fact, despite initial appearances, the "affective" criticism practiced by critics in the second half of the twentieth century owes nothing to the ancient rhetorical tradition it seems at first to resemble, and almost everything to the formalist doctrines it claims to have overturned.

The Classical Period

We may test the validity of this observation by turning to a passage from Longinus's *On the Sublime* which deals explicitly with the way a particular locution in Herodotus affects the hearer.

> So also Herodotus: "From the city of Elephantine thou shalt sail upwards, and then shalt come to a level plain; and after crossing this tract thou shalt embark upon another vessel and sail for two days, and then shalt thou come to a great city whose name is Meroe." Do you observe, my friend, how he leads you in imagination through the region and makes you *see* what you hear? All such cases of direct personal address place the hearer on the very scene of action. So it is when you seem to be speaking, not to all and sundry, but to a single individual;—
>
> But Tydeides—thou wouldst not have known him, for whom that
>   hero fought.
>
> You will make your hearer more excited and more attentive, and full of active participation, if you keep him alert by words addressed to himself.[3]

Although Longinus's reference to a hearer who is "full of active participation" might have come from an essay by Wolfgang Iser, a modern critic influenced by Iser or Fish would not approach the passage from Herodotus as Longinus does. The modern critic would begin by showing in some detail how the language of the quotation makes the reader undergo certain mental or emotional experiences. The cognitive processes which the style forces the reader to enact would then be shown to embody some underlying principle of the work—the Herodotean concept of space and time, or the historian's characteristic manner of organizing perceptual data. A modern critic, in short, would describe the reader's experience in such a way as to provide the basis for an interpretation of the work. But Longinus quotes the passage for an entirely

different reason. He wishes to demonstrate that direct address effectively draws the reader into the scene of the action. He has no interest in
the meaning of the passage, and indeed, it is doubtful that he would
recognize "meaning" as a critical issue at all. For if the reader has become
part of the action, is caught up by the language, the question of what the
passage "means" does not arise. Once the desired *effect* has been
achieved, there is no need, or room, for interpretation.

Behind Longinus's handling of the passage from Herodotus lies an
attitude toward literature and language that is characteristic of classical
antiquity and fundamentally alien to twentieth-century modes of understanding literature and art. For Longinus, language is a form of power
and the purpose of studying texts from the past is to acquire the skills
that enable one to wield that power. It follows from Longinus's instrumental view of language that he should use Herodotus to illustrate the
efficacy of direct address, ignoring what seem to us much deeper questions, because in his perspective the ultimate goal in studying literature
is to become master of a technique. Likewise, it is because of his unspoken assumptions about the nature of literary language that a contemporary reader-response critic would use the same passage as an occasion to
discuss its meaning. All modern criticism—whether response-oriented,
psychological, structuralist, mythopoeic, thematic, or formalist—takes
meaning to be the object of critical investigation, for unlike the ancients
we equate language not with action but with signification. This explains
why the modern critic, despite his interest in audience reaction, does not
really mean the same thing by it that Plato, Aristotle, Horace, and Longinus do. The two concepts of response spring from concepts of language that are radically opposed to one another.

The concept of language as a force acting on the world, rather than
as a series of signs to be deciphered, accounts for the absence of specificity in ancient descriptions of literary response. Aristotle, although he
speaks of pity and fear as the emotions proper to tragedy, judges the
merit of poetic production in general on "vividness of impression," and
"concentrated effect," and says that the end of the art is to be "striking."[4] In other words, it is not the *nature* of the impact that concerns him,
but the degree. The concept of poetry as an instrument of power whose
value is to be measured by the force of the impression it produces takes a
more extreme form in Longinus. Longinus's notion of the sublime is
equivalent to a conception of poetry as pure power. His descriptions of
the sublime center on the effect sublime poetry produces in its hearers,
but instead of specifying this or that emotion, Longinus speaks only in
terms of intensity or strength of feeling. The sublime *is* impact, effect,
raised to the highest power. It is "intensity," "force," "irresistible might."
"Sublimity flashing forth at the right moment scatters everything before
it like a thunderbolt."[5]

The equation of language with power, characteristic of Greek thought at least from the time of Gorgias the rhetorician, explains the enormous energies devoted to the study of rhetoric in the ancient world.[6] It also explains the two most prominent characteristics of literary criticism in antiquity: its preoccupation with matters of technique and its debates over the morality of literary production. When language is believed to have an overwhelming influence on human behavior, then mastering its techniques and exercising ethical control over its uses must of necessity become the paramount critical considerations. It is the consequentiality of poetry as a political force that explains Plato's decision to banish lyric and epic poets from his republic. Only someone who accorded poetic language the highest degree of power in determining human action and behavior could regard poets as dangerous enough to exile.

Plato's expulsion of poets from the ideal state unites the two features of the classical attitude toward literature that distinguish it most markedly from our own: the identification of language with power and the assimilation of the aesthetic to the political realm in Greek life. Though Plato is the only commentator who goes so far as to exclude poetry from the civil order because of its potentially harmful influence, the ancients generally agree that the force of poetic language must be harnessed to the needs of the state. Thus Aristophanes is reflecting conventional wisdom when he has one of his characters in *The Frogs* declare that tragedians must provide "wise counsel for the making of better citizens."[7] The reader, in antiquity, is seen as a citizen of the state, the author as a shaper of civic morality, and the critic as a guardian of the public interest: literature, its producers, and consumers are all seen in relation to the needs of the polity as a whole.[8]

The integration of art and politics in Greek thought affected the status accorded to the literary text, a status which, in turn, reflects ancient attitudes toward the power and function of language. Texts are quoted and commented upon, as in the passage from *On the Sublime,* only to demonstrate by precept and example what the beginning poet should emulate and what he should avoid. The critic faces toward the future and writes in order to help poets produce new work; insofar as he looks back it is only to provide rhetorical models for works yet to be written. The text as an object of study or contemplation has no importance in this critical perspective, for literature is thought of as existing primarily in order to produce results and not as an end in itself. A literary work is not so much an object, therefore, as a unit of force whose power is exerted upon the world in a particular direction. The extent to which discourse is reified in the form of a written text is a measure of its weakness, for once frozen into letters, speech can no longer defend itself against abuse or suit its terms to the various people it wishes to address. It cannot take advantage of opportunities or forestall misprision; in short, because it lacks the power of accommodation to circumstance, it loses its power to mold circumstance in its own image.

> I cannot help feeling, Phaedrus, that writing is unfortunately like painting; for the creations of the painter have the attitude of life, and yet if you ask them a question they preserve a solemn silence. And the same may be said of speeches. You would imagine that they had intelligence, but if you want to know anything and put a question to one of them, the speaker always gives one unvarying answer. And when they have been once written down they are tumbled about anywhere among those who do and among those who do not understand them. And they have no reticences or proprieties towards different classes of persons; and, if they are unjustly assailed or abused, their parent is needed to protect his offspring, for they cannot defend themselves.[9]

Plato's devaluation of the written word in this famous passage exemplifies response-oriented criticism in the classical mode. His attitude toward response and his attitude toward the written text go hand in hand. Response, to Plato, means the effect that discourse has on human behavior. What matters, ultimately, is the behavior, not the discourse.

By contrast, it is the already-written text that stands at the center of the contemporary critical enterprise. And it is not the behavior of the audience but the meaning of the text that is criticism's chief concern. The critic's central activity is not setting standards for the moral content of literary works or instruction for authors who want to produce new work, but the elucidation of texts from the past. This approach does not so much ignore the question of social relevance as postpone it, assuming that until the text is rightly understood it cannot be evaluated. The function of the critic is first to interpret and only then to judge. He is responsible for the impression that literature makes on society not because he has told the author how to make it, or established a censorship code, but because he has told the reader what the text means. In effect, he is the "parent" Plato said the written word stood in need of as protection against the abuse of misreading. The written text itself creates the need for explication since it can be "tumbled about anywhere among those who do and among those who do not understand."

The stance of the contemporary critic vis à vis the text is that of the exegete because, as Plato suggests, the text is no longer in a situation that immediately clarifies its intent, and so the business of the critic, in one way or another, is always with interpretation. This stance in relation to the text is shared by schools of contemporary criticism that otherwise appear to be in mortal conflict. New Criticism, psychoanalytic criticism, structuralist criticism, myth criticism, genre criticism, style criticism, all bear the same explicatory relation to the texts they address because they all share the assumption that texts are objects to be analyzed and deciphered. In this respect, reader-response criticism is no different from the formalist criticism it claims to oppose, or from any other contemporary approach to literature. It is just that instead of arriving at literary meaning by using a vocabulary based in formalism, linguistics, genre theory, or myth, reader-critics have recourse to interpretive systems that describe various kinds of mental activity (Iser's making and breaking of gestalts, Fish's decisions and revisions, Stephen Booth's wandering among systems of coherence, Norman Holland's reproduction of identity themes). What has happened is that the locus of meaning has simply been transferred from the text to the reader. This move seems radical at close range because it undermines the notion of textual objectivity. But the transfer of meaning from text to reader appears startling only within the narrow assumptions of the modernist perspective. For although reader-oriented critics speak of the "poem as event" and of "literature as experience," meaning is still for them the object of the critical act.[10] That act, moreover, has the same shape in reader-response criticism as it does in any contemporary critical analysis: one discourse (an explication) is substituted for another (a literary work) and the first stands to the second in a relationship of equivalence. Although the description of the reader's experience may change with each reading of the text, and though the text may be said to consume itself or to disappear, and though the reader may be said to write his own text, the critic obeys the tradition of explication which takes the single text as the standard unit of interpretation. Shadow though the text may be, by convention it still provides the space within which the reader-critic performs his role.

In summary, reader-response criticism, when viewed in the perspective of critical history, looks more like New Criticism than it does like ancient discussions of response. When the literary work is conceived as an object of interpretation, response will be understood as a way of arriving at meaning, and not as a form of political and moral behavior. The distinction between response conceived as meaning, and response conceived as action or behavior, separates the current conception of literary response not only from the classical one but from the way responses to literature have been understood by most critics before the twentieth century. If one turns to definitions of literature and literary response formulated in the Renaissance and in the eighteenth century, one finds not only that they differ from the modernist definition, but that they differ from it in the same way.

The Renaissance

Perhaps what makes it so difficult for twentieth-century critics to see literature as anything other than an occasion for interpretation is the belief that it is essentially different from all other forms of discourse. Literature is "art" and, therefore, has a special relation to the life around it; it organizes that life, gives it meaning, "expresses it," in Emily Dickinson's phrase, like "the attar from the rose." Therefore, it follows that if we can only interpret the poem aright, we will be in a better position to understand the world. Literature in the Renaissance bore a different relation to the surrounding world. Rather than being a quintessence or a distillation of reality, literature was continuous with it, though not in any simple sense. When the masques at court were over, the actors and actresses, who were also members of the royal family and the aristocracy, chose partners from the audience for the dance. The masques, as Stephen Orgel has demonstrated, functioned in a multiplicity of ways as representations and extensions of royal power. In their combination of poetry, theatricality, social entertainment, and political rhetoric, they emblematize the difference between the Renaissance conception of art and ours.[11]

That conception, in its surface manifestations, is almost identical with the classical model.[12] "Poetry was by its nature an imitation or representation of reality," writes Bernard Weinberg in his *History of Literary Criticism in the Italian Renaissance,* "made to conform as nearly as possible to that reality in order to produce moral effects desirable both for the individual and for the state." The question was one of utility and instruction: Could poetry, by making men morally better, contribute to their moral instruction and hence, indirectly, to the common weal?[13] Since literature is once more defined as a shaper of public morals, its nature and value depend upon the kinds of effects it produces, effects that are equated, as before, with moral behavior and not with textual meaning. The question of meaning, again, plays no role in critical theory except when allegorical interpretation is invoked occasionally as a strategy for dealing with poems that would otherwise be considered false or immoral. But while the language of Renaissance criticism echoes the language of the ancients to an amazing degree, and differs from contemporary theory, point for point, in exactly the same ways, the circumstances within which Renaissance criticism and literature were produced cast these theoretical assertions in a new light.

Response continues to be, more than ever, the central issue. As Weinberg says: "The qualities of a poem were to be sought through the study of its effects upon an audience."[14] But the audience has changed and with it the nature and conception of literary activity. The audience is no longer constituted, as it was in antiquity, on an oratorical model—the speechmaker's audience, a crowd to be stirred or soothed—but is a small group of influential people such as might be present at a meeting of some government council, or at an evening's private entertainment. The audience consists of highly placed members of the government, the court and the aristocracy, individuals known to the poet who are in a position to dispense the patronage he needs. The poet's relation to that audience affects poetic production in every conceivable way and gives the Renaissance attitude toward literature its distinctive character. As Arthur Marotti has argued, "the term 'the literature of patronage' should not be limited to complimentary works or to works provided with complimentary dedications designed to get financial and social favors, for virtually all English Renaissance literature is a literature of patronage."[15] Consequently, its place within the socio-political system keeps literature in the Renaissance from being regarded either as a free-standing activity whose products have autonomous aesthetic value (the modernist view), or as a craft whose products, whether moral or recreational, must contribute to the common good (the classical view). For while poetry is believed to have a social function, as it did in antiquity, the content of that function does not remain the same because the social, economic, and political structures that define it have changed. The poet's dependence on his patrons, the social relations that subsist between him and his audience, give Renaissance poetry the power to carry out a host of new functions that might be summed up in the phrase "public relations." In addition to being regarded as an inculcator of civic virtue, poetry becomes, as a variety of recent studies of the period have suggested, a source of financial support, a form of social protection, a means of procuring a comfortable job, an instrument of socialization, a move in a complicated social game, or even a direct vehicle of courtship.[16]

A glance at the titles of Ben Jonson's verses furnishes an index to the kinds of services Renaissance poetry regularly performed that distinguish it both from classical and from contemporary literature: "Lord Bacon's Birthday," "An Epigram on the Court Pucelle," "The Dedication of the King's New Cellar to Bacchus," "New Year's Day Poem" (to Elizabeth, Countess of Rutland), "To Penshurst" (the home of the Sidney family), "To the Right Honourable the Lord High Treasurer of England an Epistle Mendicant," "A New Year's Gift Sung to King Charles, 1635," "Epigram to the Queen, then Lying In," "Epigram on the Prince's Birthday." Jonson pours forth a continuous stream of verse celebrating the birthdays, christenings, marriages, and sundry accomplishments of members of the royal family and the nobility and, sometimes, he begs money for himself. When it is the essence of the poet's task to express an attitude toward real persons and events—praising, blaming, memorializing, petitioning, thanking—then poems are thought of as a form of influence, a means of accomplishing specific social tasks.

This is exactly the way poetry is presented by authors of Renaissance defenses of the art. They value poetry for what it can do, and especially for what it can do for the aristocracy it serves. In Puttenham's list of the "necessary uses" of poetry, he puts celebrating "the worthy gests of noble Princes" and "the memoriall and registry of all great fortunes" first; then come "the praise of vertue and reproofe of vice," "the instruction of morall doctrines," and other contributions to the general welfare.[17] Thus, while Renaissance critics follow the ancients in valuing poetry for its social utility, they extend that concept to include more practical advantages. Sir Philip Sidney is not even half joking when he reminds poetry's detractors at the end of his defense that poems can win you favor or keep your name alive when you are dead.

Renaissance defenses of poetry have a promotional flavor partly because of the place of literary activity in the social matrix of the court, where poetry had to compete with pursuits such as hawking and hunting for its share of patronage and prestige.[18] Sir Philip Sidney's story, at the opening of his *Apologie,* about John Pietro Pugliano, instructor in horsemanship at the court of the emperor, is not merely a charming preamble to the main argument, but a knowing comment on the position poets occupied at court:

> Hee sayd, Souldiours were the noblest estate of mankinde, and horsemen the noblest of Souldiours. Hee sayde they were the Maisters of warre, and ornaments of peace; speedy goers, and strong abiders; triumphers both in Camps and Courts. Nay, to so unbeleeued a poynt hee proceeded, as that no earthly thing bred such wonder to a Prince as to be a good horseman. Skill of gouernment was but a Pedanteria in comparison. Then would hee adde certaine prayses, by telling what a peerlesse beast a horse was . . . that if I had not beene a peece of a Logician before I came to him, I think he would haue perswaded mee to haue wished my selfe a horse. But thus much at least with his no fewe words hee draue into me, that selfe-loue is better than any guilding to make that seeme gorgious wherein our selues are parties. Wherein, if *Pugliano* his strong affection and weake arguments will not satisfie you, I wil giue you a neere example of my selfe, who (I knowe not by what mischance) in these my not old yeres and idelest times, hauing slipt into the title of a Poet, am prouoked to say somthing unto you in the defence of that my unelected vocation.[19]

Sidney makes fun of the way Pugliano magnifies the importance of his own vocation but prepares in the next breath to do the same thing for *his.* He knows that in the competition for royal favor and support, poets must strive alongside riding-masters, and that the key to success is "making that seem gorgious wherein our selues are parties."

Besides being an advertisement for himself, Sidney's *Apologie* is written as a reply to Gosson's scathing Puritan denunciation of poetry's vicious moral influence, a circumstance not at all unusual in an age when Christian and Platonic attacks on poetry were common.[20] His theoretical claims therefore must be viewed in the context of the historical circumstances which called them forth. When Sidney writes "Onely the

Poet . . . dooth growe in effect another nature. . . . Her world is brasen,
the Poets only deliver a golden," he is not describing the perfect poetic
microcosm of formalist theory but offering a rare experience to poetry's
loyal supporters.[21] The mode of Renaissance criticism, given the social
context in which it was practiced, is not one of explication but of advo-
cacy. Thus the extravagant claims poets make for poetry are not advanced as doctrinal truths in a system of belief, to be understood as
ontological definitions of poetic making, but rather as ingenious advertisements for a vocation.

The sense of audience that motivates these advertisements is what
finally distinguishes Renaissance attitudes toward literature from ours.
Criticism and poetry alike are aimed at a particular audience and are
designed to achieve particular effects. Literature exists in order to serve
its clientele and is subject to the audience's judgment. In the modern
period, on the other hand, the work is not written for a known constitu-
ency, nor is it intended to have such well-defined results. Instead of
moving the audience and bringing pressure to bear on the world, the
work is thought to present another separate and more perfect world,
which the flawed reader must labor to appropriate. The work is not a
gesture in a social situation, or an ideal model for human behavior, but
an interplay of formal and thematic properties to be penetrated by the
critic's mind. The imputation that a poem might break out of its self-
containment and perform a service would disqualify it immediately from
consideration as a work of art. The first requirement of a work of art in
the twentieth century is that it should *do* nothing.

The belief that literature is above politics and does not act directly to
bring about results has determined the way contemporary reader-
centered critics define their task. Whereas in the Renaissance, literature's effects are often conceived in socio-political terms—effects on the
dispositions of princes, on the national self-image, on the moral climate
of the age—modern reader-critics understand effects as entirely a matter of *individual* response. They may focus on the reader's cognitive
processes as he moves from line to line, or on the motivational patterns
that govern his interpretations of a work, or on the identity theme that
mediates the work for him, but however the responses are characterized,
and whatever their moral benefits are said to be, the consequences of
reading are normally confined to the self considered in isolation. Nor is
there any recognition, in contemporary discussions of response, of poetry's ability to accomplish social tasks—such as courtship, flattery, obtaining favors, or displaying one's technical skill—because in the modern era
poetry is not conceived as a means of carrying out social transactions
between persons known to each other, but as a collection of artifacts in
the public domain, available to everyone for study and appreciation.
Reader-response critics who are interested in individual reactions to lit-

erature, therefore, do not describe them as responses to a social situation, but as projections of the reader's psyche onto the text. The situation of the reader vis à vis the text determines completely the nature of the text as well as the definition of response. In a modern academic setting, instead of being the instrument of a social transaction, the poem is the occasion for acquiring literary competence, if the reader is a student; and if the reader is a professor, it is the occasion for advancing his professional career when he publishes a new interpretation of it. Defining the text as an object of interpretation, in both instances, satisfies the demands of the institutional context. By making the reactions of individual readers a legitimate basis for literary interpretation, reader-response critics have extended the power and usefulness of the interpretive model that they inherited from formalism.

The Augustan Age

The conception of literature and of literary response in force in the Augustan age is even more opposed to the contemporary interpretive model, if that is possible, than the Renaissance conception. The tailoring of verse to some particular person or situation assumes its most obvious form and achieves its most spectacular results in the genre that dominates poetry in the late seventeenth and early eighteenth centuries—satire. In his introduction to a collection of essays on satire, Ronald Paulson points directly, if unintentionally, to the chasm that divides the Augustan conception of literature from ours. He says, in effect, that the Augustans had no poetics of satire because their discussions of the genre consider only its social function and the motives of the satirist; these discussions, moreover, are carried on principally by the satirists themselves, who are "essentially defenders of their own practice." "Only in the last few decades," he concludes," has a poetic of satire been attempted and to a large extent worked out."[22] Paulson's judgment that the Augustans had no theory of the genre at which they excelled is based, of course, on a particular notion of what poetry is. If the poem is thought to be an "organic system of relationships," then it is true that eighteenth-century critics have nothing to say in the matter.[23] But if poetry is thought of as a weapon to be hurled against an opponent, as a partisan activity whose purpose is to advance individual and factional interests, then its social function and the motives of its users inevitably occupy the center of critical discussion. J. V. Guerinot, in a discussion of pamphlet attacks on Alexander Pope, pushes Paulson's position even further when he finds fault with the Augustan critics who attacked Pope in the *Dunciad* for failing to see "that the *Dunciad* was a poem." Instead of reading the poem "as a poem," "as an organic unity," they took it as an attack on themselves. Not realizing that Pope had lifted his poem out of "historical reality" and given it "universal significance," they did not separate satirist and *persona,* for "to them the speaker of the poem was quite simply Pope."[24] The Augustans, in short, had not read Maynard Mack's essay, "The Muse of Satire," which provides New Criticism with a way of handling polemical verse. Such poetry does not express "the poet's actual feelings about a contemporary," Mack argues, but "the strong antipathy of Good to Bad." The historical author of the poem, he maintains, is not the same as its dramatic speaker; and hence, the poetry reflects a "general fictive situation" which is characterized by "impersonality."[25]

Such a definition of satire alters the Augustan notion of satire's intended effects beyond recognition. Instead of conceiving the poem as a missile designed to inflict damage on the objects of its ridicule, and to rouse public opinion against them, it reconceives the work as a container of universal truths, which the diligent and perceptive reader may retrieve if he understands the formulae in which they are encoded. It is precisely this attempt to transform historical features into dramatic features, and to read particular allusions as vehicles for moral universals, which, according to Edward Rosenheim, destroys satire's very essence. In a frontal attack on the formalist interpretation of the genre, Rosenheim asserts: "Punitive satire is distinguished by the presence of *both* the historically authentic and the historically particular; in the absence of either, the satiric quality disappears."[26] Emphasizing the specificity of satire's objects, Rosenheim continues: "Swift's chief target is the Royal Society rather than vanity in general, Walpole rather than man's venal tendencies, Puritan Enthusiasm rather than the vice of affectation." The audience of satire, he insists, is specific, the satirist's mission "limited by historical circumstances," his motives, "genuine but ephemeral." Far from being separated from its temporal human origins by a literary *persona* or by translation to a level of universal significance, eighteenth-century satire is embedded in the historical setting, engendered by it, and responsive to it in detail.[27]

The dynamic nature of poetic utterance that Rosenheim claims for satire pushes the classical identification of language with political power to an extreme and implies that literary production and reception are the moral equivalents of physical combat. The exactitude of this description is illustrated nicely by an anecdote connected with the verse "Essay on Satire," which Dryden composed with the Earl of Mulgrave. "Men aim rightest when they shoot in jest," they write, defending the social usefulness of satire, and go on, in the body of the poem, to "hit" some of the greatest people of the day. One night shortly thereafter, on his way home, Dryden was cudgeled in an alley by three ruffians. No one knows who hired them, since, as the editor notes, "no omnibus satire of the period could have been more offensive to more powerful people in a

position to retaliate."[28] But whoever they were, the ability of a poem to
elicit such a response, and the equivalence between poetry and cudgeling
that the response implies, dramatize in a crude but forceful way the kind
of power that poetic discourse had when Dryden wrote.

Poetry of the late seventeenth and early eighteenth centuries traffics
in power both in the broad sense of exerting influence on personal
behavior and public opinion, and in the narrower sense of dealing
explicitly with political issues.[29] Pope's "Essay on Criticism," written, like
Sidney's *Apologie,* as a reply to an attack on literature, concerns the
supposed alliance between wit (which was identified with literature) and
disruptions of the peace and threats to civil order during the preceding
century—the religious heresy and violence of the Civil Wars, the decline
in public morals and increase in religious skepticism under Charles II,
and the growth of impiety during the reign of William III.[30] To defend
poesy, for Pope, was to take up a position in the debates raging over the
political and religious events of the day, because poetry was assumed to
have influenced the course of those events, whether for good or ill. The
extent to which poets were involved in political controversy in this period
can be summed up by an observation J. V. Guerinot makes in describing
Pope's political affiliations. If a political pamphlet begins by attacking
Walpole, he says, it will be very likely to favor Pope, but if it praises the
Prime Minister, Pope is sure to come in for a beating.[31] The interdigita-
tion of poetry and politics that this remark takes for granted is unthink-
able today.

I have emphasized the extent to which poetry from the Renaissance
to the middle of the eighteenth century was enmeshed in English social
and political life in order to provide some perspective on what it means
to talk about literary response. When poetry takes its place parallel to
and in reciprocal relation with other kinds of human activity, and when
the author's relation to his audience is direct and intimate, audience
response so crucially determines the nature and direction of literary
activity that its importance is simply assumed. Given that response is
what all poems aim at, the chief critical issues are how to achieve that
response and the kinds of effects that poetry ought to produce. By
contrast, the questions to which contemporary reader-response critics
have addressed themselves—whether or not it is legitimate to discuss
response at all, whether response can be considered part of poetic meaning, whether meaning should be located in the text or in the reader—do
not arise until artistic activity has become cut off from the centers of
political life and the art product loses its power to influence public opinion on matters of national importance. Once this process is underway,
definitions of literature and of literary response begin to change accordingly. The stark opposition between the formalist definition of literature
and those that prevailed in the classical period, the Renaissance, and the

early eighteenth century starts to weaken. As the conditions of life—economic, social, political—come more and more to resemble those of the present day, conceptions of literature take on a more and more familiar outline. The development of literary theory from the pre-Romantics onward leads in a straight line to literary formalism, effecting a total reversal of the assumptions that had been in force since the Renaissance. This remarkable shift—so profound, yet gradual and continuous at close range—registers itself most tellingly in the changing definition of literary response, which, ever at the center of critical attention, comes paradoxically but inevitably to be redefined out of existence.

The Advent of Formalism: Kames to I. A. Richards

The process of separation between literature and political life begins to occur in the second half of the eighteenth century when the breakdown of the patronage system, the increase in commercial printing, and the growth of a large reading public change the relation of authors to their audiences.[32] Christopher Caudwell notes that as long as the poet continues to write for a patron and those who form his patron's circle, he speaks a "more or less current language," and "writes for an audience he has directly in mind, to whom perhaps he will presently read his poems and so be able to watch their effect."[33] But, once authors become dependent for their means of support upon the sales of their printed work, the personal relation to their audience is severed and the relationship becomes more purely economic. Manuscripts no longer circulate by hand among a coterie of friends and associates; poems are no longer read aloud in groups; sonnets are not exchanged among acquaintances. Instead, literature assumes the fixed condition of print. The literary work becomes endlessly reproducible, available to anyone who can read. Hence, the possible distance in time and space between the originator of the work and its readers becomes virtually limitless. "From this moment on," writes Bertrand Bronson in a study of author-reader relations in the late eighteenth century, "gradually but increasingly there develops a race of authors who write to an indefinite body of readers, personally undifferentiated and unknown, who accept this separation as a primary condition of their creative activity and address their public invisibly through the curtain, opaque and impersonal, of print."[34] Instead of taking place within the context of a social relationship, the production and consumption of literature go on independent of any social contact between author and reader. Literature becomes simultaneously both impersonal and privatized. Instead of writing a dedicatory poem on the King's new cellar, the poet writes an "Ode to Joy."

The literature of feeling that emerges in the second half of the eighteenth century—sentimental novels, Gothic novels, the poetry of sensibility—is designed to give the reader certain kinds of emotional experience rather than to mold character or guide behavior, and is aimed at the psychic life of individuals rather than at collective standards of judgment on public issues. A corresponding development in the field of criticism moves attention away from literature's social and moral effects and toward the psychology of reading, so that the concept of literary response, from having been primarily a social and political one, now becomes personal and psychological. The nature of this critical movement can be inferred from its tremendous interest in Longinus, whose sole concern had been the means of producing transport. However, while the eighteenth-century critics share Longinus's belief that poetry should evoke intense feelings, they are less interested than he in the method of producing such effects and much more interested in the assumptions about mental functioning that such a method must imply. Arguing for the effectiveness of concrete details in rendering a scene vivid to a reader, Lord Kames writes: "The power of language to raise emotions depends entirely on raising such lively and distinct images as are here described; the reader's passions are never sensibly moved till he be thrown into a kind of reverie, in which state, forgetting that he is reading, he conceives every incident as passing in his presence, precisely as if he were an eyewitness. . . ."[35] As in the passage from Longinus with which this essay began, the subject under discussion is how to transport the reader into the world of the description, making him feel he is there on the scene. Longinus recommends a particular technique for achieving this effect and illustrates it twice. But Kames wants to establish a point about the way the mind works (it can be aroused only by images that are "lively and distinct") and to describe the mental condition of the rapt reader (a state of "reverie"). Unlike Pope and Sidney, Kames feels no need to write a polemic or an encomium on poetry's behalf. When he compares imaginative to historical writing a few sentences later, it is not in order to make literature look good at history's expense, but to show that "fable" can produce "sympathy" and "vivacity of . . . ideas" more effectively than fact.[36] Patiently and systematically, Kames constructs a detailed theory of the relationship between language and emotional response, not to urge the noble uses of poetry, but in order to enlarge his reader's understanding of a new subject.

That subject is aesthetics—the study of the perception and evaluation of works of art. With the work of Kames and his contemporaries—Richard Hurd, Edmund Burke, Alexander Gerard, Sir Joshua Reynolds—who use emotional responses to literature and the other arts as evidence for their speculations on the universal laws of the mind, literary criticism becomes a science. The reception of works of art comes to be treated not as an event in the social world with social consequences for author and audience, but as an object of scholarly and scientific investigation. The kinds of experience that come under scrutiny—experiences of the sublime, the romantic, the picturesque, the pathetic, the beautiful—have little to contribute to the making of better citizens; the emotions are considered desirable and interesting in themselves. And once literary experience is seen as occupying a realm of its own, one whose frame of reference, in R. S. Crane's phrase, is "not the republic, but the republic of letters," the way is open to seeing the poet as a special kind of person and the literary work as a special kind of object—more like an icon than a cudgel, and less likely than before to do anyone any harm.[37] Or, one might add, any good.

Literary theory at the beginning of the nineteenth century, however, is still at pains to demonstrate how much good the poet can do. After the French Revolution the study of sensibility for its own sake turns into an effort to show that poetry's power over the feelings can bind men together by appealing to their deepest human sympathies. Wordsworth emphasizes the moral benefits of poetry both as a force for human brotherhood and as a civilizing agency. He believes that the need for poetry's refining influence has been created by the "increasing accumulation of men in cities," which has "blunted the discriminating powers of the mind. . . . The uniformity of occupations," moreover, "produces a craving for extraordinary incident, which the rapid communication of intelligence hourly gratifies." Wordsworth affirms that his poetry will counteract this trend by enlightening the understanding, strengthening and purifying the affections, and enlarging the mind's capacity to become excited "without the application of gross and violent stimulants."[38] But although Wordsworth's rationale for the kind of poetry he writes is political, his concept of response is not. A poem should not incite any particular feeling or form of behavior but rather should improve the faculties that mediate experience. The ministry of poetry, apparently, is secret. It may work invisible alterations in the human heart, but it will not decrease the accumulation of men in cities or diversify human occupations. Nor should it attempt to do so. In order to achieve maximum effectiveness, poetry must operate at the most profound level of human experience, rather than dissipate its force on any particular social issue.

If the ambitious scope of Wordsworth's humanitarian aims leads him to formulate poetry's goals in general rather than in concrete terms, this is even more true of Shelley, who believes that because poetry is man's best hope it cannot be used to shape human action to any particular, and therefore limited, end.[39] Because he wants to preserve for poetry what he conceives as the most potent and lasting form of influence on human life, Shelley strips it of its traditional function as a regulator of social behavior and instrument of civic virtue. "A poet," he says, "would do ill to embody his own conceptions of right and wrong, which are usually those of his place and time," for "poetical creations . . . participate in neither." "Eternal poets," on the contrary, scorn to "affect a moral aim."[40]

At the same time that it makes statements such as these, Shelley's "Defense" attributes the rise of Western civilization directly to poetry's influence. Poetry, for example, is made responsible for the abolition of slavery and the emancipation of women.[41] Yet for all his eagerness to demonstrate the "effects of poets, in the large and true sense of the word, upon their own and all succeeding times," Shelley's concept of poetry is determinedly ahistorical.[42] In order to make the highest possible claims for poetry, Shelley must declare that it is neither produced by nor responsive to finite historical circumstances, for if it were otherwise, poetry would be trapped in the finite sphere of materiality and perpetual flux. Shelley's declaration that poetry transcends these limitations, which is remarkable for its imperialism on poetry's behalf, signals the beginning of a movement whose momentum is not yet played out; and that is the separation of poetry from ordinary life through a denial of its local origins and effects, and a simultaneous elevation of its function to that of a repository of eternal values.

This change points to a number of other, similar, and apparently contradictory, developments in the way literature was talked about in the nineteenth century, developments which lead directly to the view of art that has dominated criticism in the twentieth. At exactly the time when a consciousness of history becomes fundamental to critical thought, poetry is spoken of as transcending the influences of place and time. Just when the most grandiose claims are made for the power of poetry to transform human consciousness—poets are the "unacknowledged legislators of the world," who "bind together the vast empire of human society"—the poet starts to be described as lonely and ineffectual, a "nightingale who sits in darkness and sings to cheer its own solitude with sweet sounds."[43] And while literature is hailed as England's most important national resource, greater than the entire Empire of India, it is also spoken of as one of the worst possible ways to make a living.[44]

These apparent contradictions can be accounted for by the gap that had opened up in the nineteenth century between literary activity and social and political life. When poets begin to be described as heaven-sent, God-gifted, divinely inspired individuals, more sensitive, more passionate, more responsive to life than ordinary people, they are no longer the associates of powerful men. They write for a faceless, unpredictable public rather than for a small, highly influential elite. And while poetry is said to be "divine" and to have a future that is "immense," the kind of poetry for which these claims are made sells poorly on the marketplace. The *Lyrical Ballads*, typically, were remaindered, while exotic verse tales of the East sold in the thousands.[45] For the first time in history, as Caudwell notes, poetry had become a commodity for sale along with socks and shoes.[46] There was no longer any way for the poet to measure the impact of his work on an audience, since the author and his audience were no longer personally known to each other. Perhaps this explains why poets began to make grandiose claims as to who their audience was.

Wordsworth proclaims that the poet writes to "all human beings," "in spite of differences of soil and climate, of language and manners, of law and customs"; Shelley imagines poetry participating in "the awakening of a great people"; Carlyle heralds the poet as the "articulate voice" of a nation; and Arnold believes that criticism can mold a classless cultural elite.[47] But in fact, the audience for literature in the nineteenth century was the new urban middle class, enriched by the industrial developments that the Romantic and Victorian poets feared and condemned.[48]

The difference in tone between defenses of poetry written during the Romantic age and those written before it testify to the uneasy position poets had come to occupy in relation to the rest of society. Sidney's geniality, flamboyance, and self-mockery, Pope's witty sententiousness and smug polemicism give way to Wordsworth's earnest manifestoes, shot through with anxiety and defensiveness, Shelley's desperate intensity, and the braggadocio and bombast of Carlyle. But alongside these nervous proclamations that literature is a universal force for good with power over the hearts of millions, there runs another definition of poetry that reflects more accurately its separation from public life. John Stuart Mill, for whom poetry had in fact constituted a salvation of a sort, understood it to be a "culture of the feelings," divorced from "struggle and imperfection"; insofar as a poem seeks to move men to action, it is not poetry but "eloquence."[49] Mill's pronouncements demonstrate clearly the split that has developed between poetry and the world of affairs. Literature becomes synonymous with emotionalism, individualism, and the contemplative life; science and politics with the intellect, power over the material environment, the life of action. Thus, Pater's declaration at the end of his essay on Wordsworth—that "the end of life is not action but contemplation—*being* as distinct from *doing*"— indicates the direction poetic theory will take for the rest of the century. "Not to teach lessons, or enforce rules, or even to stimulate us to noble ends; but to withdraw the thoughts for a little while from the mere machinery of life, to fix them with appropriate emotions, on the spectacle of those great facts in man's existence which no machinery affects. . . . To witness this spectacle with appropriate emotions is the aim of all culture."[50]

By making the absence of material influence on the environment into an essential characteristic of art, the literary theorists of the nineteenth century turned the artist's progressive alienation from society into a positive principle. Poetry is regarded as the highest manifestation of culture and the greatest force for the attainment of an advanced state of cultural development *because,* unlike other forms of discourse, it has no particular uses, no loyalties, no causes to plead. For Matthew Arnold, freedom from sectarian interests of any kind is the sign of a true classic. Because he believes that classic poetry is the custodian of the "high destinies" of "our race," Arnold feels compelled to exclude from this category any work that savors of the "professional and exclusive."[51] Criticism, like poetry, should never be the "organ of men and parties having practical ends to serve," but ought to promote "the free play of mind on all subjects, steadily refusing to lend itself to any ... ulterior, political, practical considerations."[52] In order to endow literature with the greatest possible historic mission, Arnold, like Shelley, must remove literature from history. Classic poetry must descend from a sphere of unchanging values—otherwise it loses its claim to universality and hence its redemptive function.[53]

Formalism and Beyond: The Triumph of Interpretation

The deification of poetry that occurs in the nineteenth century pre- pares the way for the interdict against affective response that arises in the twentieth by conferring on poetry a function so high that it ends by escaping from this world altogether. Paradoxically, the critic whose work is responsible for making the discussion of emotional response to poetry illegitimate in academic criticism is I. A. Richards, the most response- centered critic of his time. Richards's notion of the function of criticism, which he inherits from Arnold, is extremely traditional, in the sense that both critics believe literature's essential function is to civilize men. But "civilization" by the end of the nineteenth century had come to be de- fined in opposition to material production and political action. It is, in Pater's phrase, *being,* not *doing.* The highest point of moral development is no longer Sidney's "virtuous action" but a Paterian state of aesthetic contemplation. But whereas for Pater "to witness the human spectacle with appropriate emotions" meant being in a state of high excitement, of startled observation, of passion, or of ecstasy, to Richards it means bal- ance, order, and control. He defines the ideal human condition as one of equilibrium, a perfect adjustment and conciliation of conflicting im- pulses, a condition in which no single emotion predominates and "inter- est is not canalised in any one direction."[54] The function of great poetry, according to Richards, is to induce this state in the reader, and so to advance and preserve civilization.[55]

Richards's belief that poetry can "save us" by organizing our dispa-

rate impulses at once repeats and contradicts the ancient conception of
poetry's function. When he represents poetry as capable of making better citizens Richards follow the classical and Renaissance conception of
poetry's civilizing mission; when he says that the sign of great poetry is
that it leaves the reader uncommitted to any particular course of action,
he is writing as the heir of Wordsworth, Shelley, and Arnold. Plato
banishes poetry from the republic because it stirs the passions; Richards
looks to poetry for salvation because it keeps the passions under control.

The idea that poetry is an ordering force that can provide a stay
against a world in confusion becomes a major tenet of twentieth-century
critical belief. It is a belief that has its roots in the conviction—fostered by
nineteenth-century critics—that poetry must be detached from the
world in order to save it. But it takes their position one step further by
making poetry act not simply to purify and refine the feelings but to
neutralize them completely through a process of mutual cancellation.
This crucial step prepares the way for the criticism of T. S. Eliot and his
disciples, which ends by repudiating affect and removing poetry from its
historical circumstances altogether.

Eliot begins, in the Romantic tradition, by distinguishing the "ordinary man's experience," which is "chaotic, irregular, [and] fragmentary,"
from "the poet's mind," which is "constantly amalgamating new
wholes."[56] But the source of the wholeness that Eliot desires lies not so
much in the poet's mind as in the poem, which contains the "objective
correlative" of the poet's experience.[57] Eliot emphasizes the objectification of emotion in the poetic artifact for the same reason that Richards
makes the purpose of poetry an ordering of the feelings: a desire to keep
emotion under control, to eliminate the "chaotic" and "irregular" from
experience. This need also motivates Eliot's insistence that there is no
one-to-one correlation between the emotions of the poet and the emotions of the poem he creates. What the poet has to express is not a
"personality" but a "medium." What he produces is not the expression of
emotion but "a new thing resulting from the concentration of a very
great number of experiences," because finally, "poetry is not a turning
loose of emotion, but an escape from emotion; it is not the expression of
personality, but an escape from personality."[58]

Thus Eliot effects two major changes in poetic theory simultaneously. He severs the tie between the poem and its origins more completely than has ever been done before by denying that there is any
direct relationship between the life of the work and the life of its maker.
And second, he transforms Richards's theory that poetry balances the
warring impulses of the reader from a theory of reading into a theory of
the poem itself. The poem now becomes the place of order and equilibrium; it is the condition of harmony toward which humanity strives. Not
only is the poem not the expression of a particular personality or feeling

or moment in history, but it represents the end of history. The poem, like the Grecian urn in Cleanth Brooks's interpretation of Keats's "Ode," is a simulacrum of eternity. Whereas Romantic and Victorian critics attributed to poets the powers they wished poets had, twentieth-century critics attribute to poetry the qualities they feel are missing in modern life.

Another way to describe the change that Eliot's ideas made in modern critical theory is to say that they transferred the ultimate locus of value from the context of poetry to poetry itself. In the formalist view, poetry is not conceived as existing to serve the needs of the state by making better citizens, or to promote the brotherhood of man by binding men together through their deepest human sympathies, or to raise the level of civilized existence by refining the organs of perception or producing a state of rapt contemplation or balancing the warring impulses of the reader's psyche. Rather, poetry serves men by providing them with an image of perfection, a goal toward which they can aspire. In the scale of values, it is superior to nature and to human life. It has no transitive function, is not an agent or an instrument but an end. Literary response, consequently, becomes a meaningless category, since the chief object of critical concern is not the effects that poems have but their intrinsic nature. And so, with the arrival of formalist criticism, the issues that had occupied literary critics from Plato onwards simply drop from sight.

But while the focus of critical theory has shifted from prescribing poetic function to defining poetic structure, the broad aim of the critical enterprise is still the same as it was for Pope and Sidney: to defend poetry from its detractors, increase its importance, and establish its claims on ever surer ground. And this task the New Critics performed with truly spectacular results.

The kind of competition the New Critics faced—namely, competition from science—determined, in large part, the shape of their poetic theory just as Puritan attacks on poetry had shaped literary theory in the Renaissance. The attack on poetry in the twentieth century, unlike previous attacks, has nothing to do with poetry's effects—its power to deceive or corrupt its hearers—but concerns instead the kind of knowledge poetry affords. The reason for this lies in the attitude toward language implicit in the positivist epistemology that undergirds the scientific perspective. Language, according to this model, is a neutral, transparent medium for the transcription of facts about the physical world. "On the one hand and *first* there is the content of the scientific message, which is everything; on the other hand and *next,* the verbal form responsible for expressing that content, which is nothing."[59] Language has no power of its own; it cannot do anything but mirror the image of a preexistent reality. Literature, therefore, which depends on the manipulation of language to achieve its ends, has no power of its own either; it, too, can only transmit knowledge that has already been made available by other means. The knowledge that literature transmits, moreover, lies in areas that are not well-suited to scientific measurement—human attitudes, feelings, and values. Literary studies, consequently, whose subject matter is not quantifiable, whose methods are not formalized, and whose results are not able to be objectively verified, cannot compete with science for an equal share of prestige and economic support in a society where positivist values prevail.

This line of argument suggests that the only way to defend the literary enterprise would be to challenge the positivist conceptual framework on which science depends for its prestige. And in fact, this is what reader-response criticism, in its later phase, has done. But the New Critics responded by attempting, in effect, to beat science at its own game. The first step was to declare poetic language ontologically distinct from scientific language, and the objects of its investigation ontologically separate from (and by implication superior to) the objects of scientific research. "Scientific precision can be brought to bear only on certain kinds of material. . . . Poetry . . . also represents a specialization of language for the purpose of precision; but it aims at treating kinds of materials different from those of science. . . ."[60] These materials— "attitudes, feelings, and interpretations"—have the status of eternal truths; they are the universals of human nature just as scientific laws are the universals of physical nature. But the language that expresses truth in poetry, unlike the language of science, is inseparable from the message it conveys; poetic language, therefore, is ontologically different from scientific language because its content is unparaphrasable and unreproducible by any other means.

The New Critical effort to generate a definition of literature as "an object of knowledge *sui generis* which has a special ontological status," not only meets the positivist objections to literary study but establishes the whole enterprise on a new footing.[61] Once the literary work has been defined as an object of knowledge, as meaning not doing, interpretation becomes the supreme critical act. The kind of interpretation that the formalist definition of literature requires, moreover, cannot be performed by the man on the street. Since the literary work is formally and semantically unique ("special," "*sui generis*"), it requires interpreters specially schooled in the intricacies of the poetic medium. The formalist definition of the literary work, in sum, calls for the institutionalization of literary study on a new basis.

Because literary discourse is ontologically distinct from all other discourse, the discipline of criticism must be carefully set off from the neighboring disciplines of history, biography, sociology, and psychology. Textbook writers like Brooks and Warren warn their readers that poetry must be studied *as* poetry and not as any of the other forms of linguistic expression with which it is likely to be confused.[62] Poetry's special status legitimizes the development of a special vocabulary for describing the properties of poems and the establishment of standard methods of explication, which, by regularizing the practice of literary interpretation, make it suitable for teaching on a mass scale in colleges and universities. The formalization of interpretive techniques simultaneously provides critics with the means of producing explications of literary works that serve as demonstrations of their professional expertise. The definition of criticism as an activity requiring professional expertise justifies the credentialling system of graduate education and gives support to professors of literature in their competition with natural and social scientists for institutional resources. The theory of poetry that proclaims poems to be the least practical of man-made things proves, in the long run, to be the most practical answer to the pressures of the cultural and institutional context.

The powerful relationship between formalist theory and institutional praxis cannot be overemphasized. The triumph of interpretation as the dominant mode of twentieth-century critical discourse has determined the shape of even the most concerted attempts to break with formalist doctrine. For whatever direction the revolt against formalism may take, the assumption that criticism is synonymous with interpretation, the belief that the discovery of meaning is the goal of the critical enterprise, remains unquestioned. The evolution of response-centered criticism is a case in point.

Response-centered criticism in the 1960s and 1970s arises from a set of cultural and institutional pressures, much as the New Criticism did. Having walled itself off from neighboring fields in order to establish disciplinary autonomy, and having ruled out the discussion of personal feelings in order to emulate scientific objectivity and rigor, formalist criticism stood in danger of becoming too narrow and specialized a pursuit to attract the necessary student clientele and too far removed from changes in the intellectual climate to adapt itself to the times. By legitimizing the inclusion of personal responses to literature in the process of textual explication, reader-centered critics appeared willing to share their critical authority with less tutored readers and at the same time to go into partnership with psychologists, linguists, philosophers, and other students of mental functioning. The brunt of their attack on formalism, therefore, was directed against Wimsatt and Beardsley's famous essay on the Affective Fallacy. In reply to the statement that when affective responses are taken into account "the poem itself, as an object . . . tends to disappear," reader-response critics argue against locating meaning in the text, against seeing the text as a fixed object, and in favor of a criticism that recognizes the reader's role in making meaning.[63] They bring forward in support of their positions the kind of evidence

Wimsatt and Beardsley had specifically ruled out—the reports of individual readers on their experience of a text—and, in flat contradiction of the claim that what must be avoided at all costs is a "confusion between the poem and its results (what it is and what it does)," declare that the poem *is* what it does.[64]

In opening the door to the discussion of personal experience in literary interpretation, these critics appear to be undoing the effort of New Criticism to hold the line against science. The formalists had labored to prove that their discipline was as rigorous as any science by mounting a discourse that was tough-minded, logical, detached, and above all, objective. Reader-critics, on the other hand, by inviting readers to describe in detail their moment-by-moment reactions to a text, appeared to be letting back into literary criticism all the idiosyncrasy, emotionality, subjectivity, and impressionism that had made the literary enterprise vulnerable to attack by science and that the New Critics had worked so hard to eliminate from critical practice.

But in fact response-centered critical theory is engaged in exactly the same power struggle with science that played so large a role in the formation of New Critical doctrine. The difference is not one of goals but of tactics. Instead of trying to come up with a defense of poetry that will satisfy positivist demands for objectivity and verifiability, as the formalists did, reader-oriented critics attack the foundations of positivism itself. Instead of protecting literature from unfavorable comparison with science by maintaining that literary language is uniquely constitutive of meaning whereas scientific language merely reflects it, response-centered theory, in its most recent formulations, denies the existence of any reality prior to language and claims for poetic and scientific discourse exactly the same relation to the real—namely, that of socially constructed versions of it. All language, in this view, is constitutive of the reality it purports to describe, whether it be the language of mathematical equations or that of a Petrarchan sonneteer. This assertion deprives science of its privileged position in relation to other forms of knowledge by declaring that the objectivity on which science bases its superiority is a fiction.

But it is one thing to make such assertions and another thing to make them stick. The success of formalist criticism in meeting the intellectual challenge of scientism on its own grounds, and, even more important, the extent to which formalism has built itself into the structure of the institutions where literary criticism is practiced, presents formidable obstacles to any critical movement that attempts to overturn its doctrines. This is true not because of the outright opposition that any such challenge is likely to encounter but because New Critical assumptions determine the format within which such a challenge can be articulated and put into practice. What is most striking about reader-response criticism and its close relative, deconstructive criticism, is their failure to break out of the mold into which critical writing was cast by the formalist identification of criticism with explication. Interpretation reigns supreme both in teaching and in publication just as it did when New Criticism was in its heyday in the 1940s and 1950s. In the long perspective of critical history, virtually nothing has changed as a result of what seems, from close up, the cataclysmic shift in the locus of meaning from the text to the reader. Professors and students alike practice criticism as usual; only the vocabulary with which they perform their analyses has altered.

In the classroom, an account of one student's moment-by-moment experience of the text, though it differs in every substantive respect from a formalist analysis of image patterns, still treats meaning as the goal of critical inquiry, still takes the text as the primary unit of meaning, and still perform its operations on the same texts that were used to illustrate irony, paradox, ambiguity, complexity, organic unity, and the use of the *persona*. The text remains an object rather than an instrument, an occasion for the elaboration of meaning rather than a force exerted upon the world. A recent article by Walter Michaels entitled "*Walden*'s False Bottoms" shows how little difference reader-centered theory has made in the practical criticism that appears in even the most avantgarde of professional journals.[65] We no longer interpret *Walden* as an organic unity, Michaels argues, or even as being unified by the reader's experience of it, but as a contradictory text which puts the reader in the untenable position of having to decide what reality is while simultaneously taking away from him the basis on which he could make any such decision. The fact that Michaels's interpretation of *Walden* calls into question the possibility of ever arriving at a final interpretation of anything does not alter the message delivered by the traditional format of his essay, which, in time-honored fashion, challenges previous interpretations of *Walden* and offers a new reading of the text. The essay assumes that interpretation is its task—no matter whether it is a task that can ever be completed or not—and cannot imagine that criticism could be engaged in any process but an interpretive one. It seems, then, that there is no escape from interpretation, not because the text is undecidable, as the deconstructionists would have it, but because the institutional context within which the critic works—a context created by the doctrines of literary formalism—dictates that interpretation is the only activity that will be recognized as doing what criticism is supposed to do.

But if we take seriously Michaels's own theoretical assertion, in "The Interpreter's Self," that perceptual categories define the world and give reality the only shape it can ever have, then a shift of critical emphasis would seem to be in order, a shift away from the analysis of individual texts and toward an investigation of what it is that makes texts visible in the first place. Such an investigation would entail more than the anatomizing of interpretive conventions that Jonathan Culler calls for in *Structuralist Poetics;* for if, as the post-structuralists claim, reality itself is language-based, then the study of language necessarily takes on a political character.[66] The insistence that language is constitutive of reality rather than merely reflective of it suggests that contemporary critical theory has come to occupy a position very similar to, if not the same as, that of the Greek rhetoricians for whom mastery of language meant mastery of the state. The questions that propose themselves within this critical framework therefore concern, broadly, the relations of discourse and power.[67] What makes one set of perceptual strategies or literary conventions win out over another? If the world is the product of interpretation, then who or what determines which interpretive system will prevail?

The similarity between contemporary critical theory and the criticism of antiquity, if such a similarity exists, lies not in the common focus on literature's audience, for to the extent that contemporary critics occupy themselves with the responses of readers it is within the framework of a formalist conception of the text. The similarity lies rather in the common perception of language as a form of power. It is this perception, which so far has been confined almost entirely to the level of theory in contemporary writing, that constitutes the real break with formalism and promises the most for criticism's future.

Notes

1. For example, Wolfgang Iser and Michael Riffaterre, neither of whom renounces formalism entirely, make statements such as "the reader's enjoyment begins when he himself becomes productive," and the "semiotic process really takes place in the reader's mind." Walter Slatoff reduces the importance of the text even further: "works of literature," he says, "have scarcely any important qualities apart from those that take shape in our minds." Psychoanalytically oriented critics go further still, putting the reader in place of the text as the prime object of critical investigation. Norman Holland writes: "The point is to recognize that stories . . . do not 'mean,' in and of themselves, . . . people do, using stories as the occasion . . . for a certain theme, fantasy, or transformation." And David Bleich generalizes the point to make it include all utterances: "The meanings of individual words, and of aggregates of words, depend altogether on those who read the words and tell the meanings to others." Finally, reader-critics influenced by structuralism not only deny that literary texts have meaning in and of themselves, but also that individual readers can create their own meanings. Thus, Jonathan Culler writes: "the poem . . . has meaning only with respect to a system of conventions which the reader has assimilated," and Stanley Fish declares: "the objectivity of the text is an illusion"; "there are no fixed texts but only interpretive strategies making them." Wolfgang Iser, *The Act of Reading: A Theory of Aesthetic Response* (Baltimore: The Johns Hopkins University Press, 1978), p. 108; Michael Riffaterre, *The Semiotics of Poetry* (Bloomington: Indiana University Press, 1978), p. 4; Walter Slatoff, *With Respect to Readers: Dimensions of Literary Response* (Ithaca: Cornell University Press, 1970), p. 23; Norman N. Holland, *5 Readers Reading* (New Haven: Yale University

Press, 1975), p. 39; David Bleich, *Subjective Criticism* (Baltimore: The Johns Hopkins University Press, 1978), p. 7; Jonathan Culler, *Structuralist Poetics, Structuralism, Linguistics, and the Study of Literature* (Ithaca: Cornell University Press, 1975), p. 116; Stanley E. Fish, "Literature in the Reader: Affective Stylistics," *New Literary History* 2, no. 1 (Autumn 1970): 140 (chapter 6 in this volume); idem, "Interpreting the *Variorum*," *Criticial Inquiry* 2, no. 2 (Spring 1976): 484 (chapter 10 in this volume).

2. W. K. Wimsatt, Jr., and Monroe Beardsley, "The Affective Fallacy," in *The Verbal Icon: Studies in the Meaning of Poetry* (Lexington: The University Press of Kentucky, 1954), p. 22.

3. Longinus, *On the Sublime*, trans. W. Rhys Roberts (Cambridge: Cambridge University Press, 1899), as reprinted in James H. Smith and Edd Winfield Parks, eds., *The Great Critics: An Anthology of Literary Criticism* (New York: W. W. Norton & Co., 1951), pp. 92–93.

4. Aristotle, *Poetics*, trans. S. H. Butcher, *Aristotle's Theory of Poetry and Fine Art* (London: Macmillan, 1895), as reprinted in Smith and Parks, eds., *The Great Critics*, p. 61.

5. *On the Sublime*, I, 4. The sublime as a property of the text is described as "intense utterance," "vehement passion," "speed, power, and intensity," "force"; its effects on the hearer are "overpowering." He is "carried away," "utterly enthralled," in a state of "transport." When the sublime is an attribute of the poet, he is "carried away by enthusiasm and passion," "possessed," "inspired," able to "consume by fire and carry away all before him," "inflaming our ardour and illuminating our path."

"Intensity" is used to describe the sublime in I,4; XI; IX,13; III,1; "force" in VIII; and "irresistible might" in I,4.

6. In the *Encomium of Helen*, one of the strongest statements of the Greek belief in the power of persuasion, Gorgias compares speech to magic, sorcery, and drugs, arguing that Helen should be exonerated because "speech the persuader forces the persuaded mind to agree with what is said and approve what is done. The persuaded, because she is compelled by speech, deserves no abuse"(*Ancient Literary Criticism: The Principal Texts in New Translations*, ed. D. A. Russell and M. Winterbottom, trans. D. A. Russell [Oxford: The Clarendon Press, 1972], pp. 6-8). On the Greek conception of language, see Nancy Struever, "The Background of Humanist Historical Language: The Quarrel of Philosophy and Rhetoric," in *The Language of History in the Renaissance* (Princeton: Princeton University Press, 1970), pp. 5–39.

7. Aristophanes, *The Frogs*, trans. Gilbert Murray (New York: Longmans, Green & Co., 1916).

8. Atkins, *Literary Criticism in Antiquity*, 2. vols. (Cambridge: Cambridge University Press, 1934), I, pp. 6-7; Rosemary Hariott, *Poetry and Criticism Before Plato* (London: Methuen & Co., 1969), p. 109.

9. Plato, *Phaedrus*, trans. Benjamin Jowett, in *The Dialogues of Plato*, 5 vols., 2nd ed. (Oxford: The Clarendon Press, 1875), II, pp. 154–55.

10. Louise Rosenblatt, "The Poem as Event," *College English* 26, no. 2 (November 1964): 123–28; Fish, "Literature in the Reader," pp. 129, 131; Norman Holland, *The Dynamics of Literary Response* (New York: Oxford University Press, 1968), p. xiii.

11. Stephen Orgel, *The Illusion of Power: Political Theater in the English Renaissance* (Berkeley: University of California Press, 1975).

12. The two kinds of criticism prevalent in the classical period persist in the Renaissance: the technical treatise, or *ars poetica*, in Puttenham's *Arte of English Poesie*, Campion's *Observations in the Art of English Poesie*, and Gascoigne's *Certayne Notes of Instruction;* and moral criticism in the defenses of poesy such as Sidney's, Heywood's, and Harington's or combinations of the two as in Samuel Daniel's *Defense of Ryme* and Chapman's *Preface to the Odyssey*.

13. Bernard Weinberg, *A History of Literary Criticism in the Italian Renaissance*, 2 vols. (Chicago: The University of Chicago Press, 1961), II, pp. 801, 805.

14. Ibid., II, 806.

228   JANE P. TOMPKINS

15. Arthur Marotti, "John Donne and the Rewards of Patronage." *Patronage in the Renaissance,* ed. Stephen Orgel and Guy Lytle (Princeton: Princeton University Press, 1981).

16. A number of recent studies have emphasized in various ways the integration of literature into Renaissance social life. Daniel Javitch, for example, argues in *Poetry and Courtliness in Renaissance England* (Princeton: Princeton University Press, 1978) that writing a poem and being a courtier are activities governed by identical principles of decorum. He demonstrates that Puttenham's *Arte of English Poesie* is a book of etiquette at the same time that it is an *ars poetica* because the conception of poetry it embraces regards poetic success as a matter of proper conduct. John Stevens, in *Music and Poetry in the Early Tudor Court* (London: Methuen & Co., 1961), defines the Tudor lyric as "a *symptom* of a certain kind of social activity" (p. 151). He describes the composition of the lyric as a pastime exactly parallel to dancing, games, or conversation—activities which expressed the governing fiction of leisure class life, the code of courtly love. The poems, which often accompanied a gift or a love token, were not artifacts, in his view, but gestures in a social relationship and derived their significance from the position they occupied in a system of social transactions. Richard Lanham makes the same kind of point from yet another angle in a recent essay, "*Astrophil and Stella:* Pure and Impure Persuasion" (*English Literary Renaissance* 2, no. 1 [Winter 1972]: 100-115). The essay attacks a host of critics for failing to recognize what Sidney's poetic enterprise really is: the courtship of Penelope Rich. The sonnet sequence, Lanham argues, is not to be analyzed in terms of its thematic structure, its narrative progression, or its putative persona, but as a series of acts of persuasion designed to produce results in the real world. *Astrophil and Stella,* he concludes, is not philosophical poetry aimed at expressing universal truth, but "applied poetry which aims directly at making something happen" (108).

17. George Puttenham, *The Arte of English Poesie* (a facsimile reproduction of the 1906 reprint published by A. Constable and Son), intro. by Baxter Hathaway, ed. Edward Arber (Kent, Ohio: Kent State University Press, 1970), p. 39.

18. On the establishment of literary criticism as a discipline and the literary critic as a professional in competition with other professionals, see Vernon K. Hall, Jr., *A Short History of Literary Criticism* (New York: New York University Press, 1963), pp. 43-44.

19. Sir Philip Sidney, *An Apology for Poetry, Elizabethan Critical Essays,* 2 vols., ed. G. Gregory Smith (Oxford: Oxford University Press, 1959), I, pp. 150-51.

20. In the Introduction to his collection, *Elizabethan Critical Essays,* G. Gregory Smith notes that "the greater forces which stimulated this literary defence [the 'Apologies' for Poets and Poetry] were themselves unliterary. . . . They denounce Poetry because it is often lewd, the theatre because it is a school of abuse: their argument is social, political, personal" (p. xiv). On the nature of Renaissance attacks on poetry, see also Weinberg, *A History of Literary Criticism in the Italian Renaissance,* II, pp. 797-804.

21. Sidney, *An Apology for Poetry,* p. 156.

22. Ronald Paulson, ed. *Satire: Modern Essays in Criticism* (Englewood Cliffs, N.J.: Prentice-Hall, Inc., 1971), p. ix.

23. This is the definition of a poem offered by Cleanth Brooks and Robert Penn Warren in their Introduction to the first edition of *Understanding Poetry* (New York: Henry Holt and Co., 1938), p. 37.

24. J. V. Guerinot, *Pamphlet Attacks on Alexander Pope, 1711-1744: A Descriptive Bibliography* (New York: New York University Press, 1969), pp. iv, vii.

25. Maynard Mack, "The Muse of Satire," in Paulson, ed., *Satire: Modern Essays in Criticism,* pp. 201, 193-94.

26. Edward Rosenheim, "The Satiric Spectrum," in Paulson, ed., *Satire: Modern Essays in Criticism,* pp. 318, 326.

27. Ibid., p. 326.

28. John Dryden and John Sheffield, Earl of Mulgrave, "An Essay upon Satire," in *Anthology of Poems on Affairs of State: Augustan Satirical Verse, 1660–1714*, ed. George deF. Lord (New Haven: Yale University Press, 1975), pp. 86, 184.

29. The headings under which George Lord groups the entries in his seven-volume collection of social and political satire written between 1660 and 1714 reflect both of these characteristics: "The War of Words," describing poems that attack other poems and their authors, accurately characterizes the sense in which literary discourse was an exchange of blows at a personal level; headings such as "The Popish Plot and the Exclusion Crisis, 1677–1681," "The Trial and Death of Shaftesbury," "Monmouth's Rebellion, June–July 1685," and "Invasion Fears, Spring–Summer 1688," name major topics of poetic debate. Imagining a modern counterpart to this—hundreds of poems written on the Strategic Arms Limitation Treaty negotiations, inflation, or a presidential election—measures the distance between our conception of what poetry is and the Augustans'.

30. See Edward Niles Hooker, "Pope on Wit: The 'Essay on Criticism,'" *Seventeenth Century, Studies in the History of English Thought and Literature from Bacon to Pope by Richard Foster Jones and Others Writing in His Honor*, ed. Francis R. Johnson et al. (Stanford: Stanford University Press, 1951), pp. 225–46.

31. Guerinot, *Pamphlet Attacks on Alexander Pope*, p. xiv.

32. For an excellent account of process, see A. S. Collins, *Authorship in the Days of Johnson, Being a Study of the Relation Between Author, Patron, Publisher, and Public, 1726–1780* (London: Robert Holden & Co., 1927).

33. Christopher Caudwell, *Illusion and Reality* (London: Laurence and Wishart, 1937), p. 86.

34. Bertrand H. Bronson, *Facets of the Enlightenment* (Berkeley and Los Angeles: University of California Press, 1968), p. 302.

35. Henry Home, Lord Kames, *Elements of Criticism*, in *Literary Criticism in England, 1660–1800*, ed. Gerald Wester Chapman (New York: Alfred A. Knopf, 1966), pp. 310–11.

36. Ibid., p. 311.

37. R. S. Crane describes the distinction between classical and neo-classical criticism succinctly. Of the latter, he writes,

its characteristic appeal, on all issues that involved the end or good of art, was not (as in the *Republic* or the *Phaedrus*) to the knowledge of the philosophers or (as in the *Laws*) to the sagacity of statesmen, but rather to the trained taste and sensitive judgment of men expert in the enjoyment of poetry, painting, or music. Its frame of reference, in short, tended to be not the republic but the republic of letters; and, although the larger context of morals or civil philosophy was seldom left entirely out of account, . . . it still remains true that the utility of criticism in this tradition was normally conceived in terms of the needs of men, not as moral beings or as seekers after truth, but as poets and artists, readers and spectators, listeners and connoisseurs.

"English Neoclassical Criticism: An Outline Sketch," in *Critics and Criticism, Ancient and Modern*, ed. with an introduction by R. S. Crane (Chicago: University of Chicago Press, 1952), p. 376.

38. William Wordsworth, *Observations Prefixed to the Second Edition* (of *Lyrical Ballads*), in Smith and Parks, eds., *The Great Critics*, p. 502.

39. This belief stems from a conception of human life based on the Platonic opposition between material and spiritual existence. In Shelley's view, there are two kinds of good in the world: spiritual good, which is "durable, universal and permanent," and material good, which is transitory and particular. Good of the second kind means banishing the "importunity of the wants of our animal nature, . . . surrounding men with security of life, . . . dispersing the grosser delusions of superstition, and . . . conciliating such a degree

of mutual forbearance among men as may consist with the motives of personal advantage." These goals are far inferior to those which poetry can achieve, for poetry (and we hear the echo of Wordsworth) "strengthens and purifies the affections, enlarges the imagination, and adds spirit to sense."

40. Percy Bysshe Shelley, *A Defense of Poetry*, in Smith and Parks, eds., *The Great Critics*, pp. 563–64.

41. The poetry of Dante, who "understood the secret things of love," lit the spark that ignited the Renaissance; and the poets of the Renaissance made possible the birth of modern science. Shelley, *A Defense of Poetry*, pp. 571–77.

42. Ibid., p. 575.

43. Ibid., pp. 562–583; Wordsworth, *Observations*, p. 509. This trend became exacerbated as the century progressed. "The description of the typical poet was . . . plainly immoderate . . . and one is forced to the conclusion that, in fact, there was something a little monstrous in the Early Victorians' wishful fantasy of the poet." Alba H. Warren, Jr., *English Poetic Theory, 1825–1865* (New York: Octagon Books, 1966), p. 216.

44. Thomas Carlyle, "The Hero as Poet," in *On Heroes, Hero-Worship and the Heroic in History*, ed. with an introduction by Carl Niemeyer (Lincoln: University of Nebraska Press, 1966), p. 113.

On the economic and social relationship of Romantic artists to their society, see J. W. Saunders, *The Profession of English Letters* (London: Routledge and Kegan Paul, 1964), pp. 146–98.

45. Saunders, *The Profession of English Letters*, pp. 161, 163.

46. Caudwell, *Illusion and Reality*, p. 102.

47. Wordsworth, *Observations*, p. 509; Shelley, *A Defense of Poetry*, p. 583; Carlyle, "The Hero as Poet," p. 14.

48. Saunders, *The Profession of English Letters*, pp. 160–61; Warren, *English Poetic Theory*, p. 222.

49. John Stuart Mill, *The Early Draft of John Stuart Mill's Autobiography*, ed. Jack Stillinger (Urbana: University of Illinois Press, 1961), p. 125; John Stuart Mill, "What Is Poetry?" in *Essays on Poetry*, ed. F. Parvin Sharpless (Columbia: University of South Carolina Press, 1976), p. 12. For a useful survey of Mill's views on poetry, see Warren, *English Poetic Theory*, pp. 67–78. My own view of Mill is especially indebted to Raymond Williams's discussion in *Culture and Society, 1780–1950* (New York: Harper and Row, 1958), pp. 62–70.

50. Walter Pater, *Appreciations, with an Essay on Style* (London: MacMillan and Co., 1895), pp. 61, 62.

51. Matthew Arnold, "The Study of Poetry," *Essays in Criticism, Second Series* (London: MacMillan and Co., 1958), pp. 2–3; Matthew Arnold, "Sweetness and Light," Chapter 1 of *Culture and Anarchy*, rpt. in *Lectures and Essays in Criticism*, ed. R. H. Super (Ann Arbor: The University of Michigan Press, 1962), p. 113.

52. Matthew Arnold, "The Function of Criticism at the Present Time," in Super, ed., *Lectures and Essays in Criticism*," p. 270.

53. The revolution that occurs in the definition of literature between the beginning of the eighteenth century and the end of the nineteenth century emerges sharply in the changing attitudes toward the poetry of Pope, who, from having been the preeminent poet of his time becomes, along with Young, the nineteenth century's favorite "exemplar of malpractice." (See Warren, *English Poetic Theory*, p. 6.) Joseph Warton's two volume *Essay on the Genius and Writing of Pope* (London: 1806) sets the tone for subsequent criticism of Pope and reveals the standards by which poetry in the nineteenth century would come to be judged. Warton says in his conclusion that Pope "has written nothing in a strain so truly sublime as the *Bard of Gray*" (405). He characterizes Pope as the "great Poet of Reason," whose "writing . . . lies more level to the general capacities of men, than the higher flights of more genuine poetry" (403). "Genuine poetry," it is clear, has been identified with the

capacity to stir the passions of the reader. "The largest proportion of [Pope's works] is of the *didactic, moral,* and *satiric* kind; and consequently, not of the *poetic* species of *poetry*" (401-2). "The perusal of him affects not our minds with such strong emotions as we feel from *Homer* and *Milton;* so that no man of a true poetical spirit, *is master of himself while he reads them*" (403). Wordsworth, in 1815, takes his cue from Warton and, as part of his sour argument that true genius is never appreciated in its own time, accuses Pope of stooping to certain "arts" with which he "contrived to procure" himself a reputation, instead of relying on "his native genius" (*The Prose Works of William Wordsworth,* ed. W. J. B. Owen and Jane Worthington Smyser [Oxford: The Clarendon Press, 1974], p. 72). A year earlier Leigh Hunt had condemned Pope for his "rhyming facilities" and classed him as a member of the "artificial school," while later in the century Ruskin censured him for the coldbloodedness of his conceits. But it is Matthew Arnold whose attack on Pope finally prepares the way for the modernist definition of good poetry. Having set himself the task of explaining how to determine what a true classic is in "The Study of Poetry," Arnold prepares to deny that title to the works of Dryden and Pope. First he praises their age for having freed England from its obsession with religion, but as a result "our excellent and indispensable eighteenth century," as Arnold somewhat patronizingly calls it, neglected and impaired the "imaginative" and "religious life of the soul" ("The Study of Poetry," *Essays in Criticism,* pp. 23-24). The age had the properties requisite for the development of good prose—"regularity, uniformity, precision, balance"—but these are the very qualitites which repress and silence poetry ("The Study of Poetry," p. 23). Dryden and Pope, therefore, are proclaimed the great inaugurators of an "age of prose and reason," and precisely on that account lose their claim to greatness as poets ("The Study of Poetry," p. 23). But unlike the Romantics, Arnold does not accuse Pope of coldness and contrivance. He believes that Pope failed of classic stature because he lacked "high seriousness, or even, without that . . . poetic largeness, freedom, insight, benignity" ("The Study of Poetry," p. 24). These qualities befit a poetry whose function is, as it is for Arnold, to supplant philosophy and religion. It is because he has entrusted poetry with the promulgation of eternal values and the salvation of all mankind that Arnold cannot admit to its canon the work of literary infighters and committed partisans like Pope, who used his skill for the purpose of attacking his professional rivals and defending his own beliefs and practices. For Arnold, sectarian interests of any kind are inherently opposed to the advancement of culture, which "seeks to do away with classes," and "to make men live in an atmosphere of sweetness and light, where they may use ideas, as it uses them itself, freely—nourished, and not bound by them" ("Sweetness and Light," *Lectures and Essays,* p. 130).

54. I. A. Richards, with C. K. Ogden and James Wood, *The Foundations of Aesthetics* (New York: George All and Unwin, 1925, 2nd edition), pp. 74-78.

55. I. A. Richards, *Science and Poetry* (New York: W. W. Norton and Co., 1926), p. 20.

56. T. S. Eliot, "The Metaphysical Poets," *Selected Prose of T. S. Eliot,* ed. with an introduction by Frank Kermode (New York: Harcourt Brace Jovanovich, Farrar, Straus and Giroux, 1975), p. 64.

57. T. S. Eliot, "Hamlet," in ibid.

58. T. S. Eliot, "Tradition and the Individual Talent," in ibid., pp. 42-43.

59. Roland Barthes, "Science versus Literature," *The Times Literary Supplement* (September 28, 1967), as reprinted in *Structuralism: A Reader,* ed. Michael Lane (New York: Basic Books, 1970), p. 411.

60. Brooks and Warren, *Understanding Poetry,* p. xxxvii.

61. René Wellek and Austin Warren, *Theory of Literature* (New York: Harcourt, Brace and Co., 1956), p. 144.

62. Brooks and Warren, "Letter to the Teacher," *Understanding Poetry,* p. xi.

63. Beardsley and Wimsatt, "The Affective Fallacy," in *The Verbal Icon,* p. 21. The earliest explicit reactions against the Affective Fallacy can be found in the work of Louise Rosenblatt, Norman Holland, and Stanley Fish, cited above.

64. Beardsley and Wimsatt, "The Affective Fallacy," p. 21.

65. Walter Benn Michaels, "*Walden*'s False Bottoms," *Glyph 1: Johns Hopkins Textual Studies,* ed. Samuel Weber and Henry Sussman (Baltimore: The Johns Hopkins University Press, 1977), pp. 132–49.

66. Culler, *Structuralist Poetics,* pp. 118–19.

67. Discourse in the sense described by Michel Foucault in *The Archaeology of Knowledge,* trans. A. M. Sheridan Smith (New York: Harper & Row, 1972) and applied by Edward Said in *Orientalism* (New York: Pantheon Books, 1978).

BIBLIOGRAPHY

The purpose of this bibliography is to provide a comprehensive listing of recent work in the field of reader-response criticism. The bibliography is divided into two sections, theoretical and applied. In psychology, psycholinguistics, and sociology, the listings are highly selective; in literary theory they are inclusive. In order to guide the reader, therefore, I have annotated the entries wherever possible and have starred those items that seem to me essential to a mastery of the field. The material in single entries has been organized alphabetically in the following manner: books first, essays second, and edited volumes third.

I. Theoretical

Abrams, Meyer Howard. "Pragmatic Theories." Part 3 of his introduction "Orientation of Critical Theories" to his *The Mirror and the Lamp: Romantic Theory and the Critical Tradition,* pp. 14–21. New York: Oxford University Press, 1953.

  "[T]he central tendency of the pragmatic critic is to conceive a poem as something made in order to effect requisite responses in its readers; to consider the author from the point of view of the powers and training he must have in order to achieve this end; to ground the classification and anatomy of poems in large part on the special effects each kind and component is most competent to achieve; and to derive the norms of the poetic art and canons of critical appraisal from the needs and legitimate demands of the audience to whom the poetry is addressed." To this general definition of pragmatic criticism, Abrams adjoins a brief survey of pragmatic theorists from the rhetoricians of antiquity through Samuel Johnson.

Altick, Richard. *The English Common Reader: A Social History of the Mass Reading Public, 1800–1900.* London: Chatto and Windus, 1932.

  Describes the social composition and educational experience of working- and middle-class readers in the nineteenth century: who they were, what they read, when and how they obtained it. Studies the influence of religion, utilitarianism, education, the labor movement, public libraries, the book trade, and periodical publications on the formation and growth of the English reading public. An essential reference work, extremely well-written.

Barner, Wilifried. "Rezeptionsästhetik—Zwischenbilanz (III): Neuphilologische Rezeptionsforschung und die Möglichkeiten der Klassischen Philologie." *Poetica* 9 (1977): 499–521.

Barnouw, Dagmar. Review of *The Act of Reading* and *The Implied Reader* by Wolfgang Iser. *Modern Language Notes* 94 (December 1979): 1207–13.

A sharp, informative critique of Iser's major work.

Barthes, Roland. *The Pleasure of the Text.* Translated by Richard Miller. New York: Hill & Wang, 1975.

A series of lyrical meditations on reading written so as to evoke the erotic dimension of the literary experience they celebrate.

* _____. *S/Z.* Translated by Richard Miller. New York: Hill & Wang, 1975.

Performs a structural analysis of Balzac's *Sarrasine* in terms of five "codes" in order to show that "the meaning of a text can be nothing but the plurality of its systems . . . [that] with regard to the text there is no 'primary,' 'natural,' 'national,' 'mother,' critical language." A tour de force.

_____. "The Death of the Author." In *The Discontinuous Universe: Selected Writings in Contemporary Consciousness,* edited by Sallie Sears and Georgianna W. Lord, pp. 7–12. New York: Basic Books, 1972.

"A text consists of multiple writings, issuing from several cultures and entering into dialogue with each other, into parody, into contestation; but there is one place where this multiplicity is collected, united, and this place is not the author, as we have hitherto said it was, but the reader."

Bauschatz, Cathleen. "Montaigne's Conception of Reading in the Context of Renaissance Poetics and Modern Criticism." In Suleiman and Crosman, eds. *The Reader in the Text.*

Beaujour, Michel. "Exemplary Pornography: Barres, Loyola and the Novel." In Suleiman and Crosman, eds. *The Reader in the Text.*

Berger, Carole. "Viewing as Action: Film and Reader Response Criticism." *Literature—Film Quarterly* 6 (Spring 1978): 144–51.

Discusses ways in which Fish and Iser's theories of reading can be applied to film theory.

Black, Stephen A. "On Reading Psychoanalytically." *College English* 39 (November 1977): 267–75.

* Bleich, David. *Readings and Feelings: An Introduction to Subjective Criticism.* Urbana, Illinois: National Council of Teachers of English, 1975.

Offers a program for the teacher of literature whereby students, encouraged to become more aware of their individual responses to literature, can discover an internal motive for reading and thinking about literature, namely, "the awareness that reading can produce new understanding of oneself." (For reviews see Chabot and Elliott.)

* _____. *Subjective Criticism*. Baltimore: The Johns Hopkins University Press, 1978. (Chapter 9 in this volume is found in the above.)

After locating the feelings and associations of individual readers at the center of critical attention, Bleich views the reading process as the point of intersection of a series of larger problems in philosophy, psychology, and linguistics. He draws on authoritative work in these fields in order to attack not only the orthodoxies of literary interpretation but the traditions of American pedagogy as well. (For review see Tompkins below.)

_____. "The Determination of Literary Value." *Literature and Psychology* 17 (1967): 19-30.

Analyzes responses to D. H. Lawrence's "Piano," a poem used by I. A. Richards in his *Practical Criticism,* to establish that readers determine the literary value of a work according to the degree of defensive action it calls for in confronting the reader with unconscious material.

_____. "Emotional Origins of Literary Meaning." *College English* 31 (October 1969): 30-40.

Uses a reader's response to Pinter's "The Caretaker" "to demonstrate how a fact of literary meaning is made; how it develops from the subject's emotional response to the work, and moves along its projective path to the status of (at least provisional) fact."

_____. "The Logic of Interpretation." *Genre* 10 (Fall 1977): 363-94.

Bleich argues that interpretation is not a decoding or an analytical process but "a synthesis of new meanings based on the assumptions that old shared meanings of words and works are not in question, but that the *present perception* of these meanings has created the experiential circumstances for resymbolization."

_____. "Motives and Truth in Classroom Communication." *College Composition and Communication* 26 (December 1975): 371-78.

A student's writing "is most productively discussed as a reflection of the real inward purpose of the writer," a purpose derived from the student's sense of what role the teacher might play in the student's subjective calculus of wishes, fears, intentions, and plans.

_____. "Negotiated Knowledge of Language and Literature." *Studies in the Literary Imagination* 12 (Spring 1979): 73-92.

Bleich proposes that students and professors should gain confidence in their own negotiated knowledge of literature and refuse to yield authority to an elite group of scholars who have traditionally controlled the criteria for validity in literary interpretation.

_____. "Pedagogical Directions in Subjective Criticism." *College English* 37 (January 1976): 454-67.

Outlines areas for further research in subjective criticism especially concerning its application in the classroom. (See also "Comment and Response" in *College English* 38 [November 1976]: 298-301.)

_____. "Psychological Bases of Learning from Literature." *College English* 33 (October 1971): 32-45.

Uses two readers' responses to *The Death of a Salesman* to show that "when an individual is instructed by a work of literature, it means that it has recovered for him a precept or a principle once known but lost and which was originally offered him by an individual who had authority over him."

_____. "The Subjective Character of Critical Interpretation." *College English* 36 (March 1975): 739–55.

"Interpretive knowledge is different from the formulaic knowledge of the physical sciences both in its origins and its consequences. . . . It is constructed from the uncontrolled experience of the interpreter, and the rules of construction are only vaguely known by anyone observing the interpreter." Attacks the epistemology of Holland's model of reading.

_____. "The Subjective Paradigm in Science, Psychology, and Criticism." *New Literary History* 7, no. 2 (Winter 1976): 313–34.

After T. S. Kuhn, Bleich describes the change in "thought paradigm" from one of objectivity to one of subjectivity in the twentieth century. "Under the subjective paradigm new truth is created by a new use of language and a new structure of thought. The establishment of new knowledge is the activity of the intellecting mind adapting itself to ontogenetic and phylogenetic developmental demands. Knowledge is made by people and not found." Holland responds in an essay "The New Paradigm: Subjective or Transactive?" in the same issue.

_____. "Teleology and Taxonomy in Critical Explanation." *Bucknell Review* 28 (Spring 1980).

* Booth, Wayne C. *The Rhetoric of Fiction.* Chicago: University of Chicago Press, 1961.

In the section "Beliefs and the Reader" Booth refutes the general rule of criticism that readers should become objective and dispassionate when approaching a text. This is nonsense, he claims, and he illustrates how the reader's emotions and beliefs are constantly called into play in the reading of a text.

Bourniquel, Camille. "Création, lecture sans visibilité." *Esprit* 42 (November 1974): 852–65.

Bové, Paul. "The Poetics of Coercion: An Interpretation of Literary Competence." *Boundary 2* 5 (Fall 1976): 263–84.

Critiques Jonathan Culler's concept of "literary competence" on the grounds that it implies a fallacious model of reading.

Brisman, Leslie. Review of *Self-Consuming Artifacts* by Stanley Fish. *Diacritics* 4, no. 2 (Summer 1974): 24–27.

Argues that Fish's model of reading is similar to that of the formalists except that it is able to account for the sense of growth in consciousness which a reader experiences while reading a text.

Brooke-Rose, Christine. "The Readerhood of Man." In Suleiman and Crosman, eds. *The Reader in the Text.*

Brooks, Peter. "Competent Readers." *Diacritics* 6, no. 1 (Spring 1976): 23–26.

Review of Jonathan Culler's *Structuralist Poetics.*

Bürger, Peter. "Rezeptionsästhetik—Zwischenbilanz (III): Probleme der Rezeptionsforschung." *Poetica* 9 (1977): 446–71.

Discusses the relationship between *Gegenstandsentwichlung* and *Theoriebil-dung* in order to discover the criteria for the evaluation of artistic and literary theories. Topics: the empirical sociology of art, the concept of identification in the reception-aesthetic of Jauss, and a model for a histor-ical theory of the functional development of art.

Burns, Elizabeth, and Burns, Tom, eds. *Sociology of Literature and Drama.* Har-mondsworth, Middlesex, England: Penguin Books, 1973.

Essays by Lucien Goldmann, Kenneth Burke, George Steiner, Roland Barthes, Northrop Frye, and many others on topics such as "The Social Context of Literary Criticism," "Literature as Rhetoric," "Marxism and the Literary Critic." See especially part 5, "Readers and Audiences," with pieces by Ian Watt, Eric Auerbach, and D. W. Harding.

Cain, William E. "Constraints and Politics in the Literary Theory of Stanley Fish." *Bucknell Review* 28 (Spring 1980).

Chabot, C. Barry. "Three Studies of Reading." *College English* 37 (December 1975): 426–30.

Reviews Bleich's *Readings and Feelings*, Geoffrey Hartman's *The Fate of Reading*, and Eleanor J. Gibson and Harry Levin's *The Psychology of Read-ing.*

Champagne, Roland A. "Alice and the Looking Glass: Roland Barthes as the Reader in History." *Bucknell Review* 28 (Spring 1980).

Charles, Michel. *Rhétorique de la lecture.* Paris: Seuil, 1977.

An analysis of four literary works *about* reading (by Lautréamont, Rabelais, Constant, and Montaigne) that demonstrates how each one teaches its reader the strategies by which he can as a reader of that text engage in the process of signification.

Charvat, William. "Melville and the Common Reader." In *The Profession of Au-thorship in America, 1800–1870,* edited by Matthew J. Bruccoli, pp. 262–82. Columbus, Ohio: Ohio State University Press, 1968.

Sketches the relationship between Melville's authorial personality and the reception of his fiction, and speculates on Melville's struggle to gain both popular and critical acclaim by combining both popular and private ma-terials in his novels. Charvat thinks Melville's failure was due to his in-ability to "think in narrative" and to his penchant for allegory and speculative commentary. Scholarly and provocative.

Clifford, John. "Transactional Teaching and the Literary Experience." *English Journal* 68 (December 1979): 36–39.

Finds Rosenblatt's concept of transactional criticism better as a theoretical base for teaching high school English than either New Critical objectivity or Bleichian subjectivism.

Cohen, Gillian. "The Psychology of Reading." *New Literary History* 4 (Autumn 1972): 75–90.

Surveys current research in psychological studies of the reading process, covering topics such as visual processing, phonemic processing, semantic processing, and reading difficulties. Ends with a tentative list of "strategies which characterize the performance of a skilled reader."

Compare Ross, "On the Concepts of Reading," and Goodman, *The Psycholinguistic Nature of the Reading Process.*

Coward, David. "The Sociology of Literary Response." In *The Sociology of Literature: Theoretical Approaches,* edited by Jane Routh and Janet Wolff, pp. 8–17. Keele, England: University of Keele, 1977.

Craig, George. "Reading: Who Is Doing What to Whom?" In *The Modern English Novel,* edited by Gabriel Josipovici, pp. 15–36. New York: Barnes & Noble, 1976.

Crews, Frederick, ed. *Psychoanalysis and the Literary Process.* Berkeley: University of California Press, 1970.

Psychoanalytic investigations of Dickens, Melville, Joyce, Pater, and Shakespeare, with an important introductory essay by Crews entitled "Anaesthetic Criticism." Crews attacks Frye's notion that literature "shapes itself and is not shaped externally" and asserts that literature functions as a vehicle for repressed fantasy, establishing a transitory complicity between reader and writer in which both achieve a measure of libidinal freedom.

Crosman, Inge. "Bibliography of Audience-Oriented Criticism." In Suleiman and Crosman, eds. *The Reader in the Text.*

Crosman, Robert. "Do Readers Make Meaning?" In Suleiman and Crosman, eds. *The Reader in the Text.*

———. "Some Doubts about 'The Reader of *Paradise Lost.*'" *College English* 37 (December 1975): 372–82.

Critics who posit an "ideal reader" of *Paradise Lost* are actually arguing for a particular interpretation of the poem (theirs), which they implicitly believe is the one Milton intended.

Crosman, Robert, and Deutelbaum, Wendy, eds. *Reader: A Newsletter of Reader-Oriented Criticism and Teaching.* Iowa City: University of Iowa, January 1977–.

* Culler, Jonathan. *Structuralist Poetics: Structuralism, Linguistics, and the Study of Literature.* Ithaca: Cornell University Press, 1975. ("Literary Competence," a chapter in the above work, is chapter 7 in this volume.)

One of the best introductions to structuralist and post-structuralist thought in English. Covers Saussure, Lévi-Strauss, Jakobson, Greimas, Barthes, Derrida, Kristeva, and Genette. Focuses on the importance of constitutive conventions in literary study and calls for a criticism that investigates the way conventions work rather than analyzing individual masterpieces.

———. "Apostrophe." *Diacritics* 7, no. 4 (Winter 1977): 59–69.

The rhetorical figure of apostrophe in lyric poetry calls attention to the "temporality of writing" as it resists the temporal sequence of narrative. The reader is drawn to forget temporality and to embrace a fictional time, the strangeness and total fictionality of which has caused critics to be embarrassed by apostrophes and to repress them in their discussions of lyric poetry.

———. "Beyond Interpretation: The Prospects of Contemporary Criticism." *Comparative Literature* 28 (Summer 1976): 244–56.

New Criticism institutionalized the concept of literary criticism as interpretation, so much so that important new approaches to criticism (the psychoanalytic school and Stanley Fish's affective stylistics) have not been able to free themselves from the burden of interpretation. Culler suggests that critics should now turn their attention to "ways of literature and of reading which have been repressed or displaced during the reign of interpretation."

_____. "The Critical Assumption." *Society for Critical Exchange Reports* 6 (Fall 1979): 77–84.

_____. "The Frontier of Criticism." *Yale Review* 64 (June 1975): 606–12.

A review of several books on reader response, including Iser's *The Implied Reader.*

_____. "Prolegomena to a Theory of Reading." In Suleiman and Crosman, eds. *The Reader in the Text.*

_____. Review of Norman Holland's *5 Readers Reading. JEGP* 75 (July 1976): 461–62.

_____. Review of Michael Riffaterre's *Semiotics of Poetry. French Forum* 4 (May 1979): 185–86.

_____. "Stanley Fish and the Righting of the Reader." *Diacritics* 5, no. 1 (Spring 1975): 26–31.

Culler attacks Fish's notion of the "informed reader" as a facile construct which ignores the complex interworkings of literary conventions which create the reading experience.

Dällenbach, Lucien. "Actualité de la recherche allemande." *Poétique* 39 (September 1979): 258–60.

Davis, Frederick, ed. *The Literature of Research in Reading with Emphasis on Models.* New Brunswick: Rutgers University Press, 1971.

DeMaria, Robert, Jr. "The Ideal Reader: A Critical Fiction." *PMLA* 93 (May 1978): 463–74.

Argues that every critical school has its own version of the ideal reader, a figure whose characteristics reflect the literary form of the critical work that contains him. This thesis is demonstrated in the work of Johnson, Dryden, Coleridge, and Frye.

Deutelbaum, Wendy. "Two Psychoanalytic Approaches to Reading Literature." *Bucknell Review* 28 (Spring 1980).

Dilligan, Robert J. "Effective Stylistics: A Response to Affective Stylistics." *Cahiers de lexicologie* 30 (1977): 24–37.

* Dillon, George. *Language Processing and the Reading of Literature: Towards a Model of Comprehension.* Bloomington: Indiana University Press, 1978.

Constructs a model of the way we read that describes in detail the perceptual strategies readers employ as they make their way through the words, phrases, and sentences of a literary text. Presents extraordinarily sensitive, scrupulous, and lucid analyses of linguistic experience, with examples drawn from the work of Spenser, Milton, James, Stevens, and Faulkner. Highly technical, but well worth the effort.

Eco, Umberto. *The Role of the Reader: Explorations in the Semiotics of Texts.* Bloomington: Indiana University Press, 1979.

Nine sophisticated, lucid essays written between 1959 and 1978. Part 1 deals with "open" texts (e.g., *Finnegans Wake,* the music of Pierre Boulez), which invite the reader's collaboration in the production of meaning; part 2 deals with "closed" texts (e.g., Superman comics, James Bond novels), which evoke a predetermined response; part 3 speculates on how the codes available to the reader determine what the text means to him.

Elliott, Susan M. "A New Critical Epistemology." *Hartford Studies in Literature* 7 (1975): 170–89.

Reviews Bleich's *Readings and Feelings.*

Elrud, Kunne-Ibsch. "Rezeptionsforschung: Konstanten und Varienten eines Literaturwissenschaftlichen: Konzepts in Theorie und Praxis." *Amsterdamer Beiträge zur neuren Germanisk* 3 (1974): 1–36.

Erlich, Victor. "Reading Conscious and Unconscious." *College English* 36 (March 1975): 766–75.

Holland and Fish both conceive of the reading experience as therapy: for Holland it is a way for the reader to disburden himself of repressed matter; for Fish it is a way to disburden oneself of illusion. But Holland's emphasis on unconscious processes and Fish's on conscious acts fail to account for the complexity of the reading experience as both conscious and unconscious therapy.

Escarpit, Robert. *Sociology of Literature.* Translated by Ernest Pick. Lake Erie College Studies, vol. 4. Painesville, Ohio: Lake Erie College Press, 1965.

A somewhat random discussion of circumstances surrounding the production, distribution, and consumption of literature. Written in a popular vein and theoretically naive, but full of interesting information.

Faulstich, Werner. *Domänen der Rezeptionsanalyse: Probleme, Lösungsstrategien, Ergebnisse.* Kronberg Ts.: Athenäum, 1977.

See the annotation under Henry J. Schmidt for a general comment on this text.

Fetterley, Judith. *The Resisting Reader: A Feminist Approach to American Fiction.* Bloomington: Indiana University Press, 1979.

"A self-defense survival manual for the woman reader lost in 'the masculine wilderness of the American novel.'" Fetterley argues, forcefully, that American literature is male, that to read it is perforce to identify as male, that the female reader of most American literature is therefore required to identify against herself. The book describes the male bias of supposedly "universal" representations of the human condition in works by Irving, Hawthorne, James, Anderson, Faulkner, Hemingway, Fitzgerald, and Mailer.

* Fish, Stanley E. *Is There a Text in This Class? The Authority of Interpretive Communities.* Cambridge, Mass.: Harvard University Press, 1980.

Collects all of Fish's theoretical essays in one volume, including the previously unpublished title essay, the fullest formulation of his position thus far.

*_____. *Self-Consuming Artifacts: The Experience of Seventeenth-Century Literature.* Berkeley: University of California Press, 1972.

Analyzes the way in which works by Donne, Herbert, Bunyan, Burton and others involve the reader in evaluating, deducing, and interpreting, only to declare his conclusions invalid or premature and to undermine his confidence in the ability of human reason to understand the world. (For review see Brisman above.)

*_____. *Surprised by Sin: The Reader in* Paradise Lost. London and New York: St. Martin's Press, 1967.

Paradise Lost is full of "little moments of forgetfulness" in which the reader allows himself repeatedly to become beguiled by Satanic rhetoric and then catches himself and recognizes his lack of vigilance, his distance from innocence, his need of Grace. The reader thus repeats the actions of Adam and Eve, becomes involved in the sin of the fall, and is forced to recognize and judge his involvement. (For discussion see Crosman's essay, "Some Doubts About 'The Reader of *Paradise Lost.*'")

_____. "How Ordinary Is Ordinary Language?" *New Literary History* 5, no. 1 (Autumn 1973): 41–54.

Fish attacks the distinction between "ordinary" and literary language: "ordinary language is extraordinary because at its heart is precisely that realm of values, intentions and purposes which is often assumed to be the exclusive property of literature."

_____. "How to Do Things with Austin and Searle: Speech Act Theory and Literary Criticism." *MLN* 91, no. 5 (October 1976): 983–1025.

Fish first performs a speech act analysis of *Coriolanus,* then examines the premises and limitations of that theory: its practitioners are unwilling to relinquish the distinction between fictional discourse and serious discourse and to realize that both fiction and "reality" are constituted by the same speech acts.

*_____. "Interpreting the *Variorum.*" *Critical Inquiry* 2 (Spring 1976): 465–85. (Chapter 10 in this volume.)

(See introduction to this volume. See also Mailloux's comment and Fish's response in *Critical Inquiry* 3 [Autumn 1976]: 183–90.)

*_____. "Literature in the Reader: Affective Stylistics." *New Literary History* 2, no. 1 (Autumn 1970): 123–62. (Chapter 6 in this volume.)

(See introduction to this volume. For comment on Fish's theory see also Dilligan, Holland's "Stanley Fish, Stanley Fish," Horton, Mailloux's "Evaluation and Reader Response Criticism," Rader, and Ray's "Supersession and the Subject.")

_____. "Normal Circumstances, Literal Language, Direct Speech Acts, the Ordinary, the Everyday, the Obvious, What Goes without Saying, and Other Special Cases." *Critical Inquiry* 4 (Summer 1978): 625–44.

Fish demonstrates from a variety of perspectives that the facts and significances that seem to us obvious and inescapable are always the product of assumptions and are therefore "normal" or "standard" only within those assumptions.

————. "Structuralist Homiletics." *MLN* 91 (December 1976): 1208-21.

> Reads a sermon by Lancelot Andrews as a Christian attack on the bad
> faith of referential language.

* ————. "What Is Stylistics and Why Are They Saying Such Terrible Things
About It?" In *Approaches to Poetics,* edited by Seymour Chatman, pp.
109-52. New York: Columbia University Press, 1973.

> Stylistics as an attempt to put criticism on a scientific basis fails because of
> the absence of any constraint on the way in which the stylistician moves
> from description to interpretation. Affective sytlistics posits the context
> of the reader's experience as such a restraint, and by focusing attention
> on the acts whereby a reader constitutes the meaning of a text collapses
> the descriptive and interpretive functions of criticism.

Fokkema, Douve Wessel, and Elrud, Kunne-Ibsch. *Theories of Literature in the
Twentieth Century: Structuralism, Marxism, Aesthetics of Reception.* New York:
St. Martin's Press, 1978.

Fowler, Roger. "'The Reader'—A Linguistic View." *Cahiers Roumains d'Etudes
Litteraires* 4 (1977): 47-60.

Frey, Eberhard. "What Is Good Style? Reader Reactions to German Text Samples." *Modern Language Journal* 56 (1972): 310-23.

> Demonstrates how literary training and other factors influence reactions
> to and evaluations of literature.

Fried, Michael. *Absorption and Theatricality: Painting and Beholder in the Age of
Diderot.* Berkeley: University of California Press, 1980.

> French painting and art criticism between the middle of the eighteenth
> century and the advent of David were crucially concerned with issues
> raised by "the primordial convention that paintings are made to be be-
> held."

————. "The Beholder in Courbet: His Early Self-Portraits and Their Place in
His Art." In *Glyph 4: Johns Hopkins Textual Studies,* edited by Samuel
Weber and Henry Sussman. Baltimore: The Johns Hopkins University
Press, 1978.

> Courbet's paintings are seen as seeking to achieve a particular relation to
> the beholder, who in the first instance was Courbet himself.

————. "Towards a Supreme Fiction: Genre and Beholder in the Art Criticism
of Diderot and His Contemporaries." *New Literary History* 6 (Spring
1975): 543-86.

> Fried discovers a paradox in French art criticism and theory of the
> eighteenth century: the recognition that paintings are made to be beheld
> issued in a demand that the beholder's presence be actualized; but only
> by establishing the fiction of the beholder's absence could his placement
> before and enthrallment by the painting be secured.

* Gadamer, Hans-George. *Truth and Method.* London: Sheed and Ward, 1975.

> One of the fundamental contributions to the study of hermeneutics in
> this century. Gadamer investigates understanding as a mode of experi-
> ence in relation to language, historical consciousness, scientific method,

and aesthetics, with particular reference to Kant, Dilthey, Husserl, and Heidegger.

* Gibson, Walker, "Authors, Speakers, Readers, and Mock Readers." *College English* 11 (February 1950): 265–69. (Chapter 1 in this volume.)

(See introduction to this volume.)

Glowinski, Michal. "Der potentielle Leser in der Struktur eines poetischen Werkes." Translated by Grazyna Szarszewska. *Weimarer Beiträge* 21, no. 6 (1975): 118–43.

Attempts to provide an answer to the question, "How does the structure of the poetic work determine the role of the recipient?"

———. "Reading, Interpretation, Reception." Translated by Wlad Godzich. *New Literary History* 11 (Autumn 1979): 75–81.

Offers definitions of reading and interpretation, preliminary to formulating the goal of reception-aesthetics: to reconstruct the general properties of reading (i.e., styles of reception) specific to a given era through the analysis of literary interpretations.

* Gombrich, E. H. *Art and Illusion: A Study in the Psychology of Pictoral Representation.* London: Phaidon Press, 1962.

Goodman, Kenneth S., ed. *The Psycholinguistic Nature of the Reading Process.* Detroit: Wayne State University Press, 1968.

A collection of papers presented at a symposium on the application of linguistics and psychology to an understanding of the reading process. The editor comments in a foreword: "It will be obvious that there is by no means any consensus among the symposium participants on what the psycholinguistic nature of the reading process is."

Grimm, Gunter. "Rezeptionsforschung als Ideologiekritik: Aspekte zur Rezeption Lessings in Deutschland." In *Über Literatur und Geschichte: Festschrift für Gerhard Storz,* edited by Bernard Hüppaut and Dolf Sternberger, pp. 115–50. Frankfort: Athenäum, 1973.

———. "Rezeptionsgeschichte: Prämissen und Möglichkeiten historischer Darstellungen." *Internationales Archiv für Sozialgeschichte der deutschen Literatur* 2 (1977): 144–86.

A basic survey of the literature on reception history.

———, ed. *Literatur und Leser: Theorien und Modelle zur Rezeption literarischer Werke.* Stuttgart: Reclam, 1975.

Analyses of reception-history according to diverse theories supplied by such contributors as Wilfried Barner, Hans Christoph Berg, Hartmut Eggert, Klaus Geiger, Gunter Grimm, Rolf Kellner, Günther Mohal, Paul Mog, Michael Rutzchky, Manfred Günther Scholz, Jochen Schulte-Sasse, Horst Steinmetz, Horst Turk, Gotthart Wunberg, and others.

———, ed. *Rezeptionsgeschichte: Grundlegung einer Theorie: mit Analysen und Bibliographie.* Munich: Fink, 1977.

Contains extensive bibliography of works on reception-history. See the annotation under Henry J. Schmidt for a general comment on this text.

Groeben, Norbert. *Literaturpsychologie: Literaturwissenschaft zwischen Hermeneutik und Empire.* Stuttgart: Kohlhammer, 1972.

Gumbrecht, Hans Ulrich. "Persuader ceux qui pensent comme vous: Les fonctions du discours épidictique sur la mort de Marat." Translated by Ruth Fivaz-Silbermann. *Poétique* 39 (September 1979): 363–84.

————. "Rezeptionsästhetik—Zwischenbilanz (I): Konsequenzen der Rezeptionsästhetik oder Literaturwissenschaft aus Kommunikationssoziologie." *Poetica* 7 (1975): 388–413.

Discusses the phases traversed by literary discussion concerning the problem of the reader. Examines the social actions involved in text production and text understanding; attempts to develop a new perspective on interpretation through the differentiation between *normative* and *descriptive* reception-history.

————. "Soziologie und Rezeptionsästhetik—Über Gegenstand und Chancen interdisciplinarer Zusammenarbeit." In *Neue Ansichten einer künftigen Germanistik,* edited by Jürgen Kolbe. Munich: Hauser, 1973.

Hamlin, Cyrus. "Patterns of Reversal in Literary Narrative." In *Interpretation of Narrative,* edited by Mario J. Valdés and Owen J. Miller, pp. 61–77. Toronto: University of Toronto Press, 1978.

Using the theories of I. A. Richards and Wolfgang Iser, with some additional insights drawn from Hölderlin and Hegel, Hamlin analyzes the phenomenon of reversal in narrative and concludes that "the moment of reversal is transformed into an act of discovery and recognition by the reader," or, more generally, that "the constitution of meaning in literature also requires an act of self-reflection and self-validation."

Hans, James S. "Gaston Bachelard and the Phenomenology of the Reading Consciousness." *Journal of Aesthetics and Art Criticism* 35 (Spring 1977): 315–27.

Criticizes Bachelard for adopting the phenomenological method without adopting an appropriate ontology. A sophisticated philosophical critique of Bachelard's theoretical position, with reference to Ingarden, Husserl, Heidegger, Derrida, Merleau-Ponty, and Gadamer.

Harding, D. W. "Psychological Processes in the Reading of Fiction." *British Journal of Aesthetics* 2 (April 1962): 133–47.

Attacks the concept of "identification" as a way of describing the only or even the primary relationship between the reader and characters in fiction. Offers instead an analogy between the reader and an onlooker at an event.

————. "Reader and Author." In his collection *Experience into Words: Essays on Poetry.* London: Chatto and Windus, 1963, pp. 163–74.

The author must carefully control the reader's responses to his text, and the reader must not "read into" the work meanings the author could not have intended, since, otherwise, the social relation implicit in the act of publishing a literary work will be severed.

* ————. "The Role of the Onlooker." *Scrutiny* 6 (December 1937): 247–58.

Considers the socially-determined nature and function of spectatorship, and particularly the likeness between the reader of literature and the hearer of gossip.

Hartman, Geoffrey. "The Interpreter: A Self-Analysis." *New Literary History* 4 (Winter 1973): 213–28.

"It should be the interpreter who unfolds the text, but the book begins to question the questioner, its *qui vive* challenges him to prove he's not a ghost."

Heuermann, Hartmut; Hühn, Peter; and Röttge, Brigitte, eds. *Literarische Rezeption: Beiträge zur Theorie des Text—Leser—Verhältnisses und seiner empirischen Erforschung.* Paderborn, Germany: Ferdinand Schöningh, 1975.

Contains articles on reception-aesthetics by Gunter Martens, Heinz Hillman, Norbert Groeben, and others.

Hileman, William. Review of *The Implied Reader* by Wolfgang Iser. *Style* 10 (Summer 1976): 344–47.

Hohendahl, Peter Uwe. *Literaturkritik und Öffentlichkeit.* Munich: Piper & Co., 1974.

_____. "Introduction to Reception Aesthetics." Translated by Marc Silberman. *New German Critique* 10 (Winter 1977): 29–63.

Outlines the present state and historical background of reception-aesthetics in East and West Germany.

_____, ed. "Rezeptionsforschung." (Special issue.) *LiLi* 4 (1974).

Articles on reception-aesthetics by Bernhard Aimmermann, Harold Wentzlaff-Eggebert, Egon Schwartz, Norbert Groeben, Eberhard Frey, Hans Leuschner, and Peter Conrady.

_____, ed. *Sozialgeschichte und Wirkungsästhetik: Dokumente zur empirischen und marxistischen Rezeptionsforschung.* Frankfort: Athenäum, 1974.

* Holland, Norman N. *The Dynamics of Literary Response.* New York: Oxford University Press, 1968.

The reader of a text responds to that text as a morally, socially, and intellectually acceptable transformation of unconscious fantasy. This fantasy is the basis from which all readings of the text are derived. Literary meaning consists in the pleasurable act of transforming content from the unconscious to the conscious level.

* _____. *5 Readers Reading.* New Haven: Yale University Press, 1975.

A study of the reactions of five students to William Faulkner's short story "A Rose for Emily." The meaning of the story for each student is determined by his or her "identity theme." (For reviews see Noland, Tompkins, and Waldoff below.)

_____. *Poems in Persons: An Introduction to the Psychoanalysis of Literature.* New York: Norton, 1973.

A reader's response to a text is an expression of his individual "identity theme," the organizing configuration with which his ego mediates among the forces acting on it. Holland examines the identity themes of one poet (H. D.) and three readers.

————. "*Hamlet*—My Greatest Creation." *Journal of the American Academy of Psychoanalysis* 3 (1975): 419-27.

Holland illustrates his thesis that in reading we reproduce ourselves by showing how his interpretation of *Hamlet* mirrors his own identity theme.

————. "How Can Dr. Johnson's Remarks on Cordelia's Death Add to My Own Response?" In *Psychoanalysis and the Question of the Text*, edited by Geoffrey Hartman, pp. 18-44. Baltimore: The Johns Hopkins University Press, 1978.

————. "A Letter to Leonard." *Hartford Studies in Literature* 5 (1973): 9-30.

————. "Literary Interpretation and Three Phases of Psychoanalysis." *Critical Inquiry* 3 (Winter 1976): 221-23.

————. "Literature as Transaction." In *What Is Literature?*, edited by Paul Hernadi, pp. 206-18. Bloomington and London: Indiana University Press, 1978.

————. "The New Paradigm: Subjective or Transactive?" *New Literary History* 7, no. 2 (Winter 1976): 335-46.

————. "Poem Opening: An Invitation to Transactive Criticism." *College English* 40 (September 1978): 2-16.

————. "Reading and Identity: A Psychoanalytic Revolution." *Academy Forum* (American Academy of Psycholanalysis), 23, no. 2 (Summer 1979): 7-9.

————. "Recovering 'The Purloined Letter': Reading as a Personal Transaction." In Suleiman and Crosman, eds., *The Reader in the Text*.

————. "Stanley Fish, Stanley Fish." *Genre* 10 (Fall 1977): 433-41.

Holland questions several tenets of Fish's "affective stylistics" including his "bi-active" theory of reading and his construct of the "informed reader."

————. "Transacting My 'Good-Morrow,' or, Bring Back the Vanished Critic." *Studies in the Literary Imagination* 12 (Spring 1979): 61-72.

————. "A Transactive Account of Transactive Criticism." *Poetics* 7 (September 1978): 177-89.

————. "Transactive Criticism: Re-Creation Through Identity." *Criticism* 18 (Fall 1976): 334-52.

————. "Transactive Teaching: Cordelia's Death." *College English* 39 (November 1977): 276-85.

Discusses the responses of two groups, one of women and one of men, to Cordelia's death in *King Lear* to illustrate his transactive approach to literature.

————. "The 'Unconscious' of Literature: The Psychoanalytic Approach." In *Contemporary Criticism*, edited by Malcolm Bradbury, pp. 130-53. New York: St. Martin's Press, 1971.

* ————. "UNITY IDENTITY TEXT SELF." *PMLA* 90, no. 5 (October 1975): 813-22. (Chapter 8 in this volume.)

(See introduction to this volume.)

_____. "What Can a Concept of Identity Add to Psycholinguistics?" In *Psychoanalysis and Language,* edited by Joseph H. Smith, M. D., pp. 171–234. New Haven: Yale University Press, 1977.

Holland, Norman N., and Bleich, David. "Comment and Response." *College English* 38 (November 1976): 298–301.

Holland, Norman, and Schwartz, Murray M. "The Delphi Seminar." *College English* 36 (March 1975): 789–800.

Reports on a graduate seminar that became "a self-study group to discover how the distinctive character of each of our minds affects the literary transactions we engage in and the critical statements we make."

Horton, Susan R. "The Experience of Stanley Fish's Prose or The Critic as Self-Creating, Self-Consuming Artificer." *Genre* 10 (Fall 1977): 443–53.

Hunter, J. Paul. "The Loneliness of the Long-Distance Reader." *Genre* 10 (Winter 1977): 455–84.

"Reading is fundamentally a lonely experience, and the reading of novels intensifies and extends the experience because of the magnitude of novels." Hunter uses this concept to account for various aspects and preoccupations of the genre.

* Ingarden, Roman. *The Cognition of the Literary Work of Art.* Translated by Ruth Ann Crowley and Kenneth Olson. Evanston, Illinois: Northwestern University Press, 1973.

Explores the various acts through which the reader participates (in a limited way) in constituting a literary work of art, and broaches the question of what it means for a reader's response to be "faithful" to the text.

* _____. *The Literary Work of Art: An Investigation on the Borderlines of Ontology, Logic, and the Theory of Literature.* Translated with an introduction by George G. Grabowicz. Evanston, Illinois: Northwestern University Press, 1973.

In his initial study, Ingarden explores the structure of the literary work and the ways in which that structure is "concretized" by the reader, whose filling in of indeterminate areas in the text and actualization of potential elements transforms the objective artistic work into an object with aesthetic value.

_____. "Artistic and Aesthetic Values." *British Journal of Aesthetics* 4 (July 1964): 198–213.

Draws an distinction between artistic values which are found in specific characteristics of the work of art itself, and aesthetic values which manifest themselves to the observer only at the moment when he achieves some apprehension of the work. Thus Ingarden creates a space for further studies of aesthetic response.

_____. "Psychologism and Psychology in Literary Scholarship." Translated by John Fizer. *New Literary History* 5 (Winter 1974): 213–23.

"Psychologism in literary scholarship is a *falsification* of the peculiar nature of the subject matter it investigates and specifically of the literary work through its identification with a certain multiplicity of experiences either of the author or of the reader."

Ingen, Ferdinand van. "Der Revolt des Lesers oder Rezeption versus Interpreta-
    tion: Zu Fragen der Interpretation und der Rezeptionsästhetik." *Amster-
    damer Beiträge zur neuren Germanisk* 3 (1974): 83–148.

* Iser, Wolfgang. *The Act of Reading: A Theory of Aesthetic Response.* Baltimore:
    The Johns Hopkins University Press, 1978.

    An extended treatment of the ideas first broached in his essay on "inde-
    terminacy," this volume considers in detail the ontological status of the
    literary text, the mental operations readers perform on texts, and the
    textual "spurs" to the interaction of text and reader, or what the author
    calls the text's "communicatory structure," which constitutes it as a matrix
    of potential effects. (For review see Barnouw above.)

* ———. *Die Appellstruktur der Texte: Überstimmtheit als Wirkungbedingung literarischer
    Prosa.* Konstanz: G. Hess, 1970.

    One of the seminal works of the German reception-aesthetics movement,
    Iser's study of the "structure of address" considers the audience's partici-
    pation in the interpretation of a literary work.

* ———. *The Implied Reader: Patterns of Communication in Prose Fiction from Bunyan
    to Beckett.* Baltimore: The Johns Hopkins University Press, 1974. (Chap-
    ter 5 in this volume is contained in the above).

    Based on the notion that literary meaning requires the active participa-
    tion of the reader for its realization, this study surveys the kinds of
    responses demanded of readers by representative novels from the seven-
    teenth to the twentieth centuries. (For reviews see Barnouw, Hileman,
    and Scholes.)

———. "The Current Situation of Literary Theory: Key Concepts and the Im-
    aginary." *New Literary History* 11 (Autumn 1979): 1–20.

    Iser outlines his notion of the key concepts of literary theory: structure,
    which describes the production of meaning; function, which gives con-
    crete definition to meaning; and communication, which elucidates the
    experience of the meaning. These concepts, however, reduce the poten-
    tial of the literary text which always escapes semantic transformation,
    since the ultimate dimension of the text is not semantic but "imaginary."
    It is "the experience of the imaginary" that reception-aesthetics attempts
    to describe.

———. "La fiction en effet: Éléments pour un modele historico-fontionnel des
    textes littéraires." Translated by Jean Kaempfer. *Poétique* 39 (September
    1979): 275–98.

———. "Indeterminacy and the Reader's Response in Prose Fiction." In *Aspects
    of Narrative,* edited by J. Hillis Miller, pp. 1–45. New York: Columbia
    University Press, 1971.

    Iser examines the ways in which readers interact imaginatively with a text
    in their attempts to fill in the indeterminacies within the text and to pin it
    down to a specific meaning. Texts that resist such actions, such as *Ulysses,*
    afford the most valuable reading experiences.

———. "Interaction Between Text and Reader." In Suleiman and Crosman, eds.,
    The Reader in the Text.

———. "Narrative Strategies as a Means of Communication." In *Interpretation of*

Narrative, edited by Mario J. Valdés and Owen J. Miller, pp.100–17. Toronto: University of Toronto Press, 1978.

Expanding on the premises of his essay, "The Reality of Fiction," Iser examines the strategies placed in the text by the author to direct the reader in the creation of the aesthetic object. Variations and deviations of both literary and extra-literary norms stimulate the reader into giving the aesthetic object its particular shape. Iser also discusses how the author's regulation of perspectives within a narrative contributes to this process.

———. "The Reality of Fiction: A Functionalist Approach to Literature." *New Literary History* 7 (Autumn 1975): 7–38.

The reader and the literary text are partners in a process of communication, the prime concern of which is not the *meaning* of that text, but its effect. Discusses speech-act theory and the ways in which readers build contexts to understand texts.

Iser, Wolfgang; Crosman, Inge; Crosman, Robert; and Henkle, Roger. "In Defense of Authors and Readers: For the Readers." *Novel* 11 (Fall 1977): 19–25.

* Jauss, Hans Robert. *Literaturgeschichte als Provokation*. Frankfort: Suhrkamp, 1970.

In this seminal work in reception-aesthetics, Jauss proposes the rewriting of literary history as a history of readers' reactions to literature, a history of the interplay of text and reader and the way in which the former is transformed by the latter.

———. "The Alterity and Modernity of Medieval Literature." *New Literary History* 10 (Winter 1979): 181–229.

A practical application of Jauss's notion of reception-aesthetics to the study of medieval literature.

———. "La jouissance esthétique: Les expérience fondamentales de la poiesis, de l'aisthesis et de la catharsis." Translated by Michel Zink. *Poétique* 39 (September 1979): 261–74.

———. "Levels of Identification of Hero and Audience." Translated by Benjamin and Helga Bennett. *New Literary History* 5 (Winter 1974): 283–317.

Constructs a typology of literary heroes according to the various levels of rection on which the spectators, readers, or listeners of earlier periods could identify with them.

* ———. "Literary History as a Challenge to Literary Theory." Translated by Elizabeth Benzinger. *New Literary History* 2 (Autumn 1970): 7–37.

"If literary history is to be rejuvenated, the prejudices of historical objectivism must be removed and the traditional approach to literature must be replaced by an aesthetics of reception and impact. The historical relevence of literature is not based on an organization of literary works which is established *post factum*, but on the reader's past experience of the 'literary data.'"

———. "Paradigmawechsel in der Literaturwissenschaft." In *Methoden der deutschen Literaturwissenschaft*, edited by Viktor Zmegac, pp. 274–90. Frankfort: Athenäum, 1972.

_____. "Racine und Goethes Iphigenie: Mit einem Nachwort über die Partialität der rezeptionsästhetischen Methode." *Neue Hefte für Philosophie* 4 (1973): 1-46.

_____. "Rezeptionsästhetik—Zwischenbilanz (I): Der Leser als Instanz einer neuen Geschichte der Literatur." *Poetica* 7 (1975): 325-44.

Three essays delivered at the German Romanists' Day convention on the topic "Interest in the Reader." "The history of literature, as of art, has been all too long a history of authors and their works. It has supressed or ignored its 'third state,' the reader, listener, or observer."

_____. "Theses on the Transition from the Aesthetics of Literary Works to a Theory of Aesthetic Experience." In *Interpretation of Narrative,* edited by Mario J. Valdés and Owen J. Miller, pp. 137-47. Toronto: University of Toronto Press, 1978.

Jauss discusses the implications of reception-aesthetics for historical criticism. He examines the consequences of turning attention away from works considered as historical objects whose contexts need to be restored, to a study of the historical reader and the norms and expectations he brought to texts.

Jauss, Hans Robert, and Segers, Rien T. "An Interview with Hans Robert Jauss." Translated by Timothy Bahti. *New Literary History* 11 (Autumn 1979): 83-95.

This interview affords a glimpse of how the scholars at Constance see themselves as members of an institution, and how they see their work in reception-aesthetics in relation to the history of literary theory and other contemporary theoretical positions.

Kermode, Frank. "The Reader's Share." *Times Literary Supplement* (11 July 1975): 751.

Includes a review of Iser's *Implied Reader.*

Kincaid, James R. "Coherent Readers, Incoherent Texts." *Critical Inquiry* 3 (Summer 1977): 781-802.

Kintgen, Eugene R. "Reader Response and Stylistics." *Style* 11 (Winter 1977): 1-18.

"Stylistics will have to incorporate the perceptions and responses of readers, and the only real question is whether the best approach is idiosyncratic and anecdotal—I'll tell you mine if you'll tell me yours—or somewhat more rigorous and empirical."

Kleinau, Marion, and Isabell, Thomas. "Roland Barthes and the Co-Creation of Text." In *Studies in Interpretation,* vol. 2, edited by Esther Doyle and Virginia Hastings Floyd, pp. 139-56. Amsterdam: Rodopi, 1977.

Knuvelder, G.P.M. "Ingarden ende Receptietheorie." *Spiegel der Lettern* 20 (1978): 67-68.

Kotin, Armine. "On the Subject of Reading." *Journal of Applied Structuralism* 1 (July 1979): 11-34.

An adventurous essay that first explicates Barthes's four ways of reading (fetishistic, obsessive, paranoid, hysterical) and then applies them experimentally to the last six pages of Proust's *Le Temps Retrouvé.* Provocative.

Kritzman, Lawrence D. "Learning to Read: Literary Competence and Structuralist Poetics." *Dispositio* 2 (1977): 113–17.

_____. Review of *Rhétorique de la lecture* by Michel Charles. *Poetics Today* 1 (Au-
tumn 1979): 410–17.

Kuentz, Pierre. "A Reading of Ideology or an Ideology of Reading?" *Sub-stance*
15 (1976): 82–93.

An acute Marxist critique of the Derridean concept of textuality, which,
according to Kuentz, by bracketing the individuality of the author, au-
tonomizes the text and thus reinforces the esoteric tendencies of literary
study: the text becomes "the *mirage* of that discourse which takes place
concerning it," a discourse whose own rules remain hidden.

Kunze, Michael. "Probleme der rezeptionsästhetischen Interpretation: Über-
legungen zu Hans Robert Jauss: 'Racine und Goethes Iphigenie.'"
*Interpretationanalysen: Argumentationsstrukturen in literaturwissenschaftlichen
Interpretationen.* Munich: Fink, 1976, pp. 133–44.

Langman, F. H. "The Idea of the Reader in Literary Criticism." *British Journal of
Aesthetics* 7 (January 1967): 84–94.

"Not only correct understanding but also evaluation often depends principally upon correct recognition of the implied reader" of a literary work.

Laurenson, Diana, and Swingewood, Alan. *The Sociology of Literature.* London:
MacGibbon and Kee, 1971.

Leavis, Q. D. *Fiction and the Reading Public.* London: Chatto and Windus, 1932.

A highbrow study of the relationship between the production of fiction in
England and the capacities and needs of the reading public. A valuable
book by virtue of being one of the few studies of an important subject,
but vitiated by its condescending attitude toward popular literature.

"Lecture et lectures." Special issue. *Cahiers* 4 (1977).

Leenhardt, Jacques. "Toward a Sociology of Reading." In Suleiman and Crosman, eds., *The Reader in the Text.*

Leitch, Vincent B. "A Primer of Recent Critical Theories." *College English* 39
(October 1977): 138–52.

Reviews three recent critical theories: reception-aesthetics (Fish), Geneva
criticism (J. Hillis Miller), and Buffalo criticism (Holland).

* Lesser, Simon O. *Fiction and the Unconscious.* Boston: Vintage, 1957.

Lesser paves the way for later psychoanalytic analyses of the reading
experience by positing that "we read because we are beset by anxieties,
guilt feelings and ungratified needs. The reading of fiction permits us, in
indirect fashion, to satisfy those needs, relieve our anxieties and assuage
our guilt."

Link, Hannelore. *Rezeptionforschung. Eine Einführung in Methoden und Probleme.*
Stuttgart: Kohlhammerer, 1976.

See the annotation under Henry J. Schmidt for a general comment on
this text.

Mace, C. A. "On the Directedness of Aesthetic Response." *British Journal of
Aesthetics* 8 (April 1968): 155–60.

Argues that the aesthetic response is directed to a complete object even though we seek the cause of that response in various smaller features of the work.

McFadden, George. "Aesthetics and the 1976 Meeting of the Modern Language Association." *JAAC* 35 (Spring 1977): 389-90.

Comments on the "Do Readers Make Meaning" Forum.

Macrorie, Ken. "The Objectivity-Subjectivity Trap." *Antioch Review* 24 (Winter 1964-65): 479-88.

"To preserve sanity and produce art and science we must alternate between moments . . . of objectivity and subjectivity," although the two are really one.

Mailloux, Steven J. "Evaluation and Reader Response Criticism: Values Implicit in Affective Stylistics." *Style* 10 (Summer 1976): 329-43.

"Though outwardly embracing only the descriptive capabilities of his method, Fish appears to be restraining a desire to bring in evaluative criteria." Mailloux shows, however, that "the assumptions and methodology of Affective Stylistics are value-laden."

* _____. "Learning to Read: Interpretation and Reader-Response Criticism." *Studies in the Literary Imagination* 12 (Spring 1979): 93-108.

Outlines the assumptions of and the critical strategies common to the reader-response criticism of Iser, Fish, and Stephen Booth. Discusses reader-response criticism as a "manifestation of interpretive conventions that constitute a text and its effects."

* _____. "Reader-Response Criticism?" *Genre* 10 (Fall 1977): 413-31.

Establishes a useful schema for reviewing the work of Fish in relation to that of Bleich, Holland, Iser, and Culler. An excellent introduction to the field.

_____. "Reading-Texts." *Bucknell Review* 28 (Spring 1980).

_____. "*The Red Badge of Courage* and Interpretive Conventions: Critical Responses to a Maimed Text." *Studies in the Novel* 10 (Spring 1978): 48-63.

By analyzing critical responses to the damaged Appleton text of Crane's novel, Mailloux illustrates how "traditional literary conventions function as interpretive conventions—shared strategies for making sense of texts."

_____. Review of David Bleich's *Subjective Criticism*. *JAAC* 38 (Winter 1979): 211-13.

_____. "Stanley Fish's 'Interpreting the *Variorum*': Advance or Retreat?" *Critical Inquiry* 3 (Autumn 1976): 183-90.

Accuses Fish of "denying the assumptions upon which his own critical strategy is based: the priority (in the critical act) of describing the experience of the reader in his interaction with the text." Fish responds in the same issue, asserting that the description of the reader's response in his earlier writings was always the product of an interpretive strategy posing as objective description.

Mandel, Barrett John. "Text and Context in the Teaching of Literature." *English Journal* 68 (December 1979): 40-44.

Believes that a teacher should create a "contextless" situation in the classroom in which reading, for the student, becomes "a direct encounter with the work of literature, with minimal interference from prior beliefs or structures of knowledge."

———. "What's at the Bottom of Literature?"*College English* 38 (November 1976): 250–62.

Maranda, Pierre. "The Dialectic of Metaphor: An Anthropological Essay on Hermeneutics." In Suleiman and Crosman, eds., *The Reader in the Text.*

Marin, Louis. "Toward a Theory of Reading in the Visual Arts: Poussin's *The Arcadian Shepherds.*" In Suleiman and Crosman, eds., *The Reader in the Text.*

Marlow, James. "Fish Doing Things with Austin and Searle." *MLN* 91 (December 1976): 1602–12.

Maurer, Karl. "Rezeptionsästhetik—Zwischenbilanz (III): Formen des Lesens." *Poetica* 9 (1977): 472–98.

A general introduction to the concepts of reader reception. Examines the artificial concept or myth of the author, the "interest in the reader" in literary science, the position of the reader in relation to the author, the question of "point of view" and identification, the elementary needs of the reader, and the reader's need for "orientation."

Melnick, Daniel. "Fullness and Dissonance: Music and the Reader's Experience of Modern Fiction." *Modern Fiction Studies* 25 (Summer 1979): 209–22.

Twentieth-century writers and composers used "dissonance," with its revelation of disorder, to assault the reader and evoke an active response; "in the face of disintegrating experience the Dionysian effect of the modern novel is yet to stir in the reader a creative self-realizing 'delight' and 'desire for existence.' Dissonance in the modern novel forces us to carefully examine the experience of the reader as he explores the fullness of possibility which modern fiction imagines."

* Michaels, Walter Benn. "The Interpreter's Self: Peirce on the Cartesian 'Subject.'" *The Georgia Review* 31 (Summer 1977): 383–402. (Chapter 11 in this volume.)

(See introduction to this volume.)

Miller, Owen J. "Reading as a Process of Reconstruction: A Critique of Recent Structuralist Formulations." In *Interpretation of Narrative,* edited by Mario J. Valdés and Owen J. Miller, pp. 19–27. Toronto: University of Toronto Press, 1978.

Speculates on the possibility of reconciling French linguistic and semiotic criticism with German phenomenological criticism, using the work of Tzvetan Todorov as a point of departure.

Mills, Gordon. *Hamlet's Castle: The Study of Literature as a Social Experience.* Austin: University of Texas Press, 1976.

Takes up questions of interpretation and reader-response primarily as they relate to social interaction among the readers of a text, particularly in the classroom. Mills's subject, as he puts it, is "to see, in principle, what the concept of social experience within the environment of the text means." Wide-ranging in its references to philosophy, science, and anthropology.

Miner, Earl. "The Objective Fallacy and the Real Existence of Literature." *PTL* 1 (January 1976): 11–31.

Discusses the formalist concept of the objectivity of the work of art and Ingarden and Wellek's early attempts to revise that concept to account for the participation of the subject in the creation of aesthetic objects.

————. Review of Stanley Fish's *Self-Consuming Artifacts. JEGP* 72 (October 1973): 536–43.

Mullen, Judith. "Some Readings on Reading with a Brief Introductory Initiation into Structuralism." *Rackham Literary Studies* 9 (1979): 77–87.

Nardo, Anna K. "Fantasy Literature and Play: An Approach to Reader Response." *Centennial Review* 22 (Spring 1978): 201–13.

Discusses the idea that "reading animates a game of the imagination which takes place in a 'potential space' between text and reader" with reference to the works of Tolkien and C. S. Lewis and John Gardner's *Grendel.*

Naumann, Manfred. "Autor—Adressat—Leser." *Weimar Beiträge* 17, no. 11 (1971): 163–69.

Examines the "degree to which it is permissible to abstract from the reader and from the public during discussion of the problems of literary creation."

————. "Literary Production and Reception." Translated by Peter Heath. *New Literary History* 8 (Autumn 1976): 107–26.

Opposed to the analysis of various aspects of literature in isolation, Naumann argues for a method "which permits us to grasp the complexity of the processes actually occurring in the intersection between the writing and reading of literature, among author, work, and reader": reception-aesthetics.

————. "Rezeptionsästhetik—Zwischenbilanz (II): Das Dilemma der 'Rezeptions-ästhetik.'" *Poetica* 8 (1976): 451–66.

Discusses the "war" between reader and author and traces its origin to a "socialization process of literary relationships."

————, ed. *Gesellschaft, Literatur, Lesen: Literaturrezeption in theoretischer Sicht.* Berlin: Aufbau, 1976.

A series of essays dealing with such diverse topics as: the theoretical and methodological problems of reception-history (Naumann), the reception problem in bourgeois literary concepts (Barck), literature in history (Naumann and Kliche), socialist culture and literary reception (Kliche), the literary work as a starting point for reception and problems of its mastery (Schlenstedt), and productive functions of literature (Schlenstedt and Lenzer).

Nelson, Cary. "Reading Criticism." *PMLA* 91 (October 1976): 801–15.

Criticism is a particularly ambivalent and compromised form of writing; the critic attempts to efface himself in the presence of the reader, but his interests and attitudes are inevitably revealed in his writing, often in the form of apologies. (See also responses to this article in *PMLA* 92 [March 1977]: 307–12.)

Nelson, Lowry, Jr. "The Fictive Reader and Literary Self-Reflexiveness." In *The Disciplines of Criticism: Essays in Literary Theory, Interpretation, and History*, edited by Peter Demetz, Thomas Green, and Lowry Nelson, Jr., pp. 173–91. New Haven: Yale University Press, 1968.

"Both the fictive role of the reader and the self-reflexiveness of the work have in common a playing with the reality of the fiction, or, more strongly, the exposure of the fiction to the end, paradoxically, of reinforcing it."

Newbauer, John. "Trends in Literary Reception: Die Neuen Leiden der Wertherwirkung." *German Quarterly* 52 (January 1979): 69–79.

Noland, Richard W. "The Psychological Criticism of Norman Holland." *Hartford Studies in Literature* 6 (1974): 72–79.

Review of Holland's *5 Readers Reading*.

Norman, Liane. "Risk and Redundancy." *PMLA* 90 (March 1975): 285–91.

"There are two kinds of risks in the act of reading: that the reader will not understand what the author wants him to and that the emotional or moral risk involved in such understanding will be so great that the reader may reject it. . . . Redundancy assures that the reader will understand, or that he will receive the message accurately and draw the intended conclusions, and it reassures him so that he will be able to tolerate the lessons he learns."

Odell, L., and Cooper, Charles R. "Describing Responses to Works of Fiction." *Research in the Teaching of English* 10 (1976): 203–25.

Oeuvres et Critiques 2 (Winter 1977–78).

Devoted to " 'Rezeptions asthetik'—Contributions allemandes récentes à une nouvelle approche critique: L'esthétique de la réception."

O'Hara, Daniel. Review of *The Act of Reading* by Wolfgang Iser. *Journal of Aesthetics and Art Criticism* 38 (Fall 1979): 88–91.

Ong, Walter J., S. J. "Beyond Objectivity: The Reader and Writer Transaction as an Altered State of Consciousness." *CEA Critic* 40 (November 1977): 6–13.

"Not only do [readers] read. . . , casting themselves in the fictionalized recipient role that the author has negotiated for them and with them, but they also, paradoxically, have a great deal to say that goes into the texts they read."

――――. "The Writer's Audience Is Always a Fiction." *PMLA* 90 (January 1975): 9–21.

Every author writes for an audience he constructs in his imagination, and the reader must play the role in which the author has cast him.

Pagliaro, Harold E. "The Affective Question." *Bucknell Review* 20 (1972): 3–20.

Against Wimsatt and Beardsley's famous interdict Pagliaro argues that "affect may provide the primary and irreducible ground of criticism," and suggests that critics acknowledge the (inevitable) subjectivity of their responses to literature so as to avoid the conformity of professionally "appropriate" readings, to respond more fully to the whole work, and to promote a willingness to see their own reading complemented or displaced.

Peckham, Morse. *Man's Rage for Chaos: Biology, Behavior, and the Arts.* New York: Schocken Books, 1967.

Art works, which exist within a "potential space," provide the observer with a range of experiences that increase his capacity for survival in a real-world environment.

Perry, Menakhem. "Literary Dynamics: How the Order of a Text Creates Its Meanings, with an Analysis of Faulkner's 'A Rose for Emily.'" *Poetics Today* 1 (Autumn 1979): 35–64, 311–61.

An admirer of Benjamin Hrushovsky and heavily influenced by Ingarden and Iser, Perry expounds at length a theory of the reading process that depends on the concepts of "primacy" and "recency" effects as developed in experimental psychology. In rather impenetrable language and in great detail, he answers the questions "how important are first impressions?" and "how do they get altered?" by an exhausting analysis of Faulkner's "A Rose for Emily."

Picard, Michel. "Pour la lecture littéraire." *Littérature,* no. 26 (May 1977): 26–42.

Piwowarczyk, Mary Ann. "The Narratee and the Situation of Enunciation: A Reconsideration of Prince's Theory." *Genre* 9 (Summer 1976): 161–77.

* Poulet, Georges. "Criticism and the Experience of Interiority." In *The Structuralist Controversy: The Languages of Criticism and the Sciences of Man,* edited by Richard A. Macksey and Eugenio Donato, pp. 56–72. Baltimore: The Johns Hopkins University Press, 1972. (Chapter 4 in this volume).

(See introduction to this volume.)

* Prince, Gerald. "Introduction to the Study of the Narratee." *Poétique* no. 14 (1973): 177–96. (Chapter 2 in this volume.)

(See introduction to this volume.)

———. "Notes on the Text as Reader." In Suleiman and Crosman, eds., *The Reader in the Text.*

Purves, Alan C., ed. *How Porcupines Make Love: Notes on a Response-Centered Curriculum.* Lexington, Mass.: Xerox Publishing Co., 1972.

Suggestions for a response-centered program in the classroom that emphasizes making the readers of literature secure in their own responses, aware of the causes of their responses, and sensitive to the responses of other readers.

Purves, Alan C., and Beach, Richard. *Literature and the Reader: Research in Response to Literature, Reading Interests, and the Teaching of Literature.* Urbana, Ill.: National Council of Teachers of English, 1972.

Bibliographic essay covering an extensive number of studies concerned with various aspects of the reader's response to literature; concentrates on studies of the actual responses of real readers.

Purves, Alan C., and Rippère, Victoria. *Elements of Writing About a Literary Work: A Study of Responses to Literature.* Urbana, Ill.: National Council of Teachers of English, 1968.

Rabinowitz, Peter. "Truth in Fiction: A Reexamination of Audiences." *Critical Inquiry* 4 (Autumn 1977): 121–41.

Opens up the study of audience response by defining four audiences of a text: the actual audience, the authorial audience, the narrative audience, and the ideal narrative audience.

———. "'What's Hecuba to Us?' The Audience's Experience of Literary Borrowing." In Suleiman and Crosman, eds., *The Reader in the Text.*

Rader, Ralph. "Fact, Theory, and Literary Explanation." *Critical Inquiry* 1 (December 1974): 245–72.

Rader attempts "to conceive and render explicit the objective basis of our tacit experience" of literature. The reader understands a text, he asserts, by building hypotheses of the author's "positive constructive intention" and testing them against the "problematical facts of the text." Attacks Fish's theory for failing to discover "the general quality of literature," and for denying "the preexistent fact of meaning." In his reply Fish criticizes Rader for dismissing those elements of the reading experience that do not contribute to the realization of a single coherent meaning as "negative," and defends "affective stylistics" as a more comprehensive account of what actually goes on in the process of constituting meaning in a text.

Ray, William. "Recognizing Recognition: The Intra-textual and Extra-Textual Critical Persona." *Diacritics* 7, no. 4 (Winter 1977): 20–33.

Review of works by Iser, Prince, and Piwowarczyk.

———. "Supersession and the Subject: A Reconsideration of Stanley Fish's 'Affective Stylistics.'" *Diacritics* 8, no. 3 (Fall 1978): 60–71.

Regis, Edward, Jr. "Literature by the Reader: The 'Affective' Theory of Stanley Fish." *College English* 38 (November 1976): 263–80.

Attacks Fish's theory from an "anti-revolutionary" (i.e., formalist) stance. Denies the relevance of the reader's mental processes to the discovery of meaning in a text, reasserts the referentiality of language, and restates the doctrine of determinate meaning in a text that is the source of the reader's experience and the proper object of literary criticism.

Reichert, John. *Making Sense of Literature.* Chicago: University of Chicago Press, 1977.

In Chapter 3, "Writer and Reader," Reichert outlines an approach to literary response that rests on a belief in determinate meaning. He attacks Culler's theory of "enabling conventions" by arguing that in order to interpret a text in accordance with any system of conventions a reader must see it as the expression of a real author's intention.

———. Review of Louise M. Rosenblatt's *The Reader, the Text, the Poem: The Transactional Theory of the Literary Work. JAAC* 38 (Fall 1979): 91–93.

Rendall, Steven. "The Critical *We.*" *Orbis Litterarum* 35 (1980): 32–49.

What does it mean when a critic uses the conventional "we" of literary criticism to describe readers' reaction to a text (e.g., "we fear for Oreste at this point")? Rendall answers, via a concise summary of recent reader-theory, that the the "critical we" is an attempt to create an interpretive community; it does not so much describe reader-response as legislate the role the critic thinks the reader ought to play in responding to another author's text.

* Richards, I. A. *Practical Criticism: A Study of Literary Judgement.* 1929; rpt. ed., New York: Harcourt, Brace & Co., 1935.

Richards's famous experiment analyzes the responses of Cambridge undergraduates to a group of thirteen poems in order to describe the preconceptions that underlie literary judgment. The originality of the work lies in the focus on the cultural assumptions and psychological mechanisms that govern the reader's response to literature. A touchstone for modern literary theory.

* _____. *Principles of Literary Criticism.* 1924; rpt. ed., New York: Harcourt, Brace & Co., 1959.

Richards's full-scale attempt to develop a psychological theory of literary communication and evaluation. Discusses attitudes, emotions, pleasure, and memory in literary experience. See especially the chapter entitled "The Analysis of a Poem."

Riffaterre, Michael. *Semiotics of Poetry.* Bloomington: Indiana University Press, 1978.

The detailed exposition of a complicated theory of the meaning, significance, and poeticity of poems that relies heavily on an elaboration of the concepts of mimesis, semiosis, intertextuality, and overdetermination, as well as on the dynamics of the reader's experience of the text.

* _____. "Criteria for Style Analysis." *Word* 15 (April 1959): 154-74.

Informants supply the stylistician with reactions to the text that, when emptied of content, become objective criteria for the existence of stylistic stimuli in the text. "Once stylistic facts have been identified, linguistic analysis, applied to them only, will be relevant."

* _____. "Describing Poetic Structures: Two Approaches to Baudelaire's 'Les Chats.'" *Yale French Studies* 36-37 (1966): 200-42. (Chapter 3 in this volume.)

(See introduction to this volume.)

_____. "Interpretation and Descriptive Poetry: A Reading of Wordsworth's 'Yew Trees.'" *New Literary History* 4 (Winter 1973): 229-56.

_____. "The Reader's Perception of Narrative: Balzac's *Paix du ménage.*" In *Interpretation of Narrative,* edited by Mario J. Valdés and Owen J. Miller, pp. 28-37. Toronto: University of Toronto Press, 1978.

Riffaterre formulates his familiar thesis, succinctly, as follows: "Instead of looking for rules regulating narrative structures, I propose that we look for rules regulating the actualization of such structures in the text. . . . Without actualization rules, there is no accounting for the text's ability to function as a set of constraints upon interpretation." Using the concepts of metonomy and metaphor, Riffaterre demonstrates how the narrative sturcture and surface form of Balzac's story enforce a particular reading.

———. "The Referential Fallacy." *Columbia Review* 57 (Winter 1978): 21–35.

"The naive faith in a direct contact or relation between words and referents is a fallacy," but one that is part of the literary phenomenon. "The reader trying to interpret referentially ends up with nonsense; this forces him to look for sense with the new frame of reference supplied by the text. This new sense is what we call significance."

Rosenblatt, Louise. *Literature as Exploration.* New York: Appleton-Century-Crofts, 1937; rp. ed., New York: Noble, 1968.

Calls the attention of teachers of English to "the living and unstereotyped nature of the reading experience." Discusses the importance of the instructor's understanding of his or her students' responses to literature and suggests ways in which he or she can guide students toward more articulate and mature responses in order to achieve a host of humanistic goals.

———. *The Reader, the Text, the Poem: The Transactional Theory of the Literary Work.* Carbondale: Southern Illinois University Press, 1978.

Rosenblatt further develops her theory of literature as "a coming together, a compenetration of a reader and a text," and its implications for both teaching and criticism.

———. "On the Aesthetic as the Basic Model of the Reading Process." *Bucknell Review* 28 (Spring 1980).

* ———. "The Poem as Event." *College English* 26, no. 2 (November 1964): 123–28.

A poem "must be thought of as an event in time. It is not an object or an ideal entity. It is an occurrence." Gives examples of how real readers responded to a poem, and speaks of the New Critics' reluctance to recognize the role of the reader.

———. "Towards a Transactional Theory of Reading." *Journal of Reading Behavior* 1 (Winter 1969): 31–47.

Presents readers' responses to "It Bids Pretty Fair" by Robert Frost to introduce her theory of reading: "The transactional view of the reading process not only frees us from notions of the impact of distinct and fixed entities, but also underlines the essential importance of both elements, reader and text, in the dynamic reading transaction."

* Ross, James F. "On the Concepts of Reading." *The Philosophical Forum* 6 (Fall 1972): 93–141.

An extremely intelligent, informative account of current psychological and linguistic theories of reading that arrives at this conclusion: "There is no one *reading activity* (specified by its yielding a particular output) which is present in every reading activity. . . . There is no one reading ability which is utilized to produce in whole or in part *every* reading outcome."

Ruhe, Ernstpeter. "Rezeptionsgeschichte und Trivialliteratur: Ein Leser der *Nouvelle Héloïse* im Jahre 1838." *Neuphilologische Mitteilungen* 78 (1977): 1–17.

Uses the reader-reception of *La Nouvelle Héloïse* as a focus for remarks
prefatory to the development of a "history of readers."

Schauber, Ellen, and Spolsky, Ellen. "Readers, Language, and Character."
Bucknell Review 28 (Spring 1980).

Schmidt, Henry J. "'Text-Adequate Concretizations' and Real Readers: Reception Theory and Its Applications." *New German Critique* 17 (Spring 1979):
157–69.

Brief, but useful, introductory history of the growth of reception theory
out of the "ideological conflict within West German academic literary
criticism during the later 1960s." Against this background, Schmidt reviews four new German studies in reception theory and criticizes them
for being overly theoretical and esoteric and for failing to fully respond
to Hans Robert Jauss's appeal for "critical self-awareness."

Scholes, Robert. "Cognition and the Implied Reader." *Diacritics* 5, no. 3 (Fall
1975): 13–15.

Review of Iser's *Implied Reader.*

Schor, Naomi. "Fiction as Interpretation/Interpretation as Fiction." In Suleiman
and Crosman, eds., *The Reader in the Text.*

Schücking, Levin. *The Sociology of Literary Taste.* Translated by E. W. Dickes.
London: Paul, Trench, Trubner & Co., 1944.

Schwartz, Murray. "The Space of Psychological Criticism." *Hartford Studies in
Literature* 5 (1973): x–xxi.

In this introduction to a special issue of "metapsychological literary criticism" Schwartz discusses the work of Norman Holland and other writers
of the psychoanalytic school.

* ———. "Where Is Literature?" *College English* 36 (1975): 756–65.

Against the demand for objectivity in critical method to which students
are required to submit, Schwartz proposes a context for criticism (derived
from psychoanalysis) that recognizes a "provisional space" created by the
reader's experience of the text, which can be recreated as an act of criticism.

* Segers, Rien T. "Readers, Text, and Author: Some Implications of *Rezeptionsästhetik.*" *Yearbook of Comparative and General Literature,* no. 24 (1975):
15–23.

A survey of the major theories developed in the German movement and
the major criticisms leveled against it with suggestions as to how
reception-aesthetics might fit into the study and teaching of literature,
especially comparative literature.

* Shklovsky, Victor. "Art as Technique." *Russian Formalist Criticism: Four Essays.*
Edited and translated with an introduction by Lee T. Lemon and Marion
J. Reis. Lincoln: University of Nebraska Press, 1965, pp. 5–24.

The most important theoretical statement of early Russian Formalism,
this essay introduces the concept of "defamiliarization," which it heralds
as the goal of art. "The purpose of art is to impart the sensation of things
as they are perceived and not as they are known. The technique of art is

to make objects "unfamiliar," to make forms difficult, to increase the difficulty and length of perception because the process of perception is an aesthetic end in itself and must be prolonged."

Shroades, Caroline. "The Dynamics of Reading: Implications for Bibliotherapy." *Etc.* 18 (1961): 21–32.

Singer, Harry, and Ruddell, Robert B., eds. *Theoretical Models and Processes of Reading.* Newark, Del.: International Reading Association, 1976.

A compendium of forty-seven articles on the psychology and pedagogy of reading.

Slatoff, Walter. *With Respect to Readers: Dimensions of Literary Response.* Ithaca: Cornell University Press, 1970.

One of the first book-length inquiries into the nature of the reader's role in producing literary meaning, Slatoff's work raises a variety of issues pursued by later critics, among them the nature of "objectivity" in criticism, the divergence of literary response, and the importance of the narrator in guiding reader response.

———. "Some of My Best Friends Are Interpreters." *New Literary History* 4 (Winter 1973): 375–80.

"To be a formal interpreter is . . . a curious role to play and I guess all I'm really asking for is more self-consciousness about the role and about the reasons one performs it. In place of an army of interpreters with set faces and impersonal voices trampling confidently over the pages of books, can't we have people with a variety of voices talking in a friendly or eager way, or even hesitantly, about some things they've read?"

Smith, Frank. *Understanding Reading: A Psycholinguistic Analysis of Reading and Learning to Read.* New York: Holt, Rinehart, and Winston, 1971.

An excellent basic textbook on the range of problems involved in reading and learning to read. The author surveys essential background information in communication theory, linguistics, language acquisition, habit-formation, the physiology of the eye and brain, and discusses at some length the relationship between word identification and the comprehension of meaning.

Sorescu, Roxana. "La Lecture et la critique roumaine." *Cahiers Roumains d'Etudes Litteraires* 4 (1977): 4–21.

Steiner, George. "'Critic'/'Reader.'" *New Literary History* 10 (Spring 1979): 423–52.

The critic functions at a distance from the text, of which he is judge and master, and with which his own text competes; the reader "serves" the text, is the "shepherd" of its "being," and seeks to transcend himself through submission to it. Steiner thinks there should be more readers and fewer critics.

Steinmetz, Horst. "Der bergessene Leser: Provokatorische Bemerkungen zum Realismus-Problem." In *Dichter und Leser: Studien zur Literatur,* edited by Ferdinand van Ingen, E. Kunne-Ibsch, H. de Leeuwe, and F. Maatje, pp. 113–33. Groningen: Wolters-Noordhoff, 1972.

Discusses the central question in the realism debate: "How can it be that some works should be more real than others when all are fiction and illusion?" Poses the corollary question, "Are we dealing with a particular (special) form of fiction and illusion in so-called realistic writing?" Conclusion: "Realism has its place in the imagination of the reader. It is as creative as the writer's power of imagination."

_____. "Rezeption und Interpretation: Versuch einer Abgrenzung." *Amsterdamer Beiträge zur neuren Germanisk* 3 (1974): 37–82.

Stempel, Wolf-Dieter. "Aspects genériques de la réception." *Poétique* 39 (September 1979): 353–62.

Sternberg, Meir. *Expositional Mode and Temporal Ordering in Fiction.* Baltimore: The Johns Hopkins University Press, 1978.

Outlines and discusses in detail various methods by which authors use exposition in narrative; occasionally considers, in Iserian terminology, the ways in which the ordering of information affects the reader's responses. Hard-to-read, jargon-ridden prose.

Stierle, Karlheinz. "The Reading of Fictional Texts." In Suleiman and Crosman, eds., *The Reader in the Text.*

_____. "Réception et fiction." Translated by Vincent Kaufmann. *Poétique* 39 (September 1979): 299–320.

_____. "Rezeptionsästhetik—Zwischenbilanz (I): Was heisst Rezeption bei fiktionalen Texten?" *Poetica* 7 (1975): 345–87.

Believes that reception-criticism has a mission to revive an awareness of literature as something that acts in the public sphere. This mission would be fulfilled by the "systematic and historic construction of the possibility of the reception of fictional texts."

Stonum, Gary Lee. "For a Cybernetics of Reading." *MLN* 92 (December 1977): 945–68.

In an intelligent and provocative essay, Stonum points out that there has yet to appear any general theory of reading and suggests that theorists should look to cybernetics: "Cybernetics recommends itself to reading theory not because it can supply a prefabricated content, but because it has been developing the kind of logic that a comprehensive theory requires." He discusses the theories of Iser, Fish, and Derrida.

Strzalkowa, Maria. "Entre l'auteur et le lecteur." *Proceedings of the Sixth Congress of the International Comparative Literature Association.* Stuttgart: Beiber, 1975, pp. 509–12.

Suleiman, Susan. "Interpreting Ironies." *Diacritics* 6, no. 2 (Summer 1976): 15–21.

_____. "Introduction: Varieties of Audience-Oriented Criticism." In Suleiman and Crosman, eds., *The Reader in the Text.*

* Suleiman, Susan, and Crosman, Inge, eds. *The Reader in the Text: Essays on Audience and Interpretation.* Princeton: Princeton University Press, 1980.

Todorov, Tzvetan. "Reading as Construction." In Suleiman and Crosman, eds., *The Reader in the Text.*

Tompkins, Jane P. "Criticism and Feeling." *College English* 39 (October 1977): 169–78.

Argues that "critics have turned from systematizing the work to systematizing the reader" and urges that readers ought to "read and write, not as if they were somebody else, or as if they weren't human at all, but as and for themselves, whoever they are."

————. Review of *5 Readers Reading* by Norman Holland. *Journal of Modern Literature* 6 (1977 supplement): 536–38.

Criticizes Holland for the incoherence of his position on determinate meaning.

* ————. Review of *Subjective Criticism* by David Bleich. *MLN* 93 (December 1978): 1068–75.

"Bleich's theory of knowledge denies the possibility that there is an objective standard of truth to which individuals must submit. But the same theory also denies the possibility of knowing anything in a direct, unmediated way—including the self and its experiences. Thus Bleich's epistemology undercuts the notion of an independent self, which is the very notion that subjective criticism was originally intended to preserve."

Torbe, Mike. "Modes of Response: Some Interactions between Reader and Literature." In *Literature and Learning*, edited by Elizabeth Grudgeon and Peter Walden. London: Ward Lock Educational, 1978.

Uphaus, Robert W. *The Impossible Observer: Reason and the Reader in Eighteenth-Century Press.* Lexington: University of Kentucky Press, 1979.

In the only theoretical passage of the book, Uphaus rejects any critical theory that relies on determinate, objective meanings found in the text and declares himself for reader-response criticism. He argues "that some of the principal texts of eighteenth-century English literature elicit their meaning by deliberately juxtaposing the expectations of rationality, objectivity, and aesthetic closure against the larger and more problematical experiences of reading about, and imaginatively identifying with, characters and situations which are continually human though not consistently determinate."

Van Rees, C. J., and Verdaasdonk, H. "Reading a Text vs. Analyzing a Text." *Poetics* 6 (March 1977): 55–76.

Many current studies in reader response rest on erroneous assumptions about the nature of the reading experience, namely that "the textual facts present themselves in such a way that the observer cannot but note their relevance." The authors propose that attention be turned to poetic concepts by which a reader manipulates texts "for the purpose of applying them to his own situation and of clarifying this situation."

Waldoff, Leon. "Perceiving and Creating in Interpretation." *Hartford Studies in Literature* 7 (1975): 154–69.

Reviews Holland's *5 Readers Reading.*

Warning, Rainer. "Pour une pragmatique du discours fictionnel." Translated by Werner Kügler. *Poétique* 39 (September 1979): 321–37.

————, ed. *Rezeptionsästhetik: Theorie und Praxis.* Munich: Fink, 1975.

Essays on reception aesthetics by Ingarden, Jauss, Iser, Gadamer, Vidicka, Fish, and Riffaterre.

Weimann, Robert. "'Reception Aesthetics' and the Crisis of Literary History." Translated by Charles Spencer. *Clio* 5 (1975): 3–33.

Considers reception-aesthetics as a reaction to trends in Marxist and formalist criticism.

Weinrich, Harald. "Für eine Literaturgeschichte des Lesers." In *Methoden der deutschen Literaturwissenschaft,* edited by Victor Amegac, pp. 259–73. Frankfort: Athenäum, 1972.

————. "Les temps et les personnes." *Poétique* 39 (September 1979): 338–52.

Wellek, René. "Zur methodischen Aporie einer Rezeptionsgeschichte." In *Geschischte—Ereignis und Erzahlung,* edited by Reinhart Koselleck and Wolf-Deiter Stempel, pp. 515–17. Munich: Fink, 1973.

Criticizes the lack of progress in the evolution theory of the Russian Formalists and Czech Structuralists and in Jauss's conception of reception-history. "Reception-history is primarily valuable because it clarifies the different historical positions of those who receive; nevertheless, much remains either hidden or undiscovered in a literary history focusing on reception."

Wells, Larry D. "Indeterminacy as Provocation: The Reader's Role in Annette von Droste-Hülshoff's 'Die Judenbuche.'" *MLN* 94 (April 1979): 475–92.

Welsh, Richard K. "Professionals, Laymen, and the Literary Experience." *Etc.* 14 (Summer 1957): 274–79.

Critics and teachers who attempt to objectify the literary work obscure that which makes literature valuable to us: our dynamic participation in the literary process, one of the prime means whereby the reader achieves self-knowledge and knowledge of other selves.

Winterowd, W. Ross. "The Rhetorical Transaction of Reading." *College Composition and Communication* 27 (May 1976): 185–91.

————. "The Three R's: Reading, Reading, and Rhetoric." In *A Symposium in Rhetoric,* edited by William E. Tanner, J. D. Bishop, and S. K. Turner, pp. 51–64. Denton: Texas Women's University Press, 1976.

Zimmermann, Bernhard. *Literaturrezeption im historischen Process: Zur Theorie einer Rezeptionsgeschichte der Literatur.* Munich: Beck, 1977.

See the annotation under Henry J. Schmidt for a general comment on this text.

II. Applied

A dagger (†) following an entry indicates that a full reference has already been given in Section I.

* Alpers, Paul J. *The Poetry of "The Faerie Queene."* Princeton: Princeton University Press, 1967.

One of the earliest and best studies of a literary work that makes the reader's developing psychological experience of it the primary ground of interpretation.

Anderson, Howard. "*Tristram Shandy* and the Reader's Imagination." *PMLA* 86 (October 1971): 966–73.

Sterne's presentation of character, linguistic gamesmanship, and formal innovations force the reader to confront his own limitations by making him form judgments and expectations that later prove faulty.

* Barthes, Roland. *S/Z.*†

Beall, Chandler B. "Dante and His Reader." *Forum Italicum* 13, no. 3 (Fall 1979): 299–343.

Bender, John. *Spenser and Literary Pictorialism.* Princeton: Princeton University Press, 1972.

A detailed study of Spenser's pictorial techniques that takes into account their psychological effects.

Berger, Carole. "The Rake and the Reader in Jane Austen's Novels." *Studies in English Literature* 15 (Autumn 1975): 531–44.

Austin develops her rake figures anticlimatically: our conventional expectations of the dangers posed to a hero and heroine by these figures fail to materialize. "The effect is to underscore the power of a deep and seasoned love (with the aid of Providence) to brush aside the usual external obstacles. . . . Readers who have admitted further impediments to this marriage of true minds may feel themselves admonished for a lack of faith."

Bleich, David. "Emotional Origins of Literary Meaning."†

———. "Psychological Bases of Learning from Literature."†

* Booth, Stephen. *An Essay on Shakespeare's Sonnets.* New Haven: Yale University Press, 1969.

An original and brilliant description of the line-to-line experience of reading Shakespeare's sonnets. "The reader, whatever else he is engaged with, is constantly revising his own conception of the poem before him. . . . Each reading . . . is the experience not of recognizing the mutable nature of the human condition, but of participating in an actual experience of mutability." Essential.

* ———. "On the Value of *Hamlet.*" In *Reinterpretations of Elizabethan Drama,* edited by Norman Rabkin, pp. 77–99. New York: Columbia University Press, 1969.

Describes brilliantly what *Hamlet* does to the mind of the audience. Through constantly interrupting itself, thwarting the expectations it arouses, fracturing the coherences it establishes, making once-pertinent information seem irrelevant, it offers the mind an experience of miraculously holding incompatible elements together in colloid-like solution.

———, ed. *Shakespeare's Sonnets.* With an analytic commentary. New Haven: Yale University Press, 1977.

An unusual edition of the sonnets whose purpose is the resurrection of a Renaissance reader's experience. "Both my text and my commentary are

determined by what I think a Renaissance reader would have thought as
he moved from line to line and sonnet to sonnet." Booth's interesting
preface justifying his reader-centered analytic method is more than
vindicated by the extraordinary achievements of his commentary.

* Cain, William E. "'Lycidas' and the Reader's Response." *Dalhousie Review* 58
(Summer 1978): 272–84.

"The reader's response to "Lycidas" continually develops and structures
itself from line to line, and the history of the responses of different
readers can be found in the critical work." The reader's experience of
"Lycidas" is characterized by surprise, discontinuity, and failure of expectation; and "what the reader . . . finally takes away as consolation depends
upon how he sees—whether he rests on literal facts, or creates new ones."

Charles, Michel. *Rhétorique de la lecture.*†

Charvat, William. "Melville and the Common Reader." In *The Professions of Au-
thorship in America, 1800–1870,* edited by Matthew J. Bruccoli, pp. 262–
82. Columbus: Ohio State University Press, 1968.

Chase, Cynthia. "The Decomposition of the Elephants: Double-Reading *Daniel
Deronda.*" *PMLA* 93 (March 1978): 215–25.

Eliot's novel presents itself to be read in two conflicting ways: as a narrative in the realistic mode, "a history of the effects of causes," and as a
deconstruction of the concepts of causality, identity, and the referential
function of language, concepts that the narrator of the novel assumes.
The novel is thus both a reconstruction of the sequence of events in an
imaginary human life, and a deconstruction of the assumptions that
make such a history possible.

Crosman, Robert. *Reading* Paradise Lost. Bloomington: Indiana University
Press, 1980.

DeMaria, Robert, Jr. "The Ideal Reader: A Critical Fiction."†

———. "'The Thinker as Reader': The Figure of the Reader in the Writing of
Wallace Stevens." *Genre* 12 (Summer 1979): 243–68.

With a few glances at general reader-response theory, DeMaria concentrates on Stevens's identification of the reader and the poet in statements
about his own poetry. Neither a theoretical essay nor an application of
reader-response theory, this intelligent essay seems, however, to have
been made possible by contemporary speculation about the relations between reading and writing.

* Dillon, George. *Language Processing and the Reading of Literature: Towards a
Model of Comprehension.*†

Easson, Roger R. "William Blake and His Reader in *Jerusalem.*" In *Blake's Sublime
Allegory: Essays on the "Four Zoas," "Milton," "Jerusalem,"* edited by Stuart
Curran and Joseph Anthony Wittreich, Jr., pp. 309–27. Madison: Uni-
versity of Wisconsin Press, 1973.

Presents a conventional analysis of the "fourfold drama" concealed in
Blake's poem and hangs this on the concept of the author-reader relationship.

Elliott, Susan M. "New Solutions to Pinter's Puzzles." *Hartford Studies in Literature* 9 (1977): 237–43.

Fetterly, Judith. *The Resisting Reader: A Feminist Approach to American Fiction.*†

* Fish, Stanley E. *Self-Consuming Artifacts: The Experience of Seventeenth-Century Literature.*†

* ———. *Surprised by Sin: The Reader in* Paradise Lost.†

———. "Inaction and Silence: The Reader in *Paradise Regained.*" In *Calm of Mind: Tercentenary Essays on "Paradise Regained" and "Samson Agonistes" in Honor of John S. Dikhoff,* edited by Joseph Anthony Wittreich, Jr., pp. 25–47. Cleveland: Case Western Reserve University Press, 1971.

In *Paradise Regained,* Milton presents the reader with a Christ whose actions are puzzling and even unsympathetic. In the effort to understand those actions the reader internalizes the values from which they issue, and thus becomes, in the course of the reading experience, an imitator of Christ.

———. "Letting Go: The Reader in Herbert's Poetry." *ELH* 37 (December 1970): 475–94.

———. "Problem-Solving in *Comus.*" In *Illustrious Evidence,* edited by Earl Miner, pp. 115–31. Berkeley: University of California Press, 1975.

The problems posed by Milton's masque are not meant to be solved, but to be used by the reader in his efforts to understand, and by understanding share, the virtue of the heroine. The crucial moment occurs when the Lady declines to specify the "sage and serious doctrine of virginity," and invites the reader to supply what she omits and thus demonstrate the trueness of his ears. ("List mortals, if your ears be true.")

———. "Question and Answer in *Samson Agonistes.*" *Critical Quarterly* 11 (Autumn 1969): 237–64.

Milton's poem provides its readers an experience structured so as to leave unanswered important questions that the poem itself raises. The reader is left uncertain as to the motivation of human actions and the connection between events in the world of man and the will of God.

———. "Structuralist Homiletics."†

* ———. "What It's Like to Read *L'Allegro* and *Il Penseroso.*" *Milton Studies* 7 (1975): 77–99.

L'Allegro encourages the reader to read with pleasure and without responsibility; it diffuses his attention and does not require that he put things together. On the other hand, *Il Penseroso* requires consistantly strenuous activity on the part of the reader; it concentrates his attention forcing him to create contexts and make connections.

Fowler, Roger. "Language and the Reader: Shakespeare's Sonnet 73." In his *Style and Structure in Literature, Essays in the New Stylistics,* pp. 79–122. Ithaca: Cornell University Press, 1975.

A detailed linguistic analysis of "That time of year thou mayst in me behold" built on insights gleaned from the work of Riffaterre, Fish, and

Booth. Fowler claims that if one obeys the "constraints of a precise communal syntax," thus paying attention both to the temporality of the reading experience and to the cultural code that that experience activates, one will recognize that the sonnet emphasizes the vitality and potency of the speaker as well as his deterioration.

Greenstein, Susan. "Dear Reader, Dear Friend: Richardson's Readers and the Social Response to Character." *College English* 41, no. 5 (January 1980): 524–34.

People normally respond to characters in fiction as if they were real, in the sense of liking or disliking them, getting angry at them, wanting to give them advice. According to Greenstein, this "social" response to character, which has embarrassed twentieth-century critics, must become part of any attempt to understand the full experience of reading a novel.

Higgins, Brian, and Parker, Hershel. "Sober Second Thoughts: The 'Author's Final Version' of Fitzgerald's *Tender Is the Night.*" *Proof* 4 (1975): 129–52.

Holland, Norman N. *5 Readers Reading.*†

———. *Poems in Persons: An Introduction to the Psychoanalysis of Literature.*†

———. "*Hamlet*—My Greatest Creation."†

———. "Recovering 'The Purloined Letter': Reading as a Personal Transaction."†

———. "Transacting My 'Good-Morrow,' or, Bring Back the Vanished Critic."†

———. "Transactive Teaching: Cordelia's Death."†

Holland, Norman N., and Sherman, Leona F. "Gothic Possibilities." *New Literary History* 8 (Winter 1977): 280–94.

Hutcheon, Linda, "'Snow Storm of Paper': The Art of Reading in Self-Reflexive Candian Verse." *Dalhousie Review* 59 (Spring 1979): 114–28.

* Iser, Wolfgang. *The Implied Reader: Patterns of Communication in Prose Fiction from Bunyan to Becket.*†

———. "The Art of Failure: The Stifled Laugh in Beckett's Theater." *Bucknell Review* 28 (Spring 1980).

———. "The Pattern of Negativity in Beckett's Prose." *The Georgia Review* 29 (Fall 1975): 706–19.

Jauss, Hans Robert. "The Alterity and Modernity of Medieval Literature."†

———. "'La Douceur du foyer': The Lyric of the Year 1857 as a Pattern for the Communication of Social Norms." *Romanic Review* 65 (May 1974): 201–229.

———. "Racine und Goethes Iphigenie: Mit einem Nachwort über die Partialität der rezeptionsästhetischen Methode."†

Knight, Douglas. "The Dramatic Center of *Paradise Lost.*" *South Atlantic Quarterly* 63 (Winter 1964): 44–59.

An original, astute, and highly condensed discussion of the reader's role in *Paradise Lost* that anticipates much later work. Milton, according to

Knight, involves the reader in his poem initially through similes that force him to participate in the complex process of connecting perspectives here juxtaposed for the first time, and then through his growing identification with Adam and Eve whose predicament he comes to share as he struggles to find a perspective from which to view an action (interpretation) of which he is already a part.

Leverenz, David. "On Trying to Read *Gravity's Rainbow*." In *Mindful Pleasures: Essays on Thomas Pynchon,* edited by George Levine and David Leverenz, pp. 229-50. Boston: Little, Brown, 1976.

Levine, Jennifer. "Rejoycings in *Tel Quel*." *James Joyce Quarterly* 16 (Fall 1978/ Winter 1979): 17-26.

Offers a brief introduction to French deconstructive readings of Joyce's *Ulysses* and *Finnegans Wake* and compares them with those produced by Anglo-American criticism.

Lund, Michael. "Beyond the Text of *Vanity Fair*." *Studies in the Novel* 2 (Summer 1979): 147-61.

"In his response to one of the novel's two main characters, Becky Sharp, the reader finds himself called upon to purify his understanding of causality in *Vanity Fair,* to resist the temptation to approve of the unprincipled exploitation of the corrupt social system to which he pays a certain measure of allegiance in real life. In his response to the other major figure, Amelia Sedley, the reader's compassion is succeeded by a recognition that she has, to some degree, created her own misfortune."

McDonald, Christie V. "The Model of Reading in Rousseau's *Dialogues*." In *Interpretation of Narrative,* edited by Mario J. Valdés and Owen J. Miller, pp. 11-18. Toronto: University of Toronto Press, 1978.

A deconstructionist reading of Rousseau's *Dialogues* that argues, somewhat predictably, that Rousseau posits a model of reading that is to reveal truth and then undermines this model by the practice of his own writing.

McGann, Jerome J. "The Aim of Blake's Prophecies and the Uses of Blake Criticism." In *Blake's Sublime Allegory: Essays on the "Four Zoas," "Milton," "Jerusalem,"* edited by Stuart Curran and Joseph A. Wittreich, Jr., pp. 3-21. Madison: University of Wisconsin Press, 1972.

Focuses on the intended *effect* of Blake's epic poems rather than on their meaning, and argues that, unlike the reader of Coleridge and Keats for whom experience is mediated by the poet, Blake's reader is "forced to a direct experience of a verbal process which can have no precise signification . . . until he himself has given the language his own personal meaning." Blake's art, McGann argues, is "to seem *not* to interpret . . . but to offer signs without a point of view from which to understand their significance."

Male, Roy R. *Enter, Mysterious Stranger: American Cloistral Fiction.* Norman: University of Oklahoma, 1979.

See especially the chapter entitled "The Curiously Receptive Reader and the Mysterious Author."

Mistacco, Vicki. "Reading *The Immoralist:* The Relevance of Narrative Roles." *Bucknell Review* 28 (Spring 1980).

_____. "The Theory and Practice of Reading *nouveaux romans:* Robbe-Grillet's *Topologie pour une cite fantome.*" In Suleiman and Crosman, eds., *The Reader in the Text.*

Mundhenk, Rosemary. "The Education of the Reader in *Our Mutual Friend.*" *Nineteenth-Century Fiction* 34 (June 1979): 41–58.

The application of vaguely Iserian techniques to Dickens's *Our Mutual Friend.* By manipulating the reader's knowledge, by temporarily confusing the reader, Dickens forces him "into a more active role of discovery."

Nardo, Anna K. "Fantasy Literature and Play: An Approach to Reader Response."†

Norman, Liane. "Bartleby and the Reader." *New England Quarterly* 44 (March 1971): 22–39.

A skillful and persuasive account of how the reader's identification with the lawyer-narrator leads him eventually to judge himself, to see the shortcomings of American society, and to celebrate the persistence of the Christian-democratic principle embodied in Bartleby.

Perry, Menakhem. "Literary Dynamics: How the Order of a Text Creates Its Meanings, with an Analysis of Faulkner's 'A Rose for Emily.'"†

Preston, John. *The Created Self: The Reader's Role in Eighteenth-Century Fiction.* New York: Barnes & Noble, 1970.

Preston shows how a reader invented by the author makes the fictional worlds of *Moll Flanders, Clarissa, Tom Jones,* and *Tristram Shandy* work and discusses how the real reader interacts with his fictional counterpart.

Rawson, C. L. "Gulliver and the Gentle Reader." In *Imagined Worlds: Essays on Some English Novels and Novelists in Honour of John Butt,* edited by Maynard Mack and Ian Gregor, pp. 51–90. London: Methuen, 1968.

Swift alienates and insults his mock reader even as he solicits his further indulgence.

Reeves, Charles Eric. "Continual Seduction: The Reading of *Don Juan.*" *Studies in Romanticism* 17 (Fall 1978): 453–63.

Constantly defending himself from the judgments of a reader conditioned by conventional poetic discourse, Byron assumes an antagonism between himself and his reader that produces the very dynamic of the poem itself. Ultimately Byron does not lead his reader to a static ideological viewpoint, but, by demanding of him complete mobility, a willingness to shift perspective rapidly and frequently, Byron leads his reader to an appreciation of *difference*—valued for its own sake.

Rendall, Steven. "Dialectical Structure and Tactics in Montaigne's 'Of Cannibals,'" *Pacific Coast Philology* 12 (1977): 56–63.

Montaigne's essay is read as "a series of strategies" designed to move the reader "through a dialectical experience, leaving him, at the end, with an opinion precisely the reverse of that which he started with." A deft Fishian analysis of Montaigne's text.

Riffaterre, Michael. "Interpretation and Descriptive Poetry: A Reading of Wordsworth's 'Yew Trees.'"†

_____. "The Reader's Perception of Narrative: Balzac's *Paix du ménage*."†

Ruhe, Ernstpeter. "Rezeptionsgeschichte und Trivialliteratur: Ein Leser der *Nouvelle Héloïse* im Jahre 1838."†

* Shklovsky, Victor. "Sterne's *Tristram Shandy:* Stylistic Commentary." In *Russian Formalist Criticism: Four Essays,* edited and translated with an introduction by Lee T. Lemon and Marion J. Reis, pp. 25–57. Lincoln: University of Nebraska Press, 1965.

Applies the principles enunciated in "Art as Technique" to Sterne's novel, which, Shklovsky claims, "is the most typical novel in world literature." "By violating the form [Sterne] forces us to attend to it; and, for him, this awareness of the form through its violation constitutes the content of the novel."

Sosnoski, James. "Reading Acts and Reading Warrants: Some Implications for Readers Responding to Joyce's Portrait of Stephen." *James Joyce Quarterly* 16 (Fall 1978/Winter 1979): 43–63.

Reviews critical disputes over how Joyce's *A Portrait of the Artist as a Young Man* should be read, and calls for a theory of criticism that would yield an answer to the question: "How can multiplication of critical readings be *explained* without subverting the study of literature?"

Squire, James R. *The Responses of Adolescents While Reading Four Short Stories.* Urbana, Illinois: National Council of Teachers of English, 1964.

Suleiman, Susan. "Ideological Dissent from Works of Fiction: Toward a Rhetoric of the *Roman à Thèse.*" *Neophilologus* 60, no. 2 (April 1976): 162–77.

The reader of a novel finds himself "unable to cooperate," i.e., unable to assume the role the text assigns him, when he becomes aware that certain formal devices in the novel are masks for the author's attempt to manipulate his (the reader's) values.

Thomas, Brook. "Not a Reading *of,* but the Act of Reading *Ulysses.*" *James Joyce Quarterly* 16 (Fall 1978/Winter1979): 81–93.

In the face of the vast Joycean critical-exegetical industry, Thomas asks, "What is it about *Ulysses* that makes it so capable of generating so much criticism?" After describing the act of reading *Ulysses,* he notes that the trap of reader-response theory is total subjectivity. Enlisting the aid of Michaels, Thomas attempts to avoid that trap.

Uphaus, Robert W. "The 'Equipoise' of Johnson's *Life of Savage.*" *Studies in Burke and His Time* 17 (Winter 1978): 43–54.

"Both Johnson and the reader are required to penetrate through the ostensible facts of Savage's life to the common human experience which Johnson and Savage are assumed to share, and which the reader will be led to share."

_____. "*Gulliver's Travels, A Modest Proposal,* and the Problematical Nature of Meaning." *Papers on Language and Literature* 10 (Summer 1974): 268–78.

Swift challenges the reader's interpretive abilities by forcing him to establish provisional meanings based on his own experience of the text—on the interactions between his expectations and assumptions and the various "events" in the text.

Wadlington, Warwick. *The Confidence Game in American Literature*. Princeton: Princeton University Press, 1975.

See especially his chapter "Godly Gamesomeness: Selftaste in *Moby-Dick*."

Wells, Larry D. "Indeterminacy as Provocation: The Reader's Role in Annette von Droste-Hülshoff's 'Die Judenbuche.' "†

Wilson, James R. *Responses of College Freshmen to Three Novels*. Urbana, Illinois: National Council of Teachers of English, 1966.

Wyatt, David M. "Spelling Time: The Reader in Emerson's 'Circles.' " *American Literature* 48 (May 1976): 140–51.

"In following the verbal action of 'Circles' we can discover ourselves becoming active souls. We are processed by a stucture aspiring at once to closure and continuity. While reading 'Circles' we enjoy a sense of re-solved being and unstayed becoming."

NOTES ON CONTRIBUTORS

DAVID BLEICH is professor of English at Indiana University. In his NCTE monograph *Readings and Feelings* (1975), in numerous articles on the psychological and pedagogical aspects of literary study, and most recently in *Subjective Criticism* (1978), he has maintained that criticism of literature should concern itself with the responses of individual readers on the grounds that since all knowledge is ultimately subjective, knowledge of personal psychology is the most useful kind we can have.

JONATHAN CULLER's *Structuralist Poetics* (1975) introduced the Anglo-American community to the bases of French Structuralism and post-structuralism. Professor Culler, who teaches at Cornell University, has written extensively on problems of interpretation, the reader, and literary convention, and is the author of full-length studies of Flaubert and Ferdinand de Saussure. He is currently completing a book on Roland Barthes and is preparing for publication two works on contemporary critical theory: *The Pursuit of Signs: Semiotics, Literature, Deconstruction* and *On Deconstruction: Literary Theory in the 1970s.*

WALKER GIBSON is professor of English at the University of Massachusetts, Amherst. His conception of the mock reader reflects his longstanding interest in matters of language and style. He has edited *The Limits of Language* (1962), co-edited *The Play of Language* (1971), and is the author of *Tough, Sweet, and Stuffy: An Essay on Modern American Prose Styles* (1966) as well as of numerous other books and articles on writing and the creative process. He was president of the National Council of Teachers of English in the early 1970s and has since served as chairman of the MLA's Division on the Teaching of Writing. Recently he has directed several NEH seminars for college teachers on writing and style.

STANLEY E. FISH, William R. Kenan, Jr., Professor of English at The Johns Hopkins University, wrote the first full-scale reader-oriented analysis of a literary work: *Surprised by Sin: The Reader in* Paradise Lost (1967). Since then he has written a number of articles focused on the reader of Renaissance literature and has supplied the movement with two of its most important theoretical statements, both of which are reprinted in this volume. His books include *John Skelton's Poetry* (1965), *Self-Consuming Artifacts: The Experience of Seventeenth-Century Literature* (1970), and *The Living Temple: George Herbert and Catechizing* (1978). His volume of theoretical essays, *Is There a Text in This Class?: The Authority of Interpretive Communities* (1980) is the most outstanding recent contribution to Anglo-American literary theory.

NORMAN N. HOLLAND is James H. McNulty Professor of English at the State University of New York at Buffalo and founder and director of SUNY's Center for the Psychological Study of the Arts. He completed a program for nonmedical candidates at the Boston Psychoanalytic Institute and is a member of the Boston and Western New York psychoanalytic societies. Professor Holland, who has written over one hundred articles and reviews, as well as three books on Shakespeare, is the leading psychoanalytic interpreter of literary response. He has written three highly influential books in the field: *The Dynamics of Literary Response* (1968), *Poems in Persons* (1973), and *5 Readers Reading* (1975).

WOLFGANG ISER, who has taught at major universities throughout Europe and the United States, is currently professor of English and comparative Literature at the University of Konstanz and the University of California, Irvine. He is the author of books on Fielding (1952), Pater (1960), Spenser (1970), and Beckett (1979), but he is best known as the founder (along with Hans Robert Jauss) of German reception-aesthetics. In a series of essays and in three major books—*Die Appelstruktur der Texte* (1970), *The Implied Reader* (1974), and *The Act of Reading* (1978)—he has formulated a theory of the reader's role in creating literary meaning and has developed a method of describing the experience of literature that has generated large quantities of reader-centered criticism in the past several years and continues to be extremely influential.

WALTER BENN MICHAELS teaches English at the University of California, Berkeley. His essays in literary theory concern questions of belief and reference and the problem of interpretation in the law. He has written articles on James, Eliot, Thoreau, and Dreiser and is currently completing a book on American literary theory entitled *American Epistemologies: Literary Theory and Pragmatism.*

GEORGES POULET is the leading figure in the Geneva School of phenomenological criticism. He has held posts at the University of Edinburgh, The Johns Hopkins University, where he was chairman of the

Department of Romance Languages, the University of Zurich, where he was director of the Romanisches Seminar, and the University of Nice, where he held the Chair in French. His major works include the four-volume *Etudes sur le temps humain* (1949, 1952, 1964, 1968), two of which have been translated into English as *Studies in Human Time* (1956) and *The Interior Distance* (1959); *Les Metamorphoses du cercle* (1961); *L'Espace proustein* (1963), translated as *Proustian Space* in 1977; *Trois essais de mythologie romantique* (1966); *Qui était Baudelaire?* (1969); *La Conscience critique* (1971); and most recently, *Entre moi et moi, Essais critiques sur la conscience de soi* (1977).

GERALD PRINCE's article on the *narrataire,* which appeared in *Poétique,* touched off a number of studies devoted to describing the reader implied by or inscribed in the literary text. While he has written a book and several articles on twentieth-century French literature, his more recent work has been devoted to literary theory. *A Grammar of Stories* (1973) and shorter pieces on the "diary-novel" and "metanarrative" extend the approach to the study of narrative developed here. He has recently completed a book-length manuscript entitled *Narratology: The Form and Functioning of Narrative* and is now preparing a *Dictionary of Narratology.* He teaches at Pennsylvania State University.

MICHAEL RIFFATERRE is Knopf Professor of French at Columbia University where he has been chairman of the Department of French and Romance Languages since 1974. His early articles on prose style, especially "Criteria for Style Analysis" (1959) and "Stylistic Context" (1960), have been extremely influential. His most famous essay, reprinted here, established the pattern for his distinctive brand of close textual analysis. Its practical application is reflected in the essays collected in *La Production du texte* (1979), while its theoretical propositions have been extended and refined upon in *Semiotics of Poetry* (1978). Professor Riffaterre has held professorships and lectureships at colleges and universities throughout the United States and Canada. He is the general editor of *The Romanic Review* and is on the editorial board of a dozen journals in French, Comparative Literature, and literary theory.

JANE P. TOMPKINS teaches American literature and literary theory at Temple University. In addition to the present volume, she has edited a collection of critical essays on James's short fiction, *Twentieth-Century Interpretations of* The Turn of the Screw *and Other Tales* (1970). She has written articles and reviews on American fiction, autobiography, and literary theory and is currently writing a book on American popular fiction entitled *American Melodrama: The Novel as Social Theory in Brockden Brown, Cooper, and Harriet Beecher Stowe.*